Two Oxen Ahead

Two Oxen Ahead

*Pre-Mechanized Farming
in the Mediterranean*

Paul Halstead

WILEY Blackwell

This edition first published 2014
© 2014 Paul Halstead

Registered Office
John Wiley & Sons, Ltd, The Atrium, Southern Gate, Chichester, West Sussex, PO19 8SQ, UK

Editorial Offices
350 Main Street, Malden, MA 02148-5020, USA
9600 Garsington Road, Oxford, OX4 2DQ, UK
The Atrium, Southern Gate, Chichester, West Sussex, PO19 8SQ, UK

For details of our global editorial offices, for customer services, and for information
about how to apply for permission to reuse the copyright material in this book please
see our website at www.wiley.com/wiley-blackwell.

Library of Congress Cataloging-in-Publication Data

Halstead, Paul.
    Two oxen ahead : pre-mechanized farming in the Mediterranean / Paul Halstead.
        pages cm
    Includes bibliographical references and index.
    ISBN 978-1-4051-9283-5 (hardback)
1. Agriculture–Economic aspects–Mediterranean Region.   2. Farm management–
Mediterranean Region.   3. Land use, Rural–Mediterranean Region.   I. Title.
    HD2055.7.H35 2014
    630.937–dc23

                                                                    2013036924

A catalogue record for this book is available from the British Library.

Cover image: *Threshing with oxen in Crete, c. 1927–30*, photograph by Nelly's
(Elli Souyioultzoglou-Seraidari) © Photographic Archive of the Benaki Museum, Athens.
Cover design by Simon Levy

Set in 10.5/13.5pt Palatino by SPi Publisher Services, Pondicherry, India
Printed in Malaysia by Ho Printing (M) Sdn Bhd

1   2014

Contents

Contents

Preface

This is a study of how Mediterranean farmers grew crops and raised families before mechanization and industrialization. With the ultimate aim of enriching ancient historians' and prehistorians' understanding of Mediterranean farming societies in the distant past, it explores pattern and diversity in the practices and decision-making of twentieth-century premechanized farmers. Much of this book is based, therefore, on first-hand observation of and interviews with residents of the Mediterranean countryside (Chapter 1).

Anthropologists often disguise the identity of informants and host communities, but real toponyms are used here to place agricultural practices and decisions in their ecological and social context. Informants were not asked deeply personal questions, although some volunteered sensitive information about themselves or neighbors. Many would happily have been named in print, but most have been more or less anonymized, occasionally out of discretion, but mainly because it would be confusing to name them all. Those named are identified by first names, for brevity, and sometimes by pseudonyms to differentiate between homonymous neighbors. A few informants are named frequently, because they were important sources and to place what they said in the context of their particular circumstances or life history. Informants did not sign "informed consent" forms. Some, whom I had known for decades, would have treated any such request with disbelief. Others I met for the first time when I "interviewed" (i.e., talked with) them, and any invitation to sign a printed form would have ended our acquaintance before it began. A few were illiterate, some had failed eyesight, and several died before I thought of writing about what they told me. Informants often provided greatest insight when they strayed from the preplanned questions that a consent form would have covered. None of the information used was intentionally acquired by subterfuge.

Acknowledgments

To my largely elderly sources, named and unnamed, I am deeply indebted for generously sharing their time, knowledge, and, often, food and drink. In northern Greek Assiros, the barber, Fotis Alexiou, introduced customers by occupation ("current goat herder," "retired pig farmer"), while my regular evening companion in the *kafenío*, Apostolis Papafotiou, invited to our table experts in whatever aspect of rural economy had caught my interest. Introductions were similarly provided in north Greek Paliambela and Kolindros by Yannis Stangidis; in central Greek Tharounia on Euboea by Giorgos Palogos ("Skantzouris'"); on southern Greek Kithira by Despina Isaakidou; on Crete by Stavros Amianakis, Gerald Cadogan, Angeliki Karagianni, Spiros Liapakis, Yannis Papadatos, Antonis Vasilakis, and Kostas Venianakis; in Tuscan Garfagnana by Mariangela Filippi; around Haute Provençal Sault by Jean-François Devaux; in Asturias by Valentina Palacios; and in Andalucian Zuheros by Leonor Peña-Chocarro. Companions in information gathering included Bill "ethnokafenologist" Alexander, Amy Bogaard, Artemis Brofidou, Mike Charles, Pat Collins, Jack Davis, Michele Forte, Angelos Gkotsinas, Eleni Hatzaki, Valasia Isaakidou, Glynis Jones, Ingrid Mainland, Vaso Tzevelekidi, Tony Wood, and, as infant passports to households closed to unaccompanied adults, Georgina and Huw Halstead. Directly or indirectly, the Arts and Humanities Research Council (and preceding AHRB), British Academy, Institute for Aegean Prehistory, Natural Environment Research Council, King's College Cambridge, University of Cambridge Faculty of Classics, University of Cincinnati, and University of Sheffield funded fieldwork. The British School at Athens library, Gennadius Library (American School of Classical Studies at Athens), and Spoudastirio Laografias (Aristotle University of Thessaloniki) provided a wealth of Greek literature. Tina Badal, John Bennet, John Bintliff, Amy Bogaard, Cristina Fernandez Bustamante, Kostis Christakis, Michele Forte, Yannis Galanakis, Andy Garrard, Angelos Hadjikoumis, Debi Harlan, Eleni Hatzaki, Valasia Isaakidou, Kostas Kotsakis, Nancy Krahtopoulou, John Moreland, Mark Nesbitt, Gianna Siamidou, Christina Tsoraki, Duska Urem-Kotsou, and Todd Whitelaw shared unpublished information or published sources. Ferran Antolín, John Bennet, Amy Bogaard, and Valasia Isaakidou helpfully commented on draft chapters. Nikos Valasiadis provided the maps and Valasia Isaakidou some of the photographs.

1

Introduction
Mediterranean Farming between Longue Durée and Contingency

For the last 8000–10000 years, the peoples of the Mediterranean have overwhelmingly subsisted on cultivated plants and domestic animals. Historians and archaeologists have studied ancient farming for insight into changing economy, society, and landscape, but available evidence has significant limitations. Literary sources assume much background knowledge and, to varying degrees, address moralizing or romantic content to elite readers. Iconography is selective and poses problems of distinguishing normal practice from rare innovations or fantasy. More mundane archaeological evidence (tools, seeds, bones) is potentially more representative and socially inclusive but provides ambiguous traces of many practices, a fragmentary picture of farming regimes, and at best circumstantial insight into why people farmed in particular ways. Scholars have drawn extensively on recent "traditional" (nonmechanized, preindustrial) farming, therefore, to infer uses of tools (e.g., Byzantine digging implements – Bryer, 1986), practices (e.g., Roman harvesting

Two Oxen Ahead: Pre-Mechanized Farming in the Mediterranean, First Edition.
Paul Halstead. © 2014 Paul Halstead. Published 2014 by John Wiley & Sons, Ltd.

methods – Spurr, 1986), land-use regimes (e.g., Bronze Age cereal–olive–vine polyculture – Renfrew, 1972), or production parameters (e.g., area yields for classical Greek grain crops – Gallant, 1991) for which direct evidence is lacking or ambiguous and to identify likely rationales for documented practices (e.g., nonspecialized, classical Greek oil- and wine-processing facilities reflecting limited production for market – Foxhall, 2007).

Many accounts of traditional Mediterranean farming overgeneralize, however, or conversely highlight local customs, and few explore the balance between "practical" and "cultural" influence on methods. Moreover, detailed studies of particular aspects (e.g., tillage, reaping) may obscure the extent to which decisions shape outcomes and choices at subsequent stages of the agricultural cycle. The *relevance* of traditional farming to the past also requires critical consideration. Emphasis on relatively *timeless* constraints (e.g., Semple, 1932; Blanchard, 1945; Grigg, 1974; Braudel, 1975) of environment (e.g., low rainfall), technology (e.g., "primitive" wooden plows) and perhaps know-how (e.g., presumed ignorance of crop rotation) has encouraged uncritical extrapolation to antiquity. Traditional practice was highly variable, however, and demonstrably shaped also by medium-term historical contingencies (e.g., land tenure, markets – Silverman, 1968; Halstead, 1987; Forbes, 1993) and cultural preferences and by short-term tactical decision-making. These influences must be disentangled to enable judicious use of recent practices as analogies for the past.

This study attempts an overview of traditional Mediterranean farming practice and a critical evaluation of its potential to illuminate ancient farming. It explores what recent farmers did and how, why, and with what consequences. For reasons of space, it concentrates on staple Old World grain crops, dealing briefly with fruit, fiber, oil and vegetable crops (primarily where relevant to farmers' overall cropping decisions and rotation practices), and livestock (primarily as aids to or beneficiaries of arable farming). Geographically, it focuses on Greece, with patchier coverage of the northwest and eastern Mediterranean to encompass greater ecological and cultural diversity; inclusion of upland Asturias on

2

the Atlantic façade of northwest Spain, characterized by wet summers, offers a useful contrast with typically Mediterranean regions of mild, rainy winters and hot, dry summers.

Evidence is drawn partly from published agronomic, ethnographic, and folkloric studies but in large measure from firsthand observations and oral-historical accounts, because this makes accessible a substantial body of original information and facilitates contextualized exploration of farmers' decisions. These observations and oral histories were collected over four decades in Spain, southern France, Italy, Cyprus, and especially Greece (Figure 1.1). Much of this information is a by-product of ethnoarchaeological projects, investigating whether particular farming practices leave distinctive material traces: crop processing in the Greek islands (Jones, 1984); irrigation in northern Spain (Jones *et al.*, 1995); intensive "gardening" of pulses in central Greece (Jones *et al.*, 1999) and cereals in Asturias (Charles *et al.*, 2002); extensive einkorn growing in Provence; and woodland management in northwest Greece (Halstead and Tierney, 1998; Smith, 1998). Much has also been gathered during archaeological fieldwork in Greece, with subject matter depending on local land use, informants' experiences, and my evolving interests.

1.1 Fieldwork

Many interviewees expressed delight at finding someone interested in their experiences. A farmer on the Greek island of Amorgos solicited questions to prolong breaks in the *kafenío*, while his son sweated on the threshing floor. One May in Khionades on the mountainous Greek–Albanian border, a blind woman of 85 initiated conversation from behind closed shutters. She had outlived her husband, siblings, and children and, other than periodic shouted exchanges with a housebound neighbor, I was her first social contact since the previous summer. In northern Greek Assiros, the neighborhood grandmothers regularly invited me for morning coffee, entertaining me (and themselves) with half-forgotten dialect words and customs

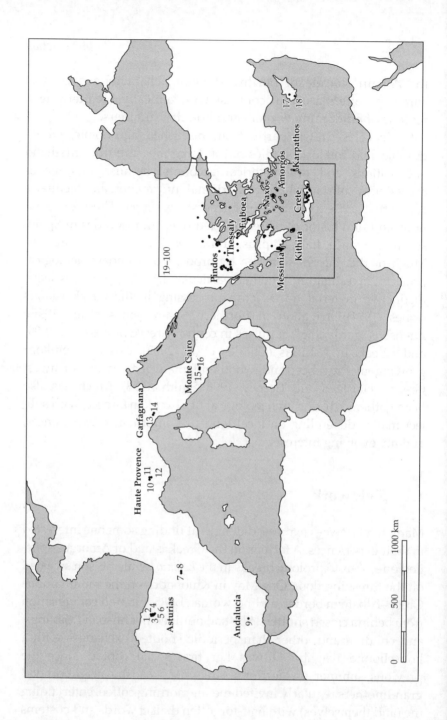

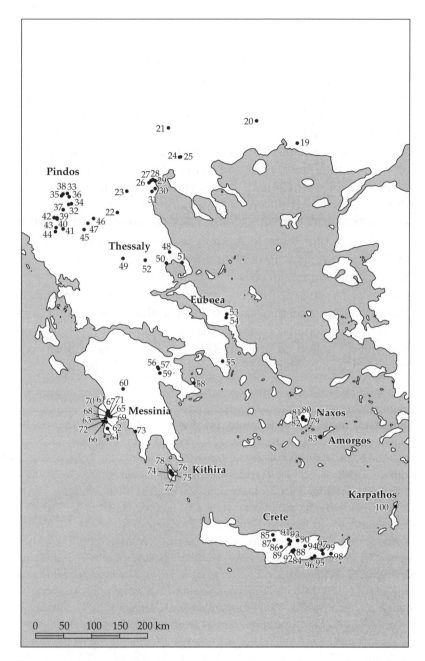

Figure 1.1 Map of Mediterranean Europe, showing locations described by informants. Key: 1. Zureda, 2. Tiós, 3. Xomezana, 4. Carraluz, 5. Piñera, 6. Llanos de Somerón, 7. Ambel, 8. Borja, 9. Zuheros, 10. Mollans-sur-Ouvèze, 11. Brantes, 12. Sault, 13. Piazza al Serchio, 14. Castiglione di Garfagnana,

or embarrassing stories about male villagers. Conversely, some individuals were reluctant to recall grinding poverty or civil war. Others were wary of a stranger but perhaps relented on seeing friendly exchanges with neighbors. As an outsider, being foreign was sometimes advantageous in that curiosity was attributed to eccentricity or ignorance rather than official snooping. Once, mention of an émigré mutual acquaintance, who had not written home for months, proved difficult, but normally introductions from an insider greatly eased information gathering. Frustratingly, women carers occasionally limited access to housebound individuals, out of embarrassment for their decrepitude, misplaced concern that they would bore me, or fear of their revealing family secrets – often already heard from neighbors.

Ethnoarchaeological projects, involving systematic sampling of plant or animal specimens from fields, threshing floors, and barns, required completion of standardized questionnaires, but most "interviews" defied close control. In the mountains of northwest Greece, a Vlach herder and anthropologist's father had firm ideas

---

Figure 1.1 (*Cont'd*) 15. Casalattico, 16. Monforte, 17. Gerakies, 18. Kouklia, 19. Neo Sidirokhori, 20. Prasinada, 21. Mouries, 22. Lazarades, 23. Skafi, 24. Assiros, 25. Mavrorakhi, 26. Kastania, 27. Kolindros, 28. Paliambela, 29. Aiginio, 30. Kitros, 31. Nea Trapezounta, 32. Agia Paraskevi, 33. Aetomilitsa, 34. Fourka, 35. Khionades, 36. Likorakhi, 37. Pigi, 38. Plikati, 39. Agios Minas, 40. Aristi, 41. Dikorfo, 42. Mavrovouni, 43. Ligopsa, 44. Zitsa, 45. Metsovo, 46. Kipourio, 47. Kranea, 48. Kanalia, 49. Prodromos, 50. Sesklo, 51. Vizitsa, 52. Zoodokhos Pigi, 53. Manikia, 54. Tharounia, 55. Markopoulo, 56. Arkhaia Nemea, 57. Dervenakia, 58. Methana, 59. Mikines, 60. Karitaina, 61. Asoutaina, 62. Iklaina, 63. Khora, 64. Kinigou, 65. Kontogoni, 66. Korifasio, 67. Makraina, 68. Metaxada, 69. Milioti, 70. Palaio Loutro, 71. Potamia, 72. Tragana, 73. Stoupa, 74. Aroniadika, 75. Frilingianika, 76. Kastrisianika, 77. Mitata, 78. Potamos, 79. Filoti, 80. Kourounokhori, 81. Melanes, 82. Potamia, 83. Kolofana, 84. Agia Semni, 85. Aloides, 86. Ano Asites, 87. Anogia, 88. Arkalokhori, 89. Arkhanes, 90. Kalo Khorio, 91. Knossos, 92. Miliarisi, 93. Skalani, 94. Pinakiano (Lasithi plateau), 95. Anatoli, 96. Mirtos, 97. Pakhia Ammos, 98. Stavrokhori, 99. Vasiliki, 100. Olimbos.

on note-taking ("that is important, write it down"). Some informants overestimated my interest in warfare (men) and miraculous icons (women), but often such lack of discipline proved invaluable, because my questions reflected the limits of my understanding and the most revealing "answers" were unsolicited.

The words of Mediterranean farmers, like those of academics, cannot be treated uncritically. Sometimes participant observation provided a check and, wherever possible, multiple oral sources were compared. Once, a recent interviewee reacted angrily to my asking his neighbor the same questions, but most informants seemingly attributed such behavior to slow learning. While conversations with one person at home were easiest to follow, group discussions, as with the old men outside the cobbler's workshop in Assiros, revealed who embroidered their experiences – for dramatic effect or in a misguided attempt to be helpful. It was often clear from context whether answers were pessimistic ("life was hard in the old days") or optimistic ("I had the best-fed and most powerful oxen in the village"), and generalizations were easier to evaluate when leavened with specific examples ("in 1934, when it did not rain from October 18 to March 18, we only harvested 20 loads of wheat"), the accuracy of which was often confirmed by other informants. A common response to questions, as Binford found among the Nunamiut, was "it depends" (Binford, 1978; also Forbes, 1992, 92), and the contingent nature of decisions and their outcomes accounts for many apparent discrepancies between informants. Thanks to the close interest that Mediterranean farmers take (for sound reasons – Section 7.4) in neighbors' activities, informants could often identify differences of needs or means that might account for such discrepancies.

Given the rapid pace of technological, economic, political, and social change in the twentieth-century Mediterranean, it is essential to establish a chronological framework for oral histories – despite the tendency of elderly informants to use "recently," "the year before last," or even "the day before yesterday" to refer to events 50 or 60 years ago. A positive consequence of this logarithmic perception of time is that informants' memories focus on adolescence and early adulthood rather than providing a pastiche of experiences throughout their lifetimes. Informants in their 90s and occasional centenarians thus provided vivid firsthand accounts of life near the beginning of the twentieth century, even if they could not remember breakfast on the day of interview. Indeed, one 90-year-old, close as a teenager to a centenarian grandfather, provided oral history reaching back in two steps to the early nineteenth century. The building of oral histories with time depth from informants of successive generations is invaluable in revealing how "traditional" agricultural practices have altered with changing circumstances. Fortunately, most informants distinguished readily between experiences as members of their parental household and subsequently as independent householders. Women especially linked experiences to the life cycles of close kin ("I was breast-feeding my son when we first harvested that field") and could recall or calculate dates of births, marriages, and deaths. Men routinely recalled whether experiences pre- or postdated military service or work abroad. For both men and women, war and civil unrest provided indelible temporal signposts. Insofar as interviews could be stage managed, therefore, the first step was to establish a potted biography for the informant, identifying areas of firsthand expertise and events (marriage, military service) that could date experiences.

1.2 Scales of Analysis

Variability in traditional farming is explored in turn through the *annual* cycle of grain production, from tillage and sowing (Chapter 2) to harvest (Chapter 3) and processing for storage or consumption (Chapter 4); then the *interannual* cycle of practices such as crop rotation and manuring (Chapter 5); and finally the *generational* cycle of shifting balance between households' consumption needs and available labor, land, and livestock (Chapter 6). Attention is drawn to how decisions on a generational and interannual scale inform those taken during the annual crop production cycle and how the latter shape choices at subsequent stages of this cycle. Diversity of practice is explored in terms of *cultural* "ways of doing" and *practical* adjustment to circumstances, the latter on timescales ranging from the timeless *longue durée* through the medium-term *conjoncture* to the short-term *événement* of Braudel (1975). Each chapter examines the contexts and consequences of alternative practices (e.g., tillage with hoe or plow, yoking of oxen or cows), offers order-of-magnitude estimates of costs and benefits (e.g., speed of tillage or reaping, fodder requirements of draft animals), and suggests how this information might shed light on ancient Mediterranean farming, drawing examples from the earliest Neolithic to Greco-Roman antiquity. Although largely dealing with very practical matters, much of this book is concerned with human decision-making. Chapter 7, therefore, discusses how traditional Mediterranean farmers acquired information and skills, how they made decisions, and the extent to which they were rational actors making predictable choices, before assessing the potential of traditional farming to provide relevant and illuminating analogies for the distant past. Because traditional farming was not timeless, the temptation will be resisted to write agricultural history just from recent analogy.

References

Binford, L.R. (1978) *Nunamiut Ethnoarchaeology*, Academic Press, New York.

Blanchard, R. (1945) *Les Alpes occidentales 4: les préalpes françaises du sud*, Grenoble & Paris, Arthaud.

Braudel, F. (1975) *The Mediterranean and the Mediterranean World in the Age of Philip II, volume 1*, Fontana, London.

Bryer, A. (1986) Byzantine agricultural implements: the evidence of medieval illustrations of Hesiod's 'Works and Days'. *Annual of the British School at Athens*, 81, 45–80.

Charles, M., Bogaard, A., Jones, G. *et al.* (2002) Towards the archaeobotanical identification of intensive cereal cultivation: present-day ecological investigation in the mountains of Asturias, northwest Spain. *Vegetation History & Archaeobotany*, 11, 133–142.

Forbes, H. (1992) The ethnoarchaeological approach to ancient Greek agriculture: olive cultivation as a case study, in *Agriculture in Ancient Greece* (ed. B. Wells), Swedish Institute at Athens, Stockholm, pp. 87–101.

Introduction

Forbes, H. (1993) Ethnoarchaeology and the place of the olive in the economy of the southern Argolid, Greece, in *La production du vin et de l'huile en Méditerranée* (eds M.-C. Amouretti and J.-P. Brun), École française d'Athènes, Athens, pp. 213–226.

Foxhall, L. (2007) *Olive Cultivation in Ancient Greece*, Oxford University Press, Oxford.

Gallant, T.W. (1991) *Risk and Survival in Ancient Greece*, Polity Press, Cambridge.

Grigg, D.B. (1974) *The Agricultural Systems of the World: An Evolutionary Approach*, Cambridge University Press, Cambridge.

Halstead, P. (1987) Traditional and ancient rural economy in Mediterranean Europe: plus ça change? *Journal of Hellenic Studies*, 107, 77–87.

Halstead, P. and Tierney, J. (1998) Leafy hay: an ethnoarchaeological study in NW Greece. *Environmental Archaeology*, 1, 71–80.

Jones, G. (1984) Interpretation of archaeological plant remains: ethnographic models from Greece, in *Plants and Ancient Man* (eds W. van Zeist and W.A. Casparie), Balkema, Rotterdam, pp. 43–61.

Jones, G., Charles, M., Colledge, S., and Halstead, P. (1995) Towards the archaeobotanical recognition of winter-cereal irrigation: an investigation of modern weed ecology in northern Spain, in *Res Archaeobotanicae – 9th Symposium IWGP* (eds H. Kroll and R. Pasternak), Oetker-Voges, Kiel, pp. 49–68.

Jones, G., Bogaard, A., Halstead, P. *et al.* (1999) Identifying the intensity of crop husbandry practices on the basis of weed floras. *Annual of the British School at Athens*, 94, 167–89.

Renfrew, C. (1972) *The Emergence of Civilisation: The Cyclades and the Aegean in the Third Millennium BC*, Methuen, London.

Semple, E.C. (1932) *The Geography of the Mediterranean Region: Its Relation to Ancient History*, Constable, London.

Silverman, S.F. (1968) Agricultural organization, social structure, and values in Italy: amoral familism reconsidered. *American Anthropologist*, 70, 1–20.

Smith, D. (1998) Beyond the barn beetles: difficulties in using some Coleoptera as indicators of stored fodder. *Environmental Archaeology*, 1, 63–70.

Spurr, M.S. (1986) *Arable Cultivation in Roman Italy c.200 B.C.–C.A.D. 100*, Society for the Promotion of Roman Studies, London.

2

Working the Earth
Tillage and Sowing

"What does 'farmer' mean?" Alexis answered his own question: "two oxen ahead and one ox behind"; in Greek, *vódhi* (ox) symbolizes stupidity rather than strength. At 81, Alexis was lame and his sight failing. He no longer had draft animals and his tools gathered cobwebs in the barn, but he enjoyed reenacting his craft. He yoked virtual oxen to a wooden ard that "scratched" a furrow, rather than turning the soil like a modern plow, in the dirt road outside the barber's shop in north Greek Assiros. He paced out a 10 m-wide strip for broadcast sowing, marked the edges by plowing a single furrow, and then walked up one edge and back down the other, pulling imaginary seed from a double bag on his shoulder and casting it 5 m towards the middle of the strip. From time to time, he reversed the bag on his shoulder to keep the weight of unsown grain balanced. Then, he walked up and down the middle of the strip, casting seed towards the edge. He maintained a steady rhythm by synchronizing hand movements with

Two Oxen Ahead: Pre-Mechanized Farming in the Mediterranean, First Edition.
Paul Halstead. © 2014 Paul Halstead. Published 2014 by John Wiley & Sons, Ltd.

paces. "That's how we 'locals' sowed." Thracian refugees from European Turkey, who arrived in the 1920s, sowed by casting alternately left and right and, he reckoned, achieved less even coverage; he could identify "locals" and Thracians from afar by their sowing rhythm.

After stopping for a real cigarette, he plowed the strip to cover the seed before birds could rob it; migratory flocks of geese were a particular worry. He placed the iron share tip of the ard at the start of the first furrow. Then, with one hand steering the ard from behind and the other brandishing a goad that doubled as a spatula for scraping mud off the share, he trudged up and down the sown strip. As he walked, he called instructions to the oxen to keep straight and then turn at the end of the field, where he lifted the ard and positioned it to start the next furrow. He reckoned the oxen pulled the ard back and forth 15–25 times to cover over the 10 m-wide "sowing," with furrows overlapping to avoid leaving untilled strips in which weeds would grow and compete with the crop. If the ground was heavy, he kept stopping to scrape mud off the share. "Next, if possible, you harrowed the field, but the animals were slow and the weather was a problem. We started plowing in October, as soon as the first rains softened the ground, but we could not work when the ground was wet and, by early December, frost often made the ground too hard."

As dusk fell, Alexis pulled up a chair. "Then, from late January, when the weather allowed, we plowed the fallow fields." Each year, half of the fields were sown with wheat and half left fallow. "We plowed the fallow in one direction and then a second time, after it had rained, crosswise. Before April or May, we plowed a third time, in the same direction as the first. If you had good animals, you plowed four or five times." In March to May, some fallow fields were planted in summer crops (e.g., maize, sesame), and once these were harvested, the fields should be plowed again. The number of plowings grew as Alexis warmed to his theme. Other elderly villagers claimed that earlier generations had plowed *nine* times, citing a false folk etymology for *niáma*, the word used in many parts of Greece to denote tilled fallow or the first plowing of the fallow period. However exaggerated, these accounts underline the value placed on repeated plowing of fallow – echoed by the Cretan and Cypriot term for tilled fallow (*kalourgiá, kalourká*), which literally means "good working."

Alexis' reenactments were somewhat idealized – he had not been the most thorough farmer. Much of his performance is echoed, however, for sound practical reasons, in descriptions of ard plowing elsewhere in Greece (e.g., Loukopoulos, 1983, 182–183) and the wider Mediterranean (e.g., Palmer, 1998). The characteristic back–forth movement is necessary for effective tillage with an ard (Forbes, 1982, 215). A sowing strip about 10 m wide is widespread, as is the explanation that 5 m is a practicable distance over which to scatter seed and that throwing seed from both edges and perhaps also the middle achieves even broadcasting. The length of sowing strip is more variable but limited by size of field, strength of draft animals, and the need to cover seedcorn promptly; farmers feared not only robbing by birds but also interruption by rain or snow. At Anogia in highland Crete, a man had just sown a terrace far above the village and was plowing in the seed, with his pregnant wife behind breaking clods with a pick when she announced that her waters had broken. He helped her onto the donkey and told her, "hold tight [to the unborn baby!] and hurry"; he followed down the mountain as soon as he had covered the seed. Fear of interruption before the job was complete, coupled with the slowness of plow animals, strongly favored sowing small strips, enabling cropping decisions to be taken on a much smaller scale than with mechanized agriculture (Section 6.5).

Despite many common features in the tillage and sowing of fields for Old World cereals and pulses, there are also important variations in several interrelated aspects: the type of tool used for tillage and what (or who) provides the labor to operate it, how often and when the ground is tilled, and the method and timing of sowing. Some of this variability is found in Alexis' Assiros and some further afield.

2.1 Two-Oxen Households in Paliambela

The lowland hamlet of Paliambela lies 45 km southwest of Assiros, below the town of Kolindros. The workforce of a Turkish agricultural estate occupied Lotzano, as it was then called, until the early twentieth century, when the area was incorporated within the Greek state and a syndicate from Kolindros bought the land. A few estate workers remained in Paliambela and were joined in 1922 by Thracian refugees from European Turkey. The Thracians had fled their homes temporarily a few years previously, but in 1922, knew they were leaving for good. "My father loaded my mother and us girls on the oxcart with the chickens, hand-mill, loom, cooking utensils, sickles, and two sacks of grain. Then, he emptied the remaining sacks, drained the wine barrels, and turned loose the rest of the animals. As we pulled away, one sack of grain fell off the cart."

In Thrace, most of the refugees had been farmers with their own plow oxen. For the first few years in Paliambela, they were landless and several families shared the abandoned two-room houses of the estate workers. They survived by plowing and harvesting for "local" landowners and, once they accumulated some cash, by renting a few fields to cultivate on their own account. In the late 1920s, each family was allocated 3–4 ha of land, depending on the number of children. The more industrious households rented, and eventually bought, additional fields so that they cultivated up to 5–6 ha of autumn- or winter-sown cereals and pulses and perhaps 1–1.5 ha of summer crops (e.g., maize). Nikos, born in 1929, orders two glasses of *tsípouro* (the north Greek equivalent of Italian *grappa*) before filling in some details. "Our fathers all had a pair of oxen. With one good pair, you could not sow more than 50–60 *strémmata* (5–6 ha) of winter crops, because every field had to be plowed twice: after the first rains, to break the stubble, and then crosswise after sowing, to cover the seed. After that, to break clods and make the field level, we harrowed with a bundle of wild pear branches – it has very tough wood." The Paliambela Thracians had too little land to sow only half of their fields every winter (as Alexis had done in Assiros). Fallowing was limited to the small area of summer crops, and most stubble fields were plowed only once, at the end of summer, before being sown again.

The Thracians used oxen for plowing and carting the harvest, whereas "locals" in Paliambela and many in Kolindros, perched on a hill, favored horses and mules for plowing as these served as pack animals on steep paths, carrying produce from distant fields and transporting merchandise over the hills to the town of Veria. Thracians and "locals" agreed that oxen plowed more thoroughly than horses or mules. Some "locals" also used oxen, but the refugees regarded a pair of oxen as a source of pride and, in their first years in Paliambela, these animals must have been the only material sign of their status as *farmers*. The first generation of Thracians maintained and, when necessary, replaced these costly assets, although initially they cannot have used them fully.

As Nikos' generation entered their teens, surpluses produced with oxen enabled some purchases of additional fields. By the 1950s, however, those born in Paliambela were marrying and setting up separate households, leading to subdivision of landholdings. Nikos stayed with his father, to accumulate property for his sisters' dowries, and continued plowing with oxen. Many of his contemporaries, starting independent households with only 1–2 ha of fields and lacking the cash to rent more, could not maintain oxen and started plowing with cows. Like horses and mules in Kolindros, draft cows had uses other than plowing – in this case, producing calves for sale to urban butchers. Mitsos, the oldest man in Paliambela, takes up the story over morning coffee. "My father plowed with oxen, big animals that he brought from Thrace. The older generation was proud of their oxen and they could really work. When I got married, I made up a lame pair of two little cows, thinking I could make money from the calves, but they could not do much work. I had to work them gently at the start of each season, until a callus formed on the neck where the yoke rubbed. It was the same with oxen, but they were stronger. They worked longer hours and plowed a bigger area; and the furrow went deeper and did a better job. The cows could not plow the heaviest soils, and some people only used them instead of

15

oxen after tractors came in and could be hired for the difficult fields. Oxen also lasted longer, working until they were 12 or 15 years old, whereas cows were worn out by 10–12 or even younger." Some of the oxen that came from Thrace in 1922 must have worked until they were over 20 years old, as Eleni and others of her age recall them around the village in the late 1930s.

Cows were less effective plow animals than oxen because they were smaller, less powerfully built, and sometimes worked while pregnant. Kostas, born in an oxcart en route to Paliambela, joins in: "we also worked them too young. Our fathers trained oxen from three or four years old, starting with pulling a cart – it is lighter work than plowing. They would not work them until they were four or five years old and strong. We sometimes worked the cows at two or three years because we had no other means of plowing." Diet affected the strength of both oxen and cows. In Kolindros, landownership was far more uneven than among the Paliambela Thracians, and some farmers owned enough fields to leave half fallow each winter. One such was Iraklis, who in his youth plowed with oxen and horses. Once the winter crops were sown, Kolindros farmers with well-fed oxen plowed their fallow fields in late winter, then again in spring, and a third time in autumn to sow the following crop. Pasture is very poor in late winter, however, and poorer farmers, who could not spare much grain for fodder, had to delay plowing fallow fields until May, when the new grass had restored their draft cattle's strength.

While some Kolindros inhabitants had enough land to practice biennial fallow or even leave large areas uncultivated, others owned a garden or small vineyard and few fields. They gathered every morning in the town square, armed with tools appropriate to the season, and waited to be hired for the day. I am nursing *tsípouro* to repel the mosquitoes, but Nikos says he is used to giving blood. As manual cultivators interest me, he calls over Vasilis, who married into Paliambela in the 1940s after growing up in Kolindros. "In spring we dug vineyards for other people. In summer we harvested. In winter we cleared new fields, but only when the weather was good. If it was raining or snowing, there was no paid work." Vasilis' father owned a 0.3 ha vineyard, from which he

16

produced wine and *tsípouro* for sale, and 2.5 ha of fields. He had a donkey for transport but too few fields to support oxen or even cows for plowing. "We sowed three quarters of the fields with wheat and the rest with maize. We got someone with oxen or horses to plow the wheat fields, and repaid them in cash or kind – three days of manual labor for one day's plowing. In spring, sometimes someone else plowed the maize field and we then dug and planted it, but sometimes we did the whole job by hand because we were rested after the winter break when we could not work. One spring, my father and I planted maize in a field here in Paliambela. It was not plowed and we took two weeks to dig it. In autumn, after months of hard labor digging and harvesting, we were too tired to cultivate the wheat fields by hand." Nikos, who later bought Vasilis' maize field, added that it measured 0.65 ha.

Nikos and the other Paliambela Thracians also had plentiful experience of digging fields with pick and mattock but supplementing rather than replacing the plow. Hand tools played a minor role in preparing fields for autumn sowing. "The oxen worked the fields well, but as a teenager I had to follow behind with a mattock, digging up the brambles that the plow did not dislodge." Sometimes, the mattock or pick went ahead so that brambles or saplings would not hold up the plow. Fields sown in spring, however, were worked more thoroughly to destroy weeds, which would compete vigorously as the weather warmed up, and to retard evaporation of scarce moisture from the soil (cf. Forbes, 1976; 1982, 205, 436–438). While the male household head drove the plow team, women and older children followed behind, digging out weeds and breaking clods to create a clean and even seedbed (Figure 2.1). Such scenes can still be seen in upland areas, such as Asturias or the Pindos Mountains, during late spring sowing of maize and potatoes. For farmers of moderate means, like Nikos' father, the area sown with summer crops depended on the number of household members fit enough for digging and hoeing. "We only sowed a few summer crops because the whole field had to be hoed after plowing and that was very hard work." In the case of maize, further hoeing was needed once the young plants had become established. Wealthier farmers

(a)

(b)

Figure 2.1 Tillage for planting maize and potatoes at Plikati, northwest Greece. (a) Two mules pulling an ard. (b) Manual weeding and clod breaking follow a mule-drawn ard.

could plant more maize because they hired poor neighbors, like Vasilis and his father, for the hard labor.

In both Kolindros and Paliambela, as throughout the Mediterranean, small gardens in backyards and in more distant locations with light tractable soils or accessible water produced onions, cabbages, salad plants, and so on for domestic consumption. They often

Figure 2.2 Manual cultivation of a vegetable garden at Plikati, northwest Greece.

contained a few rows of pulses (e.g., broad beans or peas, perhaps also grown as field crops) and in Asturias even small patches of spelt/emmer. Many such gardens were cultivated entirely by hand (hence the selection of light soils) because they are too small to maneuver a plow team (Figure 2.2). In Asturias, two experienced practitioners independently stated that they would yoke draft animals for half a day's plowing (400 m² – Section 2.6.1) but dig by hand plots half this size. A recent survey (Charles *et al.*, 2002) found that plots up to 200 m² were indeed tilled by hand, but some even smaller (conveniently long and thin) strips in open fields were plowed.

2.2 Scratching a Living in the Hills of Messenia

Within living memory, use of the plow was also restricted in many hilly regions by natural obstacles. Metaxada in Messenia, southwest Greece, is now largely depopulated, and the surrounding slopes are

19

extensively overgrown, but widespread traces of terracing and field boundaries are visible. Ilias, in his early 80s and too lame to negotiate the path down to the *kafenío*, welcomes visitors to his balcony overlooking the steep-sided valley where he has spent a lifetime herding goats and growing cereals, vines, and olives. Like Nikos in Paliambela, he learned to plow with his father's oxen. "Those who produced only 500–1000 kg of wheat plowed with little cows. Big farmers, real husbandmen like my father, only plowed with oxen. They were big animals that scattered stones and bushes when we cleared new fields. If you stood next to one of these animals, you could not see someone standing on the other side. But they needed feeding to work at their best. Wealthy farmers fed their oxen all year round with oats, hay and straw, but the poorer ones left them, once the sowing was over, to graze prickly oaks [evergreen bushes] on the mountain. Even some cows were strong if they were well fed."

Ilias plowed where possible, but digging with hand tools was necessary around rocks and near terrace edges; because of the width of the plow team, he could plow no closer to walls and boulders than perhaps half a meter. Working such slopes by hand was hard because the soil was full of stones. One day in 1950, Ilias and his brother with their young wives (they still maintained a joint household) were working on a stony high terrace. His sister-in-law cut her foot with the pick and started crying, in despair as much as pain. It seemed an opportune moment to suggest pooling their savings to buy land around the nearby town of Khora. "Do you want to dig with a mattock instead of a pick, and in soft earth?" The prospect of using a broad-bladed mattock, though by no means light work, persuaded his hobbling sister-in-law. Some households in Metaxada had too little land to maintain work animals and either hired a pair of oxen for an agreed amount of grain or exchanged two or three days of manual labor per day of plowing. In other hill villages, men and women of Ilias' generation described cultivating fields with so many boulders that the plow was not used at all.

Compared with the gentle slopes round Paliambela, plowing was inevitably slower on the steep and stony fields of Metaxada because of repeated interruptions to negotiate boulders or move the team between terraces that accommodated only a few short furrows. In such terrain, areal measurement of landholdings is neither easy nor meaningful, and farmers are consistently less willing than their lowland counterparts to offer such figures; they often refer to days of plowing (e.g., Methana, Peloponnese (Forbes, 2000a, 348, n. 8); Kalo Khorio and Skalani, central Crete), days of sowing (e.g., Agia Paraskevi, Pindos Mountains), or quantities of seedcorn (e.g., Anogia, highland central Crete) rather than areas sown (cf. Petropoulos, 1952, 89–92). Nonetheless, it seems that significantly smaller areas of winter cereals and pulses were sown per pair of oxen at Metaxada than at Paliambela. The fields of Metaxada were divided into two alternating bands of winter cereals/pulses and fallow. In the fallow zone, the best fields were plowed twice in March and planted with maize, New World beans, or chickpeas, while the rest were grazed uncultivated. In autumn, the poorer fields were sown with barley or oats "on the face of the earth" and then plowed only once to cover the seed. "If you had strong animals, you plowed the [remaining] good fields once after the first rains and then, two weeks later, sowed wheat and plowed them a second time to cover the seed." The two-week delay allowed weeds to appear and be destroyed by the second plowing. In fields too narrow for second plowing at right angles to the first, the furrows were aligned at a slight angle to reduce the chances of leaving ground untilled.

2.3 Tillage Time and Sowing Season from Assiros to Asturias

Despite Alexis' normative performance, methods of tilling and sowing were very variable in Assiros, reflecting farmers' variable circumstances. Assiros lies just north of the city of Thessaloniki. When Alexis was born in 1908, much of the arable land in the village was owned by a handful of Ottoman *beys* and cultivated by sharecroppers, often using oxen provided by the *beys*; these oxen were big and well fed, and the few villagers old enough to have seen them recalled their size and strength with admiration. Most of the remaining men of the village gained their livelihood by digging vegetable gardens on the outskirts of Thessaloniki or driving horse-drawn carts between the city and the towns of Serres and Nigrita. During the first two decades of the twentieth century, as the Ottoman Empire was dismembered, some of the more dynamic sharecropper households acquired substantial blocks of land from the departing *beys* and, in the late 1920s, land reform allocated smaller holdings of 3–5 ha to the rest of the community (Karakasidou, 1997, 164–169). Many in the latter category initially plowed by yoking a cow to that of a neighbor, later buying a horse to combine part-time farming with carting. Those with larger holdings (and, as in Paliambela, a few Thracian refugees) initially used oxen and later switched to horses. In 1940, when the Greek army mobilized the horses, rich farmers reverted to oxen, while their poorer neighbors used cows or buffalos and a few tried cultivating small areas of cereals by hand. Many Assiros elders thus had first-hand experience of several alternative means of tillage. By almost universal consent, oxen plowed more thoroughly than horses, but the latter were faster and more useful for carting. An enabling factor was the spread of iron plows designed for a single horse, which reduced the costs of equid traction.

Like all his neighbors old enough to have plowed with animals, Alexis emphasized the problems posed by weather during the autumn and spring sowing seasons. Around Assiros, there are both heavy and light soils, the former being more fertile but harder to work – especially when wet. Accordingly, farmers with access to both soil types, and also to strong work animals, prioritized sowing of heavy soils before repeated rainfall made them unworkable. "But, if it rained, we sowed light soils until wind dried out the heavy ones." Alexis grew oats to feed two horses that carried grain to and from the family's water mill in another village. As oats are undemanding and the quality of the harvest was not a vital concern, he sowed some oats directly onto the previous year's wheat stubble, plowing the field only once to cover the seed. As well as increasing the area available for sowing, this relaxation of the "norm" of alternate-year fallowing extended the effective length of the autumn sowing season because stubble could be worked immediately after rain, whereas tilled fallow fields needed first to dry out a little. As soon as the first rains made the ground soft, therefore, Alexis sowed and plowed in oats on stubble until last year's fallow plots were dry enough to start sowing the main wheat crop. When it rained again, he switched back to sowing oats on stubble until he could return to sowing wheat. Such tactics for making the most of the autumn tillage period were widespread. In Paliambela, Mitsos also sowed oats on stubble while aiming to plow his wheat and barley fields both before and after sowing, and in Haute Provence, einkorn was likewise sown on stubble (Duplessy *et al.*, 1996, 55). In Metaxada, Ilias worked stony terraces on rainy days when his better fields were too sticky for access, and he too aimed to plow wheat fields more thoroughly than those sown with the less demanding and less valuable oats and barley. In Kinigou, another hill village nearby, fodder lupines were sown on unplowed stubble, and in some regions, sowing was begun even before the first rains (e.g., *xirovolí* (dry broadcasting) in Kouklia, southwest Cyprus).

One year, lack of rain delayed the start of sowing at Paliambela until St Nicholas' Day, December 6. By this date, local farmers normally aimed to have *finished* sowing and, in neighboring Kolindros, the feast of *Panagía Xespirítsa* (Our Lady of the End of Sowing) on November 22 marked this aspiration (just as the feast of St George the Sower on November 3 signaled the start of sowing on Rhodes – Vrontis, 1938–1948, 111). At Assiros, Alexis also reckoned, with good weather, to finish sowing winter cereals before Christmas, again ideally before the end of November. By December, the cumulative effects of rain might make fields unworkable or overnight frosts might delay the start of plowing until late morning (to allow the ground to thaw). When sowing continued into January, there was a significant risk that heavy frosts would kill germinating wheat. "I remember one year, when the rains started late and I was still struggling to plow and sow the fields in March. With the frost, it was terrible, but I had no choice." Normally, however, he devoted any good weather in January and February to plowing fallow fields and in March started sowing these with pulses, maize, and sesame. Alexis was a moderately large landowner, who at one stage cultivated more than 10 ha of fields, so putting himself under considerable time stress during the autumn–winter sowing season. A few villagers managed substantially larger holdings by employing farmhands and running several plow teams, while neighbors with a single plow team but fewer fields (up to, say, 5–7 ha) normally sowed both cereals *and pulses* before Christmas.

Uneven landownership and access to work animals thus affected the timing of tillage and sowing. The variable responses from Assiros regarding sowing dates of pulses, in particular, are paralleled widely in Greece. The New World beans (*Phaseolus* spp.) and Old World black-eyed bean (*Vigna unguiculata*) seem invariably to have been sown in spring, and chickpea (*Cicer arietinum*) was normally sown at the same time or slightly earlier. Lentil (*Lens culinaris*), bitter vetch (*Vicia ervilia*), broad bean (*Vicia faba*), pea (*Pisum arvense*), and several *Lathyrus* species, however, seem variously to have been sown in autumn–early winter or early spring, as also in ancient Greece (Theophrastus *Enquiry into Plants* 8.1.4) and twentieth-century AD Jordan (Palmer, 1998, 157). In Paliambela, Koula and Marika insist that peas and broad beans sown in spring had to be picked green – the onset of summer drought prevented them from ripening, but elsewhere both autumn- and spring-sown pulses are harvested dry. Another consideration is that whereas wheat was normally a staple and sometimes an important cash crop, these pulses were – quantitatively speaking – of secondary dietary and economic importance, and their date of sowing seems sometimes to have been adjusted to avoid scheduling conflicts. Similarly, in northeast Turkey, where macaroni wheat recently displaced emmer, small-scale sowing of the latter for locally consumed cracked wheat or *bulgur* is now delayed until spring (Hillman, 1981, 147–148).

The date of onset of winter conditions of course varies with latitude and altitude. After the end of November, farmers in Assiros could not *rely* on good plowing and sowing weather, but their counterparts in the low hills just to the north *half-expected* snow cover. The residents of Plikati, at 1200 m in the Pindos Mountains, faced an even more restricted sowing season. Only the month of October could be depended on for sowing the highest terraces, where the snow settled first, and these were sown before the lower fields around the village to make the most of this narrow window. As elsewhere in the Pindos, villagers sowed wheat, barley, oats, and rye in autumn, before the snow came, and then again in spring (March–April), before planting maize, potato, and *Phaseolus* bean summer crops. In the case of wheat, barley, and rye, at least, distinct fast-growing varieties (e.g., "two-month" or "three-month" wheat and barley) were sown in spring. The autumn varieties were more productive, and both autumn and spring varieties failed or yielded poorly when sown out of season. Lentil and bitter vetch too were variously sown in autumn or spring, though it is said that those sown in spring "did not grow [in years] when it did not rain."

In the absence of scheduling conflicts, early sowing is normally favored, not only because wet or cold weather in midwinter may prevent tillage or reduce its thoroughness but also because a long growing season enhances yields. The former consideration exercises farmers especially in the northern Mediterranean and at higher altitudes, while the latter is critical further south, where rainfall during the winter–spring growing season is modest on average and very variable from year to year and rapidly gives way to summer drought. Early-sown crops benefit from relatively dependable winter precipitation, while late-sown crops are dependent on less reliable spring rainfall or, as they say in parts of Greece, "the early[-sown crop] is blessed by God, the late[-sown] by luck." Italian folk wisdom is even clearer: "early sowing is rarely a mistake" (Spurr, 1986, 42). Probably for this reason, in the early twentieth century, the growing of separate spring varieties of wheat and barley seems to have been significantly less common in lowland Greece than in the Pindos, where the brevity of the autumn sowing season strongly encouraged this practice. "Three-month wheat? Here? This place is dry. Even the winter crops don't grow if it doesn't rain," replied an octogenarian at Markopoulo in lowland Attica, central Greece. The same verdict was delivered at Anatoli in the dry southeast of Crete, but some central Cretan farmers sowed in March a little *Martáki*, descriptions of which suggest two-row barley (*Hordeum vulgare* ssp. *distichum*), because it produced

25

whiter and lighter bread than the staple six-row barley (*H. vulgare* ssp. *hexastichum*) sown in autumn–early winter. This spring barley only grew on the better fields, however, in the fallow year when these had been plowed repeatedly "like chickpeas" and even then was more at the mercy of spring rainfall than its less desirable six-row counterpart. Other farmers saw their neighbors' results with *Martáki* and did not try it themselves.

A distinctive ecological niche, in which spring-sown grain crops may, unlike *Martáki*, neither require intensive tillage nor risk water deficit late in the growing season, is the seasonally exposed margins of lakes and large rivers. In early nineteenth-century Thessaly, central Greece, Leake saw cereals sown in spring on the margins of Lake Karla when low water levels had ruined the fishing (Leake, 1967, 424). In 1974, the oldest residents of Kanalia, a village on the shore of Karla, recalled similar opportunism in 1895 when "three-month wheat" was broadcast without tillage on the dried-up bed of the lake; more modest falls in water level exposed reed beds rather than bare ground and could not be exploited. The floodplains of the larger rivers of northern Greece also posed problems. At Aiginio near the mouth of the Aliakmon, before the latter was canalized, New World beans and maize were sometimes sown in the alluvium left by retreating floodwaters. The spring (March–May) floods, fed by snowmelt in the mountains, were dependable, but their number and timing varied and renewed flooding sometimes swept away growing beans and maize. Earlier sowing of Old World cereals and pulses on this part of the floodplain was not worth attempting. Despite abundant moisture and rich soil requiring little or no tillage, therefore, the alluvial margins of Mediterranean lakes and rivers, without extensive drainage works, offer unreliable opportunities for spring sowing of most Old World grain crops (Section 5.1).

Within the main autumn–early winter season, the timing and order of sowing responded to several considerations. Even in semi-arid areas, late sowing of the heavier fields entailed some risk that harvests would be poor in rainy winters because wet ground was inadequately tilled. On the dry Cycladic island of Amorgos, farmers tended to sow the productive flat fields, on which they primarily depended, before the lower-yielding and more risk-prone terraces. Conversely, at Kalo Khorio in the hills of central Crete, the poorer terraces were sown before the heavier fields to allow time after the first rains for weeds to appear on the latter and be eradicated by the plow that covered the seedcorn. Moreover, especially in semiarid areas, farmers have to balance the disadvantages of late sowing (a short growing season and low yields) against the risk that the first rains might suffice for seed to germinate but not for seedlings to become established. Accordingly, on Amorgos, inessential broad beans and fodder pulses (common vetch and grass pea) were sown in November, before staple barley and wheat (Halstead and Jones, 1989). Similarly, in Jordan, wheat is sown at the optimum time, with barley and pulses scheduled before and after (Palmer, 1998, 146).

While fodder crops may be sown early on inadequately tilled ground to lengthen the plowing season, cereals may also be sown early on *fertile* land to encourage vigorous growth for "early-bite" grazing or green fodder. In Assiros, owners of sheep flocks sowed barley (less commonly oats and occasionally wheat) for this purpose (*khasíl*) on plots that, thanks to heavy manuring, were easily worked as well as fertile. In Asturias, spelt/emmer to be cut as green fodder (*alcacer*) for cattle was sown as early as August. Conversely, sowing may be *delayed* by choice rather than scheduling conflicts. In Asturias, the sowing of spelt/emmer or *pan* (literally "bread") for grain, now on a trivial scale and largely restricted to heavily manured infield plots, has recently shifted from November–December to December–January or even February, partly because of milder winters and partly to shorten the growing season and so reduce excessive crop growth and the risk of lodging (stem collapse). The same tactic was employed, albeit more selectively, in central Crete on the more fertile fields. In the same region, sowing of both chickpeas and *Martáki* spring barley was sometimes delayed to reduce the likelihood of heavy rain thereafter compacting the surface of the sown and plowed field and so making it difficult to harvest these short crops by uprooting. In the case of pulses eaten fresh, such as broad beans, sowing may also be staggered to ensure a longer season of green produce.

Finally, crops are sometimes sown late because an earlier sowing has failed (e.g., because severe frost has killed sprouting wheat). Common millet (*Panicum miliaceum*) can be sown very late in the growth cycle of the staple winter cereals and, being very small seeded, also requires little investment of seedcorn (also Spurr, 1986, 96–97). Alexis used to sow millet in April for fodder grain, broadcasting as little as 20–30 kg/ha – a tenth of the seedcorn normal for wheat or barley in Assiros. Occasionally, a farmer wishing to take advantage of actual or hoped-for early summer rainfall sowed millet here as late as June for cutting as green fodder. Tall Andonis did this in mid-June 1989, and although the field was very wet and so was plowed very poorly, a harvestable crop developed.

2.4   Juggling with Seedcorn

The amount of seedcorn used varies between crops. Alexis recited an old saying that advocated "sow broad bean upon broad bean [densely] and chickpeas with big gaps between [sparsely]" (*koukkí apáno sto koukkí kai to revíth' edó ki ekeí*). In Asturias, traditional advice is: "if you don't want to leave the shop [if you want to keep buying staple grains], sow spelt thinly and maize thickly [so that both yield poorly]." Around Sault in Haute Provence, southeast France, einkorn is sown far more sparsely than bread wheat because it tillers more strongly – each germinating grain produces more shoots. For broadcast sowing of cereals, a rule of thumb repeated in different parts of Greece (e.g., Loukopoulos, 1983, 182, n. 2), and again attributed to past generations, is that there should be four to five grains in the hoofprint of an ox. Although practical application of this mnemonic is hard to imagine, the implied sowing rate of perhaps 150–250 kg/ha (assuming a 10–12 × 10–12 cm hoofprint and 1000 wheat grains/50 g (cf. Gill and Vear, 1966, 258)) falls within the range for broadcast wheat in northern Greece.

In practice, farmers diverge from such general guidelines for several reasons. With broadcasting, an even coverage of seedcorn is needed to avoid weeds growing up in unseeded gaps and then outcompeting or pulling down the crop. Broadcasting evenly requires considerable skill, and some farmers sowed densely to compensate for lack of dexterity. Other things being equal, however, farmers prefer low sowing rates to minimize costs. In small-scale "garden" cultivation, they often sow by dropping seeds into small holes (dibbling) or a furrow (row sowing) and covering them with their foot or a hoe. Dibbling and row sowing need significantly less seedcorn than broadcasting: for broad beans, a third or half as much, according to two farmers from Skalani in lowland central Crete and Manikia in the hills of Euboea, respectively. Such anecdotal estimates match well those from controlled observation of seed drills in nineteenth-century AD Britain (McConnell, 1883). Without a mechanical seed drill, however, broadcasting is the fastest method of sowing, although row sowing may be speeded up, in plots large enough to till with animals, by using a plow both to create the furrow and to cover the seed afterwards.

Dibbling and row sowing ensured more even distribution and reliable covering of seed than broadcasting, while row sowing, at least, facilitated weeding of the growing crop (Section 5.5). Row sowing was the norm for summer crops (e.g., maize, chickpea), which need intensive hoeing, and was fairly common in Greece for small-scale pulse crops, even when sown in autumn or winter. For example, in a study of pulse gardens and fields around Tharounia in Euboea (Jones *et al.*, 1999, 171–175, table 2), dibbling and row sowing with a hoe were restricted to small plots of up to 34 m², while row sowing with a plow and broadcasting were practiced on plots as large as 1000–2000 m² (0.1–0.2 ha). Dibbling and row sowing seem to have been commoner with the larger-seeded pulses (e.g., broad bean around Tharounia, broad bean and chickpea at Assiros), and broadcasting seems more usual with smaller-seeded species (e.g., winged vetchling (*Lathyrus ochrus*) around Tharounia; lentil, grass pea (*Lathyrus sativus*), and common vetch (*Vicia sativa*) at Assiros). This contrast, also observed in Jordan (Palmer, 1998, 146), reflects greater difficulty both of evenly broadcasting large grains and of individually planting small grains.

Some elderly Greek farmers report past attempts at sowing wheat in rows, either to facilitate weeding or, especially during

World War II occupation, to economize on seedcorn. At Iklaina in the hills of Messenia, "Farmakis" ("Poison," after a failed attempt at the age of 10 to make coffee in his father's *kafenío*) claimed to have used only one third of the normal amount of seedcorn on a good field that he regularly row-sowed with wheat. In Kolindros in the early 1940s, 12-year-old Nikolaos and his three younger brothers helped their parents hoe 1 ha of row-sown wheat to obtain clean seedcorn. Farmers found manual row sowing prohibitively labor-intensive for large-scale application, however, and either abandoned the attempt or applied it to just the odd field to produce clean seedcorn, perhaps for sale. In Asturias, an ethnoarchaeological study of intensively cultivated spelt/emmer (Charles *et al.*, 2002) encountered two row-sown plots of 15 m^2 and 60 m^2, but broadcasting was more usual and consistently reported to have been the norm in past years, when spelt/emmer was grown on a larger scale.

Farmers also vary sowing rates to manipulate how crops grow. Cereals grown as pasture or green fodder were sown more densely than those to be harvested for grain: for example, 240–280 kg/ha for pasture barley versus 200 kg/ha for grain barley in Assiros; 350 kg/ha for pasture barley versus 300 kg/ha for grain barley in Filoti, on the Cycladic island of Naxos; and 50–60 kg/ha for pasture millet versus 20–30 kg/ha for grain millet in Assiros. Similar variation in sowing rates is reported from central Italy for forage and grain rye, barley, oats, maize, broad beans, lupins, and vetch (Camera di Commercio, Industria e Agricoltura, Frosinone, 1954). Sowing densely increases the volume of pasture or forage and also its quality. A farmer in Khora, Messenia, was growing a few rows of closely set maize plants in the garden for his two milk goats: "sowing thickly produces slender stems that the goats can eat – otherwise they are too hard and only cattle can eat them."

As noted in Section 2.3, cereals grown for pasture or green fodder were often sown on well-manured plots to secure lush growth. Crops for grain also tended to be sown more densely on fertile, heavy, and flat fields, "because they could support it," than on poor, light, and sloping land: a "hoofprint-of-ox" guideline recorded in 1932 in central Crete was 5–10 seeds on heavy and 2–3 on light soil

(Pagkalos, 1983, 6). Heavy sowing of light land may yield poorly, as a result of excessive competition for scarce nutrients and moisture, while light sowing of rich land may allow weeds to take advantage of favorable growing conditions. In Greece, Spain, and Italy (e.g., Spurr, 1986, 57), while some farmers increased sowing rates on fertile plots so that a dense crop smothered weeds, the reverse also occurred quite widely. Informants at Iklaina in Messenia and Knossos on Crete sometimes sowed fertile plots sparsely to promote tillering and thus a shorter crop stand that was less vulnerable to lodging. Light sowing also reduced the risk of vigorous plant growth exceeding water supply, and sowing rates on Crete, though usually reported per day of plowing rather than unit area, seem to have been consistently low (about 100–150 kg or less per hectare vs. 150/200–250 kg/ha in lowland northern Greece).

2.5   Flexible Farmers

While recent premechanized tillage and sowing practices exhibited broad similarity in different parts of the Mediterranean, there is considerable variability in the manner, timing, and frequency of their execution. In part, this reflects regional differences in climate: for example, the order in which different cereals and pulses were sown (and whether or not these included distinct spring varieties of wheat and barley) was influenced by the extent to which low growing-season rainfall posed a greater hazard to crop production than severe winter weather that hindered tillage. Other differences reflect local variability in terrain (e.g., more intensive tillage of level than sloping fields) or medium-term shifts in weather (e.g., milder winters enabling later sowing in Asturias) or production goals (e.g., changes in staple crops affecting the scheduling of sowing). Also relevant (and often interrelated) are the size of plots and their distance from home (Jones, 2005): small plots tend to be worked by hand and planted by dibbling or row sowing, while large fields are plowed and broadcast; and nearby fields are more likely to be manured (Section 5.3.1.3), with potential implications for ease of

31

tillage and the density and timing of sowing. Farmers also make a wide range of flexible adjustments to interannual fluctuations in growing conditions (e.g., late sowing of millet to capitalize on a wet summer or compensate for a failed winter crop). These, coupled with differences in treatment between crop types and plots with contrasting soils or topographic situations or cultivation histories, may obscure any overall pattern in decision-making. Moreover, local or temporary conditions may occasion not merely adjustment, but reversal, of general principles: for example, level and fertile fields are generally sown early and thickly but may be sown late and thinly if there is a risk of excessive growth. Apparently conflicting advice from different Roman writers on sowing density and the like may reflect contrasting (but unstated) assumptions regarding such contingent variables (e.g., Spurr, 1986, 57).

Individual farmers often do things differently, because they are more or less industrious, conservative, proud, burdened with dependents to feed, or blessed with "hands" to help. Much of the variability of practice described earlier can be understood, however, in the context of broader differences of strategy between large- and small-scale cultivators. Fotis was one of a small group of octogenarians that assembled every evening on the bench outside the cobbler's shop in Assiros. The others made approving noises as he summed up the difference between "us poor" and the *tsorbatzídes*, the few big landowners who could afford to feed their farmhands with *tsorbás* – a nutritious porridge (cf. Karakasidou, 1997, 271 n. 41). "The rich left half their fields fallow every year because they could not sow them all [in autumn-early winter]. The poor sowed nearly all their fields every year, because otherwise they did not have enough to eat." By common consent, wheat gave higher yields after tilled fallow than after another winter cereal or pulse (Section 5.2.1). Fallow also allowed those with plentiful land to spread the labor of repeated plowing and so till their fields more frequently, and hence more thoroughly, than would otherwise have been possible with animal traction. They sowed in autumn on a field plowed perhaps three times during the fallow year and so relatively free of weeds, providing a well-worked seedbed favorable to root development and presenting a fine and even surface that facilitated infiltration of rainfall. Smaller-scale farmers, forced to sow their fields every year, plowed the previous stubble once at best before sowing, if rain in late summer or early autumn softened the ground enough for it to be worked (even without rain, their large-scale counterparts could probably plow in the stubble of any summer crops planted on the well-tilled fallow). A field plowed only once since the previous autumn tended to be weedier, had a poorer seedbed, and absorbed rain less effectively, and, of course, these problems were exacerbated if the stubble was plowed when the ground was still dry and hard or if the field had been poorly plowed in the previous autumn. When Alexis in Assiros sowed oats directly on stubble, he expected a poor crop because the share would jump as he plowed in the seed, leaving untilled patches where competing weeds could flourish. Thus, although thorough tillage was of great importance for successful crops, the extent of a farmer's land influenced the frequency and timing of plowing – provided she/he had the means to plow the land. Those without plow animals were in the worst position: to sow their fields, they had to rely on the good will or avarice (depending on the agreement made) of a neighbor or relative with underused plowing capacity and so tended to till late or poorly and sometimes left land uncultivated.

The following section explores further the relationship between scale of cultivation and sources of power for tillage, looking at the benefits and then costs of different forms of plowing and manual cultivation.

2.6 Ard, Hoe, and Scale of Cultivation

2.6.1 Ard versus hoe: Benefits

Across the Mediterranean, before adoption of the standard hectare of $10000\,m^2$, land was widely measured in terms of the notional area that could be plowed in a day: the Roman *iugerum* (cf. *iugum* = yoke) of 0.25 ha, the *dia de bueyes* (= oxen day) of 0.08 ha in upland eastern Asturias, the nineteenth-century Greek *strémma* (= turning, perhaps referring to the *boustrophedon* movement of the animals) that varied locally between 0.09 and 0.16 ha (Psikhogios, 1987, 24–25), and the Turkish *dönüm* (also = turning), the value of which similarly varied. Comparable terms for the area (usually of vines) that could be cultivated manually per person per day are less common but much smaller: the nineteenth-century Greek *axinári* (cf. *axína* = mattock, hoe) of 0.05 ha (Psikhogios, 1987, 34) and its Venetian equivalent, the *zapada* (cf. *zappa* = hoe), of perhaps 0.03 and 0.05 ha in different parts of southern Greece (Forbes, 2000b, 321). Of course, these "norms" for plowing and hoeing represent administrative conventions, as illustrated by the confusion surrounding imposition of Venetian metrical standards in southern Greece around 1700 (Forbes, 2000b; Davies, 2004, 113–116). The experiences of non-mechanized Mediterranean farmers predictably reveal a more complex reality.

First, "plowing" covers several different tillage operations, for which farmers routinely use different words. Alexis in Assiros reckoned that the first "cutting" (*kópsimo*) or "breaking" (*khálasma*) of stubble in late winter was harder and slower work (0.1 ha/pair of oxen/day) than the subsequent second and third plowing of fallow in spring (0.15–0.2 ha/day), plowing in of harvested maize or sesame in late summer (≤0.2 ha/day), or covering of seed in autumn–early winter (≥0.1 ha/day, including delays for sowing). The Roman author Columella offered a similar ranking of four successive tillage operations for alternating fallow–wheat (Spurr, 1986, 137), and in modern Paliambela, where repeated plowing of fallow was not the rule, Mitsos also considered the "opening" (*ánoigma*) of stubble (≤0.15 ha/pair of oxen/day) slower than the subsequent covering of seed (≤0.2 ha/day). While subsequent workings of fallow are often described in Greece simply as *divólisma* (second plowing), *trivólisma* (third plowing), or *stávroma* (cross-plowing), the first plowing is widely distinguished as an arduous process of "breaking" or "cutting" or "turning up" (e.g., for Crete, Pagkalos, 1983, 3; southern Spain, Peña-Chocarro, 1999, 32). For this reason, farmers sometimes broke fallow with more widely spaced furrows (perhaps 50 cm apart), whereas overlapping furrows (say, 30 cm apart) were needed to cover over seedcorn. Moreover, as iron plows (plows, sensu stricto, that turned the soil) became widely available in Greece during the twentieth century, many farmers used them primarily to break stubble and retained their wooden ards to cover seed after sowing because they left a flatter surface that did not need to be harrowed. Likewise, in Asturias, a heavy plow (*cambiecha*) broke hard ground, while the lighter "Roman ard" (*arado Romano*) covered the seed after sowing. The turning plow tilled the ground more thoroughly than the ard, but farmers who have used both are divided on which of the two was faster. Some suggest that the plow was easier to pull, because it threw the soil aside, and others that it was more demanding of draft animals, because it turned rather than scratched the soil. This disagreement supports a third group of respondents who perceive choice of iron plow or wooden ard as not critical to speed of tillage.

[margin handwritten: "mixed modernity = co-existence of ard & iron plow]

Secondly, speed of plowing is significantly affected by the heaviness of the soil, and again, farmers tended to use the "new" iron plows (which were more effective against weeds) on heavy and wooden ards on lighter soils. Partly for this reason and partly because the ard is better suited to stony ground, iron plows were favored in valleys and wooden ards on slopes. Some farmers, in both northern Greece and Asturias, also favored the ard on slopes because it caused less soil erosion than the plow. This selective adoption of new tools highlights how ecologically contingent may be the relative merits of primitive and advanced technology and also how technologically contingent the distinction between marginal and prime arable land. While the lighter soils of the hills and mountains are in general easier to till, however, than their heavier counterparts in the valleys, this is often more than offset in upland farming by the small size and dispersal of fields or terraces, steepness of slopes, and abundance of boulders. In about 40 estimates, from various parts of Greece, of the area plowed in a day by two cattle, most lowland farmers suggested between 0.15 and 0.3 ha, while upland farmers suggested between 0.1 and 0.2 ha (or considered such figures meaningless in broken terrain). Corresponding figures from Jordan are similar: 0.3–0.4 ha in the plains and 0.15 ha in the hills (Palmer and Russell, 1993, 48).

A third significant variable in tillage speed is type of muscle power. Where individual informants offered comparative figures, thus minimizing differences of soil, equipment, and tillage frequency, a fairly consistent rank order emerged. Pairs of horses (≤0.4–0.5 ha/day) were faster than single horses (about 0.3 ha/day), which matched or outperformed pairs of oxen (0.2–0.3 ha/day). Oxen worked faster than cows (0.1–0.2 ha/day), although well-fed cows of improved breed used by the last generation of non-mechanized farmers sometimes matched earlier oxen. On Kithira, pairs of donkeys (usually yoked like cattle but sometimes harnessed with a collar like horses) plowed perhaps half the area worked by cows and were generally avoided for large fields or heavy soils. In each case, the daily rates cited are suggested modal figures for plowing in gentle terrain; figures from upland villages in more difficult terrain, for example, in Asturias or the Pindos, tend to be substantially lower. Finally, well-fed oxen were not only faster than cows but tilled more thoroughly (deeper, wider, and more even furrows – also Palmer, 1998, 142) and broke heavier ground than cows or horses. In some areas, the "ears" or "wings" on the old wooden ards were set further apart for oxen than cows to create a wider as well as deeper furrow.

A fourth consideration is the number of hours worked, and level of exertion tolerated, per day. As Iraklis in Kolindros observed, "two horses can plow up to 5 *strémmata* (0.5 ha) in a day, but only if the farmer is young enough to keep up – that means a lot of walking." In Kalo Khorio, Crete, we drank strongly scented sage tea, listening to Kostis, now in his 60s. He had been so dynamic a plowman in his youth, I learned afterwards, that he managed the unusual feat of tiring his big Serbian horse. Draft cattle worked more slowly, so the limiting factor was less likely to be the plowman. In Assiros, Vangelis had come out of retirement to help excavate the nearby Bronze Age settlement. A workaholic, he grumbled when photography or planning forced him to rest his handpick. I found him in the *kafenío* one evening, passing round a few of the charred barley and bitter vetch seeds that he had found on site. The burnt barley grains reminded his companions of wartime "coffee," and they were proud to recognize the bitter vetch, unfamiliar to the tractor-driving younger men around them but once grown as fodder for oxen. The discussion moved on to oxen and Vangelis' all-too-plausible confession that he was an impatient farmer. He had pushed his oxen to plow 3–5 *strémmata* (0.3–0.5 ha) in a long day, but the next day, they would not get off their knees; 2–3 *strémmata* (0.2–0.3 ha) was more realistic. Stoïlis agreed: "I could plow and sow 2 *strémmata* per day on my own. If someone else did the sowing, I could plow 3 *strémmata*, but it wasn't worthwhile because the oxen got no rest and quickly tired out." At Llanos de Somerón in Asturias, Lucino had once similarly pushed the family's two cows to plow 0.16 ha per day, double the standard *dia de bueyes*, so as to finish plowing before starting military service. On the steep slopes around his village, however, this had tired the animals to a degree that was not sustainable.

Part of the variation in estimates of area plowed per day is thus attributable to farmers sometimes offering a realistic average during an extended period of tillage and sometimes citing the area that could be plowed, under favorable circumstances, in one day (cf. Forbes, 1982, 92). Interestingly, in various regions of southern Greece where land was measured not in units of standard area but in days of plowing, the local rule-of-thumb conversions of the latter seem consistently to have been optimistic: 0.3 ha/day for the Cycladic island of Milos (Wagstaff and Augustson, 1982, 131), 0.2–0.25 ha/day for Cycladic Naxos (Kasdagli, 1999, 410) and Methana in the Peloponnese (Forbes, 2000a, 348, n. 8), 0.2–0.3 ha/day for Skalani in central Crete, and 0.15–0.2 ha/day for Kalo Khorio, also in central Crete but in more difficult terrain. Thus, the "day of plowing" (like the Roman *iugerum* and the old Turkish *dönüm*, also of 0.25 ha – Davies, 2004, 115) seems to refer to the area that could be tilled by a reasonably fit pair of *oxen* over a full working day, even though many of the farmers using this term plowed (more slowly) with cows or single mules. This "optimism" reflects the contexts in which villagers used days of plowing to estimate land area. In the broken terrain where this currency had not been displaced by standardized measures of absolute area, days of plowing

37

were of little use for calculating the sale value, productivity, or taxation potential of a farmer's land. Their primary use was in assessing the cost, to a farmer without, of hiring plow animals. In Kalo Khorio, we have finished the sage tea. Fountoulonikolis is a retired farmer and miller in his late 80s. He is tired, but will not take his afternoon nap until satisfied that I have understood. A 0.25 ha group of boulder-strewn terraces included a significantly smaller area of cultivable soil and yielded far less grain than a level field of the same overall extent. With allowance for the delays caused by boulders and terrace walls, however, the two blocks of land took a similar length of time to till, and on this basis, both were described as *miás zevgarás* (one day's plowing) and cost the same (in cash or days of manual labor) to have plowed. The *zevgará* was the area cultivable in a day by a pair of *well-fed oxen* because the owners of *powerful* work animals were more likely to have spare plowing days, and less likely to fear harming their team through overwork, than those (like Mitsos in Paliambela) who struggled to till their own land with underfed cows.

In this light, the nineteenth-century Greek *strémma* and Turkish *dönüm* of 0.09–0.16 ha appear rather small for official measures based on the area plowed per day. It has been suggested that they represented square fields of 30 × 30 or 40 × 40 paces (Petropoulos, 1952, 89; some informants volunteered the same), suitable for cross-plowing, but on the plains of north and central Greece, where fields are *relatively* regular in size and shape and land measurement in areal extent is most meaningful, rectangular fields (around both old villages and newer settlements of 1920s refugees) are usually oblong rather than square. Moreover, fields of 30 × 30 or 40 × 40 paces would provide rather short sowing strips – at least, for oxen on flat land. While hill farmers in Crete recall strips only 25–50 m long, dictated by uneven terrain or the limited strength of draft cows, stronger oxen in the plain round Paliambela plowed strips as long as 100–150 m; where a field was too long for the stamina of draft cattle, it was divided into two or more sets of shorter strips to allow more frequent pauses, while the plow was turned between furrows, and more frequent grazing breaks while the next strip was sown.

Questioned about the size of *strémma* used in Kolindros, Nikolaos replied, "1000 square meters, that is, 10 meters [the width of a sowing strip] by 100 meters; that's a good distance for oxen to plow – any more and they tire." Depending on terrain, fragmentation and dispersal of plots, weather, and strength of draft animals, a farmer might sow and plow two, three, or even four strips in a day. The *strémma/dönüm* of 0.09–0.16 ha may thus originally have represented not the area plowed in a day, but the strip(s) sown and then plowed before oxen were stood down to graze; this is consistent with the Roman *iugerum* of 0.25 ha representing the sum of *two* blocks of 35 m (a Roman *actus* or furlong) by 35 m. Alternatively, the *strémma/dönüm* may have represented the area plowed per day by a pair of small draft cows.

The speed of manual cultivation is subject to the same contingent considerations as plowing with animals. The initial breaking of stubble, probably with a narrow-bladed pick, tends to be far more arduous than subsequent seedbed preparation or weed control with a broader mattock. Heavy soils and weedy plots require more work than light soils with few weeds. On average, young adults dig faster and more thoroughly and can work a longer day than children and the elderly. While plowing was normally a male task, women frequently did digging. Nikolis, a *tavérna* owner in Skalani, has tired of teaching me to extract snails from their shells – I am a lost cause – and turns his attention to my younger companions whose technique is beyond reproach. "In the old days, girls of their age were tough; they dug the vineyards. Any girl like these three – soft and white (he used the same words to praise bread made from spring barley) – would be stolen. A young man would gather his cousins, they'd break down the door and take her away – whether she wanted to go or not." We learned later that Nikolis had firsthand experience of this custom.

Hired workers often dug vineyards and so norms for the number of vines to be dug per day are volunteered reasonably freely. Nikolis reckoned something like 0.04 ha (120 vines spaced 2 m by 1.80 m apart) per day was reasonable, although the local soils are fairly heavy. In nearby Knossos, Giorgis, one of Arthur Evans' old workmen, reckoned on 0.03 ha (or 100 vines) per day for hired diggers. Reported figures from the Peloponnese, of 0.03 ha/day for Methana (Forbes, 2000b, 322), 0.05–0.06 ha/day for Elis and Messenia (Topping, 1972, 78), and 0.05 ha/day for Khora in Messenia, are broadly similar and match those already cited for the Venetian *zapada* and Greek *xinári*. Digging of vines, however, took place in spring and sometimes followed plowing between the rows with a mule and, on both counts, is not an ideal analogue for manual cultivation of grain crops sown in autumn–early winter. An elderly market gardener from Assiros suggested that workers in Thessaloniki were expected to dig a certain number of rows, amounting to 0.02–0.05 ha/day depending on the tractability of the soils. Market gardening entails exceptionally intensive tillage (with hand cultivation often supplementing initial plowing), however, and so is usually practiced on light soils, again posing potential problems for extrapolation to manual grain growing. At Kastrisianika on Kithira, I watched Babis, on his day off from work as a builder's laborer, dig a garden last cultivated only a few months previously. Working steadily but sustainably, he needed a day to dig over about 100 m² or 0.01 ha to one spade depth. On a larger scale, at Paliambela in lowland northern Greece, Vasilis' and his father dug their 0.65 ha maize field at a rate of 0.02 ha/man-day, although he also suggested that two people needed a whole week to dig 0.1 ha, equivalent to less than 0.01 ha/man-day.

For manual cultivation to sow autumn–winter cereals and pulses, relentless questioning of reluctant informants elicited broadly similar responses. In the Pindos Mountains, the following estimates were offered, mostly by elderly men for digging by their wives, sisters, and daughters: "perhaps 10–15 days for 3 *strémmata*" (0.02–0.03 ha/man-day) at Zitsa; "four people took two days to dig perhaps 500 square meters" (0.006 ha/man-day) at Pigi, Konitsa; "perhaps a quarter of a *strémma* per woman per day" (0.025 ha/man-day) at Dikorfo in the Zagori; "one week per *strémma*" (say, 0.015 ha/man-day) at Agia Paraskevi; and "two or three families, say, ten persons in all, would get together and might dig one *strémma* in a day, but it was tiring and they could only keep it up for one week" (0.01 ha/man-day) at Metsovo. An elderly man in Kranea, near Metsovo, added that "you cannot dig if you put on weight – your belly gets in the way."

40

At Zureda in Asturias, Severina spoke from personal experience in suggesting "eight or ten hours for half a *dia de bueyes* but spread over several days because it was tiring" (say, 0.03 ha/woman-day). Hajnalová and Dreslerova (Hajnalová and Dreslerova, 2010, 176) report an elderly woman burning, raking, and hoeing 0.01 ha in one day in Romania. These estimates of 0.006–0.03 ha/man-day are reasonably consistent, given the variability in soils and composition of the workforce, and bracket the range of 0.01–0.02 ha/man-day for hoeing inferred from late third-millennium BC texts in Mesopotamia (Maekawa, 1990, 140–142, tables 6 and 8), while the upper figure matches that suggested for nineteenth-century manual cultivation of cereals in the Var region of southern France (Amouretti, 1986, 201–202). Being lower than the more widely available norms for digging vines (and than comparative figures of 0.02–0.05 ha/man-day under different climatic/edaphic and agronomic conditions – Russell, 1988, 114, table 19), they accentuate the gulf in tillage rates between manual cultivation and plowing with animals.

Arguably more informative are the reasons why farmers were reluctant to give estimates for manual tillage of autumn–winter cereals and pulses. One practical reason is that manual cultivation usually *supplemented* animal-powered tillage (see Section 2.6.3), replacing the plow mainly in terrain where measurement of land area was difficult or rather meaningless. Similarly, as some of the examples cited make clear, farmers working their own land tended to spread the arduous task of digging, making it difficult to estimate labor expenditure; as one Cretan widow commented on her lifetime of hard labor, "I never thought to measure how much I dug." Manual labor was hired for digging relatively high-yielding vegetable gardens and vineyards, leading to the establishment of norms for a full day's work – as with plowing, such norms are a by-product of the commoditization of labor. Conversely, unproductive terraces sown with grain crops did not justify hiring workers, but were dug by household members or by larger groups of kin and neighbors gathered on the basis of reciprocal assistance to make the task less tedious. "We dug our own fields or swapped labor" is a common refrain in Crete. Plots accessible to the plow, however, were usually prepared for autumn–winter grain crops with work animals – if necessary, borrowed or hired from someone else.

Arrangements for hiring, sharing, or borrowing plow animals are discussed in the succeeding text (Section 6.7), but of interest here is the widespread practice of exchanging a plow team for manual labor. Such manual labor might include tasks like reaping or beating olives but most commonly involved breaking clods and digging weeds behind the plow. In Metaxada and Palaio Loutro in Messenia, Kalo Khorio and Skalani in Crete, Kolindros in northern Greece, Agia Paraskevi and Kipourio in the Pindos Mountains, and Casalattico on Monte Cairo, central Italy (Forte, 2009), one day's plowing was normally reciprocated with two or three person-days of hoeing, an exchange sometimes rationalized as 2 hoers/diggers = 2 draft cattle and 3 hoers/diggers = 2 draft cattle + 1 plowman. By contrast, in eighteenth- to nineteenth-century southern Italy, as many as 5 or 10 laborers could be hired for the same sum, *in money*, as a pair of oxen (Delille, 1977, 147) – a rate of exchange more compatible with the contrasting speeds of manual cultivation (0.01–0.03 ha/person-day) and plowing with cattle (0.1–0.3 ha/day). The significance of the low rate at which a day's plowing was reciprocated with manual labor is discussed in the succeeding text (Section 6.8). It was not dictated by scarcity of manual labor, however, as is made clear by accounts of landless laborers gathering every morning in the square of Kolindros in the hope of being employed for the day. Giorgis in Knossos makes the same point over his excellent *rakí*, homemade from *moskháto* grapes. "Most people here worked as day laborers for a huge estate with kilometers of vines. His foreman drank too much and, one evening, went in turn to all the *kafenía* of the villages around, having a few glasses in each and asking for workers to dig a vineyard. When they all turned up, at dawn the next day, they were far too many and started fighting over who would work."

More important perhaps than daily tillage rates is the area cultivable *per season*. The size of landholding issued to farmers (Tsopotos, 1974, 140) for cultivation with oxen, and sometimes identified as a Greek *zevgári*, Turkish *çift*, or Venetian *para di bo* (literally "pair [of oxen]"), is fairly consistent: for Byzantine estates, 8–10 ha in the eleventh to twelfth century AD (Harvey, 1989, 54) and 5–7 ha in a thirteenth-century document (Davies, 2004, 116); for Ottoman estates, about 9 ha around 1600 AD in Macedonia (Moskof, 1979, 60), 8–9 ha in early eighteenth-century Messenia (Parveva, 2003; Zarinebaf, Bennet, and Davis, 2005, 192–193), and about 20 ha for two to three pairs of oxen in eighteenth-century Boeotia, central Greece (Asdrakhas, 1988, 188); for seventeenth-century Venetian occupation of the Peloponnese, perhaps 8–9 ha (Davies, 2004, 116); for early nineteenth-century Greece, perhaps 7.5–8 ha *per plow team* (Palaiologos, 1833, 93); and in late nineteenth-century Thessaly, 9–15 ha *per plow team* (Prontzas, 1992, 266, table 47). A survey from early twentieth-century southern Italy indicates that farmers with oxen could cultivate 10 ha (Delille, 1977, 128–129). Excepting the Thessalian data (linked to a three-year rotation – Prontzas, 1992, 298–299), most of these figures probably refer to land under alternate fallow, implying that a farmer with one pair of draft cattle could sow 4–5 ha of autumn–winter cereals and plow another 4–5 ha of fallow (some perhaps sown with summer crops) annually. Even ignoring uncertainties over rotation regimes, metrical systems, and possible inclusion of unplowed pasture, these figures reflect contractual arrangements for exploiting human labor rather than measurements of the potential of draft cattle. In some cases, farmers probably worked land in addition to that documented (e.g., Laiou-Thomadakis, 1977, 69–71), and given that the word for "oxen" in Greek, Italian, and Spanish (*vódia, buoi, bueyes*) is also used loosely to refer to draft *cows*, the identity of any recorded plow animals is ambiguous.

Oral accounts of tillage in twentieth-century Greece provide a little contextual detail. At Assiros and Paliambela, in the favorable terrain of lowland northern Greece, most farmers came close to Nikos' estimate of up to 5–6 ha of winter crops with a single pair of oxen (cf. 4.2–7.5 ha in Jordan – Palmer, 1998, 139). Higher figures were suggested for horses in the same terrain and variable but lower figures for oxen in hilly or mountainous areas and for cows in both steep and gentle terrain. Even in Assiros and Paliambela, estimates of the area of winter crops sown with the aid of a pair of cows ranged between 1–2 ha and 4–5 ha. The higher figure related to recent improved breeds, which rewarded more generous feeding with greater size and strength as well as a supply of milk. The lower figures were for local breeds – tolerant of minimal feed, producing no milk, and performing a modest amount of work – but the limiting factor in some cases may have been land rather than draft power. For poorly fed cows that also produced occasional calves, a figure of 2–3 ha of winter crops seems realistic and is consistent with suggestions from lowland Crete and northern Greece and from the Pindos Mountains that owners of a single cow, making a pair with a neighbor who also owned one draft animal, might expect to cultivate 1–2 ha of winter crops.

In the light of these twentieth-century figures, historically attested allocations of 8–10 ha under biennial fallow were surely farmed with the aid of oxen sensu stricto and would have made fairly full use of the plowing capacity of such a team. As with the area that can be plowed in a day, therefore, the term for the unit of land that can be plowed in a year (*zevgári*, *çift*) is associated with high performance levels. A farmer cultivating with draft *cows*, rather than *oxen*, plowed on a smaller scale, because cows worked more slowly and for shorter periods. Moreover, if cows were also used for breeding, then calving in winter or spring was likely to interrupt autumn–early winter sowing or plowing of fallow fields and sowing of spring field crops. In Asturias, cows routinely worked until the seventh month of pregnancy and occasionally calved in the yoke, but the area they plowed per day was small. Cows also cut shallower and less even furrows than oxen, favoring the development of patchy and weedy crop stands – especially given that sowing was less likely to take place after plowed fallow. Less thorough tillage in turn increased the need for subsequent hoeing and clod breaking, while plowing with understrength animals often involved a second person to lead or even drag the team, in addition to one steering the ard from behind. Plowing with cows, rather than oxen, may thus have demanded significantly more human labor, as well as being substantially slower and less effective. And if unfavorable weather or scheduling conflicts led to a heavy field remaining untilled for a year, a pair of cows might struggle to bring it back into cultivation. One May in Paliambela, Mitsos' small draft cows could barely break the surface of a heavy field that had been left unplowed for nearly two years, and he had to hire a pair of powerful male buffalo to bring it back into cultivation.

Few historical sources shed light on the amount of land that a farmer without plow animals might take on: in the Byzantine case, a quarter (i.e., 2–2.5 ha, again probably including biennial fallow) of the allocation to a farmer with a plow team (Harvey, 1989, 52); and, in southern Italy, from 2–3 ha intensively farmed to 3–4 ha (perhaps 4–5 ha in less fertile areas) under extensive cropping, with winter grain crops in each case making up half or less of the total (Delille, 1977, 128–129, 131, 136, n. 89). Oral estimates of the area of winter crops cultivable by hand are also few and difficult to interpret, as they tend to relate to areas of difficult terrain and/or to households lacking sufficient manpower to secure access to work animals even by hiring or in exchange for manual labor. At Palaio Loutro in Messenia, families supplemented plowed winter cereal fields with manual cultivation of perhaps 0.1–0.3 ha of less accessible plots – in addition to small vineyards dug later in the year. At Zitsa in the hills of northwest Greece, it was suggested that a household may have cultivated by hand perhaps 0.3–0.5 ha of land too steep or rocky for the plow. At Plikati, high in the Pindos, a figure of only 0.1–0.2 ha of manual cultivation was suggested "for the poorest families, but other people lent them oxen after they had finished plowing their own fields." In these cases, informants were estimating something they had never had reason to measure, in terrain unsuited to areal measurement, and manual cultivation had *supplemented* plowing. At Mavrorakhi in the hills above Assiros, an elderly refugee woman had seen manual cultivation by poor farmers with no plow animals in early twentieth-century central Turkey. She suggested that two adults could work up to 1.0–1.5 ha, perhaps comparable with the Byzantine figures and lower estimates from southern Italy.

The area cultivable by hand of course depends on the number of workers: some higher figures from southern Italy involved mobilization of a family labor force including grown or teen-age children, as well as parents (e.g., Delille, 1977, 130), which will only have been possible at optimal points in the domestic cycle (cf. Gallant, 1991, 78–81). Although elderly Mediterranean villagers are often remarkably sprightly, it is not uncommon to see old women who are permanently "bent double" – broken by tasks like hoeing and reaping. That physical toil also takes its toll of men is illustrated by the Albanian migrant workers who latterly did most of the manual labor of tobacco growing in Paliambela. As one employer (who worked alongside them) observed, "the Albanian men are used to work, hard and resilient, but they are in their 20s and early 30s – after that they are finished." Only with early marriage and prompt birth of healthy children, therefore, could a household of manual cultivators expect to enjoy the benefit of fit adult workers from two generations. The strength of manual laborers, like that of draft animals, was also liable to seasonal variation, especially if nutritional standards were low – as in Kolindros, where Vasilis and his father lacked the strength to dig their own cereal fields in winter.

Finally, like plowing, manual tillage was dependent on favorable weather and ground conditions. Like many of his generation, Nikolis in Skalani espouses practice over theory and has summoned us to his garden on a sunny morning in late March for enlightenment on good horticultural practice. He points to the ground that he dug over during a dry spell in late winter; it rained shortly afterwards and the earth can now be hoed with ease to plant courgette seeds. His impatient son worked the rest of the plot when the ground was wet and the rain that followed made the surface "like cement." Plainly, mistimed tillage can create soil conditions inimical to crop growth, and one disadvantage of manual cultivation must have been a reduced ability to take rapid advantage of brief windows of weather and soil conditions favorable to sowing.

With these provisos, a larger area (say, 4–6 ha) of winter grain crops could be sown with draft oxen than with cows (perhaps 2–3 ha) or manual cultivation (perhaps 1–2 ha, depending on household size and composition). The faster tillage methods also enabled timelier sowing and more thorough working of any fallow land and presumably made household labor capacity more stable over the domestic cycle. To put these figures in perspective, informants' estimates of the amount of grain needed to feed the human members of a household for a year cluster around 1000–1500 kg (probably including seedcorn but excluding modest amounts of pulses). This might be harvested from 2–3 ha of winter cereals, with low area yields of 500 kg/ha, or just 1–1.5 ha, with more optimistic, but attainable, area yields of 1000 kg/ha (Section 5.6). A household could feed itself, with more optimistic yields, by hand tillage or shared access to a pair of draft cows or, with low yields, by ownership of a pair of draft cows and would not need oxen, on either scenario, to meet domestic consumption needs.

2.6.2 Ard versus hoe: Costs

As Alexis in Assiros emphasized, premechanized plowing involved long and often cold or wet days trudging over uneven and perhaps sticky ground, coaxing more or less reluctant draft animals, and sometimes struggling to keep the share free of mud. By common consent, however, the tribulations of the plowman paled into insignificance alongside the backbreaking toil of manual cultivation. Why was the animal-drawn plow not in universal use? A simple wooden ard was not difficult to make – although some were made by specialists (e.g., in Jordan – Palmer and Russell, 1993, 38–39), many farmers made their own (e.g., in central Greece – Loukopoulos, 1983, 14–26; eastern Spain – Palanca, 1991, 22), ideally working a hard wood such as holm oak (*Quercus ilex*) or prickly oak (*Quercus coccifera* – e.g., Pagkalos, 1983, 6) with an axe, and only bought the iron share tip, often from passing gypsy smiths. Much of the skill in making an ard lay in choosing a suitably curved piece of wood (e.g., Loukopoulos, 1983, 19–21) to minimize the number of joints that were hard to make and easily broken; at Neo Sidirokhori in northeast Greece, Konstantinos' father spent much of his "leisure" time making wooden tools and, walking to and from the fields, made a mental note of any trees with a growth form suitable for making curved or angled tools like plows. The size and weight of homemade ards varied and, as Ilias in Metaxada describes, were adjusted to the strength of draft animals: small cows struggled to pull a heavy ard, but a light ard pulled by strong oxen would break if it encountered rocks. Despite selecting hard wood, the ard (usually the body, rather than the working tip) did break during plowing – especially if the wood contained knots. According to Ilias, prudent farmers kept at least two ards so as not to lose valuable time when the weather was suitable for tillage. At the end of a day's plowing, if a farmer intended to resume work the following day in the same area, the ard (after removal of the purchased iron share) might be left out overnight – it was not regarded as a major capital item.

Plowing with animals required some strength and skill, which not everyone possessed. Maria, now housebound, giggles with embarrassment as she describes her teenage attempts at plowing in the late 1930s in another Messenian hill village, Milioti. The draft animals would pull the share out of the ground and hurry to the end of the field, dragging Maria and the plow after them. With more experience, she would have pushed the share into the ground with her foot to act as a brake, as Sofia had once done in Cretan Aloides to rescue a lame male neighbor who had lost control of his draft cattle. Koula in Paliambela gave up plowing her own fields, when her husband died, because unaided she could not lift the heavy yoke to harness the draft cattle. Far more numerous, however, are stories of women who have excelled at plowing, in place of an absent husband or deceased father. Lack of physical strength or specialist skill did not normally present a serious obstacle to making or using an ard plow.

As noted earlier, the use of a plow may be impracticable in very small plots or when only small patches of soil can be tilled between boulders. Pairs of draft cattle are capable, however, of working quite steep slopes (better so than mules, it is said, although a single equid can of course plow a narrower terrace than a pair of cattle) and (*pace* Gilman, 1981) are easily trained to stop pulling when they encounter tree roots. Elderly Mediterranean farmers consistently identify lack of draft animals as the principal limitation on using the plow. In the twentieth century, as many Mediterranean farmers switched from cattle to horses or mules, the acquisition of plow animals often involved a significant cash outlay, because few arable farmers kept breeding horses. In Greece, horses and mules were usually bought from gypsies or pastoralists at the annual livestock fair in a nearby market town. Cattle had long been the usual draft animals, however, and in some regions, the verb *zeugarízo* (literally, I (work with a) pair) meant "I plow" (e.g., Crete – Pagkalos, 1983, 3), even when farmers did so with a *single* horse. Many households reared their own oxen or draft cows, retaining two bull calves if income from their sale could be spared and powerful animals were needed but otherwise yoking breeding cows. Working cattle were also bought, sometimes trained and sometimes not, from a neighbor or at the livestock fair, although some households again found this capital outlay prohibitive (cf. Psikhogios, 1987, 48), especially if restricted landholding precluded a rapid return. Calves destined for work might begin very light training in their first summer, taking a few turns on the threshing floor with older animals, and might be tied to follow the cart, before they were old enough to be yoked. Ideally, new draft animals pulled an empty cart before their first outing with the plow and were initially yoked with an experienced animal that took the lead. It was more difficult to train two novices, and sometimes, in addition to the plowman behind, a second person had to lead or pull from in front for a few days. In Paliambela, however, Koula's father made his first team from two young bullocks that he yoked and set to plow alongside his uncle's experienced pair; they learnt in eight days. Cattle, mules, and donkeys alike became accustomed to working on the left or right side of a pair, unless care was taken in training to swap them round regularly, and this was impossible if a novice was paired with an experienced animal accustomed to one side. When buying a draft animal, therefore, farmers looked for one of complementary side, and also similar size (to avoid asymmetrical draft), to its intended partner. These constraints made it even more difficult to be self-sufficient in draft animals, as farmers ideally needed not only a working pair but also both a left- and a right-sided reserve. The same constraints of compatible side and size existed when owners of a single animal sought a neighbor with whom to make up a pair.

Cattle also needed to be fed. Those that did not work could graze outdoors for much of the year, often supervised by children. For work animals, especially in the slack period between spring and autumn plowing, many village communities in Greece reserved an area of good pasture (*voidolívado*, ox pasture; *zevgarolívado*, (yoked) pair pasture; *moularolívado*, mule pasture) near the settlement (e.g., Loukopoulos, 1983, 92–95). When bad weather or lack of pasture made stall-feeding necessary, nonworking cattle could largely subsist on crop residues such as straw or maize leaves and cobs, although provision even of such by-products in sufficient quantities could be demanding. The use of straw for fodder inflated the labor of harvesting, transporting, and processing cereals (Chapters 3 and 4). "How much straw does a cow need over winter?" usually attracts disbelief or the answer "lots." In the Paliambela *kafenío*, Mitsos always thinks before responding and admonishes those who answer without firsthand experience. He suggests something like two cartloads (i.e., several cubic meters) of straw per head and the rest of the over-70s coffee circle nod or tap their sticks in approval. The period of enforced stall-feeding at Paliambela, in lowland northern Greece, was short compared to highland villages in the Pindos or Asturias and of course longer and more inevitable than in lowland Crete. At Kalo Khorio, in the hills of central Crete, Fountoulonikolis has returned from his siesta and considers the same question. Winter grazing was richer here than in Paliambela and landholdings were small, but draft cattle plowed the olive groves in winter once field crops were sown. He reckons that 20 donkey-loads of chopped straw (considerably more compact than harvested sheaves) were needed for a pair of cattle stall-fed only when working. Assuming five Cretan pack animals carried the same as one Paliambela cart (Section 3.4), these two estimates are similar, but they mean more when translated into the area of grain crops needed to produce them.

In Paliambela, Mitsos cultivated just 2 ha of grain crops with his "lame pair of two little cows," while his father maintained four to five cattle (including two draft oxen) and cultivated a little over 4 ha of grain crops. Both found that 1 ha of cereals usually produced just enough straw to overwinter one cow or ox, but straw yields (roughly half of the harvested crop, by weight) vary from year to year like those of grain. In years of poor harvest (or if rain penetrated and spoiled the outdoor straw stack), therefore, Mitsos and his father had to buy and cart straw from one of the villages in the fertile Giannitsa plain. Veteran farmers in the hills above Paliambela offered very similar figures: Nikolaos in Kolindros reported that 3 ha of cereals yielded insufficient straw for 2 oxen in bad years, while Giorgos in Kastania had in his youth maintained 10 oxen, cows, and calves on the straw from 12 ha of grain crops. Overwintering a pair of draft cattle in lowland northern Greece thus needed something like 2 ha of straw, matching or exceeding the area needed to produce grain for the human members of most recent households (see the succeeding text). On the poor soils of Kalo Khorio, in central Crete, yields of both straw and grain will have been significantly lower than around Paliambela, and area measurement of cereal plots had little meaning. Fountoulonikolis' 20 donkey-loads of chopped straw for two working cattle, however, were derived from 60 loads of harvested barley sheaves and, in a good year, these might have yielded 2.5–3 tons of barley grain – well above the grain requirements for human consumption of most recent households.

Not surprisingly, therefore, those who maintained draft animals frequently emphasize the value of cereal straw. In the Skalani *tavérna*, Nikolis is again imparting agronomic expertise to accompany his wine, pickled wild bulbs, and boiled greens. He is extolling the virtues of spring barley or *Martáki*, for making bread, so we ask why it was only grown on a small scale. One consideration was the labor involved, because the field had to be worked very thoroughly, but autumn-sown barley was also taller and yielded more of the straw needed for draft cattle and horses.

Providing straw for a pair of draft cattle may have been challenging, in both north and south Greece, for a household that cultivated grain crops just for domestic consumption. A farmer with two plow oxen, who wanted to avoid *buying* replacements, also had to feed at least one (preferably two) breeding cows and one or two bullocks that were being reared to an age and strength suitable for yoking. Such a farmer, with four to six cattle, needed straw from a significantly larger area of cereals than the grain requirements of the human members of the household dictated (an estimated 1.5–3 ha of straw to feed two oxen, a calf, and two donkeys (Halstead and Jones, 1989, 48) refers to tall cereals dressed with chemical fertilizers). In Paliambela, some Thracians who owned and reared their own draft cattle, but had modest landholdings, threshed large quantities of cereals for Kolindros farmers (both those wealthy enough to subcontract this task and those too poor to maintain their own work animals) in return for the straw from the crop. In Kalo Khorio, owners of draft cattle threshed for those without work animals on the same basis, while their counterparts in the hills of central Greece plowed the fields of those without a team in return for the straw from the eventual harvest (Loukopoulos, 1983, 157–158).

At least during the plowing season, when fodder requirements may be more than double maintenance rations (United Nations Food & Agriculture Organisation (FAO), 1972, 45–46), most farmers fed draft animals with grain: usually oats or barley for horses and mules but bitter vetch by preference for cattle. Farmers all over Greece describe coarsely ground bitter vetch as making cattle "drunk" and increasing their strength dramatically. Draft cattle were usually fed a few handfuls of grain while working, perhaps also smaller amounts while stalled over winter, and then none during idle spring and summer days when they could graze. Mitsos in Paliambela fed about 2 kg of grain per day, from October to March, to each of his small draft cows. This amounted to 800 kg per year for his plow team – "too little for the big oxen that they brought from Thrace." Estimates from Kolindros, Assiros, and Mavrorakhi, still in lowland northern Greece, ranged between 800 kg and 1–2 tons per year for a pair of draft cattle, with the higher figures linked to better-off farmers with oxen that plowed fallow as well as sown fields. On the other hand, at Assiros and neighboring villages in the first decades of the twentieth century, some households cultivating on a large scale maintained several pairs of working oxen used in rotation. Two or three pairs each worked a two- to three-hour stint, and while the plowman continued with the other team(s), the resting oxen grazed the edge of the field under the supervision of a child. Farmers using such multiple plow teams, with each ox working fewer hours and spending time at pasture, may have needed significantly less fodder per head than their counterparts with a single pair of overworked draft animals. Lower requirements of grain fodder are reported in Crete for a pair of cows plowing on a small scale: 200–300 kg in upland Lasithi and 200 kg in Kalo Khorio, where "they were only fed when they were plowing or threshing – the rest of the time they grazed outdoors." Working cows in Asturias seem not to have been fed grain, but their normal diet was hay rather than straw and their work rate was modest.

The volume of feed needed thus depended on the size of draft cattle, how much they worked, and the quality of any pasture available during the plowing season. Elderly informants often emphasized that the oxen of wealthy farmers were better fed and stronger than the cows of poorer neighbors, but draft cattle could only be underfed to a degree. In Paliambela, Koula and Marika, both in widow's black, recall a man of their fathers' generation who was known in the village for his meanness. He underfed his oxen to the point that they had to be lifted to their feet in the stable, and his children only avoided hunger because their grandfather loaned his team. For a household producing primarily for domestic needs, therefore, requiring perhaps 1–1.5 tons of cereal grain for human consumption, the maintenance of an effective pair of draft cattle would have entailed a significant increase in the scale of cultivation. Nonworking cows, by contrast, often received little or no high-quality fodder, as a story from early twentieth-century Carraluz in Asturias illustrates. A landlord sent his farmhand to the cattle byre with instructions to turn the cows loose to graze and leave the oxen indoors (to consume richer fodder). The farmhand confused his orders and turned loose the oxen, simultaneously jeopardizing their ability to work and wasting fodder on the cows. His error was immortalized because it was considered self-evident what he should have done.

Horses were often stall-fed, and with grain, year-round, so that one horse was frequently said to need as much grain as two oxen (as in nineteenth-century England – Stokes, 1853). This was often cited as a disadvantage of draft horses, but other informants emphasized the convenience of not having to take them out to graze or of being able to leave them tethered in a field, whereas oxen had to be watched. Coupled with the widespread verdict that horses tilled more quickly but less thoroughly than oxen, the implied concern for time efficiency partly reflects wider changes in the decision-making environment, including greater opportunities for paid employment, more diverse ways of spending money, and growing constraints on child labor from formal education. It also reflects pressure to modernize – "fashion" as one Assiros farmer put it.

The considerable cost of running draft animals is also underlined by estimates of the area of land devoted to fodder grains by individual farmers. In early twentieth-century Assiros, one of the big share-cropper households, which had bought large blocks of land from the Turkish *beys*, sowed 1.5 ha of bitter vetch for four to six oxen. Many smaller landowners in Assiros, Paliambela, and Kolindros used to sow 0.5 ha of bitter vetch for two draft cattle. The number of "hands" available in early summer also limited the area sown in bitter vetch, as the harvesting of this low scrambling crop, necessarily by uprooting, was particularly backbreaking (Section 3.3). To varying degrees, the coarse-ground bitter vetch was mixed with barley, maize, broad beans, or other pulses, so the recurrent figure of 0.5 ha of bitter vetch per pair of draft cattle may be a significant underestimate of the overall scale of provision. Sheep, pigs, nonworking cows, and humans also consumed these other grains, however, and farmers did not identify the area sown for draft cattle. Set against the 3–5 ha of fields allocated to farmers in early twentieth-century land reform, even 0.5 ha is a large area to devote to grain for draft cattle, and many farmers could spare less: Nikolis' grandfather in Skalani, central

Crete, sowed 0.3–0.5 ha of bitter vetch for two oxen; at Tharounia in the hills of Euboea, 0.2–0.3 ha of bitter vetch is reported for two draft cows; and Yannis at Lazarades in the hills of northern Greece sowed only 0.1–0.2 ha of bitter vetch for two oxen.

Finally, although the costs of feeding work animals and, if necessary, buying replacements were the principal obstacles to owning a plow team, farmers also draw attention to the importance and practical difficulty of housing oxen and storing their fodder (e.g., Loukopoulos, 1983, 84). Mitsos' problems with storing straw in open-air stacks have been mentioned, and he started married life by erecting a barn before building a home for himself and his wife. Straw can be stored in flimsy (e.g., wattle) structures and grain fodder was not bulky, but housing for big animals like oxen had to be fairly sturdy. One poor farmer in Assiros did not rear bullocks for sale because he lacked the means to build a stall robust enough to contain a large animal. In the mountains, the need for winter stalling is self-evident, but even at low altitude in Crete, a byre seems to be regarded as a prerequisite for owning work animals. Lack of overnight shelter during the autumn–winter plowing period would have reduced the capacity for work of draft cattle, especially if fodder rations were less than generous.

2.6.3   On balance: Hoe or ard, cows or oxen?

Unsurprisingly, the advantages of oxen over cows over human laborers in tillage are offset by higher fodder costs. Despite variability in soils, terrain, climate, and tillage regime, the area that could be worked per day by each form of labor displays some consistency across the Mediterranean for basic biomechanical reasons (FAO, 1972, 25–31; Russell, 1988, 120, table 24). The same probably holds for the area workable in a winter sowing season, although relevant figures are, significantly, much more widely available for oxen than for cows or human laborers. Farmers are less ready to volunteer estimates of fodder costs, partly because rations for draft animals tend to be subsumed within fodder for other animals and partly because the scale of provision is often dictated by availability of land and labor rather than by perceived needs. In consequence, the scale of tillage was often constrained by the level of feeding of draft animals (and indeed human workers).

Against this background, opinions inevitably vary on the scale of cultivation necessary to justify maintenance of draft oxen or cows. Nonetheless, the minimum figures offered in lowland Assiros and Paliambela, of 1–2 ha for a pair of cows and 3–4 ha for a pair of oxen, in each case *without* biennial fallow, are plausible. Something like 2 ha of cereals and pulses may have provided enough straw for a pair of cows, and *at least* 1–2 ha were probably needed before some of the grain harvested could be spared for fodder (assuming a household grain requirement of 1000–1500 kg and "optimistic" yields of 1000 kg/ha). Moreover, because plowing with oxen entailed capital costs of purchase or maintenance also of breeding cows, there were obvious attractions to plowing with cows up to their suggested limit of 2–3 ha of winter grain crops. Even farmers with holdings of 2–3 ha, however, sometimes lacked the capital to acquire work animals, like Vasilis' father in Kolindros, or perhaps supplemented farming with a second occupation (e.g., cobbler) that made it difficult to care for large animals. The availability of plow teams for hire or loan obviously played a part in the ability of some farmers to continue without work animals, although, as Alexis in Assiros put it, "they only came when they had finished their own, so it was a lottery." As well as such practical considerations, ownership of plow animals was a matter of status: for the Paliambela Thracians, only a good pair of oxen really conferred dignity on a farmer; and in a hill village north of Assiros, "one cow [yoked to another belonging to a neighbor of similar means] was enough for poverty, but with two oxen, you could buy things." Even more so, informants recalled digging fields suitable for plowing with some embarrassment, although such concerns with dignity are doubtless related to practical considerations of avoiding drudgery and reducing the risk of underproduction. Significantly, most Greek villagers with land but without work animals preferred to exchange their own manual labor for the services of a neighbor's plow team. In a society where working for others is demeaning, this preference underscores the difficulty of growing grain crops by hand.

2.7 Tillage and Sowing in the Past

Tillage and sowing are perhaps the two defining characteristics of farming, as distinct from gathering, of plants. How and when recent non-mechanized farmers performed both tasks varied greatly with climate, topography and soils, type and intended use of crop, and especially scale of cultivation. Thanks to the correspondence between muscle power and feeding costs, cultivation by hand or with small or large draft animals was associated with a trend from small-scale self-sufficiency to large-scale surplus production. For similar practical reasons, type of tillage power was related to sowing and harvesting methods and rotation and fallowing regimes and, more broadly, was a symptom and cause of social and economic inequality.

These recent observations may be applied to the past in two complementary ways: first, where archaeological or textual evidence exists for particular tillage methods or sowing seasons, to suggest contingent factors that perhaps favored or enabled these choices; second, where evidence exists for contingent constraints, to suggest likely tillage and sowing practices. In either case, such analogies must be used heuristically: to identify relevant questions, suggest likely answers, and thus target further research.

Both method of tillage and timing of sowing are central to Sherratt's (1981) argument that early European cultivation with hand tools (e.g., hoe, digging stick) was displaced by plow agriculture as part of a "secondary products revolution." Early cultivation involved fixed-plot horticulture on rich alluvial soils, with spring sowing to avoid destruction of growing crops by winter floods (Sherratt, 1980). He saw the ard and yoking of paired cattle as related technological innovations that diffused into Europe from the Near East in the fourth to third millennia BC. Animal-drawn ards facilitated colonization of agriculturally marginal areas, by rapid cultivation of lighter and less fertile soils, and promoted social inequality (Sherratt, 1981), by enabling surplus production and making arable land a scarce resource (Goody, 1976). This chapter raises several questions about this model.

First, recent farmers regarded autumn–early winter as the most productive and reliable season for sowing the cereals (other than millet) and pulses (other than chickpea) available in the prehistoric Mediterranean. When sown in late winter or early spring, these crops were at the mercy of undependable March–April rainfall, as Hesiod recognized in the eighth century BC (*Works and Days*, 479–492). Theophrastus in the fourth century BC also considered most "two-month" and "three-month" cereals less productive than their more usual early-sown counterparts (*Historia Plantarum* 8.4.4–8.4.5). In both the recent past and first millennium BC, spring sowing tended to be a response to prevention of earlier sowing (e.g., by scarce labor or unfavorable weather) or failure of an early-sown crop (e.g., from severe frost). Spring sowing of alluvial margins of lakes and rivers (especially those fed by rainfall rather than melting snow) occasionally yielded windfall harvests but was even less dependable than spring sowing away from floodplains. This suggests that Neolithic sites in alluvial environments mainly cultivated land not subject to regular flooding or normally depended for subsistence on resources other than crops. Either way, this undermines claims (contradicted by the location of many Early Neolithic sites – Wilkie and Savina, 1997) that the rapid spread of farming across Europe reflects colonization of a highly restricted alluvial niche (van Andel and Runnels, 1995).

Secondly, farmers, recent and ancient (Hesiod *Works and Days*, 432), often made their own ards and yokes. Especially for the simple types first encountered in Europe (Sherratt, 1981), carpentry skills were probably less critical than the ability to choose wood of suitable species and especially shape. Given the importance of prompt and thorough cultivation and the drudgery of manual tillage, attaching cattle to a digging stick was probably attempted independently in different regions. Rare fourth- and third-millennium BC finds of ard marks and models of yoked or plowing cattle are compatible with diffusion into Europe from the east, but the absence of earlier such finds does not preclude earlier plowing. Conversely, at Knossos on Crete, skeletal pathologies, compatible with traction-related stress, suggest the regular use of cattle (mainly cows rather than oxen) for plowing from at least the sixth millennium BC (Isaakidou, 2006). It may not be coincidental that this evidence is particularly abundant from so early on Crete, where long and severe summer drought delays the start of sowing but places a particular premium on early completion. Here, plowing with cattle would have greatly speeded up tillage and sowing and reduced the risks in growing staple crops (Isaakidou, 2008).

Thirdly, the proposed link between the ard and marginal colonization is groundless. In the recent past in the Mediterranean, manual tillage was common on light soils, because these were selected for intensively worked gardens, and on poor upland soils, because steep slopes, boulders, and small, scattered plots slowed ard cultivation, while longer stall-feeding over winter made draft animals costlier to maintain. Reliance on ard cultivation cannot be inferred, therefore, from occupation of agriculturally marginal areas (*pace* Sherratt, 1981; van Andel and Runnels, 1988).

Fourthly, recent experience suggests that the considerable costs of maintaining draft cattle, rather than technological know-how, may have been the primary limitation on use of the ard. Adoption of the ard is likely to have been piecemeal, therefore, depending on local and interhousehold differences in scale of cultivation, potential length of sowing season, and ability to feed working cattle (Isaakidou, 2008). Large, high-performance oxen (i.e., castrated males) have particularly heavy maintenance costs, can only be replaced if breeding cows are also kept, and do not provide calves or milk in addition to labor. Conversely, a pair of cows (especially if shared between neighbors) costs less to run but can plow a smaller area. The economic and social significance of the ard thus depends greatly on the type of animals that pulled it.

Indications of plowing with *cows* at Neolithic Knossos (Isaakidou, 2006), sparsely paralleled elsewhere in Europe, are compatible with early use of the ard to facilitate, and reduce the risk of, cultivation rather than extend its scale radically. Draft cows, whether shared or not, are likely to have plowed on a modest enough scale for hand tools to have followed the ard routinely, consistent with indications of intensive cultivation in Neolithic crop weed assemblages from Hungary and Bulgaria (Bogaard, 2005). Nonetheless, although compatible with a "domestic mode of production" (mostly) by and for the household, cultivation with draft cows could have enhanced output differences and facilitated competitive overproduction between households, thus promoting economic and perhaps social inequality from an early stage of the Neolithic (Isaakidou, 2008), as Bogucki (1993) has suggested for temperate Europe.

The maintenance of specialized draft *oxen*, however, was probably linked to large-scale overproduction and thus to salient social inequality, as envisaged by Sherratt for plow agriculture in general. For example, pairs of working cattle with masculine epithets, recorded in Linear B texts by palace officials at later second-millennium BC Knossos on Crete (Killen, 1993), were apparently involved in large-scale, centrally administered cereal growing (Killen, 1998) producing much of the surplus that fed several thousand palace servants and craft workers (Halstead, 1999). A similar picture emerges from at least the fourth to third millennium BC in Mesopotamia (e.g., Heimpel, 1995) where draft cattle and the plow had elite associations in iconography (Sherratt, 2006) and literature (Vanstiphout, 1984). On Crete, palatial cereal growing was apparently concentrated near major centers (Bennet, 1985), and comparison of textual with bio-archaeological evidence indicates that palatial control of regional agricultural production was both restricted and selective (Halstead, 1995; 1998–1999). Whether "nonpalatial" agriculture was dependent on tillage with cows, or even by hand, should become clearer once more faunal data are available from nonelite sites.

Variation in means of tillage and scale of cultivation is also a crucial issue for Greco-Roman antiquity. In Greece, Hesiod around 700 BC advised the use of adult male draft cattle (*Works and Days*, 436–438) and spring or summer plowing of fallow (*Works and Days*, 462–464), while Theophrastus and Xenophon in the fourth century BC implied the predominance of cereals alternating with bare fallow (Amouretti,

1986, 51–52; Isager and Skydsgaard, 1992, 24). Their descriptions resemble extensive surplus-generating agriculture of the recent past, but these authors were drawn from and writing for a class of well-off landowners (e.g., Amouretti, 1986, 233). While a few rich men in fifth- and fourth-century BC Greece owned large estates of perhaps 20–50 ha, historical and archaeological evidence suggests that the *zeugites* ("pair farmers") who served as citizen–soldier *hoplites* typically owned something like 3.6–5.4 ha (40–60 *plethra*) of arable land (Burford Cooper, 1977–1978; Amouretti, 1986, 205–207; Foxhall, 1992; Osborne, 1992). The nature of *zeugites'* draft animals is not certain, but holdings of 4–5 ha would have warranted oxen, if devoted mainly to grain crops grown in some form of rotation, or could have been farmed with cows, if grain crops alternated with fallow; they seem unlikely to have sustained draft oxen *and* biennial fallow (*pace* Isager and Skydsgaard, 1992). In addition, poorer Athenian citizens or *thetes* owned perhaps as little as 1–2 ha, an area that could perhaps have been worked by hand and certainly by shared access to draft cows and that, on either scenario, is unlikely to have permitted regular fallowing. Thus, the agricultural regime emerging from literary sources probably reflects that of the richest landowners, *possibly* including some *zeugites*, but surely not most citizen farmers. The Roman "agronomists" are likewise primarily concerned with plow agriculture and with oxen more than bulls or cows (White, 1970, 285), while Columella, at least, favors alternating cereal and fallow (Spurr, 1986, 118). Their perspective on grain growing is again that of the prosperous extensive cultivator, and much of the advice of Cato and Columella is formulated for substantial estates of about 50–60 ha (e.g., Amouretti, 1986, 224) – a world apart from allocations to resettled colonists in second century BC Italy, the smaller of which (5–10 *iugera* or 1.25–2.5 ha – Hopkins, 1978, 57, n. 81) could have been worked with draft cows or perhaps even by hand. Again, the written sources probably shed little light on the husbandry practices of these small-scale farmers. Such sharp differences in scale of Greco-Roman land tenure and cultivation are likely to have been matched by differences not only in means of tillage but also in other aspects of crop husbandry (Section 5.7).

References

Amouretti, M.-C. (1986) *Le pain et l' huile dans la Grèce antique: de l' araire au moulin*, Les Belles Lettres, Paris.

van Andel, T. and Runnels, C. (1988) An essay on the 'emergence of civilization' in the Aegean world. *Antiquity*, 62, 234–247.

van Andel, T. and Runnels, C. (1995) The earliest farmers in Europe. *Antiquity*, 69, 481–500.

Asdrakhas, S. (1988) *Elliniki koinonia kai oikonomia 18 kai 19 ai*, Ermis, Athens.

Bennet, J. (1985) The structure of the Linear B administration at Knossos. *American Journal of Archaeology*, 89, 231–249.

Bogaard, A. (2005) 'Garden agriculture' and the nature of early farming in Europe and the Near East. *World Archaeology*, 37, 177–196.

Bogucki, P. (1993) Animal traction and household economies in Neolithic Europe. *Antiquity*, 67, 492–503.

Burford Cooper, A. (1977–1978) The family farm in Greece. *The Classical Journal*, 73, 162–175.

Camera di Commercio, Industria e Agricoltura, Frosinone (1954) *Prodotto netto dell' agricoltura della Provincia, 1938–1949–1950*, Ufficio Provinciale di Statistica, Frosinone.

Charles, M., Bogaard, A., Jones, G. *et al.* (2002) Towards the archaeobotanical identification of intensive cereal cultivation: present-day ecological investigation in the mountains of Asturias, northwest Spain. *Vegetation History & Archaeobotany*, 11, 133–142.

Davies, S. (2004) Pylos Regional Archaeological Project, part vi: administration and settlement in Venetian Navarino. *Hesperia*, 73, 59–120.

Delille, G. (1977) *Agricoltura e demografia nel Regno di Napoli nei secoli xviii e xix*, Guida Editori, Naples.

Duplessy, B., Gabert, A., Valabrégue, J.P. *et al.* (1996) *Le livre de l' épeautre*, Edisud, Aix-en-Provence.

Forbes, H. (1976) The 'thrice-ploughed field': cultivation techniques in ancient and modern Greece. *Expedition*, 19, 5–11.

Forbes, H. (1982) *Strategies and soils: technology, production and environment in the Peninsula of Methana*, Greece. PhD thesis. University of Pennsylvania.

Forbes, H. (2000a) Dowry and inheritance: their relationship to land fragmentation and risk reduction on Methana, in *Contingent Countryside: Settlement, Economy, and Land Use in the Southern Argolid since 1700* (ed. S.B. Sutton), Stanford University Press, Stanford, pp. 200–227.

Forbes, H. (2000b) Appendix A: land measurement in the Peloponnesos during the Second Venetian Period, in *Contingent Countryside: Settlement, Economy, and Land Use in the Southern Argolid since 1700* (ed. S.B. Sutton), Stanford University Press, Stanford, pp. 321–324.

Forte, M.A. (2009) *A Mediterranean mountain: landscape and land use on the Cairo Massif, Central Italy, 1700–1970 A.D.* PhD thesis. University of Sheffield.

Foxhall, L. (1992) The control of the Attic landscape, in *Agriculture in Ancient Greece* (ed. B. Wells), Swedish Institute at Athens, Stockholm, pp. 155–159.

Gallant, T.W. (1991) *Risk and Survival in Ancient Greece*, Polity Press, Cambridge, UK.

Gill, N.T. and Vear, K.C. (1966) *Agricultural Botany*, 2nd edn, Duckworth, London.

Gilman, A. (1981) The development of social stratification in Bronze Age Europe. *Current Anthropology*, 22, 1–8.

Goody, J. (1976) *Production and Reproduction*, Cambridge University Press, Cambridge, UK.

Hajnalová, M. and Dreslerova, D. (2010) Ethnobotany of einkorn and emmer in Romania and Slovakia: towards interpretation of archaeological evidence. *Památky Archeologické*, 101, 169–202.

Halstead, P. (1995) Late Bronze Age grain crops and Linear B ideograms *65, *120 and *121. *Annual of the British School at Athens*, 90, 229–234.

Halstead, P. (1998–1999) Texts, bones and herders: approaches to animal husbandry in Late Bronze Age Greece. *Minos*, 33–34, 149–189.

Halstead, P. (1999) Towards a model of Mycenaean palatial mobilization, in *Rethinking Mycenaean Palaces* (eds M.L. Galaty and W.A. Parkinson), Cotsen Institute of Archaeology, UCLA, Los Angeles, pp. 35–41.

Halstead, P. and Jones, G. (1989) Agrarian ecology in the Greek islands: time stress, scale and risk. *Journal of Hellenic Studies*, 109, 41–55.

Harvey, A. (1989) *Economic Expansion in the Byzantine Empire 900–1200*, Cambridge University Press, Cambridge, UK.

Heimpel, W. (1995) Plow animal inspection records from Ur III Girsu and Umma. *Bulletin on Sumerian Agriculture*, 8, 71–171.

Hillman, G. (1981) Reconstructing crop husbandry practices from charred remains of crops, in *Farming Practice in British Prehistory* (ed. R. Mercer), Edinburgh University Press, Edinburgh, pp. 123–162.

Hopkins, K. (1978) *Conquerors and Slaves*, Cambridge University Press, Cambridge, UK.

Working the Earth

Isaakidou, V. (2006) Ploughing with cows: Knossos and the 'secondary products revolution', in *Animals in the Neolithic of Britain and Europe* (eds D. Serjeantson and D. Field), Oxbow, Oxford, pp. 95–112.

Isaakidou, V. (2008) The fauna and economy of Neolithic Knossos revisited, in *Escaping the Labyrinth* (eds V. Isaakidou and P. Tomkins), Oxbow, Oxford, pp. 90–114.

Isager, S. and Skydsgaard, J.E. (1992) *Ancient Greek Agriculture: An Introduction*, Routledge, London.

Jones, G. (2005) Garden cultivation of staple crops and its implications for settlement location and continuity. *World Archaeology*, 37, 164–176.

Jones, G., Bogaard, A., Halstead, P. *et al.* (1999) Identifying the intensity of crop husbandry practices on the basis of weed floras. *Annual of the British School at Athens*, 94, 167–189.

Karakasidou, A.N. (1997) *Fields of Wheat, Hills of Blood*, Chicago University Press, Chicago.

Kasdagli, A.E. (1999) *Land and Marriage Settlements in the Aegean: A Case Study of Seventeenth-Century Naxos*, Hellenic Institute of Byzantine and Post-Byzantine Studies, Venice.

Killen, J.T. (1993) The oxen's names on the Knossos Ch tablets. *Minos*, 27–28, 101–107.

Killen, J.T. (1998) The role of the state in wheat and olive production in Mycenaean Crete. *Aevum: Rassegna di Scienze Storiche Linguistiche e Filologiche*, 72, 19–23.

Laiou-Thomadakis, A.E. (1977) *Peasant Society in the Late Byzantine Empire: A Social and Demographic Study*, Princeton University Press, Princeton.

Leake, W.M. (1967) *Travels in Northern Greece*, 4, Hakkert, Amsterdam.

Loukopoulos, D. (1983) *Georgika tis Roumelis*, Dodoni, Athens.

Maekawa, K. (1990) Cultivation methods in the Ur III period. *Bulletin on Sumerian Agriculture*, 5, 115–145.

McConnell, P. (1883) *The Agricultural Notebook*, Crosby Lockwood, London.

Moskof, K. (1979) *Isagogika stin istoria tou kinimatos tis ergatikis taxis: i diamorfosi tis ethnikis kai koinonikis sunidisis stin Ellada*, Moskof, Thessaloniki.

Osborne, R. (1992) 'Is it a farm?' The definition of agricultural sites and settlements in ancient Greece, in *Agriculture in Ancient Greece* (ed. B. Wells), Swedish Institute at Athens, Stockholm, pp. 21–27.

Pagkalos, G.E. (1983) *Peri tou glossikou idiomatos tis Kritis, 7: ta laografika*, Kentro Erevnis Ellinikis Laografias Akadimias Athinon, Athens.

Palaiologos, G. (1833) *Georgiki kai oikiaki oikonomia*, Vasiliki Tipografia, Nafplio.

Palanca, F. (1991) Agricultura, in *Temes d' etnografia Valenciana 2: utillatge agrícola i ramaderia* (eds F. Martínez and F. Palanca), Institució Valenciana d' Estudis i Investigació, Valencia, pp. 11–181.

Palmer, C. (1998) 'Following the plough': the agricultural environment of northern Jordan. *Levant*, 30, 129–165.

Palmer, C. and Russell, K.W. (1993) Traditional ards of Jordan. *Annual of the Department of Antiquities of Jordan*, 37, 37–53.

Parveva, S. (2003) Agrarian land and harvest in south-west Peloponnese in the early 18th century. *Études Balkaniques*, 1, 83–123.

Peña-Chocarro, L. (1999) *Prehistoric Agriculture in Southern Spain During the Neolithic and the Bronze Age*, Archaeopress, Oxford.

Petropoulos, D.A. (1952) Sumvoli is tin erevnan ton laikon metron kai stathmon. *Epetiris tou Laografikou Arkhiou*, 7, 57–101.

Prontzas, V. (1992) *Oikonomia kai gaioktisia sti Thessalia (1881–1912)*, Morfotiko Idrima Ethnikis Trapezis, Athens.

Psikhogios, D.K. (1987) *Proikes, foroi, stafida kai psomi: oikonomia kai oikogenia stin agrotiki Ellada tou 19 aiona*, Ethniko Kentro Koinonikon Erevnon, Athens.

Russell, K.W. (1988) *After Eden: The Behavioral Ecology of Early Food Production in the Near East and North Africa*, British Archaeological Reports, Oxford.

Sherratt, A. (1980) Water, soil and seasonality in early cereal cultivation. *World Archaeology*, 11, 313–330.

Sherratt, A. (1981) Plough and pastoralism: aspects of the secondary products revolution, in *Pattern of the Past: Studies in Honour of David Clarke* (eds I. Hodder, G. Isaac, and N. Hammond), Cambridge University Press, Cambridge, UK, pp. 261–305.

Sherratt, A. (2006) La traction animale et la transformation de l'Europe néolithique, in *Premiers chariots, premiers araires. La diffusion de la traction animale en Europe pendant les IVe et IIIe millénaires avant notre ère* (eds P. Pétrequin, R.-M. Arbogast, A.-M. Pétrequin *et al.*), CNRS, Paris, pp. 329–360.

Spurr, M.S. (1986) *Arable Cultivation in Roman Italy c.200 B.C.–c. A.D. 100*, Society for the Promotion of Roman Studies, London.

Stokes, J. (1853) *Ox: A Beast of Draught in Place of the Horse Recommended for all Purposes of Agriculture*, John Stokes, London.

Topping, P. (1972) The post-classical documents, in *The Minnesota Messenia Expedition: Reconstructing a Bronze Age Regional Environment* (eds W.A. McDonald and G.R. Rapp), University of Minnesota Press, Minneapolis, pp. 64–80.

Tsopotos, D.K. (1974) *Gi kai georgoi tis Thessalias kata tin Tourkokratian,* 2nd edn, Epikairotita, Athens.

United Nations Food & Agriculture Organisation (FAO) (1972) *Manual on the Employment of Draught Animals in Agriculture,* FAO, Rome.

Vanstiphout, H. (1984) On the Sumerian disputation between the hoe and the plough. *Aula Orientalis,* 2, 239–251.

Vrontis, A.G. (1938–1948) Oi zevgades tis Rodou. *Laografia,* 12, 104–129.

Wagstaff, M. and Augustson, S. (1982) Traditional land use, in *An Island Polity: The Archaeology of Exploitation in Melos* (eds C. Renfrew and M. Wagstaff), Cambridge University Press, Cambridge, UK, pp. 106–133.

White, K.D. (1970) *Roman Farming,* Thames & Hudson, London.

Wilkie, N.C. and Savina, M.E. (1997) The earliest farmers in Macedonia. *Antiquity,* 71, 201–207.

Zarinebaf, F., Bennet, J., and Davis, J.L. (2005) *A Historical and Economic Geography of Ottoman Greece: The Southwestern Morea in the Early 18th Century,* American School of Classical Studies at Athens, Princeton.

3

Harvest Time

It was the beginning of June 1981 and we were on Amorgos in the Cyclades for an ethnoarchaeological study of non-mechanized reaping and crop processing. The dispersed white-washed houses of Kolofana, in the south of the island, stood out against a patchwork of gold cereal crops and brown stubble of harvested pulses that covered the plateau and lower slopes. The uppermost terraces on the surrounding slopes were abandoned. The weekly truck from the port pulled up where the dirt road ended, outside Irini's "Dolphin" *kafenío* where we spent the next six weeks. The harvest and work on the threshing floors were at an early stage and, over homemade goat's cheese and draft resinated wine (*retsína*), Irini explained that fate had providentially disabled two of the three local reaping machines, so most fields were harvested manually – many by her husband, Dimitrakis ("little Dimitris"), whose preferred use of spare time was to assist infirm or idle friends, neighbors, and relatives.

Two Oxen Ahead: Pre-Mechanized Farming in the Mediterranean, First Edition.
Paul Halstead. © 2014 Paul Halstead. Published 2014 by John Wiley & Sons, Ltd.

The cereals grown in Kolofana were barley and oats for fodder, wheat (mixed bread and macaroni wheat) for human consumption, and especially *migádi*, a wheat/barley maslin from which Irini and her neighbors made dark, coarse bread and hard rusks (*paximádia*) that needed moistened before eating. At first we received tasteless white bread, delivered on the weekly lorry for rare visitors, but this ran out and we discovered the alternative. To our dismay, the next delivery put "French bread" back on the menu, but eventually we persuaded Irini that her "demeaning" rustic rusks were preferable. The cereals were mostly grown in rotation with autumn-/winter-sown pulses: grass pea and common vetch, sown separately and together for fodder, and lentil, pea, and broad bean for human consumption. Every few years, to control weeds, fields were left under cultivated fallow, and some of these were planted with "summer crops," including salad plants, chickpea, and black-eyed bean. In July, passing farmers helped themselves to a few green pods of chickpeas "like ice cream."

Harvesting of the principal cereals and pulses around Kolofana is described in the following section, before exploring variations on this process in other parts of the Mediterranean and considering some related quantitative issues.

3.1   Amorgos: From Field to Threshing Floor

To minimize shedding of grain, Dimitrakis and Irini reaped in the early morning and, occasionally, in the evening, when pulse pods and cereal ears were less dry and brittle than at midday. They grasped the cereal stems in the left hand and cut them at about shin height with a small, curved iron sickle held in the right hand. The pulses were cut close to the ground or uprooted, using a sickle or a larger "scythe" of the same shape (i.e., with a handle in the same plane as the blade). In each case, they reaped the crop low, involving much bending, because they needed the straw as fodder for their mules and cows. Dimitrakis and Irini worked side by side, cutting a swathe the length of the field and then another parallel to the first (Figure 3.1). At regular intervals they left small piles of gathered

Figure 3.1 Reaping a strip of wheat/barley maslin at Kolofana, Amorgos, with previously harvested strip in foreground and remaining unharvested strip in background.

pulses or bunches of cut cereals, which they later amalgamated and, in the case of cereals, bound into sheaves. In the past, whole families were mobilized for the harvest, but their adult son worked away and their teenage daughter minded the Dolphin. My offer to assist, citing a few hours practice the previous summer on Karpathos in the southeast Aegean, was treated with deserved disdain. Like many agricultural tasks, reaping with a sickle looks easy, but on Karpathos I repeatedly cut my fingers and uprooted whole plants, rather than cutting the straw as instructed, and the unaccustomed bending left me unable to stand straight for days. My Karpathos reaping lesson took place in a very sparse crop, on a plot with more stones than earth, and I was supposed to reap selectively, leaving behind even unobvious weeds like darnel (*Lolium temulentum*). In Kolofana, the cereal stands were taller and denser, and Dimitrakis and Irini had more animals and so harvested lower. They were thus

Figure 3.2 Mules carrying wheat/barley sheaves from field to threshing floor at Kolofana, Amorgos.

more concerned with speed than crop purity and only left uncut the most robust and obvious weeds, such as dock (*Rumex pulcher*).

The harvested crop was perhaps left for a day or two to dry before transport to one of the many circular, stone-paved threshing floors scattered among the fields and houses. Some local farmers used two or three floors, including those of relatives who no longer farmed or had already processed any crops grown nearby. Transport to the threshing floor posed renewed risk of shedding ripe grain, so pulses especially were only carried at the beginning and end of the day, when the sun was low. Using an outlying floor closer to the field reduced transport losses but left crops vulnerable to two- or four-legged theft, so some farmers stationed a dog to guard sheaves awaiting processing. The time needed for transport depended on the volume of crop, distance involved, and number of pack animals available; ownership of three mules rather than one donkey significantly increased the amount of both grain and straw that was needed as fodder but saved time during this very busy period (Figure 3.2).

Within living memory, both the amount of land in cultivation and the availability of human labor had declined around Kolofana, obscuring whether manual reapers worked under more or less time stress than in previous generations. Either way, ripe crops – pulses followed by cereals – had to be gathered quickly, before they were scattered by birds or ruined by a rare summer storm. The landholdings of individual households were dispersed, making it difficult to monitor directly the ripeness of distant fields, but farmers noticed the state of others' crops as they walked to and from their own fields and exchanged information when their paths crossed. Thanks to such intelligence gathering, Dimitrakis adjusted his plans on a daily basis. On Amorgos, June is called *theristís* (reaper) and July *alonistís* (thresher), but in practice there is a considerable overlap between harvest and crop processing. By the time the cereal harvest was under way, Dimitrakis and his neighbors were reaping in the early morning, threshing in the midday heat, winnowing in the afternoon sea breeze, and then reaping or transporting sheaves in the cool of evening. Over six weeks, I did not see Dimitrakis sit down.

Our stay in Kolofana was entertaining as well as instructive. The amusement was apparently mutual: a colleague, passing through Kolofana in the late 1990s, stopped at the Dolphin and was regaled by Dimitrakis, over *rakí*, with tales of my hilarious ignorance of matters bucolic. The following sections explore some finer points of harvesting that I did not appreciate in 1981, as well as documenting important regional and tactical variations in when, what, and how to reap and in the treatment of crops between harvest and processing for storage.

3.2 When to Reap

In Amorgos, the harvesting of autumn-/winter-sown grain crops started in late May with pulses and continued through June with cereals – barley before wheat and finally oats; slight variation in ripening, probably reflecting differences between plots in aspect and soil, blurred rather than undermined this sequence. Spring-sown chickpea and black-eyed bean were harvested after the July threshing of the earlier crops. With important regional differences in the species and varieties involved, broadly the same sequence of ripening and harvesting is encountered throughout the Mediterranean: autumn-/winter-sown pulses → barley → bread/macaroni wheat → oats → summer crops (including millet, maize, chickpea, black-eyed bean, New World beans). Dates vary with latitude and altitude, so that barley and wheat were traditionally harvested in May in Jordan (Palmer, 1998, 150) and May–June in Cyprus (Littlejohn, 1946) and lowland Crete but in June to early July in lowland northern Greece and late July to early September in the mountains of northwest Greece. In Provence, the cereal harvest extended from late June on the coast, through July in the hills (Sault, Plateau d' Albion), to August and September in the French Alps (Martel, 1982, 47), allowing highland villagers to supplement their own meager yields with three months' work as migrant hired reapers (e.g., Blanchard, 1945, 461–462; Braudel, 1975, 47).

Although timing of the harvest is largely dictated by date of ripening (see succeeding text), the reverse holds occasionally. Around Sault in Haute Provence, einkorn (a glume wheat) ripens as late as August, a month or more after free-threshing bread wheat. This poses two risks: there is often insufficient moisture to fill einkorn grain in late June; and, conversely, strong summer rainfall may beat the crop down before harvest. Einkorn seed from other regions ripens significantly earlier than the local population, the tardiness of which probably results from inadvertent selection by late harvesting. In the days of slow manual reaping, einkorn was harvested not only after barley, bread wheat, oats, and rye but also after lavender, an important cash crop (J. Devaux, personal communication), so early-ripening einkorn plants would have shed their ears and not contributed to future seedcorn. In Asturias, harvesting of spelt and emmer (also glume wheats) in August–September is likewise constrained by the need to mow hay beforehand, and there may again have been selection for late ripening. Indeed, such a scheduling conflict may have been fairly common in upland areas, where necessarily lengthy winter stalling and scarce cultivable land often placed a premium on bulk collection of natural hay. Conversely, in the Mediterranean lowlands, where winter stalling tends to be shorter and cultivable land less scarce, provision of winter fodder often relies more on sown cereals and pulses, cut before they produce ripe grain and so too early to clash with harvesting of grain crops. In lowland northern Greece, however, other scheduling clashes seemingly produced local variation in the order of harvest and ripening: at Assiros, as elsewhere, bitter vetch was harvested early (before barley) and rye late (with or after wheat), whereas in the Paliambela–Kolindros area, these positions were reversed.

The stage of ripeness at which crops are harvested also varies. First, both cereals and pulses may be cut or grazed well before the seed fills and even in a vegetative state (Section 5.1). Secondly, harvesting of filled but unripe grains is particularly widespread with broad beans, peas, and some New World beans eaten as green vegetables but also occurs with cereals. In the eastern Mediterranean, free-threshing (bread or macaroni) wheat is sometimes harvested unripe and scorched for human consumption (Turkish *firig*, Arabic *frika*): "milk-ripe" grain is eaten in small quantities as a snack, for example, during weeding, but "dough-ripe" grain is also dried and stored in larger quantities, for boiling like *bulgur* (Hillman, 1985, 13–14; Palmer, 1998, 152). In Greece, scorched semi-ripe wheat grains (locally *psáni*) were eaten as a snack at Metaxada in Messenia (also in central mainland Roumeli – Loukopoulos, 1983, 185; in southern mainland Tsakonia – Kostakis, 1976–1978, 99; on Rhodes – Vrontis, 1938–1948, 116), while on the island of Kithira, dough-ripe barley was dried and broken into groats for storage (Section 4.2). In temperate Europe, glume wheats (spelt, emmer, and einkorn) and rye too were consumed milk ripe (Hillman, 1985, 13–14, 16). Among the Plains Indians of North America, "sweet corn" was harvested early for both gourmet and risk-buffering reasons (Will and Hyde, 1964, 115–123, 143–153). In the recent Mediterranean, early harvesting was usually rationalized as diversifying the diet and usually occurred on too small a scale for significant reduction in losses to subsequent desiccating winds or storms (Section 5.1). Sometimes, however, early harvesting was a response to scarcity. A few decades ago, Tharounia in Euboea was a classic Mediterranean hill village, with a population exceeding local grain-growing capacity, and many inhabitants worked seasonally in coastal villages, digging vines or reaping cereals. The owner of a now-defunct water mill recalls poor villagers who, running out of grain before the next harvest, reaped crops early and dried them in the oven for grinding into flour. Many resorted to these measures during the grain shortage in World War II. A few years earlier, at Aloides in central Crete, wheat was harvested early to ward off liturgical rather than subsistence crises. Amid tales of devils and divine retribution, violent deaths, and departing souls, Sofia describes how "my mother used to cut a few unripe but filled ears of wheat, just one or one and a half kilos, which she dried in the sun for one or two days to make *kóliva*." This dish, of boiled wheat grains mixed with sugar, cinnamon, nuts, fruits, and herbs, is distributed at memorial services in Greece. Households in Aloides and other villages subsisted on barley bread and only grew small amounts of wheat for ceremonial and ritual purposes including *kóliva*; Sofia's mother sometimes found herself short of this essential ingredient in the weeks before the cereal harvest.

Before mechanization, even crops harvested for dry grain and intended for long-term, bulk storage were often reaped a little prematurely. One important rationale for this was to minimize loss of grain during reaping and removal from the field. Some crops are very prone to shed seeds when ripe, and accordingly, farmers in north Greek Assiros and Paliambela harvested lentils and sometimes rye or oats before they were fully ripe. For the same reason, they harvested lentils or rye, usually grown on only a small scale, soon after dawn when they were soft enough with dew to retain their seeds. Wheat and barley were less vulnerable to shedding their grain, but reaping of "dead"-ripe crops inevitably incurred losses. Hill farmers in Messenia and Crete, in the semiarid south of Greece, consistently maintain that cereals were harvested completely dry; the grain was not considered "ready" earlier. Here, reaping even of staple cereals was often restricted to the early morning and evening, as also in southeast mainland Tsakonia (Kostakis, 1976–1978, 103) and on Amorgos. Cretan farmers started the harvest long before dawn on moonlit nights: "by mid-morning [9–10 a.m.!], you had to stop because the ears shed their grains." In northern Greece, the scale of the cereal harvest tended to be larger, but reaping of wheat and barley continued through the day rather than by moonlight. Here, the shedding of wheat and barley grain was widely reduced by reaping a little in advance of full ripeness, although – significantly – this was usually rationalized in terms of the logistical difficulty of completing the harvest promptly with slow, manual reaping; *khlorothéri* ("green harvest"), as the Paliambela Thracians called it, extended the harvest season by a week or two. Crops reaped early completed ripening on the straw while stooked in the field or stacked at the threshing floor. In Paliambela, Koula's husband only reaped barley and macaroni wheat early, because he found that "green" bread wheat and oats heated up in the sheaf and spoiled, but "green harvesting" of barley left him with swollen hands, because the crop was heavier than when reaped fully ripe. In Assiros, the practice of reaping some barley and especially wheat slightly early, known here as *proúnga*, was again primarily justified as extending the time available for harvest, but some held that cereals which finished ripening on the cut straw produced slightly heavier grain, better flour, and more nutritious straw. The same benefits were attributed in Italy to reaping at "yellow ripeness," before the grain was hard (Spurr, 1986, 67). In Haute Provence, where harvesting of sub-ripe grain was held to improve grain and straw quality and reduce risks from summer storms and birds, two sayings highlight the urgency of the harvest: "on St. John's Day [June 24th], sickle in hand" and "from St. John's Day onwards, every day is a year" (Martel, 1982, 46–47). Grain harvested early, however, was thought to store less well and make poorer seedcorn than that cut fully ripe (Gaillard, 1997, 26). At Plikati, high in the Pindos Mountains, cereals might be cut prematurely for a different reason: the reaping of Old World cereals began in late July to early August around the village, at 1200 m, and extended into September on the highest fields, up to perhaps 1700 m. If the highest crops were not ready by mid-September, they might not ripen at all and so were harvested and left to dry on threshing floors in the village.

How did farmers know when crops were ripe? As on Amorgos, mainland Greek (Loukopoulos, 1983, 240), Provençal (Martel, 1982, 46;

Gaillard, 1997, 26), and Valencian (Palanca, 1991, 153) farmers monitored the color and feel of the crop. Mitsos in Paliambela explains that a ripe ear breaks up when rubbed and the grain is hard when bitten, but straw color is also a reliable guide. For Cretan farmers, popular culture offered the following mnemonic for different cereals: "harvest barley as an old man, wheat as an upright young man, and oats half-green so the oxen don't lose out." Barley grain is not filled completely until the head bends over, but this does not hold for wheat, and oats shed their seeds if harvested dry. In northern Greece too, farmers reaped oats while still slightly green but waited for the straw of barley, wheat, and rye to turn yellow brown even for "green harvesting." Agricultural scientists use similar criteria (e.g., Percival, 1974, 141).

Timing of the harvest is more complicated in the case of maslins comprising crops with different ripening times. On Amorgos, where wheat/barley *migádi* tended to be harvested after "pure" barley, the greater ripeness of the barley component of *migádi* presumably contributed to the overrepresentation of wheat among unthreshed ears retained in the coarse sieve (Jones and Halstead, 1995, 105). At Kalo Khorio in central Crete, farmers delayed harvest of *migádi* until the wheat component was ripe. In Messenia, at least, farmers selected cereal *varieties* that minimized differential ripening. For example, in Metaxada, Ilias sowed maslin (here called *smigádi*) on poor soils, reserving his better plots for wheat. He combined barley with an early-ripening wheat variety so that the *smigádi* evaded the worst of the summer drought. In Kinigou, Nikos sowed the same maslin and remarks that the early-ripening wheat had a relatively short straw, like barley, making *smigádi* easier to reap.

Although farmers could extend the harvest period by growing a range of early- and late-ripening pulses and cereals and reaping some fields early, the limitations of manual labor often meant that some fields were reaped very ripe. In Paliambela, bitter vetch was gathered late and bone dry, suggesting that it shed its seed less easily than the lentils harvested green a month earlier. Delayed harvesting of ripe crops may also be less risky for glume wheats than free-threshing cereals. The glumes that tightly envelop the grains of the former make the ripe ear less vulnerable to scattering by wind or birds (Hillman, 1985, 5). In southern Spain, late harvesting of einkorn did not affect yields adversely (Peña-Chocarro, 1999, 33). Ripe einkorn, in particular, also bends in the manner of barley, so the ear sheds water easily, reducing the risk that rain late in the growing season will result in lodging or in wetting and premature germination. In upland Asturias, the spelt and emmer harvest used to last from mid-August to late September or even early October, partly because crops ripened later on heavy than light ground. Farmers also maintain, however, that the harvesting of ripe spelt and emmer could be delayed (with appropriate methods of reaping – see succeeding text) and this might increase yields. Any additional rain in the last stages of ripening, provided it did not cause lodging, helped fill the grain: "water in August is all flour." Nowadays, birds sometimes cause significant losses to ripe spelt and emmer, but their attention is focused on very few remaining fields. Birds were not a serious threat to glume wheats in the past, although they forced Leandro in Tiós to abandon an attempt to introduce bread wheat. Similarly, one reason why farmers on Amorgos were keen to complete the harvest of free-threshing cereals promptly was to preempt losses to birds. Perhaps selection for late ripening in Haute Provence only affected einkorn and not bread wheat, barley, rye, or oats (also grown there), because einkorn best withstood delayed harvesting. At any rate, einkorn sheaves were left in the field to dry for less time, suggesting harvest in a riper state, than those of free-threshing wheat (Duplessy *et al.*, 1996, 60).

3.3 What and How to Reap

The *method* of harvesting seed crops varies considerably in both the part(s) of the plant collected and the tool(s), if any, used. These interlinked variables are in turn related to the structure and intended use(s) of particular crops, as well as other practical and cultural considerations. The crops discussed in this chapter were harvested for their seed, but the method of harvesting depended on the extent to which the straw too was valued and the ease with which ears or pods could be harvested without it.

Uprooting was widely the norm for flax, partly because it was often grown as much for the fiber in its stems as for its oil-rich linseed and partly because the toughness of the stems (the reason for their value as fiber) makes them difficult to cut. One reason why Messenian households grew flax on a very small scale was the difficulty of uprooting it on hard ground, where the tough stems cut the hands of harvesters. At Borja in northern Spain, Alfredo recalls that flax "bit like a dog." Tall-growing rye too was often uprooted in northern Greece because its long and strong straw was valued – uncut – for thatching, stuffing saddles, and tying sheaves (see succeeding text). Similarly, in northern Greece and Messenia, in fields harvested by sickle, a few tall wheat plants might be uprooted to obtain straws long enough for binding sheaves.

Conversely, uprooting was also common for cereals too short to be cut easily with a sickle. The Cretan spring barley (*Martáki*) was usually uprooted because its short stem left little room for gathering both ear and straw (see succeeding text) with a sickle: "the sickle would hit stones when the crop was short." Other cereals of taller growth habit were normally cut with a sickle but uprooted when poor soils (e.g., Loukopoulos, 1983, 263) or unfavorable weather yielded a short stand. Uprooting of short "wasted" crops is recalled in the hill villages of Tharounia in Euboea, Metaxada in Messenia, and Kalo Khorio in central Crete and likewise reported from Turkey (Hillman, 1984, 118) and Jordan (Palmer, 1998, 150). In Assiros, Alexis once uprooted a failed wheat crop, only 30 cm high, to recover straw for winter fodder.

Sesame, an important summer cash crop in some regions, was gathered as whole plants, because its numerous small seed capsules cannot realistically be harvested otherwise. Most pulses harvested for dry grain were collected as whole plants, partly again because the pods are distributed more widely than the ears on cereal plants, and so difficult to gather selectively, and partly because the straw was often valued more than cereal straw as fodder (also Palmer, 1998, 159–160). Sesame and most Old World pulses have a more or less short or scrambling growth habit, posing similar problems for sickle-reaping as spring barley. These too were widely uprooted by hand, particularly in sparse stands that a sickle would scatter or flatten. In denser stands, however, a sickle or "scythe" might be favored because each stroke gathered more of the crop than the hand alone. Accordingly, uprooting was the norm for bitter vetch, cutting with a sickle or "scythe" was usual for common vetch, and the method for lentils and peas varied at least partly in accordance with crop density. In practice, the distinction between uprooting and sickle-reaping was often blurred by using a blunt sickle or horizontal-handled "scythe" to facilitate uprooting, as with common vetch and grass pea on Amorgos and short cereals in Turkey (Hillman, 1984, 117–118). For example, the sickle was favored for denser pulse crops in Assiros but was only used as a cutting tool where uprooting was difficult or impossible.

Broad bean, a particularly tall and robust Old World pulse, exemplifies the flexibility of reaping method: in various parts of Greece, it was uprooted where stems did not yield easily to the sickle, but cut when large roots made it difficult to pull up by hand. In general, however, Greek farmers reaped both pulses and cereals with a sickle, if practicable: to quote Fountoulonikolis at Cretan Kalo Khorio, "where the crop was tall enough, we used a sickle, but where it was too short, we uprooted." At Metaxada in Messenia, Nikos concurs, but Ilias owned more and better land. He usually faced only small patches of very short cereals that he left for his animals to graze, rather than uproot them. Uprooting was normally slower than sickle-reaping, because even small sickles have a much wider span than the human hand, and it often involved more bending. Indeed, in northern Greece, the availability of manual labor for the backbreaking task of uprooting sprawling pulses was often the limiting factor on the area sown with lentils and bitter vetch and, together with the disappearance of draft cattle, has now resulted in virtual abandonment of the latter.

Uprooting is much easier in loose than compact soil. On the heavy marls round central Cretan Skalani, therefore, Nikolis found chickpea and spring barley, both short enough to require uprooting, difficult to harvest. He delayed sowing these crops, to avoid heavy rain on the plowed and sown field, so that the surface would be loose at harvest time (Section 2.6.1). Conversely, autumn-sown barley, wheat, and oats were cut with a sickle, because their greater height made this practicable, while compaction by winter rain of the less intensively worked field surface made uprooting very difficult. In Paliambela, Mitsos gathered his small lentil crop very early in the morning, when the soil was damp with dew and the plants could be uprooted easily without scattering the seeds, but the roots pulled up dirt and contaminated the grain with grit. Grit of similar size to the lentils was not removed by winnowing or sieving on the threshing floor and, if not picked out by hand in the final stages of crop cleaning, could break human teeth. For this reason, Koula in Paliambela cut her lentils with a sickle but uprooted bitter vetch as she was not concerned about grit in the feed of the oxen. Those who harvested by uprooting often removed adhering dirt in the field, at least from crops for human consumption. Dirty roots were knocked against one of the ubiquitous stones in Metaxada, on the knee of the harvester in Assiros, or on the base of the sickle blade in Kalo Khorio (as in Turkey – Hillman, 1984, 118). When the surface of the field was hard, less dirt adhered as the roots of pulses remained in the ground and those of cereals came up clean. Uprooting in such conditions scattered more grain, however, and was slower and harder; in Paliambela, Mitsos and Eleni wore thick woolen socks as gloves to uproot bitter vetch from a dry field.

Throughout the Mediterranean, cereals reaped by sickle (oats, tall barley, most wheat, rye not earmarked for thatching or bundling) were cut low or high, again for various reasons. First, as Ilias in Metaxada commented, "if you needed a lot of straw [for fodder], you reaped low." This rationale is widespread, but reaping low involved more bending, which harvesters might avoid – particularly those with no interest in recovering straw. In Haute Provence, hired reapers heard watching employers shout "cut low, because we need lots of straw" (Martel, 1982, 40). Conversely, the need to leave stubble for grazing animals is occasionally cited, as in Valencia (Palanca, 1991, 154) and at Tharounia on Euboea, as a reason for not reaping low (cf. White, 1970, 182). Straw is also of variable digestibility, and at Monforte in central Italy, rye was sometimes reaped higher than wheat or barley, because its stiff straw (like that of einkorn in southern Spain) was not valued as fodder. Secondly, Ilias adds, "you must cut low enough to be able to tie bundles – that needs at least 60 cm of straw," which again meant harvesting short crops low. Thirdly, as 92-year-old Panagiotis observes of wheat/barley *smigádi* in the Messenian hill village of Potamia, he had to reap short crops low to catch the lowest ears but could cut good crops a little higher. The height of ears is particularly variable in late-sown crops and primitive wheats (Hillman, 1984, 119). For example, in 1991 in einkorn (sown early) at the Savoillat experimental farm in Haute Provence, the taller tillers were about 1 m high and most ears above 70 cm, but several were as low as 50 cm. In southern Spain, einkorn was reaped at mid-height to catch the lower ears (Peña-Chocarro, 1999, 34). Fourthly, wheat on manured infield plots at Tharounia was sometimes so weedy that it was cut high, leaving cattle and mules to graze the straw and weeds. Harvesting of ears (or pods) only is discussed in the succeeding text, after considering in more detail how ears were cut with straw.

The sickles used to cut cereals differed locally in size and curvature and in whether the edge was serrated or plain. For example, in north Greek communities such as Assiros and Paliambela, the "local" short-handled sickle with a strongly curved and "toothed" blade contrasted with the Thracian refugees' long-handled *leléki* ("stork") with an angled or lightly curved and un-serrated blade (e.g., Psarraki-Belesioti, 1978, 28, figs. 20 and 21). The *leléki* afforded a longer reach and so harvested more of the straw than the "local" sickle (Kizlaris, 1938–1948, 404–405). For the same reason, it could lift and cut lodged cereals in one movement, whereas the "local" sickle required two discrete actions. In Paliambela, some Thracians linked their preference for the *leléki* to needing straw for oxen, but it is unlikely that all Thracians needed more straw (or faced more severe lodging) than all "locals." On the other hand, the *leléki* tended to uproot the crop, if its blade was not sharp. It was also heavier and so regarded by some as more tiring, but others argued the reverse because the cut material gathered in the left hand was long enough to rest the base of the stems on the ground, whereas the shorter material cut with the sickle had to be held in the air. Similarly, some considered the *leléki* faster, because it cut more material at a stroke, while others emphasized the more rapid cuts possible with the sickle. In the Vlach village of Sesklo, in central Greece, the sickle is said to have given way to the *leléki* in the mid-twentieth century, because the latter cut more of the crop, but elsewhere the sickle supplanted the *leléki*. When asked to estimate the area that could be reaped per day, north Greek proponents of both tools offered similar figures, acknowledging that skill and stamina of worker were more critical than type of implement.

Some informants emphasize the importance for efficiency of using familiar tools. In Assiros, Alekos shows me five toothed sickles, all of similar shape but slightly different size and weight – and each belonging to a different family member; anyone who grabbed the wrong tool when setting off for the fields early in the morning struggled to get used to its unfamiliar handling. Such difficulties were significantly greater when reaping with an unfamiliar *type* of tool. The first-generation Thracians in Paliambela stuck to the *leléki*, while their "local" neighbors used the smaller sickle. Both groups rationalized their choice of reaping implement in terms of efficiency, probably because hardly anyone mastered both tools. Lemonia, at 85 the oldest Thracian in Paliambela, is a supporter of the *leléki* but also has a sickle. She explains that these tools require completely different bodily movements and are not readily interchangeable. Being too immobile to reach the nearest cereal field, she demonstrates by attacking weeds in her garden with *leléki* and then sickle. With the former, she wears on her left hand a *palamariá*, a wooden "glove" with projecting claw that simultaneously protects the fingers from the blade of the *leléki* and encompasses a larger bunch of straws. She gathers stems with the *leléki*, grasps them low down with the *palamariá*, and then breaks them by swinging the *leléki* across her shins. Switching tools and abandoning the *palamariá*, she grabs stems higher up with her bare left hand and cuts them by drawing the sickle towards her stomach. The first Thracian girls to marry into "local" households took a *leléki* as part of their dowry, and as late as the 1950s, Khrisoulla came to Paliambela in marriage from a Thracian village, bringing her *leléki*. By the late 1930s, however, most Thracians born in Paliambela were learning to use the "local" sickle. Koula's father had minded sheep in Kolindros as a teenager and was one of the few who handled both tools with ease; he used the *leléki* when reaping with his uncle but the sickle when working with his children. In 1941, when Koula was 12 and ready to learn, her father gave her a sickle, saying that the lighter tool would be easier to master. The *leléki* also caused practical difficulties when Thracians worked as hired reapers for "locals" in Kolindros, because it cut closer to the ground, yielding long sheaves that could not be stooked or stacked neatly with the shorter sheaves made by sickle users. To avoid the risk that rain might penetrate uneven stooks in the field or stacks on the threshing floor (see succeeding text), some *leléki*-wielding Thracian parents reaped, sheaved, and stooked separately from their sickle-using children.

The Thracians who settled around Assiros in the 1920s came from a different part of European Turkey. They also used the *leléki* but wielded it differently from those in Paliambela. Fotis, a sickle-using "local," was struck by how the newcomers gathered the corn they cut in the crook of their left arm. He never worked alongside a Thracian and insisted this was impossible: "someone working next to me with a *leléki* would have cut me as I reaped." Each group had an established way of working, not only because they learned from their parents, but also because this made teamwork easier and safer. Just north of Assiros in the hamlet of Mavrorakhi, "Pontic" refugees arrived from northern Turkey (Karakasidou, 1997) with the *leléki*, but their children again adopted the sickle. Giorgos has left some rye uncut to provide a reaping class for students excavating at Bronze Age Assiros Toumba. After a flurry of strokes with the sickle, he slows down to demonstrate. Following the first stroke, he places the cut straws between the thumb and index finger of his left hand. With successive strokes, he fills the gaps between his index and middle, middle and ring (Figure 3.3), and finally ring and little fingers before placing the accumulated handful on the ground. Fotis did this when he was young and dismisses it as suitable only for novices. In Paliambela, Koula and her friends have never seen this done and do not believe it is practicable: "how many

Figure 3.3 Giorgos grasping cut cereal bunches between fingers at Mavrorakhi, northern Greece.

straws can you fit between the fingers like that?" Nonetheless, Giorgos held a good bunch of straws between each pair of his big farmer's fingers, and our inability to follow what he was doing, when working at normal pace, suggests his method was effective enough for someone accustomed to it.

Far more widespread in Greece was the simpler procedure of accumulating cut straws from successive strokes of the sickle or *leléki* as a single bunch held between thumb and fingers. Suggestions as to the number of cuts per bunch range between two to three, for a dense crop, and five to six, for a sparse stand (also Palanca, 1991, 154). In addition, a *leléki* gathered more material in one stroke than a sickle, men with bigger hands collected larger handfuls than women or children, and the *palamariá* held more than a bare hand. Like choice of cutting tool, use of a *palamariá* or finger guards without claw extensions varied regionally across the Mediterranean (e.g., Meurers-Balke and Loennecken, 1984) but also between individuals. Around both Assiros and Paliambela, the *palamariá* was considered mandatory to protect the left hand from the sweeping movements of the *leléki*, but optional with the shorter and more closely controlled cuts of the sickle. In Paliambela, Eleni missed most of her first harvest season, at the age of 10 or 11, after the sickle sliced a lump out of her left hand – unprotected because the *palamariá* was too big to wear. Once the wound healed, she wrapped her fingers in cloth so that the finger guard fitted snugly. At Monforte in central Italy, Lina and her mother did not protect their left hands from the sickle, but the men of the family wore cane guards on three fingers because they reaped more rapidly and so were more likely to cut themselves. Finger guards also protected against pricking by thistles and barley awns – less serious than sickle cuts, but a source of irritation that slowed the harvest. In Assiros, Tasoula wore a *palamariá* when using a sickle and even, to protect her left hand against thistles, when uprooting lentils, but many of her neighbors reaped bare-handed and maintain that awns or thistles did not trouble their work-hardened fingers.

Across much of the Mediterranean, cereals were harvested with sickles until the introduction of reaping machines, but in parts of southern France, the scythe with vertical handle was adopted in the nineteenth century. In Haute Provence, some favored it for its greater speed, and others resisted it as a threat to the seasonal employment of hired sickle harvesters (Martel, 1982, 40). Widely used for mowing hay, it was less suited to cereals: unless fitted with a cumbersome cradle, it scattered the cut corn, making binding difficult and risking the loss of grain; and it was ineffective with lodged crops. It was regarded as wasteful and even sinful in Provence (Martel, 1983, 32, 37–39). In Greece, the vertical-handled scythe was used to mow sown forage crops, such as alfalfa (*Medicago sativa*), or unsown hay meadows in favorable locations (e.g., the margins of north Greek Lake Langadas; abandoned fields in the Pindos Mountains). Some farmers in Assiros tried the scythe on cereals but rejected it because it scattered the crop, did not allow them to avoid thistles (posing serious problems for bundling, as well as contaminating the crop), and did not work on thin stands. Likewise, sparse and/or restricted stands of grassy hay (sown and unsown) were usually cut with a sickle rather than mown with a scythe.

Instead of harvesting grain crops with varying amounts of straw, sometimes only the ear or pod was collected. Pulses eaten green were usually picked pod by pod, partly because unfilled pods were left for later and partly because succulent seeds or pods cannot be separated from the rest of the plant by threshing. Nonetheless, on Euboea, villagers were seen uprooting green broad bean plants, so they could pick the pods off in the shade at home. Cereal ears may likewise be picked individually for snacks of scorched milk-ripe *frika* (see preceding text), in selection of preferred varieties or qualities of seedcorn, or in gleaning after harvest. Two elderly farmers in Assiros, who had selected seedcorn in this way, stressed how time-consuming it was, requiring a workforce of "many girls"; elsewhere, prime ears for seedcorn were selected as the harvest was spread on the threshing floor (Section 4.2). Gleaning, perhaps most familiar from the Old Testament story of Ruth (Hillman, 1984, 120), was an important source of support for the poor in many parts of the Mediterranean until very recently (e.g., Loukopoulos, 1983, 247) and was sometimes protected by an enforced delay between harvesting and grazing of fields (Gaillard, 1997, 16). Lemonia recalls the first landless years of the Thracian refugees in Paliambela: "my mother-in-law reaped the fields of farmers from Kolindros and afterwards she gleaned them – it was a double income." The availability of ears for gleaning was related to two concerns of cereal growers at harvest time – the need to reap low enough to catch the shortest tillers and early enough to avoid losing too many ripe ears. After the Thracians acquired land of their own, gleaning continued but as a source of pocket money for children, who found that thorn bushes lining the narrow paths conveniently exacted a tithe from the sheaves carried by pack animals heading for Kolindros.

The bulk harvesting of ears, or ears with minimal straw, was fairly widespread in the past, on the northern margins of the Mediterranean and further afield (Hillman, 1985, 6–7; Sigaut, 1988, 19–20). In Asturias, spelt and emmer straw is sometimes used for thatching or as emergency fodder but mainly as stall litter. Dry weather during and after the late summer harvest is not dependable here, so the harvested crop cannot be dried and threshed outdoors,

Figure 3.4   Harvesting emmer with clamp (*mesorias*) at Tiós, Asturias.

as in Amorgos and many other parts of the Mediterranean. Instead, the ears are piled in sturdy, raised granaries (*hórreos*) to await manual threshing and then mechanical dehusking over winter. The straw is harvested later, with a scythe – and with difficulty where the crop has lodged. Straw harvested separately from the ears remains free of awns, probably enhancing its value as fodder; mixed straw and chaff of einkorn in Haute Provence (Duplessy *et al.*, 1996, 61) and of barley in Karpathos (Halstead and Jones, 1989, 45) were avoided as fodder because the sharp awns stuck in the gums or throats of livestock and prevented them from feeding. In Asturias, when the spelt or emmer crop is standing, the ears are harvested by clamping a group of stems between two hazel twigs or *mesorias* (e.g., Peña-Chocarro, 1993, 26, fig. 3; 1996, 135–136). The harvester stands on the base of the plants to prevent uprooting and slides the *mesorias* upwards with both hands to break the stems at or below the base of the ears (Figure 3.4); fully ripe ears break off easily, but those less mature tend to be broken off with some of the straw attached.

The ears are gathered in a basket of chestnut and hazel wood. If the crop has lodged or is very weedy, however, *mesorias* cannot be used and the ears must be plucked one by one. Inevitably, *mesorias* require skill to handle efficiently and some harvesters prefer to pluck ears even from standing corn. Ears plucked with the right hand may be dropped directly into the basket or collected in the left hand, as with sickle harvesting, and transferred to the basket by the handful. The latter procedure is presumably faster, but all forms of plucking are regarded as a very slow alternative to skilled stripping of ears with *mesorias*. Leandro in Tiós argues that the modest amount of straw collected with the ears by *mesorias* is advantageous, when the dry ears are briefly set alight to burn off the awns, and in the past the exaggerated bulk of the harvest served to impress neighbors – whence the saying "wheat and straw to the granary go." A large volume of straw, however, would have hindered both manual threshing and mechanical dehusking (Section 4.2).

Delfina, born in Asturian Xomezana in 1907, recalled that barley was also reaped with *mesorias* in the early twentieth century. In other regions, ears of both free-threshing cereals and glume wheats were apparently harvested, with sickles or reaping clamps, either to reduce the volume of crop for storage and threshing (as in Asturias) or to preserve the straw intact for thatching. For example, sickle-reaping of ears, followed by reaping of the straw for thatching, is reported from southern Spain for bread wheat and einkorn (Peña-Chocarro, 1993, 25). Leandro justifies the Asturian preference for *mesorias* on the grounds that the straw is strong and the ear fragile, so cutting ripe ears with sickles scatters the seed. On the other hand, he and his neighbors advocate harvesting emmer and spelt late in the season and when the sun is out, because ripe and dry ears break off easily in the *mesorias* or hand. The method and timing of harvesting are thus closely interrelated. Cause and effect cannot strictly be disentangled, but it may be significant that ears were cut with a sickle in the arid south of Spain, where the climate favors early and rapid ripening and so may make the harvest more urgent (Ibañez *et al.*, 1998, 139; but cf. Peña-Chocarro, 1999, 33). Conversely, *mesorias* are used in the wetter uplands of Asturias, where harvested ears cannot be dried outdoors before going into storage and so farmers are more concerned to achieve full ripening than to complete the harvest rapidly.

3.4 After Reaping: Binding, Drying, and Transporting the Harvest

Green pods of beans or peas picked for a single meal are often carried home in a gathered apron. Emmer and spelt ears harvested for bulk storage were carried to the barn in baskets in Asturias. Cereals too short to be reaped with a sickle might be gathered in a sheet in central Crete and in a basket, sack, or net in Turkey (Hillman, 1984, 121) for more or less immediate removal to the threshing floor or barn. Harvesting a lot of straw with the ears or pods substantially increased the weight and especially volume of crop collected. A rule of thumb widespread in Greece for traditional long-straw cereals was that straw and grain each contributed about half of the weight of the harvested crop – to some degree independently of absolute yields, as poor soils and bad years produced shorter straw as well as lighter ears. Because of the greater weight and volume of material harvested, the person reaping normally deposited successive handfuls of the crop in a pile on the ground, rather than dropping them straight into a container, and started a new pile once the previous one was no longer conveniently within reach. Then the crop was often tied into sheaves or bundles, rather than carried loose in baskets or sheets, and removal of the harvested crop from the field was more likely to be delayed. For the same reason, secure storage indoors, such as in the *hórreos* of Asturias, was less likely to be practicable, and the crop was usually threshed before storage (cf. Sigaut, 1988, 21). Crops had to be thoroughly dry to be threshed (Section 4.1) or put into store; stored grain that was insufficiently dry was vulnerable to both fungal attack and infestation by weevils. Before threshing, therefore, harvested crops were often left in the field or on the edge of the threshing floor for anything from a few days, if not quite fully ripe and dry, to several weeks, following "green harvest" or if available labor was fully committed to the more urgent task of reaping other fields. Control of ripening and drying was inevitably more difficult with larger volumes of crop. When a lot of straw was harvested with the ears or pods, therefore, the gathering and removal of the crop often took place over a significantly longer period and in several more stages, involving greater risks due to more prolonged exposure and more frequent handling.

Tasoula describes harvesting with her parents and sister in Assiros in the 1940s and 1950s. "Difficult years – I don't even want to think about it," but she warms to the subject. "Don't look at my size now. I had a lovely little body when I was young. That's why I have an agricultural pension – because I dug and reaped. We reaped the lentils first, starting early in the morning so as not to scatter the seed. We harvested the field in strips. The width of the strip depended on how many of us there were; we reaped a few paces apart so we had room to work. As we pulled or cut handfuls of lentils, we piled them on the ground in heaps as big as we could get our arms round – so we could lift them afterwards. You could not tie pulses into sheaves, apart from broad beans; if these were tall, my father tied them with a little wheat cut nearby. He did not sow many pulses, just a few for the household, so we would finish each field in one or two mornings and then transport the crop to the threshing floor and thresh it before we started reaping the cereals." Others left their pulses in the field for a few days, to finish ripening or until they had time to remove them, and so might collect the piles of harvested crop together in one part of the field. The tangled heaps of pulses were not easily scattered by a breeze, although a strong wind might roll away an entire heap. To transport the pulse harvest from the field, Tasoula's father piled it loose on his oxcart, but farmers elsewhere, who used pack animals, carried it in sacks or sheets, like harvested pods and ears (e.g., on Rhodes – Vrontis, 1938–1948, 116), or tied it in bundles with cereal straw; in Kalo Khorio, Crete, the lentil crop was carried in sheets, if short, and tied in bundles, if tall. In Tharounia, Euboea, each handful of lentils was tied with wild grass, and several of these small bunches were then tied with rye straw (from the previous year's harvest) into larger bundles that could be loaded onto a mule or donkey for transport to the village. At the threshing floor, the big bundles were opened up so that each small bunch could be threshed by hand. Bitter vetch, on the other hand, was tied only in large "transport bundles," because (unusually) it was fed to the animals unthreshed and so smaller bunches served no useful purpose.

Tasoula moves onto the cereal harvest. "As we reaped, we left the cut cereals in piles, several handfuls in each. At the end of each strip, we three women would gather these piles together to make up sheaves and my father would come behind to tie them with bindings of tall wheat straws prepared first thing in the morning. It needed a man to tie them tightly enough. At the end of the day, before going home, we carried the sheaves to the middle of the field and my father stooked them. He laid four sheaves flat on the ground in the shape of a cross, with the ears pointing inwards, then added two more layers and finally capped the stook with a single sheaf. In this way, he protected the ears from rain, sun and birds and from animals, because the sheep flocks would start grazing the stubble before we could remove the sheaves." Yiannis, Tasoula's husband and of "local" extraction, has woken up and shouts out that his father sometimes added an extra layer of sheaves, so the stooks (*stáves*) could each contain either 13 or 17 sheaves. Thracians in nearby villages built their stooks (*tikourtzínia*) in the morning rather than evening (again when the ears were soft and would not easily spill grain) but also used 13 or 17 sheaves (Kizlaris, 1938–1948, 405). Once the corn stooked in the field had dried and harvesting no longer demanded all available hands, the sheaves were transferred to the threshing floor and built into tall stacks, one for each type of crop, with the ears again normally facing inwards, although "locals" and Thracians built stacks of different shapes.

The way in which sheaves were stooked varied, not least because of variation in the size of sheaves (see succeeding text). For example, in Kolindros, the huge sheaves carried one on either side of a horse or mule were too heavy to stook and were simply laid flat in the fields in pairs, ready for loading. Elsewhere in northern Greece, the cross-shaped arrangement favored by both "locals" and Thracians was arguably one of many symbolic measures to avert accidents; in

Turkey, sheaves were arranged in a circular or linear form, again with the ears protected (Hillman, 1984, 120). In Haute Provence, farmers placed greater reliance on practical than symbolic protection. Stooks were again built with the ears pointing to the protected interior, but sheaves were placed vertically and more effort was made to secure the capping sheaves. A stook might contain 80–100 or even more sheaves of wheat or rye but fewer of spring barley or oats, especially in wet years, because of the risk of the stack heating up and the grain rotting, instead of ripening (Martel, 1983, 88–92). From Turkey to Provence, treatment of the crop between harvest and threshing had to balance two opposing sets of hazards. On the one hand, individual sheaves lying in the field were at risk from scattering by birds or wind, soaking by rain, "burning" by the sun (curtailing the final stages of ripening), and perhaps consumption by domestic animals (depending on restrictions on stubble grazing). Mitsos recalls one disastrous harvest at Paliambela in the early 1950s, when a violent hailstorm flattened any unreaped crops and scattered sheaves stooked in the fields but only partially damaged the big stacks at the threshing floors. Sheaves and field stooks were also vulnerable to theft: in Assiros, Yannis' father routinely removed a sheaf of oats from the base of a neighbor's stook to feed his horse; in Kolindros, Nikolaos counted his sheaves to check whether any were stolen overnight. On the other hand, large stacks built before the crop had lost some moisture and, before any green weeds had wilted, might cause the grain to rot (Martel, 1983, 88; Palmer, 1998, 151). In Paliambela, field stooks occasionally had to be dismantled, after heavy rain, to help the crop dry, and "green-harvested" cereals might be left to dry for a week in the field before being bound into sheaves. The piecemeal aggregation of the harvested crop from unbound piles (Figure 3.5a) to tied sheaves to stooks in the field (Figure 3.6) to large stacks at the threshing floor helped achieve a balance between drying the crop and moving it to safety.

In southern Greece, where cereals were reaped more or less dry and, if transport was available, removed to the threshing floor within a day or two of harvesting, sheaves were not normally stooked in the field. In Messenian Metaxada, sheaves lay in the fields a few days,

(a)

(b)

Figure 3.5 Reaping barley at Tharounia, Euboea: (a) piles of cut handfuls await sheaving for transport; (b) each handful loosely tied with wild oat (a tighter binding was used if the crop was left in the field to dry).

Figure 3.6   Progressive drying of rye in the field, from tied sheaves lying horizontally (background) to vertical stooks with ears exposed to sun (foreground) at Mavrorakhi, northern Greece.

until the farmer found time to move them, but in Cretan Aloides and Kalo Khorio, crops were usually reaped, bound into sheaves, and carried to the threshing floor on the same day. Although premature harvest of cereals in northern Greece was intended, in part, to "buy time," it seems that cereals were reaped dry in the south not simply because the area to be harvested was smaller. On the contrary, moonlight reaping and the use of hired workers indicate that the cereal harvest took place here under severe time stress, implying that the more acute summer drought accelerated the final ripening and drying of these crops (see succeeding text).

Unbound piles of harvested cereals are more easily scattered by wind than tangled heaps of gathered pulses. At Skalani in Crete, Nikolis parted the preceding handful on the ground with his thumb as he added the next to make the pile more cohesive. In Paliambela, each handful was put down with force for the same reason, but harvested crops were often left unbound overnight, and after "green harvesting" for several days, to facilitate drying. In the hills of central and southern Greece, cereals often had short straws and small ears and were reaped dry, making them particularly vulnerable to scattering by wind. At Tharounia in Euboea, each cut handful was rapidly tied with four or five straws, before being placed on the ground, to prevent the cut stems from blowing away one by one (also Karanastasis, 1952, 289; Rasmussen, 1969, 94; Loukopoulos, 1983, 242), although a looser binding with a single wild oat stem sufficed if the crop would be sheaved for transport almost immediately (Figure 3.5b). In Messenia, farmers took the same precaution in the hill villages of Asoutaina, Makraina, Milioti, and Metaxada, although Ilias considered it unnecessary for a large team, as one or two members followed the reapers and bound sheaves immediately. Above Monforte, in central Italy, harvesters tied sheaves as they reaped, laying one cut handful on the ground transversely, piling others on top lengthwise, and then binding them into a sheaf with the first handful. In Kolindros and Paliambela, individual handfuls of rye were tied and not grouped into larger sheaves, for reasons discussed in the succeeding text. Normally in Greece, however, piles of harvested cereals, whether made up of loose or tied handfuls, were aggregated and bound into large sheaves at a convenient break in reaping – the end of a strip or field or working day. These sheaves facilitated handling in the successive stages of stooking, transporting, stacking at the threshing floor, and spreading out for threshing. Ilias in Metaxada thus had good reason to advocate cutting cereals low enough for binding into sheaves.

In mainland Greece, cereals were bound into sheaves, where possible, with their own straw, both for convenience and to avoid contaminating threshed grain with other seeds. Long straws were needed, sufficiently pliable not to break during tying, so slightly green plants were sought, perhaps in the shade of a tree or at the base of a slope. These were uprooted (or cut, if tall enough to sacrifice the lowest 15 cm) first thing in the morning, ideally when moist with dew but moistened with water if necessary, and were kept in the shade or under a sheaf until needed. A handful of straws (about 15 were suggested both in Haute Provence (Martel, 1983, 86) and in

Assiros) made a binding strong enough for a single sheaf, but often two handfuls were tied together at the ears to achieve the desired length (e.g., Loukopoulos, 1983, 242; Martel, 1983, 87). In Messenian Metaxada, short barley crops might be tied with taller wheat or oats, but the long and wiry stems of rye were widely favored for binding (e.g., Loukopoulos, 1983, 242), and many farmers grew a small strip of rye for this purpose, from Borja in lowland northern Spain to Arkhaia Nemea in the southern lowlands and Plikati in the high northwest mountains of Greece. Around north Greek Kolindros, farmers considered 0.5–1 *strémma* (0.05–0.1 ha) of rye essential to tie the huge sheaves loaded on pack animals. Harvested rye was tied in small bunches and stooked vertically, ears to the sun, to speed up drying and facilitate hand-threshing, and the threshed bunches were left in water overnight to soften the straw before use to bind barley and wheat sheaves. The growing of rye to bind sheaves of barley and wheat presumably selected for its early ripening in Kolindros. In Plikati, farmers grow a single row of rye for tying bundles of leafy hay (Halstead, 1998). At Kalo Khorio, Aloides, and Anogia in central Crete, short cereal crops growing on poor soils or with sparse rainfall were bound with pliable shoots of shrubs (e.g., Spanish broom, oleander, grape vine) or trees (including deciduous oak) or even agave. A similar practice is reported from west Crete (Pagkalos, 1983, 10–11), southeast Aegean Kos (Karanastasis, 1952, 288) and Rhodes (Vrontis, 1938–1948, 116), and some southern Alpine valleys (Martel, 1983, 84).

Cereal straw for tying sheaves had to be slightly green or moist to be pliable, but once dry the binding would not come undone. The binding had to be tight, and while some farmers achieved this deftly with their hands, others compressed the sheaf with their knee and, in some areas, used a small wooden hook or needle to tighten the "knot" (e.g., Kizlaris, 1938–1948, 404; Martel, 1983, 85). Nonetheless, if a few stems fell or were pulled out during handling or transport, sheaves scattered their contents. Sheaves were particularly vulnerable to loosening if they contained short crops or were carried on pack animals, as the gait of the animals repeatedly shook the load and some ears snagged on wayside bushes. In hill villages in Greece, where these two conditions often co-occurred, sheaves were frequently made "crossed" with the ears in the middle, half pointing one way and half the other; either handfuls were placed on the ground in alternating directions during reaping or piles were grouped in alternating directions when making up sheaves. With "crossed" sheaves, the ears were less likely to slide out of the binding (also Peña-Chocarro, 1999, 33) and were protected from snagging on bushes. Conversely, where crops were tall and/or transported on carts, sheaves tended to be made up with the ears at one end, because this allowed stooks and stacks to be built with the ears pointing inwards for protection or, less commonly, outwards to facilitate drying.

The size of sheaves varied according to local custom and practical considerations. The Kolindros "locals" loaded huge sheaves, one on either side of a pack animal. These sheaves, needing two people to tie and lift, impressed the Paliambela Thracians who transported the harvest in carts and made smaller sheaves that one person could tie and lift. In lowland northern Greece, even the barley was tall enough to make large sheaves. In the hills of central and south Greece, however, cereals were often too short to be tied securely into large sheaves, even with binding material of the required length cut from trees and shrubs. Here two, less frequently three or even four, sheaves of intermediate size were loaded either side of a mule or donkey (e.g., Pagkalos, 1983, 11). Nonetheless, sheaf size *within* any one community was fairly uniform, as illustrated in Paliambela by the unusually rapid agreement of the coffee-drinking pensioners (both Thracians and "locals") on average numbers of Thracian cart-sheaves per Kolindros mule-sheaf, per full threshing floor, and even per *strémma* of good wheat field. While height of crop, length of available binding material, method of transport, and ease of lifting set obvious limits on the *maximum* size of sheaves, practical considerations also favor rough local standardization and so constrain *minimum* size. Stooks and stacks containing sheaves of varying size are unstable, and pack animals loaded asymmetrically risk shedding their burden. Farmers also count sheaves to estimate the harvest. Nikolaos in Kolindros did so to plan how many trips he needed to transport the harvest and how many times he would fill the threshing floor. In Paliambela, Mitsos estimated, while the sheaves were still in the field, whether he would need to buy grain to get through the year or could sell some. Once the grain was threshed and winnowed, he measured it accurately and so knew that his sheaves each held 2–2.5 kg of grain. In Neo Sidirokhori, Konstantinos made sheaves of the same weight (2 *okádes*), stooked them in groups of 13, and loaded 8 stooks on his cart, so he knew that each cartload represented about 200 *okádes* or 250 kg of grain. Cypriot farmers similarly counted donkeys or carts to estimate the weight of both grain and straw carried from the field, using differ- ent conversion rates for wheat, barley, oats, and bitter vetch (Panaretos, 1946, 65–66), while local officials in early nineteenth- century Kithira used numbers of sheaves to estimate the amount of grain to be paid in tithes (Leontsinis, 2000, 219). In late 1930s Crete, Sofia from Aloides, working as a hired reaper in villages up to a day's walk from home, was expected to cut 20 sheaves per day. The widespread exchange and sharing of labor at harvest time must have provided both the rationale for and means of achieving approx- imate local standardization of sheaf size.

Even where sheaf size was reasonably standardized, the way in which handfuls of harvested crop were aggregated to make up a sheaf was variable. A "handful" was usually smaller, and the number of handfuls per sheaf larger, in a sparse crop. In northern Greece, the *leléki* cut longer straw than the sickle, and the *palamariá* gathered more stems than the bare hand, so sheaves of the same weight cut with dif- ferent tools contained different numbers of handfuls and piles. In Crete, uprooted short cereals might be gathered under the left arm, so that a complete "armful" was laid on the ground rather than being built up piecemeal from a series of deposited handfuls (Pagkalos, 1983, 11). In both Greece and Spain, local dialects differ not only in using distinctive terms for these various units but also in using the same word to refer to different levels of aggregation of the harvested crop. Nonetheless, practitioners volunteer quantified guidelines that they seem to regard as local norms: at Paliambela with sickle and *pala- mariá*, 3–5 handfuls per pile or *dromí* and 3–5 piles per (cart-)sheaf; on Rhodes, 3 handfuls per pile, 2 piles per armful, 10 armfuls per sheaf, and 2 sheaves per mule load (Vrontis, 1938–1948, 117); in west Crete, 5–7 handfuls per armful, 6–8 armfuls per sheaf, and 4 sheaves per pack animal; in central Crete, 8–10 armfuls per sheaf at Skalani and Anogia and 10–12 armfuls per sheaf at Kalo Khorio, all with 4 sheaves per pack animal; and in upland Lasithi, eastern Crete, 4–5 armfuls per sheaf and 4 sheaves per pack animal. Similar norms, again varying between districts, are reported from the Valencia region of eastern Spain (Palanca, 1991, 154–155). Some local standardization was probably imposed by two practical considerations. First, where groups of harvesters collaborated, one person often tied sheaves that had been cut and gathered by others; without some consistency in the size of units into which the harvest was aggregated, sheaving would have been very slow. This point is underlined by a saying in the hills of central Greece: "I made a mess of the handfuls, and you a mess of the sheaves" (Loukopoulos, 1983, 242). Secondly, the number of cuts per handful, handfuls per pile, and so on is intimately related to the way in which the reaper moves through a field. A consistent routine aided economy of effort by each worker, successful coordination of those working together, and thus prompt completion of the harvest. Koula's account of the routine in Paliambela is instructive. "Each of us cut a strip five paces wide, which was normally enough to fill your hand; if the crop was very good or if we were doing 'green-harvesting,' we each cut only three paces wide because otherwise the weight of the corn tired your hand. Once you'd put the first cut handful down, you moved forward a pace and cut another and laid it down on top of the first one. After you had advanced five paces and had put down five handfuls, you started a new pile, but if the crop was thick you made more frequent piles." Koula's father seems to have been unusually clear in his verbal instructions, while others relied more on example in teaching children to reap, but everyone acquired a basic rhythm of cutting and an understanding of when and how to vary this. In the previous generation, two "local" brothers were judged the best reapers in Paliambela. "They were quick and did not leave an ear uncut. They left the stubble looking as though it had been cut with a spirit-level and made sheaves with the ears all pointing the same way." The neatness of their handiwork was admired for its own sake

Figure 3.7 Cutting wheat at an even height, Nikos makes sheaves that can be stood upright and stooked easily at Paliambela, northern Greece.

but was also an indicator of all-round skill and efficiency. Nikos, son of one of the champion reapers, brought his sickle out of retirement to explain some of the family secrets. Dressed in standard reaping outfit of patched trousers and shirt, he cut a strip along the edge of a wheat field that a neighbor was about to enter with his combine harvester. First, Nikos showed how cutting at an even height produced a sheaf with a flat base that could be stood upright and thus stooked easily (Figure 3.7). "A less skilful reaper who cut unevenly had to knock the base of each handful on his thigh before putting it down and that wasted time, as well as wearing holes in his trousers." Before putting the cut handful down, he rested it in the arc of the sickle blade so that the bent ripe ears all pointed in the same direction (Figure 3.8). "If the ears pointed in different directions, they rubbed against each other in the sheaf and broke off."

Finally, the organization of harvesting and binding labor displays interesting variability. In most parts of Turkey, both men and

(a)

(b)

Figure 3.8 Wheat harvest at Paliambela, northern Greece: (a) aligning ears with curved sickle blade and (b) ears aligned in same direction to avoid loss of grain.

women reap and "each sickle reaper invariably does his [or her] own sheaving" (Hillman, 1984, 118). In northern Jordan, men and women now harvest side by side, but older farmers describe sexual division of labor, with men reaping and women binding and transporting (Palmer, 1998, 151). In Calabria, southern Italy, male reapers and female binders were likewise the norm, although women undertook "simpler" forms of reaping (Rasmussen, 1969, 94). In

Greece, a man and wife reaping together perhaps shared the work fairly evenly, like Dimitrakis and Irini on Amorgos, but larger groups tended to division of labor, with binding normally a male role. In Mavrorakhi, the family reaped a strip together and then turned back to make sheaves, with the father binding and the rest gathering. If the *Vardáris* was blowing from the north, however, three persons reaped and the fourth followed behind, sheaving immediately to avoid the crop being scattered. On Crete, both men and women reaped, but hired reapers were usually women, partly because widows often harvested for a neighbor who had plowed their fields. Marked division of labor was customary among the seasonal reaping teams from Haute Provence that worked their way up from the coast of southern France each summer (Martel, 1983, 40, 57). These three-person *sauques*, originally two sickle harvesters and one binder but later one scythe harvester with a gatherer and a binder, often worked together for many years. The extent of specialization in harvesting labor thus reflected practical considerations (size and composition of workforce, weather), but gender-related division of labor was shaped by local custom and wider social values (*pace* Sigaut, 1988, 21).

3.5 Who and How Many to Reap

The Paliambela grandfathers invite me for morning coffee. Kostas has heard England is permanently fogbound. I ask which part of the agricultural year was hardest and the overwhelming consensus is the harvest. How much could they reap in a day? Occasionally, a young couple reaped up to 0.4 ha of wheat in one day, but suggested average rates for reaping and binding cluster around 0.1–0.13 ha/head/day, and even 0.1 ha is probably optimistic as a daily rate *sustainable over a few weeks*. Enquiries in nearby Kolindros and Kastania elicited identical answers, while a figure of 0.1 ha/head/day or slightly less was repeatedly offered in Assiros and Mavrorakhi, also in lowland northern Greece. These consistent estimates are offered freely, because most informants have worked as, or have employed, hired harvest-workers. The area reaped was larger if the crop was sparse and smaller if it was thick, while weeds also slowed progress. In 1939, Mitsos and three friends from Paliambela were hired to reap a large field in another village. "The field was so tangled with weeds that you could not put down the handful you had just cut. In two days, we reaped only four *strémmata* [i.e., 0.05 ha/head/day], so we gave up and came home." At Assiros, Apostolis points out a field once infested so badly with wild vetches (*Vicia* spp.) that cutting a handful of cereal shook the whole stand, scattering grain and slowing progress. A gathering of grandmothers recalls how thistles and brambles hurt their hands while harvesting, making them slow and clumsy. With shrieks of laughter, they mention the unrepeatable local name for a particularly vicious thistle that attacked anyone who squatted to reap. The ease of harvesting also differed between crops. In Paliambela, nobody enjoyed reaping barley with its sharp awns, but the soft, slightly green straw of oats was easily cut with a sickle (though difficult with a scythe in Borja, north Spain). A couple could harvest 0.5 ha of oats in two days with ease and perhaps even in one day (0.25 ha/head/day) under pressure. Of the pulses, tall broad beans were easy, but low sprawling crops involved a lot of bending and so made hard and slow work. Mitsos and Eleni together took four days to uproot 0.5 ha of bitter vetch (i.e., 0.06 ha/head/day), and Fotis in Assiros similarly reckoned to gather 0.05 ha of lentils per day. In both Paliambela and Kolindros, the difficult of uprooting was repeatedly cited as the reason for growing only modest quantities of pulses (rarely exceeding 0.5 ha, including the relatively easy broad beans). Pulses to be eaten green, and so picked pod by pod, were grown on an even smaller scale – typically just one or two furrows.

To put these north Greek figures in context, per day a fit adult could harvest with a sickle a smaller area of cereals (0.1 ha) than she/he could sow with draft cows (0.1–0.2 ha) or oxen (0.2–0.3 ha). Under favorable circumstances (early autumn rains followed by a mild winter), the autumn–winter sowing period might extend – at least in theory – over four months (October–January), whereas the harvest season is constrained to four to six weeks for a mix of barley, wheat, and oats (including "green harvesting") or perhaps five to seven weeks with the addition of early-ripening pulses. In broken terrain, with fields at different altitudes or on both north- and south-facing slopes, ripening might be staggered and the harvest extended by one or two weeks, but such terrain tended to support sparser crops. In the lowlands, recent farmers aimed to complete the harvest well within the "window" of four to six or five to seven weeks, because fully ripe standing crops were vulnerable to losses from rain, hail, wind, birds, and reaping itself. Most households could comfortably mobilize the labor needed to harvest grain for domestic consumption (say, 10–20 person-days for 1–3 ha, as the upper part of this range assumes sparse crops). A household aiming for overproduction and solely dependent on manual tillage might be busy at harvest time following a damp autumn and mild winter but heavily "underemployed" after a dry autumn or severe winter. A household making full use of a pair of draft cows or oxen, however, and so sowing in autumn–winter 2–3 ha or 4–6 ha, respectively, would need perhaps 20–30 or 40–60 person-days of harvest labor. Substantially more labor would be needed if pulses were grown on a large scale, while the time available for harvesting would be shorter if they were sown on a small scale. On paper, a married couple could reap 6 ha of cereals unaided, and one Assiros grandfather, reputedly a workaholic in his distant youth, claimed that he and his wife had achieved this target in their prime, by working day and night. In Paliambela, newlywed Koula and Mikhalis had together harvested 5 ha of grain crops, but such feats were only feasible for fit young adults in favorable weather and with a grandparent or older child to mind any livestock and small children. In practice, estimates from Assiros, Mavrorakhi, and Paliambela imply that fit adults could each harvest 1 ha of winter cereals comfortably, 1.5 ha with hard work, and 2 ha only in their prime and with consistently favorable weather. Barring misfortune, a nuclear family could harvest the area of grain crops that could be sown in autumn–winter with draft cows (2–3 ha), but not normally that sown with draft oxen. Households producing a substantial surplus with oxen thus needed external labor, for at least part of the domestic cycle, and even those producing just for domestic consumption were under some time stress, because of the risks associated with delayed reaping, and thus large- and small-scale producers alike resorted to some "green harvesting."

Southern Greek farmers faced short crops more often than their northern counterparts. Farmers in northern Karpathos (Halstead and Jones, 1989), Messenia, and Crete unanimously considered that sickle harvesting was significantly slower for short barley than tall cereals and that uprooting of very short cereals and pulses was slower still. At Milioti in Messenia, a youthful Maria found the harvest hard work in good years, when crops were tall, but a very bad experience in dry years, when stunted crops had to be uprooted. For Nikolis in Skalani, "bending over to uproot short crops, with the sun on your head, is dreadful" and standing straight to beat olives from the tree a pleasure. In the same vein, a Rhodian saying "happiness with the plow, grief with the sickle" warns that thin, easily tilled soils involve hard work for little reward at harvest (Vrontis, 1938–1948, 117; also Loukopoulos, 1983, 237). As in northern Greece, picking of individual ears or pods was so slow as to be undertaken only on a very small scale. At Pinakiano on the Cretan Lasithi plateau, source of both Old and New World pulses of outstanding quality, Manolis declared: "we cannot pick individual pods – we grow a few tons of beans. We cut the whole plant dry and thresh it." Farmers producing for domestic consumption can grow a wide range of cereals and pulses (e.g., on northern Karpathos – Halstead and Jones, 1989), with different ripening and reaping times. For those aiming at overproduction, however, the labor demands of reaping strongly encourage reliance primarily on the taller autumn-/winter-sown cereals and perhaps broad beans, at the expense of the shorter pulses and spring-sown barley, and this in turn shortens the time available for the harvest.

In the dry southeast of Greece, as in eastern Turkey, Palestine, and northern Jordan (Hillman, 1984, 120; Palmer, 1998, 150), frequent uprooting of cereals made reaping slower, while harvesting mainly in the cool of morning, when grain is less easily shed, left fewer working hours than in north Greece. The suggested daily rate for sickle-reaping cereals on southern Amorgos (0.08 ha/head) is comparable with northern Greece but on northern Karpathos (0.03–0.1 ha/head, albeit with an elderly workforce) is slower (Halstead and Jones, 1989, 47). Nikolis from Skalani was also slow, taking 20–30 days as a young adult to reap 1.2 ha of cereals *under olives* (say, 0.05 ha/day), and in northern Jordan 2–4 people reaped 0.1 ha of wheat (0.03–0.05 ha/head) in a morning by sickle and uprooting combined (Palmer, 1998, 150). Most informants in southern Greece were reluctant to estimate the *area* reaped per day and, on Crete, many cited numbers of sheaves – a better proxy measure of both labor costs and yields. Sofia's output of 20 sheaves (five donkey-loads) per day, as a fit young woman in Aloides, is widely repeated in central Crete and, at 4–5 *okádes* per sheaf, represents 100–130 kg of grain, probably comparable with the yield from 0.1 ha in northern Greece (Section 5.6). Five loads per day was a demanding target, however, achieved only by good workers in relatively dense stands. At the *kafenío* in upland Anogia, Manolis argues that a good female worker harvested only two to three loads on the best of the poor local fields, which mainly supported barley.

Despite the difficulty of interregional comparison, harvesting – of the same crops as in northern Greece – was slower in the arid southern Aegean and eastern Mediterranean and was also more time-stressed. High temperatures and severe drought in early summer, and consequently rapid ripening of grain crops (e.g., Percival, 1974, 140–142), shorten the harvest season as well as the reaping day. Ilias in Metaxada and Vangelis in Ano Asites had perhaps tried extending the harvest season by making an early start, because both reported that the straw of cereals cut slightly prematurely drew moisture from the grain, leaving the latter shriveled. Most farmers in Messenia and Crete, however, were only familiar with "green harvesting" if they had observed it during military service further north. Harvesting of cereals in a riper state in southern than northern Greece is also suggested by the length of time sheaves stood in the field before removal to the threshing floor. Crops might be dried briefly in some upland villages in the south: at Asoutaina (about 700 m) in Messenia, sheaves were stooked upright in the field to catch the sun for a few days, and at Pinakiano (>800 m) on the Lasithi plateau, cereals were not sheaved until two to three days after reaping. At lower altitudes, however, crops were usually removed from the field as soon as pack animals were available – often on the same day. Beyond the Aegean, reaping of incompletely ripe crops has already been noted for southern France and Italy, while Hillman notes drying of crops in the field for several weeks in at least the higher and wetter parts of Turkey, in contrast with rapid removal for threshing in Palestine (Hillman, 1984, 120; 1985, 7) and northern Jordan (Palmer, 1998, 150). Wheat was also reaped dry in the Valencia region of eastern Spain (Palanca, 1991, 153), and it has been noted that the harvest was more urgent in south than north Spain (Ibañez *et al.*, 1998, 139). The hiring of laborers provides anecdotal support for reaping under greater time stress in southern than northern Greece. At hilly Kalo Khorio, although arable land was scarce and poor, Fountoulonikolis reports that a married couple hired additional workers if they had 2.5–3 ha (perhaps 4 ha) of grain crops to reap; a similar area, probably representing a substantially larger harvest, was suggested for lowland northern Greece. In the fertile Knossos valley, Giorgis sowed up to 500–600 *okádes* (650–800 kg) of cereals, initially with a pair of oxen and latterly with a horse or mule. He was adamant that nobody sowed as much as 5–6 ha, so the area to be reaped probably amounted to 3–4 ha, with yields comparable to those of northern Greece at least on his better fields and in good years. To harvest this area, he hired a dozen or more women reapers, a size of team employed in Assiros only by the largest landowners cultivating tens of hectares with multiple plow teams.

For glume wheats, Provençal einkorn was until recently harvested by sickle (Duplessy *et al.*, 1996, 58), like most free-threshing bread and macaroni wheats in Greece, while Turkish emmer wheat was mostly reaped by sickle but uprooted in one region where the soil was moist at harvest time (Hillman, 1984, 118). In Asturias, where the ears of spelt and emmer are harvested separately from the straw, there is universal agreement that bulk collection with reaping clamps (*mesorias*) is much faster than plucking individual ears by hand. The latter method is only used by those who cannot handle *mesorias* efficiently or where the crop has lodged, preventing their use. Reaping with *mesorias* is often restricted to the afternoon, so that the ear is dry and breaks off easily, and cultivation is now on a very small scale, allowing elderly harvesters to execute this task piecemeal. Estimates of clamping speeds by 10 practitioners ranged from 2 or 3 to 7 or more person-days per *dia de bueyes* of 800 m². The slower rates ($\leq$0.01 ha/head/day) may have allowed for plucking patches of lodged crop, while the faster rates (0.03–0.04 ha/ head/day) referred to collaborative labor, reckoned to save time at the cost of spilling a lot of ripe grain, and anyway are substantially slower than north Greek figures for sickle-reaping (though perhaps comparable with uprooting – ignoring subsequent mowing of the straw). As a result, a few decades ago the glume wheat harvest in Asturias lasted a few weeks, even though individual households seemingly reaped quite small areas (say, 0.2–0.5 ha), thanks to high yields and heavy dietary dependence on maize and potatoes.

To the labor required for reaping must be added that to transport the harvest from field to threshing floor or barn. The Paliambela Thracians, who used oxcarts carrying 50 or more small sheaves, estimated that 0.1 ha yielded 50 cereal sheaves in a good year, perhaps 30 in a bad year. Loading the cart required one person to lift and another to arrange the sheaves (as in Valencia – Palanca, 1991, 158). The oxen moved slowly, but their fields were mostly within 1.5 km of the village, and by loading sheaves so that any shed grain fell into the body of the cart, they could work through the day, making several round trips. Two persons thus transported the harvest from 5 ha (the area cultivable with a pair of oxen) in 8–10 days and sheaves from 1 to 2 ha (enough to feed a household) in just 2–4 days. Konstantinos in Neo Sidirokhori, who loaded 104 similar sheaves on his cart, would have saved on travel time between field and threshing floor. In Kolindros, one pack animal carried two large sheaves, each equivalent to five or more Thracian sheaves, and five mules or horses were reckoned to carry the same as one oxcart. The pack animals moved much faster than draft cattle, although sheaves were ideally transported in the morning and evening, when the crop was soft, to reduce spillage of grain. Nikolaos made 10 round trips per day with two donkeys to nearby fields, but some neighbors with fields 7–8 km distant could make at most 2 round trips in a long day. In Rhodes, a pack animal loaded with sheaves of good barley was reckoned to carry about 36 *okádes* (nearly 50 kg) of grain (Karanastasis, 1952, 290), and similar figures were offered by Kostis in Kalo Khorio (30–40 *okádes*) and Ilias in Metaxada (5 *okádes* per sheaf, 6 sheaves per donkey, and 8–10 sheaves per mule or horse); in Cyprus, farmers reckoned on 30 *okádes* of barley or 20 *okádes* of wheat per donkey-load (Panaretos, 1946, 65). On this basis, a single donkey might take 20–50 round trips to carry the 1–1.5 tons of grain needed to sustain a nuclear family; an adult human carrying one large sheaf might need 40–100 trips. Whatever the mode of transport, the time taken to transfer the harvest from the fields depended on the distances and terrain involved. Even at tiny Paliambela, however, where sheaves were carried only short distances in carts pulled by draft cattle maintained for plowing, a surplus-producing farmer was busy with transport for one to two weeks after the end of the harvest, significantly delaying the start of threshing. In southern Greece, where the crop was often moved while reaping was still in progress, Messenian Ilias' verdict was that "transport of the harvest was torture." Clearly, transporting of sheaves (i.e., straw as well as ears and pods), even with the aid of draft or pack animals, added significantly to the labor costs of the harvest season.

One way of reducing, or redistributing, transport costs was to leave the straw in or near the fields. In Asturias, the straw was harvested separately, stooked in the fields, and brought to the village when needed. In parts of southern Greece, for example, at Olimbos on Karpathos (Halstead and Jones, 1989), distant fields are sometimes accompanied by threshing floors and "field houses," so that the crop can be threshed and winnowed and the straw stored more or less *in situ*, while the grain is removed to safe storage in the home village. On the higher slopes above Monforte in central Italy, sheaves were carried from the fields to nearby threshing floors on the heads of human bearers, who were considered to shed less grain than pack animals with their more uneven gait. The straw was then stored and consumed by livestock on the mountain or brought down to the village piecemeal, when needed; the threshed and winnowed grain was again carried to the village as soon as possible (Forte, 2009).

Another important means of lightening the burden of transport was collaboration. Villagers with adjacent fields on the mountain above Monforte might share a nearby threshing floor, so minimizing the distance over which sheaves were carried. Groups of households joined forces to carry the sheaves of each in turn to the threshing floor, thus ensuring efficient use of the shared facility as well as reducing the tedium of transport. As with pack animals, the sheaves were carried early in the morning, when they were damp, and so less likely to shed their grain, and when snakes lurking underneath were cold and slow moving. Several households likewise contributed to a combined team of pack animals that allowed one person to carry far more of the cleaned grain in one trip down to the village, two hours walk below, than was possible with a single donkey. In Greece, the human labor for transporting the harvest was also often minimized by mutual loans of pack animals or, as in Kolindros, by hiring teams of mules used during the rest of the year for carrying timber and other goods. In Paliambela, a farmer without a teenage son might similarly borrow a young neighbor to enable him to carry out efficiently the two-person tasks of loading sheaves onto a cart and stacking them at the threshing floor.

Collaboration also played an important part in the harvest itself. Working in a team made the task less dull, and folkloric descriptions of reaping in Greece make repeated reference to songs and jokes shared between workers (e.g., Karanastasis, 1952, 289). These drew inspiration both from the arduous nature of this task and from the rare opportunities, afforded by gang labor and sleeping outdoors, for encounters between young men and women (e.g., Slinis, 1938–1948, 100) – whose industry and stamina were meanwhile judged by potential parents-in-law (Kostakis, 1976–1978, 103). Moments of light relief and an element of competition kept members of a team working longer and faster than they did alone. When several people worked together, either as hired laborers or in mutual help, an experienced reaper might take the role of *dragoumános*, lining up the team and dictating the strip to be tackled (e.g., Kizlaris, 1938–1948, 405). On Kos, experienced reapers worked at the ends of the line and novices in the middle (Karanastasis, 1952, 289). Members of the team were spaced far enough apart (2–3 m in Kos, Crete, northern Greece, Provence (Martel, 1983, 57), and Valencia (Palanca, 1991, 153)) to have room to work, with experienced reapers taking on a wider span than novices. The size of each predefined strip represented a compromise between the need to divide up each field efficiently and to set the team morale-boosting achievable targets (Karanastasis, 1952, 289). Teams also worked more efficiently because they afforded greater opportunities for division of labor. In Greece, two, three, or four people reaping together usually stopped at intervals to gather and bind what they had cut. In a larger team, of, say, 6–10 workers, 1 or 2 often tied sheaves while the others reaped, and where crops were at risk of scattering by wind, this freed those reaping from the need to tie individual handfuls. In Metaxada, Nikos pointed out that, if one woman cooked for three households, two others were free for reaping, while elsewhere an older child might be entrusted with the children or house goats of several families (Vrontis, 1938–1948, 117). At Tharounia, while the reapers worked, ate, and slept in the fields, one person accompanied the pack animals laden with sheaves back to the village, and an elderly man, no longer fit for arduous tasks, stayed at home preparing sheaf bindings from last year's rye. Collaborative reaping also allowed timelier harvesting of ripe crops. In the north of Greece, where many crops were reaped before they were fully dry, exchange (as well as hiring) of harvest labor was not uncommon in the mid-twentieth century, but is usually rationalized as a means of reducing the tedium of the task. In southern Greece, where crops were reaped dry and the terrain is more dissected (helping to stagger ripening), exchange of labor was probably more vulnerable to scheduling conflicts but also more necessary. As Nikos in Metaxada observed, "once my field was dry, it had to be reaped immediately." Cretans repeatedly make the same point, describing how wind "threshes" or "canes" ripe barley, scattering the seed. A saying repeated in different villages underlines the need for haste: "whether May is good or bad, the sheaf must be on the threshing floor." In Kalo Khorio, according to Fountoulonikolis, the norm was for each household to reap its own fields, but a farmer with no ripe crops would help a neighbor on the understanding of later reciprocation. Many elderly Cretans, however, insist that "people went to harvest in groups and never in ones and twos," emphasizing the urgency rather than tedium of the task as the reason for collaboration. Because the window for harvesting a ripe crop was so short, small differences in ripeness between fields were exploited by exchange of labor.

3.6 Harvest Ceremonies

The beginning and end of the harvest were marked by various customs emphasizing the difficulty, urgency, importance, or partial predictability of the task. Reapers prepared for weeks of repeated bending by rubbing their backs with earth blessed in church at Pentecost (Vrontis, 1938–1948, 116) or tying round their waists the first ears cut (Karanastasis, 1952, 289). Before harvesting the first field, they might seek the almighty's blessing by cutting two strips at right angles, in the shape of a cross (Loukopoulos, 1983, 241). Reapers celebrated the end of harvesting by throwing sickles, hats and headscarves, or the final ears into the air, wishing that the pile of cleaned grain on the threshing floor would reach the same height or observing how the projectiles landed as a clue to the future (Kizlaris, 1938–1948, 405; Slinis, 1938–1948, 102; Vrontis, 1938–1948, 118; Karanastasis, 1952, 291). It was bad luck to begin the harvest on Tuesday in mainland Tsakonia (Kostakis, 1976–1978, 104) or to finish it on Saturday on Rhodes (if necessary, a final strip was left uncut to the following Monday – Vrontis, 1938–1948, 118). Around north Greek Langadas, Thracians completing the harvest hung their old shoes at the unreaped field of a neighbor, so that the risk of public ridicule provided an additional incentive to finish reaping quickly (Kizlaris,

1938–1948, 405). The last strip of crop was often left uncut "for the field," the pack animals, or gleaners (Kizlaris, 1938–1948, 405; Vrontis, 1938–1948, 118; Karanastasis, 1952, 291). The first or last ears were often cut to the accompaniment of prayers and the laying of crop or sickles in the shape of a cross. They were then plaited into a cross or "corn dolly," which might be hung on the central pole of the threshing floor and later in the house, before being mixed with the seedcorn for the following year (Vrontis, 1938–1948, 118–119; Karanastasis, 1952, 290). At harvest time, when the fruits of the previous year's toil and the basis of the following year's subsistence were at severe risk until laboriously gathered and removed from the field, Mediterranean farmers deployed a range of practical measures, religious symbolism, and sympathetic magic to ensure a rapid and successful outcome.

3.7 Reaping in the Past

The variability of recent harvesting practices in the Mediterranean reflects both local tradition and tactical responses to practical constraints. Local variation in Neolithic sickle form is richly documented in the western Alpine Foreland (Schlichtherle, 1992), thanks to the preservation of organic handles, but also apparent in use-wear on chipped-stone inserts from southeast (Gurova, 2005) and southwest (Gassin *et al.*, 2010) Europe. As regards practical considerations, two interrelated issues emerge from recent experience. First, the grain harvest took place during a narrowly constrained period and, because delay was risky, under considerable time stress, albeit to a degree that varied between farmers (depending on scale of cultivation and size of workforce), regions (with ripening more compressed towards the south), and crop types (e.g., glume wheats withstanding late harvest better than free-threshing cereals). Secondly, methods and labor costs of reaping were closely related to preceding and subsequent stages of grain production: in particular, straw was often reaped with cereal ears because it was needed as fodder or litter for work animals that, *inter alia*, helped to transport and thresh this bulkier harvest. To what extent did technological change affect these two issues?

Most recent Mediterranean farmers reaped with an iron sickle, but tools have changed considerably over the millennia, with potentially significant implications for speed and method of harvesting. Reaping experiments with replica sickles have achieved rates per head per eight-hour day of 0.02–0.05 ha with flint, 0.03–0.05 ha with bronze, and 0.1 ha with iron sickles (Russell, 1988, 116, table 20). These experiments involved different personnel and crops of contrasting height and density, but the credible implication is that reaping was significantly slower with flint and perhaps bronze than with iron sickles, while a shorter reach may have made early sickles particularly inefficient for reaping low on the straw. Even a replica Neolithic-type flint sickle, however, cut einkorn three times faster than a reaping clamp (Ibañez *et al.*, 1998, 134), and as described in Section 3.5, the latter is considerably faster in a standing crop than plucking ears by hand. The use of flint rather than iron doubtless reduced the advantage of sickle-reaping over uprooting, and the ease of uprooting depends on soil conditions and crop height, but harvesting of sprawling pulses or short cereals in this way must always have been slower and more tiring than gathering taller cereals. *Other things being equal* (see succeeding text), therefore, less effective flint (and perhaps bronze) sickles should have reduced speed of reaping, accentuating the time stress widespread in recent harvesting, and discouraged bulk gathering of straw with the grain. The following discussion considers the implications of time stress and straw gathering for early cereal harvesting methods in southwest Asia and southern Europe and, more broadly, for large-scale surplus production in the Bronze Age and later.

First, harvesting methods are central to models of cereal domestication. While wild cereal ears shatter on ripening, ensuring dispersal of seeds, non-shattering domestic cereals are unviable outside cultivation. Beating ripe wild cereal spikelets into a basket yields most grain per hour but perpetuates the shattering form in both the original stand and any gathered material that may be sown. Gradual displacement of shattering by non-shattering forms in the Near Eastern Pre-Pottery Neolithic B (Tanno and Willcox, 2012) thus implies harvesting of near- or part-ripe wild cereals by cutting or uprooting, so that ripe shattering types were scattered and non-shattering mutants selectively gathered and subsequently sown. Because the ripening of wild cereal ears is staggered, harvesting by beating must be repeated over a few days to exploit a stand fully, and on each occasion, some ripe spikelets are scattered and some plants trampled, whereas a whole stand can be cut or uprooted in one operation, achieving less time-efficient but more complete recovery of available grain. Chipped stone, consistent in morphology, hafting traces, and microwear with use in sickles for cutting plant stems, has been found with cereals of this date of both wild and domesticated morphology (Anderson, 1998, 147; Willcox, 1998) and often bears the characteristic gloss that, in experimental replication, forms only by cutting stems slightly green, when the ears are still ripening (Anderson, 1998, 150). With the development of non-shattering cereals, beating ceased to be an option for harvesting. Like recent farmers, early cereal growers doubtless used different methods in different contexts, for example, uprooting short crops in dry years or gathering fallen ears by hand, but used a sickle at least sometimes (Anderson, 1998). Hafted chipped-stone sickles offered a longer reach and, especially with a curved working surface (Ibañez *et al.*, 1998, 134), gathered more stems than a bare hand or reaping clamp and so presumably enabled faster harvesting. Reaping of cultivated cereals with a sickle selects for *more uniform* ripening, but more variable microwear now reflects cutting of stems at more diverse stages of ripeness (Anderson, 1998, 152), and this, in light of recent experience, suggests cultivation on a large enough scale to encourage very full use of the available window for harvesting.

Secondly, while the sickle seemingly played a major role in early cereal harvesting in the Near East, Sigaut (1988, 19) has argued that reaping ears with a clamp was more archaic, as well as technologically simpler, and persisted late enough in temperate Europe to give rise to the German word *Speicher* (storeroom, cf. Latin *spicarium* or store for ears). He notes that, even in the Mediterranean, surviving early "sickles" need not have cut cereals and that Roman descriptions of harvesting refer to *pectines* (combs) and enigmatic *mergae* as well as sickles (Sigaut, 1988, 21). *Pectines* and *mergae* were probably adjuncts rather than alternatives to sickles (Spurr, 1986, 67–68), however, and neither was used like a reaping clamp (Peña-Chocarro, 1999, 45). Rather than inferring generally late displacement of the clamp by the sickle, it seems safer to take Roman sources at face value – as indicating that harvesting methods, as in the recent past, varied in accordance with regional tradition and practical considerations like crop density and need for straw (Spurr, 1986, 68–73). Sigaut's main point is that storage practices are interrelated – though not deterministically (Sigaut, 1988, 25) – with methods of reaping, threshing, and so on. Thus, storage of ears is attractive in Asturias, where wet summers make bulk-threshing of sheaves outdoors and thorough drying of free grain for storage over winter more difficult than in most of the Mediterranean. Storage in the ear alone, however, does not account for the use of the reaping clamp. Asturian use of this slow reaping method is practicable, because glume wheats are grown on a modest scale, and beneficial, because wet summers favor harvesting the crop as ripe and dry as possible and hence in a brittle state that leads to heavy losses with a sickle. A further factor favoring harvest of ears alone is limited demand for glume wheat straw: Asturian farmers rely primarily on hay to stall-feed cattle and often use chestnut leaves as litter. If labor was scarcer, the harvest more extensive, the summers drier, or glume wheat straw indispensible as fodder, Asturian farmers might reap spelt and emmer ears by sickle – like einkorn growers in southern Spain (Ibañez *et al.*, 1998, 138).

Contrary to Sigaut's model, crops seemingly were harvested with chipped stone from the Early Neolithic in southern Europe, where inserts, many bearing "sickle gloss," are an important component of lithic assemblages. Morphology and microwear are ambiguous guides to use, but tasks like hide and plant processing, commonplace in the preceding Mesolithic, account less parsimoniously than reaping of grain crops for the significant changes in toolkit that often mark the Neolithic transition. Reaping clamps may have been used to gather dead-ripe and brittle cereals towards the end of the harvest period, but sickles would have enabled an earlier start to the season and faster progress. Indeed, by facilitating prompt harvesting and perhaps also gathering of straw for winter fodder, chipped-stone sickles may have been one of the components of the archaeologically durable toolkit that was most critical to survival of European farmers. Together with probable reductions in mobility and hence opportunities for embedded raw material procurement, this implies, *inter alia*, that (dis)continuity in chipped-stone technology between the late Mesolithic and Neolithic may be a particularly unsuitable medium for identifying early farmers as colonists or acculturated indigenous foragers.

Thirdly, the height of weeds represented in crop remains may also illuminate reaping methods. Neolithic assemblages from central Europe and the central Balkans include varying mixtures of low, medium, and tall weeds, indicating that at least some crops were reaped by sickle rather than uprooted or plucked (Bogaard, 2004, 65; Kreuz *et al.*, 2005), even though some were stored as ears (e.g., Maier, 1999; Marinova, 2007). In central Europe, the height of weeds in crop samples varies within settlements but exhibits no geographical patterning (Bogaard, 2004, 120), suggesting flexible reaping practices rather than regional differences in sickle form and efficiency. Possible rationales for flexibility, suggested by recent practice, include variable crop height resulting from differences in growing conditions between plots and years; variable demand for straw (reflecting availability of other fodder/litter sources, as well as numbers of animals stalled over winter); cutting of less straw in distant fields to facilitate transport; and variation in crop ripeness and hence in use of sheaves to complete ripening and drying on the stalk and facilitate handling during this process. Whatever the reasons for variable harvesting height, the lithic and archaeobotanical evidence may reflect gathering of ears and straw in two separate operations or cutting of sheaves followed by removal of ears (Section 4.9). Two-stage harvesting is depicted in a fourteenth-century AD Byzantine illustration (Bryer, 1986, 76)

117

Table 3.1 Number of man-days to harvest area tilled in one day under different combinations of tillage and reaping technology.

	Hand tillage (0.01–0.03 ha/man-day)	*Ard + cows (0.1–0.2 ha/day)*	*Ard + oxen (0.2–0.3 ha/day)*
Flint sickle (0.02–0.05 ha/man-day)	0.5	4–5	6–10
Iron sickle (≤0.1 ha/man-day)	0.1–0.3	1–2	2–3

and perhaps implied (Spurr, 1986, 67–68) in Sigaut's claimed Roman textual evidence for reaping clamps.

Fourthly, the growing of cereals for market as well as domestic consumption has accentuated some recent farmers' experience of time stress at harvest, and the scale on which crops were grown will have varied between historical contexts. It is instructive, therefore, to compare the labor demands of both reaping and tillage under different technological constraints (Table 3.1). With the autumn–winter window for sowing lasting at least twice as long as the early summer harvest period, a household using draft oxen at sowing could easily exceed the capacity of its human workers to harvest with iron sickles, while a household without draft animals might be heavily underemployed. With flint substituted for iron sickles, draft cows as well as oxen might comfortably exceed the reaping capacity of a single household, implying that cows at Neolithic Knossos were worked only lightly (arguably inconsistent with the frequency of "traction pathologies") or that only some households maintained them. The latter scenario would, given the importance of prompt sowing and the vulnerability of ripe standing crops, have favored exchanges of draft animals at sowing time for human labor at harvest, with radical implications for the development of economic and social inequality (Isaakidou, 2008). Conversely, if farmers combined *manual tillage* with flint sickles, demands on their labor at sowing and harvest time should roughly have balanced, but the use of draft cattle for the former would greatly have reduced the risk of failure. Possibly, therefore, the scarcity of "traction pathologies" in cattle outside Knossos reflects less intensive use for draft (e.g., because the ratio of cattle to people was higher) rather than reliance on manual tillage alone.

Fifthly, the range of crops grown and their ease of reaping differed between contexts. As recent southern Greek farmers emphasized, uprooting of short spring barley extended the sowing season at the cost of increased drudgery during the even more time-stressed harvest. This must have been a further disincentive, in addition to unreliable yields and the need for intensive tillage, against large-scale spring sowing of cereals in antiquity (Section 2.7). For the same reason, most recent farmers limited sowing of pulses to just a fraction of a hectare "for the household." On this basis, however, a hypothetical ancient household cultivating (with "optimistic" yields) just 1–2 ha of grain crops for domestic consumption might plausibly have sown pulses on a similar scale to cereals, enabling cereal–pulse rotation with attendant benefits of maintaining soil fertility, lengthening the harvest period, and spreading the risks of crop failure. Conversely, recent farmers engaged in large-scale overproduction focused on more easily harvested cereals and had little scope for cereal–pulse rotation. The representation of pulses and cereals in charred archaeobotanical remains is relatively balanced in very well-preserved storage deposits from Early Neolithic southern Bulgaria (Marinova, 2007) and in more haphazardly collected evidence from Neolithic and to a lesser extent Bronze Age Greece (Halstead, 1994, 204–205, table 1). This balance, which contrasts sharply with the overwhelming predominance of cereals in recent Mediterranean agriculture, suggests most prehistoric farmers cultivated on a scale small enough not to inhibit growing labor-intensive pulses. For Late Bronze Age southern Greece, however, textual evidence indicates that large-scale grain production by the Mycenaean palaces was restricted to cereals (Halstead, 1992).

Sixthly, harvesting of grain crops has attracted less attention than tillage among European prehistorians but is central to the relationship between plowing and social inequality (Section 2.7). In the recent past, while most farming households comfortably harvested the area of grain crops needed for domestic consumption, they usually hired additional labor to harvest the 4–6 ha that might be plowed with a pair of oxen and even, in the south where the onset of summer drought was more rapid, the 2–3 ha that could be plowed with cows. Large-scale *surplus* production thus typically depended not only on plow oxen but also on additional harvest labor, and the latter was frequently drawn from households lacking enough land for self-sufficiency or draft animals to work their land. In classical Athens, where slave labor in agriculture enabled citizens to participate in public life, there is anecdotal evidence that poor citizens were hired to reap for wealthier neighbors (Jameson, 1977–1978, 131–133). The urgent and highly seasonal need for additional harvesters on the bigger farms (of *zeugites* size and upwards) supports Jameson's suggestion that hired labor, regarded as demeaning for citizens, was much commoner than literary sources apparently imply. Conversely, if those with smaller landholdings struggled to support draft animals (Section 2.7), they may have exchanged seasonal harvesting labor for plowing by neighbors, as was common in the recent past, and perhaps entered thereby into long-term clientage (cf. Gallant, 1991, 139, 164–165). There are also sparse Roman literary references to hired harvest labor (Spurr, 1986, 66), and such arrangements may have become increasingly widespread through the first millennium BC and early first millennium AD, when textual references to some very large landholdings in the Mediterranean are matched by archaeobotanical evidence for weeds of extensive cultivation in southern temperate Europe (e.g., van der Veen, 1992; Jacomet and Brombacher, 2009) and zooarchaeological evidence for replacement of draft cows with oxen in both regions (e.g., Peters, 1998; MacKinnon, 2004). The implied expansion of large-scale agricultural concerns would have demanded a substantial labor force at harvest time. Broadly over the same period, glume wheats (especially emmer and spelt), which recent farmers have found more resilient to delayed harvest, were progressively displaced by free-threshing wheat in the Mediterranean and its temperate fringes (e.g., Buxó, 2008; Jacomet and Brombacher, 2009), shortening the time available for reaping staple cereals and increasing the likelihood that harvest labor was mobilized by *short-term* employment of large numbers of poorer farmers. Similarly, in late second millennium BC Greece, Late Bronze Age texts offer no hint that the palace organized the harvest of cereals apparently sown with the aid of palatial oxen, inviting speculation that local *damos* communities, on whose land these crops were probably grown (Killen, 1998), may have mobilized reapers (Halstead, 1999). One circumstantial argument in favor of this suggestion is that, taking the texts at face value, the palaces cultivated only one type of cereal (Halstead, 1995). This narrows the window for harvesting and favors short-term mobilization of a mass labor force rather than reliance on a smaller group of dependent workers, potentially recorded in surviving records but assigned therein to other seasonal tasks.

Mass mobilization of human labor for harvesting was as essential as draft oxen to the extensive surplus-producing agriculture that underpinned salient social hierarchy, from the Bronze Age Near East to early historic southern Europe. It is striking, therefore, that hierarchical societies seem to be of much greater antiquity in the semiarid regions of the Near East and southern Mediterranean than in the northern Mediterranean, where a longer window for harvesting should have reduced the amount of dependent labor needed to support a given level of surplus production and thus facilitated the maintenance of elite groups. Conversely, the greater time stress in semiarid regions, during both sowing and harvesting, inevitably accentuated the risk of failure to produce sufficient staple crops and arguably placed a premium on exchanges of plowing and reaping services, discussed in the preceding text for contexts ranging from the Neolithic to Greco-Roman antiquity. As noted previously, such exchanges may cushion households from short-term subsistence failure but escalate into long-term relations of dependence.

References

Anderson, P.C. (1998) History of harvesting and threshing techniques for cereals in the prehistoric Near East, in *The Origins of Agriculture and Crop Domestication* (eds A.B. Damania, J. Valkoun, G. Willcox, and C.O. Qualset), International Center for Agricultural Research in the Dry Areas, Rome, pp. 145–159.

Blanchard, R. (1945) *Les Alpes occidentales 4: les préalpes françaises du sud*, Arthaud, Grenoble and Paris.

Bogaard, A. (2004) *Neolithic Farming in Central Europe: An Archaeobotanical Study of Crop Husbandry Practices*, Routledge, London.

Braudel, F. (1975) *The Mediterranean and the Mediterranean World in the Age of Philip II*, vol. 1, Fontana, London.

Bryer, A. (1986) Byzantine agricultural implements: the evidence of medieval illustrations of Hesiod's 'Works and Days'. *Annual of the British School at Athens*, 81, 45–80.

Buxó, R. (2008) The agricultural consequences of colonial contacts on the Iberian Peninsula in the first millennium b.c. *Vegetation History & Archaeobotany*, 17, 145–154.

Duplessy, B., Gabert, A., Valabrégue, J.P. et al. (1996) *Le livre de l' épeautre*, Edisud, Aix-en-Provence.

Forte, M.A. (2009) *A Mediterranean mountain: landscape and land use on the Cairo Massif*, Central Italy, 1700–1970 a.d. PhD thesis. University of Sheffield.

Gaillard, E.-M. (1997) *Les blés de l' été, 3: au temps des aires*, Les Alpes de Lumière, Salagon.

Gallant, T.W. (1991) *Risk and Survival in Ancient Greece*, Polity Press, Cambridge, UK.

Gassin, B., Bicho, N.F., Bouby, L. et al. (2010) Variabilité des techniques de récolte et traitement des céréales dans l'occident méditerranéen au Néolithique ancient et moyen: facteurs environnementaux, économiques et sociaux, in *Economie et société à la fin de la préhistoire. Actualité de la recherche* (eds A. Beeching, E. Thirault, and J. Vital), Maison de l'Orient et de la Méditerranée, Lyon, pp. 19–38.

Gurova, M. (2005) Elements de faucilles néolithiques en silex de Bulgarie: evidence et contexte. *Archaeologica Bulgarica*, 9, 1–14.

Halstead, P. (1992) Agriculture in the Bronze Age Aegean: towards a model of palatial economy, in *Agriculture in Ancient Greece* (ed. B. Wells), Swedish Institute at Athens, Stockholm, pp. 105–116.

Halstead, P. (1994) The North-South divide: regional paths to complexity in prehistoric Greece, in *Development and Decline in the Mediterranean Bronze Age* (eds C. Mathers and S. Stoddart), J.R. Collis, Sheffield, pp. 195–219.

Halstead, P. (1995) Late Bronze Age grain crops and Linear B ideograms *65, *120 and *121. *Annual of the British School at Athens*, 90, 229–234.

Halstead, P. (1998) Ask the fellows who lop the hay: leaf-fodder in the mountains of northwest Greece. *Rural History*, 9, 211–234.

Halstead, P. (1999) Surplus and share-croppers: the grain production strategies of Mycenaean palaces, in *MELETHMATA. Studies Presented to Malcolm H. Wiener as he Enters his 65th Year* (eds P. Betancourt, V. Karageorghis, R. Laffineur, and W.-D. Niemeier), University of Liège, Liège, pp. 319–326.

Halstead, P. and Jones, G. (1989) Agrarian ecology in the Greek islands: time stress, scale and risk. *Journal of Hellenic Studies*, 109, 41–55.

Hillman, G. (1984) Traditional husbandry and processing of archaic cereals in recent times: part 1, the glume wheats. *Bulletin on Sumerian Agriculture*, 1, 114–152.

Hillman, G. (1985) Traditional husbandry and processing of archaic cereals in recent times: part 2, the free-threshing cereals. *Bulletin on Sumerian Agriculture*, 2, 1–31.

Ibañez, J.J., González, J.E., Palomo, A., and Ferrer, A. (1998) Pre-Pottery Neolithic A and Pre-Pottery Neolithic B lithic agricultural tools on the Middle Euphrates: the sites of Tell Mureybit and Tell Halula, in *The Origins of Agriculture and Crop Domestication* (eds A.B. Damania, J. Valkoun, G. Willcox, and C.O. Qualset), International Center for Agricultural Research in the Dry Areas, Rome, pp. 132–144.

Isaakidou, V. (2008) The fauna and economy of Neolithic Knossos revisited, in *Escaping the Labyrinth* (eds V. Isaakidou and P. Tomkins), Oxbow, Oxford, pp. 90–114.

Jacomet, S. and Brombacher, C. (2009) Geschichte der Flora in der Regio Basiliensis seit 7500 Jahren: Ergebnisse von Untersuchungen pflanzlicher Makroreste aus archäologischen Ausgrabungen. *Mitteilungen der Naturforschenden Gesellschaft beider Basel*, 11, 27–106.

Jameson, M.H. (1977–1978) Agriculture and slavery in classical Athens. *The Classical Journal*, 73, 122–145.

Jones, G. and Halstead, P. (1995) Maslins, mixtures and monocrops: on the interpretation of archaeobotanical crop samples of heterogeneous composition. *Journal of Archaeological Science*, 22, 103–114.

Karakasidou, A.N. (1997) *Fields of Wheat, Hills of Blood*, Chicago University Press, Chicago.

Karanastasis, A.M. (1952) Oi zevgades tis Ko. I zwi kai oi askholies ton. *Laografia*, 14, 201–303.

Killen, J.T. (1998) The role of the state in wheat and olive production in Mycenaean Crete. *Aevum: Rassegna di Scienze Storiche Linguistiche e Filologiche*, 72, 19–23.

Kizlaris, T. (1938–1948) Agrotikos vios ton Thrakon. *Laografia*, 12, 386–416.

Kostakis, T.P. (1976–1978) Georgika tis Tsakonias. *Laografia*, 31, 43–150.

Kreuz, A., Marinova, E., Schäfer, E., and Wiethold, J. (2005) A comparison of early Neolithic crop and weed assemblages from the Linearbandkeramik and the Bulgarian Neolithic cultures: differences and similarities. *Vegetation History & Archaeobotany*, 14, 237–258.

Leontsinis, G.N. (2000) *The Island of Kythera: A Social History (1700–1863)*, University of Athens, Athens.

Littlejohn, L. (1946) Some aspects of soil fertility in Cyprus. *Empire Journal of Experimental Agriculture*, 14, 123–133.

Loukopoulos, D. (1983) *Georgika tis Roumelis*, Dodoni, Athens.

MacKinnon, M. (2004) *Production and Consumption of Animals in Roman Italy: Integrating the Zooarchaeological and Textual Evidence*, Journal of Roman Archaeology, Portsmouth.

Maier, U. (1999) Agricultural activities and land use in a Neolithic village around 3900 BC: Hornstaad Hörnle 1A, Lake Constance, Germany. *Vegetation History & Archaeobotany*, 8, 87–94.

Marinova, E. (2007) Archaeobotanical data from the early Neolithic of Bulgaria, in *The Origins and Spread of Domestic Plants in Southwest Asia and Europe* (eds S. Colledge and J. Conolly), Left Coast Press, Walnut Creek, pp. 93–109.

Martel, P. (1982) *Les blés de l' été, 1: l' été des paysans en Haute-Provence*, Les Alpes de Lumière, Salagon.

Martel, P. (1983) *Les blés de l' été, 2: les moissons en Haute-Provence*, Les Alpes de Lumière, Salagon.

Meurers-Balke, J. and Loennecken, C. (1984) Zu Schutzgeräten bei der Getreideernte mit der Sichel. *Tools & Tillage*, 5, 27–42.

Pagkalos, G.E. (1983) *Peri tou glossikou idiomatos tis Kritis, 7: ta laografika*, Athens, Kentro Erevnis Ellinikis Laografias, Akadimias Athinon.

Palanca, F. (1991) Agricultura, in *Temes d' etnografia Valenciana 2: utillatge agrícola i ramaderia* (eds F. Martínez and F. Palanca), Institució Valenciana d'Estudis i Investigació, Valencia, pp. 11–181.

Palmer, C. (1998) 'Following the plough': the agricultural environment of northern Jordan. *Levant*, 30, 129–165.

Panaretos, A. (1946) Kupriaka metra, stathma, monades khronou kai skhetikai pros auta lexeis. *Kupriakai Spoudai*, 8, 61–82.

Peña-Chocarro, L. (1993) Los modelos etnográficos en arqueobotánica: los cereales vestidos, in *Primeras Jornadas Internacionales sobre Tecnologia Agraria Tradicional* (eds P. Barraca de Ramos and M. Soriano Berges), Museo Nacional del Pueblo Español, Madrid, pp. 21–29.

Peña-Chocarro, L. (1996) In situ conservation of hulled wheat species: the case of Spain, in *Hulled Wheats: Promoting the Conservation and Use of Underutilized and Neglected Crops 4* (eds S. Padulosi, K. Hammer, and J. Heller), International Plant Genetic Resources Institute, Rome, pp. 129–146.

Peña-Chocarro, L. (1999) *Prehistoric Agriculture in Southern Spain During the Neolithic and the Bronze Age*, Archaeopress, Oxford.

Percival, J. (1974) *The Wheat Plant*, Duckworth, London.

Peters, J. (1998) *Römische Tierhaltung und Tierzucht: eine Synthese aus archäozoologischer Untersuchung und schriftlich-bildlicher Überlieferung*, Leidorf, Rahden.

Psarraki-Belesioti, N. (1978) *Paradosiakes kalliergeies*, Benaki Museum, Athens.

Rasmussen, H. (1969) Grain harvest and threshing in Calabria. *Tools & Tillage*, 1, 93–104.

Russell, K.W. (1988) *After Eden: the Behavioral Ecology of Early Food Production in the Near East and North Africa*, British Archaeological Reports, Oxford.

Schlichtherle, H. (1992) Jungsteinzeitliche Erntegeräte am Bodensee. *Plattform*, 1, 24–44.

Sigaut, F. (1988) A method for identifying grain storage techniques and its application for European agricultural history. *Tools & Tillage*, 6, 3–32.

Slinis, M.K. (1938–1948) Agrotika ethima Drumou Makedonias. *Laografia*, 12, 92–103.

Spurr, M.S. (1986) *Arable Cultivation in Roman Italy c.200 B.C.–c. A.D. 100*, Society for the Promotion of Roman Studies, London.

Tanno, K. and Willcox, G. (2012) Distinguishing wild and domestic wheat and barley spikelets from early Holocene sites in the Near East. *Vegetation History & Archaeobotany*, 21, 107–115.

van der Veen, M. (1992) *Crop Husbandry Regimes: An Archaeobotanical Study of Farming in Northern England, 1000 BC–AD 500*, J.R. Collis, Sheffield.

Harvest Time

Vrontis, A.G. (1938–1948) Oi zevgades tis Rodou. *Laografia*, 12, 104–129.
White, K.D. (1970) *Roman Farming*, Thames and Hudson, London.
Will, W.F. and Hyde, G.E. (1964) *Corn among the Indians of the Upper Missouri*, University of Nebraska Press, Lincoln.
Willcox, G. (1998) Archaeobotanical evidence for the beginnings of agriculture in southwest Asia, in *The Origins of Agriculture and Crop Domestication* (eds A.B. Damania, J. Valkoun, G. Willcox, and C.O. Qualset), International Center for Agricultural Research in the Dry Areas, Rome, pp. 25–38.

4

Sorting the Wheat from the Chaff

During six weeks in Kolofana, we saw only one pause in the hectic activity in fields and on threshing floors. One morning, everyone abandoned crops half-processed to whitewash their houses. A woman of 102 was on her deathbed and, once she succumbed, a period of mourning would prevent whitewashing until after the festival of the local patron saint, which attracted visitors from afar. When the church bells tolled the following morning, the houses gleamed white and the threshing floors were again busy.

4.1 Amorgos: On and After the Threshing Floor

In preparation for threshing, the crop was spread across the stone-paved threshing floor for a few hours to ensure that it was completely dry. Brandishing a stick and perhaps holding a tin to catch droppings, someone (usually a man, but both sexes and various

Two Oxen Ahead: Pre-Mechanized Farming in the Mediterranean, First Edition.
Paul Halstead. © 2014 Paul Halstead. Published 2014 by John Wiley & Sons, Ltd.

Figure 4.1   Cattle and donkeys threshing wheat/barley maslin with their hooves at Kolofana, Amorgos.

ages were observed) then drove two to five cows, mules, and donkeys round the circular floor, so their hooves broke up the crop and freed the grain (Figure 4.1). Threshing in this way requires a dry and brittle crop and so took place in the middle of the day, when the sun was highest and the task most tiring, leaving farmers free to harvest late-ripening crops in the morning and perhaps evening. Once the upper layer of crop had been threshed, the contents of the floor were turned with a two-pronged wooden fork to expose underlying material to trampling. The job might be completed in a few hours on hot days but take a few days in cloudy and cool weather. Sheaves that did not fit on the floor might be placed around the edge and added piecemeal as threshing reduced the volume of the crop. Conversely, quantities of pulses too small to cover the surface of the floor were threshed by hand with a long stick.

Once the crop was thoroughly broken up, the grain was separated from the chaff (fragments of cereal ear and pulse pod) and straw by winnowing: the threshed crop was tossed in the air and the heavy grain fell to the ground, while the breeze carried the light straw and chaff a meter or two downwind (Figure 4.2a). The crop was usually tossed with a four-pronged iron fork, although small batches, such as might be flailed with a stick, were simply scooped up by hand and allowed to fall. Winnowing looks easy, but my brief apprenticeship on Karpathos a year earlier had dispelled this illusion. In Kolofana, the person wielding the fork was usually the man of the household. As he winnowed, the threshed crop before him was gradually reduced to a pile of grain with heavy pieces of straw (especially culm nodes) and unthreshed ears or pods, while the lighter chaff and straw accumulated downwind. Dimitrakis now exchanged his fork for a shovel, better suited to tossing the grain-rich contents of the threshing floor. Meanwhile, Irini swept stray bits of straw off the grain pile with a bunch of thyme and screened them in a coarse sieve to avoid losing any crop seeds (Figure 4.2b and c).

If the volume threshed was modest, the winnower might proceed in this fashion until a pile of grain remained on one side of the floor and a pile of chaff and straw on the other. With a larger volume of threshed crop, the winnower started on a strip at the windward edge of the floor and continued until this was reduced to a pile of more or less clean grain. He then worked across the floor, strip by strip. As each strip was reduced to grain with a few heavy contaminants, this was winnowed upwind to join the first pile (Figure 4.3). To save time, the light chaff and straw that accumulated on top of the unwin-nowed crop might be forked off to the built-up rim of the floor. If a crop was much too large to fit in the threshing floor, a first batch was threshed and partly winnowed, to reduce its volume, and then additional sheaves or bundles were added, and the process of threshing and winnowing started afresh. In addition, barley and barley-rich maslins were threshed and winnowed, to separate the straw, and then threshed and winnowed again, to remove the sharp awns that caused irritation if left in flour for human consumption.

With a gentle and steady breeze that did not change direction, Dimitrakis winnowed steadily for hours, but even a moderate wind forced him to stop and cover the pile of winnowed straw and chaff

Figure 4.2 Winnowing peas at Kolofana, Amorgos: (a) as the threshed crop is tossed with a fork, the lighter straw is winnowed away to the right; (b) with most of the straw winnowed away, the crop is tossed with a shovel, while remaining contaminants are raked up with a thyme bunch; (c) with winnowing nearing completion, any peas inadvertently raked off the grain pile are retrieved by coarse sieving.

Figure 4.3 Winnowing a full threshing floor of wheat/barley maslin in "strips" at Kolofana, Amorgos: as winnowing of the second strip nears completion (centre), the grain is worked across the floor to join the fully winnowed pile from the first strip (right); threshed crop (left) awaits winnowing.

with cut juniper branches to avoid it blowing away. If the breeze stopped, he could do nothing. All over Greece, farmers who have winnowed by hand are acutely aware of the direction and timing of suitable breezes, which threshing floors were sited to catch. Dimitrakis tied a ribbon to a stick on the edge of his floor to alert him to every opportunity for progress, but he often stood idle, right hand extended with fingers bent in a gesture that held the Virgin Mary personally responsible for the lack of breeze.

While Dimitrakis winnowed and Irini raked and sieved, up to five people worked on other floors, with one man winnowing, two men or women coarse sieving, and two women or children wielding thyme brushes (Figure 4.4). The coarse sieve or *dremóni*, of woven gut or punched sheet metal, had 6–10 mm apertures that allowed cereal and pulse grains (other than broad beans) to pass through but

Figure 4.4 In closing stages of processing wheat/barley maslin at Kolofana, Amorgos, one person winnows, two rake, and one coarse sieves.

retained straw segments and any unbroken ears or pods. These "cavings" retained in the coarse sieve might be added to the pile of straw and chaff or fed as a grain-rich snack to a donkey bringing sheaves for threshing. The latter stages of work on the threshing floor were flexible, with use of the *dremóni* depending on breeze, manpower, and destination of crop. Coarse sieving routinely accompanied the thyme rake to speed up the final stages of winnowing but might be omitted if winnowing had been particularly thorough or crops were destined for livestock; fodder crops were threshed and winnowed to feed straw and grain to different animals, but contamination of grain with a little straw did not matter. Conversely, on a still day, the dwindling intermediate pile of grain with heavy contaminants, which remained between "clean" grain upwind and straw downwind, might all be passed through the coarse sieve, partly replacing winnowing for small quantities of crop.

As winnowing neared completion, this intermediate pile of grain was often also visibly rich in small weed seeds (which filtered to the bottom of the grain as it was stirred by the shovel) and, in the case of *migádi* (wheat/barley maslin) and wheat, richer in barley (slightly lighter than wheat) than the "clean" grain. Sometimes farmers continued winnowing and sieving until this intermediate pile was thoroughly cleaned, sweeping up weed seeds to feed to hens, but sometimes they curtailed processing and bagged these *aposória* ("off the pile [of cleaned grain]") for use as high-quality fodder. The male household head took this decision ad hoc, presumably taking account of the availability of labor and size of harvest. The amount of grain thus diverted to fodder might be modest or substantial – up to one fifth of an individual crop in the cases observed.

Once the contents of the threshing floor were reduced to two piles (or three with *aposória*), the cleaned grain might then be passed through a *dremóni* held high enough for dust to be winnowed out as the grain fell. A single person could easily fill, lift, and shake a small *dremóni*, but larger examples were supported at one end on the tines of an upturned winnowing fork and moved back and forth by one person, while a second poured the grain. The shape of a cross was marked on the resulting grain pile, four winnowing forks and shovels were inserted equidistantly to form a cross, and sometimes a makeshift cross, fashioned from a broken stick, was placed at the apex. The "crossed" grain was then measured, put into sacks, and, with any *aposória*, removed to storage, while the threshing floor was swept clean (and the sweepings fed to hens) before the next crop was spread out. The growing pile of chaff and straw was also removed for storage, close to the animal byres, as soon as possible without delaying processing of grain (Halstead and Jones, 1989). Crops on the threshing floor were vulnerable, in descending order of severity and ascending order of probability, to destruction by lightening, soaking and perhaps spoiling by rain, and raiding by livestock. During our stay, errant goats were periodically chased off Dimitrakis' full threshing floor. The harvest was thus at risk until processed and stored, and neither the time available nor that needed for these tasks was entirely predictable. Farmers meeting on the cobbled paths in July greeted each other with "have you finished threshing?" (*polónepses?*) or "have you finished winnowing?" (*políkhnises?*).

Grain was stored indoors in wooden and stone chests. Final cleaning for human consumption was undertaken piecemeal during the year, using a fine sieve (*girokóskino*, "darnel sieve") of approximately 2–2.5 mm mesh that retained the crop but allowed small weed seeds and undersized crop grains ("tailcorn") to pass through. As the sieve was worked with a circular movement, remaining light contaminants – fragments of straw and weevil-infested grains – rose to the surface and were scooped off by hand. These scoopings ("chob"), mixed with what passed through the sieve, were fed to hens. Seedcorn too was fine-sieved, but fodder grain normally not. Grain for human consumption was also picked over by hand before milling or cooking, the by-product again being fed to hens. Wheat and *migádi* maslin were ground to flour by a specialist miller and then sieved at home through a 1 mm mesh to remove barley hulls, the stubs of barley awns, and some bran. Lentils were cooked whole, but peas were first split into *fáva* (removing the testa) in a domestic, rotary hand-mill. Fodder grains might also be coarsely ground, depending on the type of animal for which they were destined (Halstead and Jones, 1989, 46–47).

The clear normative distinction drawn in Kolofana between grain crops for human consumption (black-eyed bean, broad bean, chickpea, lentil, pea, wheat, and wheat/barley *migádi*) and those for animal fodder (common vetch, grass pea, barley, and oats) was blurred in practice by the variable composition and flexible postharvest treatment of the predominant *migádi*. The ratio of wheat to barley in harvested *migádi* depended on growing conditions and seedcorn: wheat prospered on fertile fields and in rainy years, while barley did better under less favorable conditions; and, to some degree, farmers selected seedcorn of a composition they judged suitable for each field. Despite the resulting variability in composition, farmers were fairly consistent in classifying harvested cereals as "wheat," "barley," or *migádi*: in 29 samples of winnowed and sieved grain from threshing floors, wheat made up 0–7% of "barley," 8–75% (22–75% excluding one outlier) of *migádi*, and 92–97% of "wheat" (Jones and Halstead, 1995). Anyone leaving partly cleaned *aposória*, rich in barley, for fodder raised the proportion of wheat in the cleaned crop. Farmers also manipulated the wheat to barley ratio more drastically, by sieving cleaned *migádi* through a medium-coarse mesh that selectively retained hulled grains of barley over smaller naked wheat grains. They sold the wheat grain or used it to make whiter bread, leaving the barley-rich fraction for household consumption or to feed livestock. Presumably, they also selected wheat-rich seedcorn in this way, as otherwise the greater resilience of barley to adverse conditions should gradually have converted all *migádi* crops to "barley." The *migádi* "outlier" containing only 8% wheat (see preceding text) was by far the biggest cereal crop encountered in Kolofana and was perhaps classified as *migádi* because medium-coarse sieving could extract a large *absolute* quantity of wheat (Jones and Halstead, 1995, 105).

Migádi allowed farmers simultaneously to minimize the risk of crop failure (by growing undemanding barley), capitalize on opportunities for generating cash (by growing marketable wheat), and maintain esteem (by manipulating the proportions of wheat and barley in bread, depending on the success of the harvest and the household's need for cash). The flexibility of the boundary between food and fodder was brought home by a chance encounter with a man who owned little land and lived primarily from his sheep. His donkey was carrying two sacks of grain, bought at a threshing floor that I had visited. The producer of this grain had described it as "barley," and it contained very little wheat. "For your sheep," I suggested thoughtlessly. "No," he replied, "it is *migádi* for bread at home." His neighbors knew he ate demeaning, if wholesome, barley bread, but the variable composition of wheat, *migádi*, and barley crops allowed him to maintain that he ate a culturally acceptable mix of wheat and barley.

Despite the flexibility of crop processing in Kolofana, especially in the later stages and for *migádi*, much additional variability is encountered across the Mediterranean. This is reviewed here for successive stages of processing, from threshing to storage and preparation for consumption, before considering some quantitative issues and customs relating to this part of the agricultural cycle.

4.2   Ways of Threshing

In threshing grain crops, animal hooves were sometimes supplemented by sledges or rollers and sometimes replaced by hand tools such as flails and sticks. While some variation, such as regional forms of flail in Albania (Shkurti, 1979, 102), represents alternative means of achieving the same end, much of it is related to practical differences in the structure of crops, their intended use(s), the quantity to be threshed, the labor available, and weather conditions.

First, the ease with which seeds can be threshed out of ripe ears or pods differs between crops. On Amorgos, pulses were threshed more rapidly than similar volumes of free-threshing cereals. Among cereals, practitioners widely considered oats easy to thresh, wheat difficult, and barley intermediate (e.g., Gaillard, 1997, 37). Farmers in the southern French Alps viewed rye as more difficult than wheat (Llaty, 1997, 110), probably because it matured late at high altitude and so was harvested prematurely, because Greek farmers invariably considered rye grain easy to thresh from the ear. Because crops that are easily threshed tend to shed grain in transport from the field, lentils and oats were often harvested early, and Nikolaos in Kolindros threshed small quantities of lentils and rye in the field with a stick over a sheet or rug. Conversely, hulled barley grain often needed additional threshing to remove awns: further trampling, after most of the straw had been winnowed off, on Amorgos and Tinos (Amoiralis, 1972, 379); secondary flailing or beating in Haute Provence (Llaty, 1997, 110, 113); or roasting and beating, after threshing and winnowing, on northern Karpathos (Halstead and Jones, 1989, 46).

The most difficult to process are glume wheats, as threshing (with animals or by hand) breaks the ears not into free grain and chaff but into spikelets with grains tightly enclosed in glumes. After winnowing and sieving to remove straw and weeds, the spikelets – if destined for human consumption – need further processing to free the grains from the glumes. In all but the wettest parts of Turkey, emmer spikelets were bulk-pounded outdoors with huge wooden mallets in stone or wooden mortars, large enough for two or three women to work together, in preparation for storage as free grain. In wet areas, the grain was stored as spikelets and pounded piecemeal indoors with domestic pestles and mortars. The emmer might be heated beforehand to make it dry and brittle, but the widespread belief that glume wheats *must* be parched for dehusking is unfounded (Nesbitt and Samuel, 1996, 42). Dehusking of emmer by pounding is also reported from Italy, the Balkans, and further afield (Hillman, 1984, 122–123, 129; Papa, 1996, 159; D'Andrea and Haile, 2002), although farmers with firsthand experience of growing emmer in Garfagnana, spelt/emmer in Asturias, and einkorn in southern Spain, Provence, and northern Greece consistently maintained that dehusking is impossible by hand! In Haute Provence, for initial separation of einkorn spikelets from straw, an informant in Brantes had threshed with a horse-drawn stone cylinder, while elsewhere wooden rollers with spikes were used (Duplessy *et al.*, 1996, 64). The spikelets were then dehusked in local water mills, such as that at Mollans-sur-Ouvèze, worked for more than 70 years by the laconic M. Estève. He "rolled" the unparched spikelets with a vertical millstone that revolved in a circular basin (and, with the addition of water, stripped bran from bread wheat and dehusked einkorn). Elsewhere in Haute Provence, einkorn was dehusked between two horizontal stones set further apart than when grinding grain to flour (Duplessy *et al.*, 1996, 63). In rainy Asturias, ears alone of emmer and spelt were harvested (Section 3.3) and stored intact. During winter, they were singed over a small pile of burning straw (Peña-Chocarro, 1996, 140, fig. 13), making them easier to thresh and burning off the awns and any straw and weeds that might impede subsequent dehusking. The singed ears were trampled by women wearing clogs and beaten with sticks, mallets, jointed flails, or toothed clubs (*palancas*) to break them into spikelets. After cleaning in a winnowing sieve (see Section 4.3), the spikelets were dehusked between two horizontal millstones, powered by water or hand. The resulting free chaff was sieved out and the grain put into store (Dantin Cereceda, 1941, 745; Neira Martinez, 1955, 119–120).

Hulled barley also emerges from the threshing floor with the grain tightly enclosed in protective hulls, although removal of the latter is less essential for human consumption than with glume wheats. Southern Aegean villagers normally consumed barley as bread or rusks and so ground it, without prior dehulling, to flour from which they sieved out the fragmented hulls more or less assiduously. Alternatively, barley can be dehulled by pounding in a mortar, like glume wheats, as in Turkey (Hillman, 1985) and Tunisia (Amouretti, 1986, 120). On the southern Aegean island of Kithira, some women preferred barley groats (*krithókhondro*, *kritharókhondro*) for both savory and sweet dishes, because it cooked to a "fluffy" consistency, whereas floury groats of free-threshing wheat stuck together. One variety of barley groats was made from ears cut "green but filled, as it started to turn yellow" in May (whence the name *Maiátiko khóndro*). These ears were dried in the sun or oven, beaten with a wooden handle to remove awns and hulls, broken in a hand-mill, and then stored. Such "May groats" were appreciated for their taste but probably also because the hulls of unripe ears were relatively easy to strip. Fotini insisted that the hulls of ripe barley could not be removed: "it was either given whole to animals or ground into flour for humans." Panagiotitsa *had* dehulled ripe barley, with difficulty. "You broke it in a hand-mill and then rubbed the groats on a punched-metal fine sieve, turned upside down so the holes cut. The groats fell through and the hulls remained in the sieve; any grains left in the sieve you threw back into the hand-mill." Both green and ripe barley groats were also made in Tunisia but were dehulled by pounding in a mortar (Amouretti, 1986, 120).

Secondly, the intended use of harvested material may affect method of threshing. In Turkey, Garfagnana, Haute Provence, Asturias, and southern Spain (Peña-Chocarro, 1996, 133), glume wheats were sown as spikelets rather than free grain. Seedcorn was not dehusked, perhaps because parching and pounding or "rolling" rendered it unviable. In Asturias, Antonio sowed dehusked spelt one winter in Zureda, and the crop was a failure, but ears of emmer and spelt for sowing were singed (sometimes preferentially – Peña-Chocarro, 1999, 47) before threshing into spikelets to burn off weeds and reduce the risk of damage by violent beating. Leandro in Tiós took spikelets for sowing from the bottom of the threshed pile, because they had received fewest blows. In Xomezana, where threshing could be entrusted to workers organized by the local dehusking mill, Inés and her husband beat their own seedcorn with the *palanca* club – presumably to ensure that it was not damaged.

While some cereals and pulses were harvested immature and fed to livestock as unthreshed hay (Section 5.1), ripe *grain* crops were normally threshed and winnowed for food and fodder alike. In the latter case, this allowed grain to be reserved for the most valuable working, lactating, and fattening livestock. As noted at Melanes on Naxos, small volumes of processed grain are also easier to protect from mice and rats than stacks of unthreshed sheaves. The intended use for food or fodder, however, often affects treatment of glume wheats and hulled barley *after* initial threshing and winnowing. At Aiginio in northern Greece and Zuheros in Andalucia, einkorn was fed to livestock as dry spikelets, soaked spikelets, or ground flour (depending on species of animal and farmer's preference), but not as dehusked grains. A few elderly informants in Aiginio, however, recall einkorn being dehusked "like rice" for consumption by the poor in the 1920s and 1930s. At Zuheros, in the drought-induced "year of hunger" after the Spanish Civil War, einkorn and barley were ground to flour, sieved to remove the fragmented chaff, and used in bread-making (Peña-Chocarro, 1996, 141), but one informant had also dehusked einkorn for human consumption in an adjusted flour-mill. In Valnerina in the Umbrian Apennine hills of central Italy, emmer in the husk was unambiguously classified as fodder, but with further processing became human food – albeit of low status (Papa, 1996, 163).

Rye straw was widely favored to bind sheaves and roof temporary sheep shelters or outdoor stacks of chopped straw destined for fodder. Such uses demanded intact straw and ripe rye grain is easily threshed out, so ears and straw were normally harvested together (e.g., Loukopoulos, 1983, 264), rather than separately as with glume wheats in Asturias. At Plikati in the Pindos, where households grew a strip of rye for bundling leafy hay, Kharoulla dried her crop in the sun before threshing. Grasping each sheaf by the base, she bashed the ears several times against a metal sheet

Figure 4.5 Threshing rye by hand, leaving the straw intact for bundling leafy hay at Plikati, Pindos Mountains.

(Figure 4.5), freeing most of the grains, and then hit the few short ears with a stick, because rodents nibbled any bindings containing grain and undid the stored bundles (also Gaillard, 1997, 36). The grain "by-product" she ground and mixed with commercial wheat flour to give her bread a rustic appearance. Elsewhere, rye might be threshed in the cool early hours to keep the straw intact (e.g., Shkurti, 1979, 75). At Ano Asites in central Crete, long plants of free-threshing wheat were selected on the threshing floor and beaten against a stone so the straw could be used intact for basketry, while in southern Spain, einkorn was sometimes threshed in this fashion to preserve the straw for thatching or basketry (Peña-Chocarro, 1996, 137). In Messenia, bundles of flax, grown mainly for the fiber in their stems, were likewise beaten with a stick to free seed for sowing and medicinal use, after which the bundles of stems were weighed down in water to ret (rot) "for eight days," then dried, and beaten with a wooden *mangáni* – resembling a toothed guillotine – to expose the desired fibers. For elderly Messenian women, the *mangáni* symbolizes dirty and exceptionally strenuous work.

Conversely, straw for fodder was normally broken up. Finely chopped straw was less bulky to store and widely considered more digestible (e.g., Gaillard, 1997, 48), but care was needed not to damage the grain. Barley and oats release their grain more easily than wheat, and in Greece, their softer and more digestible straw was often chopped only coarsely, allowing them to be threshed earlier in the morning. On Rhodes, they were threshed in the evening, sometimes moistened with water (Vrontis, 1938–1948, 123), and much of the coarsely chopped straw was forked off the grain with minimal winnowing. At Andalucian Zuheros, Camacho described a similar practice with a different rationale. Because livestock avoided the coarse stems of einkorn, those with sufficient barley and free-threshing wheat straw discarded that of einkorn more or less intact as soon as threshing had removed the spikelets. Others with less fodder (or more livestock) broke up the einkorn straw, finding this more time-consuming than for free-threshing wheat or barley. At Aiginio in northern Greece, Dimos recalls that tough einkorn straw was hard to reap, difficult to break up even with a sledge, and eaten reluctantly by livestock. At Brantes in Haute Provence, einkorn straw was similarly considered poorer fodder than bread wheat or barley straw, though better than rye straw.

Contamination with sharp awns could cause problems in straw destined for fodder, as in grain for human consumption. This was avoided in Asturias by separately harvesting ears and straw (used mainly as stall litter but as fodder when hay was scarce), in Haute Provence by beating out most of the grain before threshing sheaves (Duplessy et al., 1996, 61; Gaillard, 1997, 30–33), and in Valencia by cutting off the ears before threshing sheaves (Palanca, 1991, 175). In Haute Provence and Valencia, the initial removal of ears or grains was known as "(d)esbarbar," literally "to remove awns." On Karpathos, some farmers avoided barley straw as fodder (Halstead and Jones, 1989, 45), but other Greek informants maintain that awns did not trouble livestock because they were destroyed by threshing or winnowed out.

141

Cereal varieties differ greatly in strength of awns, but informants also noted that awns not removed by winnowing filter to the bottom of stores of chopped straw and some encouraged this by stirring the straw before feeding, only using the base of the pile if supplies ran low. Fine chaff also filtered through the straw as livestock fed and material in the base of the manger might be discarded daily.

Thirdly, weather in the weeks following harvest influenced the timing, location, and method of threshing. On Amorgos, where Old World pulses and cereals were harvested in late May and June, July was usually hot and dry, although farmers were keen to complete work on the threshing floor because rare summer downpours were potentially disastrous. In Cretan Ano Asites, a violent rainstorm once caught Vangelis with his barley crop threshed but not winnowed. Water running off the slope above flooded the threshing floor, and he had to breach the stone surround to drain it off. He turned the crop repeatedly for 8–10 days to aid drying, but some sprouted, leaving the grain shriveled. On the northern margins of the Mediterranean and at high altitude, where the harvest took place later in summer, bad weather was expected. In Provence, the saying in the southern lowlands was that "he who threshes before St. Magdalene [July 22] threshes care-free, he who threshes in August threshes anxiously" and in the mountains, more pessimistically, that "before August 15 threshes [anyone] who wants, afterwards [anyone] who can" (Gaillard, 1997, 75–76). Accordingly, farmers in lowland Provence threshed outdoors in the month after harvest, but those in the mountains, as in Asturias, hurried to get the crop into barns to dry for threshing during winter. Threshing in the mountains occasionally used animals, in a sheltered space under (or even inside) the barn, but this was far less effective in the cool damp conditions than in midsummer in the lowlands (Gaillard, 1997, 39). Manual processing was more normal – with sticks, with flails, or by beating sheaves on a sloping board (Llaty, 1997), as described for rye in the Pindos. Indoor threshing could be carried out piecemeal, on winter days when bad weather prevented work outdoors, but was acutely unpleasant: even on an open-air floor, dust from threshing could make breathing difficult, while fine chaff fragments penetrated clothing, hair, and skin.

A fourth factor is the volume of crop to be processed. Manual threshing is arduous and slow: in Provence, 50 or more workers with flails might thresh in a day as much wheat as 12 horses (Gaillard, 1997, 37, 42). Where weather permitted outdoor threshing, therefore, animal power was normally preferred to manual labor except for small volumes of crop, such as a single "sowing [strip]" of lentils or sesame, or pods from a row of New World beans. Conversely, animal hooves might scatter rather than thresh small quantities of crop and, if this was spread thinly, shod hooves or a threshing sledge could damage the surface of an earthen floor, contaminating the grain with dirt. Manual threshing was also considered more thorough than trampling with animals, which entailed loss of perhaps 2–3% or even 5% of grain (Cimmino, 1977; Gaillard, 1997, 42). Small-scale manual processing might take place on the threshing floor, in the yard, or on a flat roof. On northern Karpathos, the small quantities of unthreshed ears retained in the coarse sieve were normally rethreshed with a stick (likewise with a flail in Albania – Shkurti, 1979, 61). At Metaxada in Messenia, Ilias periodically improved his seedcorn by pulling the best ears from sheaves lined up on the edge of the floor and threshing them with a stick (also Karanastasis, 1952, 293; Loukopoulos, 1983, 259). In Albania, ears were sometimes *combed* from unthreshed sheaves for seedcorn (Shkurti, 1979, 64). Here, manual threshing was largely restricted to poor farmers with small harvests, but those of moderate means might thresh part of the harvest by hand to make bread without waiting until the end of processing (Shkurti, 1979, 59). In Paliambela, Kostas hand-threshed some barley (the first cereal to ripen) for the same reason during World War II. The modest quantities of ears gathered by gleaners also lent themselves to manual threshing, in Palestine (Hillman, 1984, 121–122) and among children earning pocket money in Paliambela. In Asturias, groups of women collaboratively threshed the modest harvest of spelt and emmer ears by hand (and foot). The small-scale and piecemeal execution of the task likewise facilitated manual threshing in the higher valleys of Haute Provence (Gaillard, 1997, 38; Llaty, 1997, 111). "Manual" threshing usually involved a stick, club, or flail, but very small quantities of

Figure 4.6 Rectangular threshing floor among cultivation terraces and clearance cairns with collapsing retaining walls on Monte Cairo, central Italy.

pods and ears were literally processed by hand, as when shelling green peas or beans for a single meal or rubbing off the chaff from cereal ears cut green and toasted as a snack (Section 3.2). In Asturian Xomezana, Inés – in her early 90s – cultivated spelt on such a small scale that she obtained spikelets for sowing by pulling apart a few ears, as presumably did those in Rhodes who selected seedcorn from the middle of ears (Vrontis, 1938–1948, 129).

A fifth consideration is the availability of human and animal labor. Although most Mediterranean farmers used hand tools for small or delicate threshing tasks, some were wholly dependent on manual threshing for want of alternative means. On central Italian Monte Cairo, circular, stone-paved threshing floors are interspersed with rectangular platforms (Figure 4.6). Luigi from Monforte is a retired farmer and, at 89, the oldest licensed gun owner in the province. His homemade wine and an interpreter help with the dialect, and I learn that unshod cattle dragging heavy stones or shod horses threshed on the familiar circular floors, while teams of people (from households lacking large animals) wielded flails on the rectangular platforms. Likewise, in Albania, whole families or groups of women, owning too little land to maintain large animals, flailed crops on rectangular floors. The sheaves were spread out along the center of the floor, ears facing inwards, and two lines of flailers stood on the edges, stepping forward in carefully coordinated alternation to lash the crop (Shkurti, 1979, 59–64; for northwest Spain, Fernandez Gonzalez, 1978, 144).

The number and type of animals used in threshing varied. On Amorgos, we observed mixed teams of two to five cattle, mules, and donkeys, but elsewhere, a single mule or donkey might thresh small batches. Conversely, mobile pastoralists toured lowland villages in Greece and Albania with perhaps 10–15 horses, threshing crops for a share of the harvest (e.g., Shkurti, 1979, 75; Loukopoulos, 1983, 249). Horses from the Camargue provided a similar service in Provence (Gaillard, 1997, 41). Speed was related to the number of hooves trampling the crop, but shod animals (most equids) threshed more quickly than unshod (most cattle). Cattle were sometimes shod, especially in stony terrain, and in Paliambela, where most fields are largely stone free, cattle threshed with temporary shoes that fell off over the ensuing weeks. In Albania, shod animals threshed wheat and barley, but unshod the less resilient pulses, rye, and rice (Shkurti, 1979, 75). Horses also move round the floor faster than cattle, and Ilias in Metaxada reckoned that two horses threshed in three hours what two cattle managed in a day. In the hills and mountains of Greece, therefore, where pack animals rather than oxcarts dominated transport, equids were widely preferred for threshing, even by those who plowed with cattle.

The number of animals threshing often reflected how many each farmer owned, but larger teams could be hired (see preceding text) or made up between neighbors (e.g., Shkurti, 1979, 74; Palanca, 1991, 176; Gaillard, 1997, 41). In Metaxada, Ilias and two neighbors pooled their three horses to thresh more quickly and – thanks to mutual teasing and shared consumption of a goat – pleasurably. As with animals for plowing, however, the scale of the task was critical. It was not worth borrowing additional animals for a small volume of crop and might be dangerous to rely on borrowed or shared animals for a large volume; such arrangements caused friction if cool weather delayed the first party while the second anxiously watched gathering storm clouds (Gaillard, 1997, 41). Hiring horses was less risky, but expensive: 8–10% of the cleaned crop or more in Provence (Gaillard, 1997, 42), a similar fraction in Albania (Shkurti, 1979, 75), and one sixth ("5 out of 30 tins," about 80 kg of wheat, per floor) in western Macedonia according to one Vlach informant. Given that threshing was a significant source of grain for some pastoralist households, many lowland grain farmers evidently considered payment worthwhile for getting their harvest into store rapidly. For a single horse or mule, Ilias in Metaxada recalls a similar charge of 7% of the cleaned crop, while Giorgos in neighboring Khora cited 10–15 okádes (13–19 kg) and Kostas in Tharounia one *xági* (12 okádes or 15 kg) of grain per day, but elsewhere, small-scale producers accepted payment in threshed straw (Section 2.6.2; Shkurti, 1979, 75).

Finally, the efficiency of threshing by hand or with animals could be enhanced by various tools and facilities, use of which again reflected crop type and intended use, prevailing weather, available labor, and size of task. For example, jointed flails exert more force, thresh more thoroughly, and jar the hands less than sticks (Shkurti, 1979, 62) but require more strength and skill. In early twentieth-century Provence, with a contracting harvest and increasingly elderly workforce, flails gave way to sticks in some mountain valleys although their use sometimes continued for threshing off barley awns (Llaty, 1997, 109–110). The absence of the jointed flail in the Near East (Hillman, 1984, 122) perhaps partly reflects the greater efficacy of threshing with a stick in areas where summer drought aided thorough drying of crops.

While animals on Amorgos trampled crops with their hooves, elsewhere they often pulled a threshing sledge (a heavy board with embedded "flints" on the underside) or drum (a toothed cylinder) or even a harrow (otherwise used for leveling fields after plowing). Sledges were more effective if loaded with large stones or children (e.g., Palanca, 1991, 165; Palmer, 1998, 154), and the role of juvenile "ballast" is generally recalled as a source of enjoyment. The flints embedded in sledges were often made by specialists (e.g., Whittaker, 1999), although some Paliambela Thracians made their own. Wetting the sledge periodically ensured that it gripped the stones tightly, but sledges with iron blades replacing the stones suggest this precaution was not always taken. A threshing sledge chopped straw more finely than hooves alone and so improved its value as fodder. Its use was common in Assiros, but some farmers used a smooth stone cylinder to thresh rye if they needed the straw for thatching. Nearby Thracians likewise used a sledge for finely chopping wheat straw but a wooden or stone roller for coarsely chopping the more easily threshed barley, oats, and rye (Kizlaris, 1938–1948, 407). In northern Jordan, bitter vetch and lentil were usually threshed by trampling alone (Palmer, 1998, 154), presumably because the pods thresh easily and so a sledge might damage the grain. In Greece too, some farmers threshed pulses with hooves only, or even by hand, to avoid damage, but others used a threshing sledge – in at least some cases because the volume of crop was large.

Sledges, typically pulled by two cattle or by one or two equids, made threshing with few animals faster and more thorough (e.g., Pagkalos, 1983, 14). Two sledges or rollers might be used simultaneously, drawn by two horses in series in Haute Provence (Gaillard, 1997, 95), and sometimes at Assiros for the biggest landowners, or rotating on opposite sides of large threshing floors in Valencia (Palanca, 1991, 165–166). Their use was presumably impracticable, as well as unnecessary, with a big team of animals. The size of threshing floors varied (e.g., in Albania, from 4–5 to 10–12 m or even 15 m diameter), corresponding broadly to the expected size of the harvest (Shkurti, 1979, 68–69). Given that scale of grain production was limited inter alia by access to work animals, the size of floors was perhaps loosely related to the number of animals available for threshing, but paved floors were durable, and over successive generations, their users might significantly expand or reduce cultivation.

Uniform trampling of the crop was widely managed in Greece and Albania (Shkurti, 1979) by attaching the animal(s) by rope to a pole planted in the center of the threshing floor. As the animals circulated,

147

the rope wrapped around the pole and drew the threshing team towards the center. When it ran out of rope, the team reversed direction until it reached the edge of the floor. In Provence, the *tourniquet* was a sophisticated version of the rope and pole (Gaillard, 1997, 57–61), but uniform threshing was sometimes achieved by harnessing an animal to a tapered stone cylinder that drifted towards the center of the floor, when circulating with the narrow end inwards, and then back to the edge, with the narrow end outwards (Duplessy *et al.*, 1996, 60–61). The *tourniquet*, and likewise presumably the tapered cylinder and the rope and pole, allowed a single person to thresh and so was particularly useful for small families (Gaillard, 1997, 59). A more labor-intensive alternative was for someone walking behind or seated on a sledge to steer the threshing animal(s) with reins. Where two animals pulled a sledge, however, threshing inevitably proceeded more slowly in the center and on the periphery of the floor, where the crop was only trampled, and so demanded regular turning of the threshed crop. Yannis from Miliarisi described a procedure widespread in central Crete. "We broke open 30 sheaves and spread them across the floor. As I drove the oxen round and round, their hooves threshed the crop on the center and outside of the floor, but the sledge cut up the strip in between more quickly. After a while, my father picked up the two-pronged fork and started throwing the material from the center of the floor into the path of the sledge. When this too was thoroughly threshed, he piled it in the center of the floor. He then forked the outer ring of trampled crop into the path of the sledge and broke open 10 new sheaves around the edge of the floor. We went on like this, adding 10 sheaves each time, until we had threshed the whole crop. You could not add 30 new sheaves in one go, because the sledge could not cope and became tangled." The number of sheaves laid out depended on the size of the floor and number and type of animals threshing, with sheaves spread much more deeply for horses than cattle (e.g., Shkurti, 1979, 76). By contrast, variation in how sheaves were spread on the threshing floor, as between "local" and Thracian neighbors in northern Greece (Kizlaris, 1938–1948, 410–411) or between communities in Valencia (Palanca, 1991, 175), surely represents alternative

148

traditional ways of doing things. As with reaping and sheaving, standardized routines probably promoted efficiency.

In rocky areas, threshing floors tended to be permanent, stone-paved structures, as on Amorgos or central Italian Monte Cairo, but in the lowlands, they were often remade each year with a temporary but hard-wearing surface of mud, dung, or lime plaster (e.g., Kizlaris, 1938–1948, 410; Loukopoulos, 1983, 248; Palanca, 1991, 159–161), sometimes reinforced with olive lees or bull's blood (Gaillard, 1997, 20). A paved floor, like shod animals or sledges, made threshing faster and more effective: in Tharounia, Kostas reckons five mules on a paved floor threshed as fast as six or seven on an earthen floor. In Metaxada, Ilias used a paved floor on rocky fields above the village but also a less efficient earthen floor for crops below the village "because transporting the harvest was a big problem and you could not find flag-stones easily." Shkurti (1979, 88–89) suggests that threshing sledges were preferentially used on paved floors in Albania, but in Greece sledges were routinely used in the lowlands, where unpaved floors were normal, and not in upland areas, where paved floors were common. In Haute Provence, the combination of stone roller and paved floor was considered to risk damaging grain and was avoided for lentils and beans (Gaillard, 1997, 20, 60).

In Albania, Shkurti (1979, 69–71) argues that farmers owning the land they cultivated built fixed threshing floors – paved where suitable stone was available, whereas tenants of big estates used makeshift floors. Paved floors involved a particularly large investment of labor and were sometimes built by specialists. In Provence, they belonged to rich farmers (Gaillard, 1997, 19–20), but in some regions, they were communal or shared between several related households (e.g., Loukopoulos, 1983, 248–249). In Albania, priority in use of shared floors variously followed the order of construction of houses or order of completion of the harvest or went to the person who renewed the central pole that year (Shkurti, 1979, 72). In steep terrain, where a flat area had to be built up or cut into the slope, unpaved floors too were a major investment, and their maintenance was difficult even in flat land if there was no ready source of water for replastering the surface every year.

149

Threshing floors in southern Amorgos and on Monte Cairo were somewhat dispersed among the fields and, in the latter region, nearby field houses, where straw could be stored until needed, reduced or spread the transport costs of farming distant land (Forte, 2009). Floors were often concentrated, however, in one or two localities around a village, often on common land (e.g., Palmer, 1998, 152). This partly reflected exposure to breezes suitable for winnowing and partly the tendency for completion of processing on the threshing floor to be the point at which tithe collectors and sharecroppers divided the harvest (e.g., Shkurti, 1979, 84). Sharecroppers might divide the heap of cleaned grain by filling the ubiquitous measuring tins ("one for me, one for you"), as did tithe collectors on Rhodes (Vrontis, 1938–1948, 122), but tithe collectors in northern Greece sometimes estimated the volume of grain by measuring the height of the heap with a graduated stick or simply with the handle of a winnowing fork; in Kolindros, the producer could challenge this assessment which was then judged by a group of his peers. Cleaned grain could not be lifted from the threshing floor until these obligations were settled, and in Assiros, the tithe assessor sealed each heap, with a stamped cap of mud, to prevent premature removal (also Rhodes – Vrontis, 1938–1948, 122). Threshing floors were often located in groups or close to the settlement to facilitate surveillance (e.g., Karanastasis, 1952, 295; Loukopoulos, 1983, 256–257; Gaillard, 1997, 3), whereas poor Provençal farmers *flailed* away from threshing floors to evade taxes (Duplessy *et al.*, 1996, 61).

Crops were threshed more or less in order of harvest on Amorgos (Jones and Halstead, 1995), as in Assiros and various central Cretan villages. Farmers on Rhodes threshed wheat first (Vrontis, 1938–1948, 120), however, as did Nikolaos in Kolindros "because it is the most important harvest and later the rains start; the other crops are shorter and softer and can be threshed even if slightly moist." In Paliambela, Koula's father processed wheat seedcorn first and then the rest of the wheat before other cereals to minimize contamination of the most valued crops with grain left behind from the previous threshing. On Amorgos, there was no significant relationship between the major contaminant of crop samples and the crop previously threshed on the same floor (Jones and Halstead, 1995, 110, table 3b), but the stone-paved surfaces were swept clean between batches. In Paliambela, with earthen floors, contamination was a greater problem: Koula's family processed bitter vetch last because its hard, rounded seeds impacted into the surface of the floor and cast up dirt. For the same reason, in Metaxada, owners of earthen floors processed chickpeas and lupins by hand at home.

With mechanization, threshing with animals has disappeared from most of the Mediterranean, but small quantities of beans or sesame are still beaten by hand, and farmers occasionally combine traditional and modern technologies. In summer 1983, in the Zagori district of the Pindos, a tractor driving up and down a stretch of mountain road was threshing New World beans spread on the tarmac, and on Crete, Valasia Isaakidou and Todd Whitelaw have independently witnessed cereal crops spread on public roads being threshed by passing cars.

4.3   Ways of Winnowing and Coarse Sieving

While threshing breaks up the crop, subsequent winnowing and sieving normally separate "the wheat from the chaff" and most affect the composition of both archaeobotanical samples and what is destined for food or fodder. When grain is beaten from the ear without chopping the straw, the latter may be removed simply by lifting clear the threshed sheaves (e.g., Hillman, 1984, 123). Even when both ears and straw are threshed, much of the latter may be forked or dragged off the underlying grain. Likewise, where only pods of broad beans or New World beans are picked and threshed, much of the chaff can be scooped up by hand, leaving behind the seeds. In most cases, however, winnowing is the most effective means of separating grain from lighter straw and chaff. Though requiring skill not mastered universally, winnowing is a simple process and exhibits limited variability, mostly related to the quantity of crop processed. Small quantities of threshed material are most easily gathered and lifted with bare hands or with the aid of a sieve or tin. This is how Irini on Amorgos winnowed her lentils, Voula in Tharounia cleaned a sack of threshed winged vetchling, and Giorgis in Assiros dealt with the sesame he grew behind his house. Some farmers in early nineteenth-century Campania also winnowed cereals in this fashion, though the poorly cleaned grain was not well regarded in the market (Cimmino, 1977, 44–46). As on Amorgos, however, volumes of crop large enough to thresh with animals were normally winnowed with a fork and then shovel. Although broadly similar across the Mediterranean, these winnowing tools exhibit regional variation that is again partly related to the scale of the task and size of the threshing floor (Shkurti, 1979, 78, 79, figs. 10–12, 81, 83, figs. 15 and 16).

The coarse sieve was widely considered essential threshing floor equipment, used especially *after* winnowing to remove dust and heavy chaff. It was also used *during*, and to speed up, winnowing: heavy chaff and unthreshed ears or pods, not easily separated by winnowing, were raked off the front of the strip of cleaned grain and coarse-sieved to avoid losing any free grain. This latter use was particularly important if crops contained large quantities of unthreshed ears or pods (perhaps because they were harvested a little prematurely, failed to develop fully as a result of *lívas* winds, or were threshed in cool and damp conditions) or if lack of breeze made winnowing slow and ineffective. It also enabled additional workers to speed up processing: while only one or two persons at a time can conveniently winnow a pile of grain, several more can assist with sweeping, raking, and sieving. Ears and pods retained by the coarse sieve might be rethreshed, if the quantity was large, or fed to animals, if further processing was not considered worthwhile.

In northern Jordan, two grades of coarse sieve were used, one for wheat and another with larger holes for barley and chickpeas (Palmer, 1998, 154). In Greece, the same coarse sieve was commonly used for wheat and barley, although Dimos and Dokas in Aiginio used one sieve with smaller holes for naked wheat and a second with larger holes for hulled barley and einkorn; some farmers (including Dimos) also owned one or more sieves with coarser mesh for cleaning larger grains such as oats and chickpeas and, on Amorgos, a semicoarse sieve served to separate wheat and barley. In Turkey, barley and glume wheat were again coarse-sieved with a more open mesh than free-threshing wheat, while a finer mesh removed runt spikelets from threshed (but husked) glume wheat to improve seedcorn (Hillman, 1984, 125–126; 1985, 9). In Asturias, runt spikelets sieved out of emmer and spelt were sown in late summer to provide green fodder in spring (Peña-Chocarro, 1996, 134). In the twentieth-century eastern Mediterranean, a wide range of sieves cleaned different crops to varying degrees. Itinerant specialists often supplied these sieves (Hillman, 1984, 132), but some were homemade, and there was scope for local and even individual variation in mesh size. In Asturias, Leandro's grandfather usually harvested his glume wheat later than his neighbors and so took fuller spikelets to the dehusking mill, where a sieve through which it was intended to pass retained his free grain. Here the brief singeing, which usually precedes threshing of emmer and spelt ears into spikelets, burns off most of the awns and attached fragments of straw. Any unburnt straw, and as much burnt material as possible, is then removed from the singed and threshed spikelets with a *bano* or "winnowing sieve" (Hillman, 1984, 124), effectively a leather-based coarse sieve without holes. This is held, angled upwards away from the operator, and shaken up and down so that unwanted light material rising to the farther lip can be tipped out with a jerky movement. This method of removing unwanted material, differing from the cleaned product in weight rather than size, is common also while fine sieving (see following text).

Because glume wheats for human consumption were normally (but not invariably – Hillman, 1984, 141–143) threshed and dehusked as separate operations, winnowing and sieving tended to be repeated in two cycles with different grades of coarse sieve: after initial threshing, with an open mesh through which spikelets passed, and after dehusking, with a finer mesh that retained spikelets but not free grain. Consequently, even when glume wheat was harvested as sheaves, the straw and chaff were usually removed at different stages and often used in different ways (Hillman, 1984, 126–127,

131). Otherwise, winnowing and sieving broadly follow the same flexible sequence for glume wheats as for free-threshing cereals, and the contrast in processing methods should not be overstated. The latter may also undergo a second cycle of threshing (to break up unthreshed ears or remove barley awns) and may be coarse-sieved with different grades of mesh. Moreover, the straw and chaff of free-threshing cereals, even if removed from the grain in a single operation, are partly separated by winnowing and so may also be used differentially. For example, on Kos, the fine chaff blown furthest from the pile of winnowed grain was mixed with bitter vetch and fed to oxen (Karanastasis, 1952, 294–295).

Most Greek farmers maintain that they winnowed crops fully, only leaving "rubbish" (runt grains, weed seeds) to be swept up and fed to animals, but our observations on Amorgos showed that flexible drawing of the arbitrary boundary between clean grain and rubbish could save significant amounts of processing time and generate considerable volumes of high-quality fodder. Similarly, while most Greek farmers respond that food and fodder grains alike were coarse-sieved, the thoroughness of such cleaning plainly depended on available time, labor, and energy. Some note that the presence of chaff or straw mattered less in fodder than in food grain, while an incentive for thorough cleaning of the latter was that any remaining contaminants normally had to be removed at a later stage.

4.4 Cleaning for Storage and Consumption

Once winnowed and perhaps coarse-sieved, grain might undergo further cleaning. Sometimes grain was washed, in bulk before storage, where the climate was hot enough to dry the grain quickly, or piecemeal before milling. In Karpathian Olimbos, washing was said to be the norm, and in Messenian Iklaina, Farmakis' sister also routinely washed her household's grain in a cauldron before sending it to the mill. Elsewhere, grain seems to have been washed selectively, if at all. For example, in Metaxada, Nikos recalls that "anyone who had the time washed the grain to produce whiter bread," and in Cretan Skalani, the grain was washed if threshing had dug up a lot of dirt from the earthen surface of the floor. In Haute Provence, grain threshed with animals (and so soiled by their urine and feces) was washed, whereas that flailed by hand was not (Gaillard, 1997, 74–75); where grain might prove difficult to dry, this was an incentive to thresh cereal ears by hand (Llaty, 1997, 112). On Amorgos and elsewhere, the person driving the animals sometimes intercepted feces during threshing, but many Greek farmers pragmatically accepted that droppings dried quickly in the midday heat and could be removed by hand, if whole, or winnowed out, if broken up. In Paliambela, only grain black with rust was washed (also Gaillard, 1997, 68), but immersion in water also removes weevil-infested grains and other floating contaminants (Hillman, 1984, 132) – including runt grains according to Irini on Kithira. In Greece, at least, some small-scale farmers producing for domestic consumption washed grain, but those producing on a large scale for market did not think it practicable or necessary.

Apart from dust, winnowed grain may contain heavy weed seeds, small stones (particularly after harvesting by uprooting), and straw and chaff fragments that evaded winnowing and coarse sieving. A fine sieve that retained most grain, but let runt grains, small weed seeds, and dust pass through, was used on the threshing floor in Assiros, Paliambela, and Metaxada and at home, before milling, at Kolofana and Skalani. Sometimes, the grain was fine-sieved at both stages, with cursory bulk screening on the threshing floor followed by more thorough piecemeal cleaning at home (cf. Hillman, 1984, 134). With the shaking of the sieve, any remaining chaff came to the surface and could be scooped or tossed out, as with the Asturian winnowing sieve. In Paliambela, the fine *starkó* ("wheat" sieve) was used on the lower and dirtier part of the winnowed grain pile, whereas use of its equivalent in Assiros may have been less selective. In many parts of Greece, the fine sieve is referred to as a darnel (*Lolium*) sieve, because failure to remove these small weed seeds could cause illness. Octogenarian Anastasia in central Cretan Ano Asites coarse- and fine-sieved the oats for

155

her husband's beloved mule as carefully as she cleaned the wheat and barley grain for the family. It was far more normal, however, as on Amorgos, to fine-sieve seedcorn and food grain, but not fodder grain. For example, in Andalucian Zuheros, free-threshing wheat (for food) was routinely fine-sieved, but not barley or einkorn (normally for fodder), although the latter too were fine-sieved when consumed by humans in "the year of hunger." In Milioti, Maria recalls using the fine sieve for seedcorn. In Skalani, however, Nikolis used his cleanest batch of threshed and winnowed grain for seedcorn or, if necessary, selected a few good sheaves and threshed these by hand. His wife used the fine sieve to speed up hand cleaning of grain destined for the mill. She spread the grain out on the *sofrá*, a low portable table, to sort through for stones and large weed seeds, but others searched it in the fine sieve. In Paliambela, hand sorting was considered particularly important with uprooted pulses for human consumption, because stones could break teeth, but not with those for fodder. Before the development of mechanical grain cleaners, cereals might need particularly careful sorting if heavily contaminated with the large and poisonous seeds of corncockle, *Agrostemma githago* (Gaillard, 1997, 67). In the case of glume wheats, fine sieving is doubly important in removing chaff fragments (glume bases) from dehusked grain (e.g., Hillman, 1984, 131). In Lazarades, northern Greece, Olga fine-sieved both seedcorn and food grain but only handpicked and washed the small amounts of grain destined to be broken into groats (*pligoúri*) and mixed with milk or yoghurt to make *trakhanás* (cf. Valamoti and Anastasaki, 2007).

The care taken and methods used in cleaning grain thus varied, partly depending on intended use and type and degree of contamination (in turn, influenced by quality of tillage, methods of harvesting, and thoroughness of processing on the threshing floor). Weed-rich seedcorn could jeopardize the next harvest, contaminated grain was hard to sell, and some weed seeds posed significant health risks, so farmers had strong incentives to clean grain for sowing, sale, or domestic consumption.

When and where any washing and fine sieving took place depended to a great extent on weather and availability of labor, while hand sorting seems invariably to have happened piecemeal, between storage and preparation for consumption. Pulses and free-threshing cereals were usually stored, across most of the Mediterranean, as more or less cleaned, free grain. Glume wheats store better as spikelets than free grain, in part because of damage to the latter during dehusking. In Asturias, only ears of spelt and emmer are harvested, and not being prohibitively bulky, these normally go into store intact. In Provence, einkorn was bulk-threshed outdoors in summer and, before storage, was dehusked *en masse* – for convenience because this took place in local water mills. In Turkey, glume wheats were both threshed and dehusked wholesale before storage, except in the wettest areas where open-air processing was difficult and dehusking took place piecemeal after storage (Hillman, 1984, 126).

4.5   Storage

In Asturias, newly harvested ears of spelt and emmer were usually stored in a heap, perhaps trampled to reduce their volume, on the floor of the impressive raised granaries: *hórreos* on four legs and *paneras* on six (Peña-Chocarro, 1996). The raised and well-ventilated granary protected this and other stored grains, fruits, and nuts from damp, while staddle stones at the top of each leg and a gap between the access stairs and granary doors kept out rodents. During winter, after threshing to break up the ears, spikelets for sowing remained in the raised granaries, in sacks or open baskets, while those for consumption were dehusked and then stored in the same way or in the house in a wooden chest. Several informants had sown ears or spikelets stored for two or three years, while Inés in Xomezana and Carmina in Piñera had successfully sown or consumed ears or spikelets after six and four years, respectively. Dehusked grain was significantly more vulnerable to both weevils and mold, against which the various storage containers provided no protection. Severina recalled that if weevils were seen, dehusked grain was ground "because they cannot attack flour"; most informants considered flour less vulnerable than dehusked grain to storage pests, although it became sour if kept too long. As a precaution, Candido sieved both spikelets and dehusked grain, if stored for more than a year, to clean out any weevils. According to tradition, free grain stored well if reaped, taken for dehusking, and placed in the storage chest during a waning moon; if moved or placed in the chest during a waxing moon, it was more vulnerable to weevils. If lunar cycles conflicted with practical considerations, however, Leandro was adamant that the latter took precedence.

Across the north and central Balkans, maize on the cob was often stored – to complete drying – in raised outdoor granaries of basketwork or wooden slats, loosely resembling a narrow miniature *hórreo*. Mitsos from lowland Paliambela first saw these as a soldier in upland Albania in 1940–1941, although they were also used nearer to home in villages where irrigation allowed a late maize crop harvested at the end of summer: "they could not dry their maize before storage, whereas we harvested earlier and stripped the cobs to store the grain indoors." Across most of southern Europe and Turkey, however, especially in the lowlands, Old World grain crops ripened in early summer and were usually stored in the house (the driest and most closely guarded location) or an adjacent outbuilding, contained in sacks, baskets, wooden chests, clay storage vessels, bins of unfired clay, or brick alcoves or simply heaped on the floor (e.g., Megas, 1946; Weinstein, 1973).

In addition, subterranean storage was widespread across the Mediterranean (Sigaut, 1988). In north-central Crete, Nikolis from Skalani describes how "many old houses had a circular *goúva*, like a well, unlined and 1–1.50 m wide by 1–3 m deep," cut into the soft *koúskouras* (marl) bedrock beneath the floor and covered with a stone slab so it could be walked over. Similar pits cut into other soft substrates sometimes required lining with stones. The pit was filled with cereal grain, covered with a cloth, and sealed airtight with a layer of ash that did not allow grain pests to develop. The particular concern was a moth that caused skin irritation in those who came into contact with infested grain. The irritation was sufficiently severe that those unable to cut a *goúva* stored their cereals above ground in an outbuilding well away from the house. Those with an underground store set aside enough grain for the summer and buried the rest until sowing time, a period considered long enough to neutralize these pests. After retrieval of seedcorn, grain for consumption was extracted piecemeal, with the ash layer pulled aside – by lifting one edge of the underlying cloth – and then respread. A farmer with a significant surplus of cereal grain might sell it, lend it to a neighbor in need (who would return the same quantity the following year), or open an additional *goúva* – cereals were safely stored underground for two or three years.

Elsewhere in the southern Aegean, pit storage of cereals mostly occurred in the fields. On Kos, from late July when work ended on the threshing floor to October when sowing started, wheat and barley seedcorn was placed in shallow pits and covered with ferns and chaff and then dry earth; the pits were grouped in an enclosed field whose owner acted as a paid watchman (Karanastasis, 1952, 296). On southern Amorgos, "pitting" (*lákkiasma*) was likewise recalled as a short-term measure over summer to kill pests (at the cost of losing some seed that sprouted), before grain was transferred to wooden and stone chests in the houses (Halstead and Jones, 1989, 52). On lowland Naxos, where barley was produced on a relatively large scale, farmers opened pits in fields with dry and compact soil. Perhaps after first sterilizing the pit with fire, they lined its base and sides with chopped straw and filled the pit with a cone of grain that protruded above ground so that, with a covering of straw and then earth, rainwater would drain away freely. The pit was capped with brushwood and stones to keep off animals (Sfakianos, 1979–1981, 396). On Rhodes, where again a winged insect pest caused severe skin irritation, wheat was buried in built underground stores, in which a fire was first lit to remove any residual moisture or grain pests (Vrontis, 1938–1948, 123). It is unclear whether pits were an alternative or a prelude to storage indoors on Naxos and Rhodes, but farmers across the southern Aegean seemingly perceived pit storage mainly

159

as a means of controlling grain pests by starving them of oxygen (cf. Reynolds, 1974; Sigaut, 1988), although they also appreciated the advantages of cool temperatures underground.

Some benefits of pit storage could be achieved above ground. On Amorgos and Kos, storage pits were lined with straw or chaff, presumably to minimize contamination with earth (also Palmer, 1998, 155), but on Tinos and Limnos, chopped straw was packed tight in the barn and a hole "like a *pithos*" was made in the middle for grain (Amoiralis, 1972, 379–380; cf. Sigaut, 1988, 14–15). On Kithira, Fotini's grandparents likewise kept sacks of grain inside their store of chopped straw to maintain a steady and modest temperature that kept weevils in check, as did Stamatina at Pakhia Ammos in eastern Crete with the rationale that "mice [or rats] don't go into chopped straw." In northern and central Greece, large baskets (*kofínes*) were often plastered with dung and mud, and for long-term storage, the grain was sometimes sealed airtight with a cap of grass and then dung. At Prodromos in Thessaly, grain stored like this was said to last five years or more, suggesting that dung provided an effective sealing (Halstead, 1990). Grain stored above ground was also protected against insect pests by the addition of repellents, such as origano at Messenian Khora and Aroniadika on Kithira, pennyroyal at Mitata on Kithira, and sage widely on Crete (e.g., at Aloides, Arkalokhori, and Pakhia Ammos). Fig leaves were added on the high Lasithi plateau of Crete, where sage is scarce, and are still used in north Greek Paliambela. In Tharounia on Euboea, repellents placed in storage chests included bay and walnut leaves, as well as thyme and origano. Lentils and other pulses were doused with olive oil at Tharounia and southeast Cretan Mirtos and with oil and vinegar at Mitata on Kithira. Inorganic repellents included copper sulfate in wheat seedcorn on the Cairo Massif of central Italy, ground-up potsherds in wheat and barley at Aroniadika on Kithira, lime in wheat at Assiros, and lime in wheat and old iron (perhaps of symbolic rather than practical value – see following text) in barley on Rhodes (Vrontis, 1938–1948, 123).

In addition to natural hazards, stored grain was vulnerable to theft and tithes or taxes of varying legality. On Methana in the northeast Peloponnese, farmers hid grain from brigands and officials in pits outside the village (Forbes, 1989). At Kontogoni in Messenia during the early 1940s, Velisaria's father hid some of his grain from occupying Italian and German troops in a false compartment within his wine barrel and the rest in a pit in the garden. In Paliambela, grain was hidden in pits from the last Turkish landlord around 1900. Giorgos' grandfather had described the burial of baskets full of grain, while Stefanos, reformed "archaeologist of the night," had been told of grain hidden loose in pits lined with red soil and sealed with straw and clay. In neighboring Aiginio, Theodoros, aged 104, grew up in southern Bulgaria, where Greek villagers concealed grain from nationalist *komitatzídes* in pits lined with dung and covered with branches and then earth.

Lack of summer rainfall may have contributed to the apparently greater frequency of pit storage in southern than northern Greece, especially as a short-term measure to neutralize grain pests (although not the weevils resident in aboveground storage containers). The relatively frequent storage of grain in large *pithos* jars in southern Greece, especially Crete (Christakis, 1999), probably reflects their widespread use for olive oil. Different containers had contrasting strengths and weaknesses: for example, Kiki from Messenian Khora emphasized the vulnerability of sacks to rodents, whereas Thanasis from Plikati in the Pindos dismissed rodents because he kept cats, and Mitsos from Paliambela favored sacks because they were better ventilated and so less prone to mold or weevils than jars or chests. Often, however, farmers used containers opportunistically. As a new refugee in Paliambela, Mitsos' father closed off a corner of the house with planks as a store but later made moveable wooden chests and bought from a neighboring village a dung-lined basket that held a ton or more of grain. Which crops were entrusted to which containers varied from year to year, depending on the yields of the former and capacities of the latter. For example, at Aroniadika on Kithira, Panagiotitsa's mother had two wooden chests, each with a capacity of 25 *mizoúria* (roughly 500 kg) of grain. One chest held wheat/barley maslin for consumption and the other, partitioned in the middle, variously maslin seedcorn and wheat, or wheat and broad beans; anything that did not fit went into sacks. Many households put staple cereals in big chests, bins, or baskets, each holding 500–1000 or even 2000 l, and small quantities of pulses in sacks or jars, but at Likorakhi in the Pindos, Khristos' parents devoted one of their five wooden chests to bitter vetch for their draft cattle. Many types of container also served for commodities other than grain: *pithoi* and smaller clay jars held, inter alia (Christakis, 1999, 4), olive oil, grape pressings for distilling into *rakí* (at Kalo Khorio on Crete), *mizíthra* (*ricotta*) cheeses (at Kontogoni in Messenia; Anogia on Crete), and cooked pork sealed in fat (e.g., at Monforte in central Italy; Assiros and Paliambela in northern Greece; Karitaina, Kinigou, and Metaxada in the Peloponnese; Stavrokhori in eastern Crete). Likewise, pits concealed personal belongings (e.g., Arcadian herders overwintering in lowland Messenia), stored chestnuts over winter (with regular watering – at Vizitsa on Mt Pilion, central Greece), and kept grapes fresh for a few months (suspended and sealed with dung – at Assiros in northern Greece), while fresh carcasses could be hung for a week or so deep in a well (at Mikines in the Peloponnese).

As to the scale of grain storage, elderly farmers in various parts of Greece suggested 1–1.5 tons of grain as the amount needed to maintain a family for a year, though this sometimes included a safety margin for possible losses in storage. Depending on the balance between "naked" and hulled grain, provision on this scale would require 1300–3000 l of dry storage capacity. Farmers also widely aspired to store enough grain for a second year so they could ride one total crop failure (e.g., Forbes, 1989), although the extent to which they achieved this was variable. In a study of domestic storage facilities in early twentieth-century Crete, Christakis (1999, 7–8) found that a majority of households had a capacity (for grain, oil, wine, and other foodstuffs *combined*) of up to 2200 l, meeting their subsistence needs for, at most, two years and, more often, one year or less. More anecdotal data from other parts of Greece suggests a broadly similar picture. For households that did produce a modest surplus, the choice between retention and sale was influenced by awareness that storage beyond one year increased the risk of losses to pests or mold. According to Giorgis in Knossos, "bugs don't appear in one year – they need two or more." Moisture encouraged pests as well as mold, and as Mitsos in Paliambela recalls, grain kept for a second year might be sieved and aired to extend its "shelf life." How farmers used available surpluses is discussed further in Chapter 6.

4.6 Consumption

Although culinary detail falls outside the present remit, the variable degree of refinement of grain for consumption (cf. Hillman, 1984, 140–141; 1985, 12–22) is relevant and included:

- Whole grains (normal, in Greece, for lentils, chickpeas, and New World beans; also for cereals, e.g., in memorial *kóliva* or cereal–pulse stews and soups such as Cretan *mageirgiá* or Italian *minestrone*)
- Whole cereal grains (particularly of "hard" emmer, einkorn, or macaroni wheat) stripped of their outer bran layer by wetting and pounding (perhaps after preliminary boiling, e.g., Turkish *asure* [Hillman, 1985, 15] or the *keskési* made in Crete by Christian refugees from Asia Minor) and now largely displaced by rice
- Split pulses, stripped of their testa in a hand-mill (e.g., Greek *fáva*, of various *Lathyrus* species, and sometimes peas or broad beans; split lentils for soups in Turkey)
- Coarsely ground (again hand-milled) groats of cereal grains, sometimes previously stripped of their bran (e.g., Turkish *bulgur*, some varieties of Greek *pligoúri*), sometimes not stripped (e.g., Turkish *lapa*, Cretan *khóndro*), and sometimes preboiled and dried to prevent the groats sticking together in cooking (another variety of Greek *pligoúri*)

- More or less finely ground cereal flour, with more or less bran removed (with a fine or coarse flour sieve), used to make bread, pies, dumplings, and various forms of pasta
- Fine cornstarch (Greek *nisestés*), extracted by mashing and straining wheat grains soaked for several days and used in sweets

Intensive processing and refinement, involving additional labor and "waste" of any fraction that was removed, were usually selective. For example, a finer flour sieve, removing more bran than for daily bread, was used to prepare pies for special occasions in Assiros and liturgical loaves and offerings to the priest on Samos (Dimitriou, 1976–1978). The bran removed was used as fodder (e.g., to make loaves for dogs). In times of scarcity, however, refinement was unaffordable: during the World War II occupation of Greece, bran was *added* to bread, as at Neo Sidirokhori and, with ground acorns and even chaff, at Tharounia. Human consumption of both fodder grains and weed- or chaff-rich cereals (e.g., Camporesi, 1980; Halstead, 1990; Hionidou, 2011) was widespread around the Mediterranean in such circumstances. Conversely, in good times, the most valued livestock were fed grain supplements ranging from whole hulled barley (e.g., for horses) or free wheat grains (e.g., for hens), through coarse groats of cereals and pulses (e.g., bitter vetch for oxen), to maize flour (especially for pigs).

Some bakers in Crete now sell an expensive "gourmet" barley bread containing a few chaff and awn fragments, presumably added for rustic authenticity. Sofia from Aloides, whose father during the 1930s occasionally brought a white wheaten loaf from town as a treat, finds this inversion of values extraordinary. Her father sowed his best field, only 400–500 m² in area, with wheat for special foods (coarse-ground *khóndro*), memorial *kóliva*, and white liturgical bread offered to the church, but their staple barley grain was carefully cleaned, and the flour sifted to remove any remaining awn fragments and some of the indigestible bran. On Kos, the mostly landless farmers paid field rents in wheat, eating barley bread as their daily staple and reserving wheaten flour for loaves at Christmas, New Year, and Easter and for offerings to the church

(Karanastasis, 1952, 250). On Kithira, Panagiotitsa's family ate bread of mixed wheat and barley but ideally used wheat flour only with milk or eggs to make *khilopíttes* (homemade pasta) and *trakhanás*. Similarly, at Mouries near Kilkis in northern Greece, Elli was raised on bread of maize flour, softened with a little rye, but her mother bought small amounts of wheat grain for memorial *kóliva* and wheat flour to make pasta and festive *tsouréki* bread, while her father occasionally bought a loaf of "clean" wheaten bread. On Crete, the flour of spring-sown barley (*Martáki*) was prized for its taste and light color and, probably for the latter quality, was used in Kalo Khorio to make the bread offered on Good Friday. At Agia Semni, Angela's father farmed better land and provided his family with the relative luxury of bread from mixed wheat and barley flour, with the latter sifted through a finer flour sieve to remove more of the bran. At Xomezana in Asturias, Inés' two grades of flour sieve gave her the option of making either a dark spelt bread or a lighter version "like shop-bought bread." Earlier in the cycle of cereal processing, the local millers offered the option of threshing spelt ears into spikelets with or without first singeing the ears. The latter yielded whiter bread but slowed down both threshing and dehusking (see preceding text) and damaged the grain, reducing its storage life. The sliding social scale from animal to poor human to "rich" human was thus mapped onto variation in both the grains consumed (e.g., bitter vetch/oats → barley → wheat – Section 6.6) and their degree of processing and refinement (e.g., bran → wholemeal flour → fine flour). At the bottom of the scale, human consumption of toxic fodder grains or bread rich in toxic weeds posed grave health risks (Halstead, 1990), while eating dark or unrefined bread was demeaning and unappetizing. While some households used their scarce white flour for liturgical bread from religious conviction, offerings to the church also presumably exposed a household's living standards to public scrutiny and possible shame. Certainly some Greek households, which "stretched" their flour during the hungry early 1940s with barley or even bitter vetch, were exposed by routine exchanges of bread among neighbors: "she borrowed a loaf until she next baked;

the loaf she gave me back looked lovely but tasted terrible – she had added bitter vetch flour."

4.7   Questions of Scale: Labor and Time Stress

The speed of threshing with animals depended on the type of crop, weather, use or not of a sledge or paved floor, and especially the number and type of animals. In Provence, 12 horses threshed 10,000 l (about 8000 kg) of wheat in a day (Gaillard, 1997, 42). At Miliarisi on Crete, Yannis and his father, with two large and powerful oxen working from 10 a.m. to 3–4 p.m., could thresh (but not winnow) up to 30 mule or donkey-loads (120 sheaves yielding 700–750 kg of grain) in a full day. Similar outputs of 500–650 kg (400–500 *okádes*) were offered for two cattle pulling a sledge, with one person driving the animals and a second spreading sheaves and turning the crop, at Messenian Metaxada and, including winnowing, north Greek Assiros. Threshing of only 300 kg per day is reported, however, with 7–8 animals on the island of Santorini (Sarpaki, 1992, 74–75) and for a *single* farmer with five oxen in Iran (Russell, 1988, 124). At Ano Asites, Anogia, Kalo Khorio, and Skalani on Crete, two persons with two cattle pulling a sledge threshed up to 7–10 loads (150–250 kg of grain) in the middle of the day, often harvesting in the morning and winnowing in the afternoon. Threshing outputs varied partly because the benefits of threshing in the middle of the day and winnowing with late afternoon breezes encouraged daily processing of a "floor-load" of sheaves, the number of which was determined by the volume of different crops and size of the floor as much as the availability of human and animal labor. Nonetheless, larger floors and more or stronger animals enabled economies of scale that reduced the cost in *human* labor of animal-assisted threshing.

Manual flailing of sheaves *leaving the straw intact* yielded perhaps 120 kg of wheat, 160–180 kg of barley, and 220–250 kg of oats per man-day in Provence (Gaillard, 1997, 37). For flailing ears *and straw*, veteran gun owner Luigi in Monforte, central Italy, says eight people extracted 30 *tomoli* of grain (150 kg/head) in a day, comparable with 120 kg indoors and 160–200 kg outdoors (with shorter straw) for wheat in nineteenth-century France (Sigaut, 1988, 29, n. 41). Nineteenth-century North American figures – probably flailing ears only, given the rudimentary method of winnowing – are higher (40 kg wheat or 50 kg barley/man-hour – Russell, 1988, 124–125). As Gaillard (1997, 37) notes for Provence, however, laborers paid by yield worked faster but less thoroughly, leaving more grain unthreshed, than those paid by the day. These figures represent long working days and so should be compared with the higher Greek rates of threshing wheat and barley (including straw) with cattle (250–350 kg per man-day), rather than the lower Cretan figures (equivalent to perhaps 150–250 kg per *full man-day*). Either way, manual threshing was slower, and the flailing figures represent strenuous labor by fit adults; as with digging, elderly or infirm farmers flailed in short spells that are not easily quantified. Conversely, threshing with cattle demanded tolerance of heat and dust more than physical strength and was often undertaken in Greece by individuals too young or old to cope with a day's flailing.

Unsurprisingly, apart from jobs too small or delicate, farmers threshed with animals if available, and on Crete, those without work animals usually sought help from a neighbor, in return for the straw – if this suited both parties – or for more productive manual labor. In Metaxada, nonagenarian Nikos has just climbed the path to the shrine on Mt Aigaleon for the last time "to bid farewell to the Virgin Mary." He is adamant: "thresh wheat by hand, five or six armfuls a day? No, you'd die." According to Nikolis in Skalani, manual threshing of cereals was contemplated only for one or two sheaves set aside as seedcorn or memorial *kóliva*. Pulses were easier than cereals, but Fountoulonikolis in Kalo Khorio recalls that broad beans were normally threshed with animals, even though each household sowed only 0.2–0.3 ha or less. In Paliambela, where cattle pulled sledges on earthen floors, Koula and Marika agree they would thresh 0.2 ha of pulses with animals and 0.1 ha by hand, unless the crop was unusually heavy. Here, pulses and rye might be sown on a small enough scale (e.g., "one or two furrows of beans for the house") to be threshed easily by hand, but wheat, barley, and oats were never sown in such small quantities. Elsewhere, some farmers combined crops to avoid threshing small quantities by hand. For example, on Crete, unthreshed ears of barley, wheat, and oats from the coarse sieve were often rethreshed together "at the end," and on Amorgos, one informant known for aversion to hard work had mixed pea and grass pea on the threshing floor because he could not be bothered to thresh separately [by hand] the modest returns from his careless husbandry.

Glume wheats usually required two rounds of threshing. Initial threshing by hand to produce spikelets was about as time-consuming as extraction of grain from free-threshing wheat. At Piazza al Serchio in the Garfagnana, septuagenarian Angelo and Lorenzo agree that in their prime, groups of five or six flailers produced in a day 450–525 kg (about 90 kg/head) of free-threshing wheat grain or the equivalent in emmer spikelets. In Asturias, initial hand and foot threshing of spelt and emmer ears yielded per man-day spikelets equivalent to 100–300 kg of free grain: in Zureda, Severina with her husband and two in-laws trampled the year's supply of 15–18 *fanegas* (ultimately 750–900 kg of free grain) in two days; in Llanos de Somerón, Lucino reckoned that 3–4 persons beating and two women cleaning with "winnowing sieves" processed nearly 1000 kg in a day; and in Tiós, Leandro and his father once flailed (without winnowing) 600 kg in a day (starting at 4 am!). Spikelets needed dehusking and the toil of doing so with pestle and mortar drove some Turkish women to make *bulgur* from inferior free-threshing wheat rather than superior emmer (Hillman, 1984, 140). Russell suggests that manual dehusking doubled the time needed to produce free grain by hand from glume wheats (1988, 126), and within living memory in southern Europe, this task was normally delegated to commercial mills where speed varied with the type and size of stones used and the power to drive them. Estève's Provençal mill and that used by Angelo and Lorenzo in Garfagnana ground free wheat grain to flour between horizontal stones at about 150 kg and 80–100 kg/hour, respectively. The latter dehusked emmer between horizontal stones, set slightly further apart than for flour, at 70 kg/hour, whereas Estève's vertical stone dehusked einkorn at only 11–16 kg/hour (and stripped bran from bread wheat or dehusked einkorn at 22–29 kg/hour).

Both Nikolis in Skalani and Fountoulonikolis in Kalo Khorio suggested that one person winnowing, with a favorable breeze and an assistant sweeping and coarse sieving, could deal with the threshed product of 10 loads of sheaves (containing perhaps 200–250 kg of grain) in one afternoon. For Iran, Watson (in Russell, 1988, 124) similarly suggests that 300 kg could be winnowed in 3–4 hours and coarse-sieved in 1.5–2 hours. Winnowing is thus less time-consuming than flailing and than the slower estimates for threshing with cattle but offers much less scope for investing additional labor to achieve faster completion and so remains a major task for large-scale producers using work animals in tillage and threshing. Moreover, winnowing is more likely than threshing (at least in the hotter and drier parts of the Mediterranean) to be delayed by unfavorable weather. Many elderly farmers recall years when lack of breeze halted winnowing for a week or more, increasing the risk of late summer rains beginning before crops were cleaned and safely stored.

After winnowing and coarse sieving, subsequent washing, fine sieving, and handpicking varied greatly in intensity but could be carried out piecemeal from storage and so were not pressing seasonal tasks. The final stage in processing grain for human consumption usually involved grinding to flour, and in recent decades, most Mediterranean farmers entrusted this task to a commercial mill, despite the apparently universal conviction that millers were dishonest or, as Asturian Leandro put it, "charged twice for their labor." These suspicions were not groundless according to Koula, daughter of a part-time miller in Paliambela: "the miller could not help stealing a little extra." In fairness, her father and other millers all over Greece are also remembered for generosity to needy neighbors during the famine of the early 1940s. Nonetheless, millers' overt charges were not trivial, ranging from one twentieth to one sixth of the flour in early twentieth-century Greece (Petropoulos, 1952, 71). In some remote hill villages of Greece, without access to a water mill or windmill, there is a dim recollection that grain used to be ground at home on rotary hand-mills, latterly used to make cereal groats or split pulses (e.g., Loukopoulos, 1983, 285). For the twentieth century, such memories are widespread for the hungry period of Axis occupation: at Arkhanes on Crete, one informant stole from a neighbor's field a few ripe wheat ears that his mother ground by hand to make a loaf of bread; on the island of Kea, hand-mills were used indoors at night to conceal food from neighbors (T. Whitelaw, personal communication); on Kithira, some women ground modest amounts of barley to tide their families over until they completed the harvest and could send grain to the cornmill; and in Paliambela, two households resorted to hand-milling to avoid giving scarce grain to the miller. Most Greek villagers, however, even in this time of dearth, used the local mill despite the risk of theft, if they had wheat or barley, or loss of face, if they were eating fodder grains. Grinding flour by hand, albeit with an efficient rotary quern, was laborious enough that even those producing less grain than they needed usually sacrificed some of it to avoid this task. Manual processing proved more lasting and widespread for split pulses and cereal groats, which are easier to produce than flour and consumed in smaller quantities, and traditional methods also had symbolic significance for some dishes (e.g., large-scale ceremonial breaking of wheat groats for the *rési* pilaf served at weddings in Cyprus).

How do labor inputs for crop processing compare with preceding production stages? Working with two draft oxen and one helper, Yannis at Miliarisi threshed up to 30 loads of sheaves per day, representing at least six man-days of reaping. Mitsos in Paliambela reckons more conservatively that his father with the same workforce threshed, winnowed, and sieved per day 100 Thracian sheaves, harvestable in a good year from 0.2 to 0.25 ha in something like 2.5–3 man-days, but he too insists that threshing was faster than reaping. Nikolaos in Kolindros could thresh per day the harvest from 0.5 ha, an area he plowed in two days (or four, if he plowed both before and after sowing) and reaped in five man-days. Two people working with a pair of cattle, therefore, could thresh and perhaps winnow faster than they could reap or sow the same cereal crop, and the contrast was even sharper for pulses, which were quicker to thresh and slower to reap. Although the harvest could employ a larger human workforce, work on the threshing floor was usually completed more rapidly: for example, in Paliambela, while the harvest lasted four to five weeks, threshing was completed in less than a month. Threshing by hand was more arduous than with animals and pro rata perhaps as slow as reaping with an iron sickle but significantly less time-consuming than manual tillage. For example, assuming a flailing output of 100 kg/man-day (perhaps pessimistic if barley and pulses were processed, as well as wheat) and area yields of 1 ton/ha, one person could thresh in a day the harvest from about 0.1 ha, an area needing perhaps 1 man-day to reap but 3–10 man-days to dig (Section 2.6.1). Threshing was also less urgent than reaping or tillage, because harvested crops were more dependable than those standing in the field or awaiting sowing, so work on the threshing floor, with or without animals, was not the limiting factor on production of pulses and free-threshing cereals. For glume wheats and perhaps hulled barley, *manual* dehusking was sufficiently laborious that this and initial threshing (with or without animals) together were probably more time-consuming than reaping with an iron sickle or *plow-based* (but not *manual*) cultivation, but the task could be undertaken piecemeal from storage. Indeed, there were significant advantages to doing so, even in areas with dry summers favorable to immediate dehusking in bulk (Hillman, 1981), because ears and spikelets store better than free grain.

Threshing with animals differed from manual processing in terms not only of the amount and type of labor expended but also of how this was organized. Some labor was exchanged during threshing with animals. For example, Ilias in Metaxada and Kostas in Tharounia collaborated with neighbors to mobilize a larger team of animals, and in reflecting nostalgically on mutual solidarity "in the old days," Greek villagers often recount how those who finished threshing and winnowing early went, unbidden, to assist slower neighbors and kin. There is an Albanian saying that "the help of a friend is needed above all else at funerals and on the threshing floor" (Shkurti, 1979, 73), although, with increasing inequality of land ownership, mutual assistance gave way to hiring of additional labor for the threshing floor – as for reaping (Shkurti, 1979, 74). Despite the benefits of assistance on the threshing floor, however, Greek farmers describe animal-assisted threshing and winnowing as tasks normally undertaken with household labor, in contrast to the harvest when mutual assistance and hiring of additional labor were quite commonplace. At Assiros, the biggest landowners with multiple plow teams hired "a whole gang" for the harvest but only one or two laborers on the threshing floor. On Crete, where even small-scale farmers emphasized that "at harvest, you never went in ones and twos, but in big gangs," threshing and winnowing were a largely domestic affair. For farmers with work animals, threshing was arduous and winnowing a source of anxiety, because of the need for suitable breeze, but the scope for speeding up the task with additional human labor was limited – in sharp contrast with reaping and manual tillage and also *manual* threshing of large quantities of crop. In Garfagnana, Angelo and Lorenzo describe manually threshing bread wheat and emmer in groups of five or six "from the family if you had enough sons, but otherwise with mutual help between neighbors." In Asturias, Inés recalls that initial threshing of spelt took place in January and February, in the gap between sowing winter crops and plowing for summer crops, so that neighbors were free to help – whether on a reciprocal basis or as hired labor.

There was a close relationship between methods of tillage and threshing in much of the Mediterranean: farmers with work animals normally used them in both tasks, while those without necessarily managed both by hand or secured the services of a neighbor's work animal(s). There was also some relationship between threshing practice and method of reaping. Harvesting only the ears of cereals facilitates storage of unthreshed crops (as in Asturias), whereas ears and straw harvested together are much bulkier and favor threshing before storage. Ears with straw are more easily threshed with animals, while use of straw as fodder provides a strong incentive for harvesting and threshing it. Moreover, the additional bulk and weight, when straw too is harvested, are more easily transported from the field with animals. There are thus sound practical reasons for plow cultivators to harvest sheaves and manual cultivators to reap ears, although several factors blur this opposition: wet summers discourage outdoor threshing; sharp awns favor separate harvest of ears and straw, even when the latter is needed for fodder; and farmers without work animals may harvest straw to exchange for borrowed work animals. Nonetheless, harvesting ears alone facilitates transport, threshing, and storage of unthreshed crops. The costs and benefits of harvesting ears alone or with straw (Section 3.3) must be assessed together with those of transport and threshing, therefore, and the latter are affected by availability of work animals and climatic constraints. In the southern Mediterranean, rapid ripening of grain crops exacerbates the urgency of reaping, while the ensuing hot and dry weather makes outdoor threshing of ears with straw relatively rapid and risk free. Further north, where slower ripening reduces the urgency of harvest, but outdoor threshing is risky, the harvesting of ears alone, even if more laborious, may be favored.

4.8   Threshing Floor Customs

As with tillage and reaping, work on the threshing floor was widely accompanied by customs seeking or celebrating successful completion. In Provence, the summer storms that threatened both harvest and threshing were warded off by prayer, parading of icons, ringing of church bells, and magical measures without Christian overtones (Gaillard, 1997, 76), while bull's blood was presumably used in surfacing threshing floors for its symbolic rather than practical properties. In Albania, garlands and the brush that swept the threshing floor were hung at the end of each season on the central pole. The latter assisted women with childbirth and getting pregnant and, once disused, was not burnt to avoid bad luck (Shkurti, 1979, 68, 72). As on Amorgos, the pile of winnowed grain was widely "crossed" (e.g., on Rhodes – Vrontis, 1938–1948, 121; Kos – Karanastasis, 1952, 295; Tinos – Amoiralis, 1972, 379; and at Messenian Metaxada).

Fountoulonikolis in Kalo Khorio recounted how, at the end of win-nowing, a passerby would wish "a thousand *mouzoúria* [measures] to your house" and the farmer would reply "and two thousand to yours." The same exchange was widespread on Crete, and variants are reported across the southern Aegean. At north Greek Drimos, one sheaf was left intact in the middle of the threshing floor and, at the end, covered with thorn bush and iron to make the grain durable in storage (Slinis, 1938–1948, 102–103).

Considerable significance was widely attached to the first bread baked with new grain. On Kos, the new wheat was made into an offering taken to church for blessing by the priest and into cross-shaped loaves, one for each family member and one to hang up until the following year; a loaf from the new barley was left at the spring so that the following year's supply would be as abundant as running water (Karanastasis, 1952, 290). In Albania, some of the new harvest was threshed by hand, to be ground and baked for the feast marking the end of work on the threshing floor and for distribution among neighbors (Shkurti, 1979, 85). Among Thracian refugees in northern Greece, the first bread was also shared among neighbors, who replied with wishes of good fortune (Kizlaris, 1938–1948, 413). In Drimos, appeals to magical and social sources of good luck were combined: the first bread baked with the new grain was left at the spring, and the finder shared it among the women of the neighborhood (Slinis, 1938–1948, 103).

4.9 Crop Processing in the Past

Despite detailed differences, successive threshing, winnowing, and sieving operations have fairly similar effects for the principal Near Eastern and European grain crops (e.g., Gaillard, 1997, 12; Llaty, 1997). The resulting products and by-products are thus identifiable from their constituent crop parts and weed seed types (Jones, 1987a), with important archaeobotanical applications: plants processed for use or storage are distinguishable from those discarded or consumed in season (Dennell, 1976); weed associations selected by processing are not attributed to husbandry conditions (e.g., Bogaard, Jones, and Charles, 2005); and material derived from dung may be recognized in samples of "anomalous" composition (Charles, 1998). The Kolofana study also showed that crop seeds present in grain as minor contaminants reflect what admixtures are culturally acceptable and practically avoidable (Jones and Halstead, 1995) rather than crop rotation systems (Dennell, 1978), while the urgency with which clean grain was removed from the threshing floor left scant opportunity for fire to create charred grain-rich assemblages of the sort M. Jones (1985) considered characteristic of "producer sites." The present chapter, however, has explored the *contexts* of crop-processing decisions, some implications of which for the later prehistoric and early historic past are outlined here, organized broadly in terms of successive processing stages.

First, a key variable in recent processing, with ramifications throughout the *chaîne opératoire* of grain production, was whether or not animals supplemented human labor in threshing. The antiquity of threshing with livestock has attracted less attention than their use for plowing, but Greco-Roman literary sources describe both trampling by animals and use of animal-drawn sledges (Spurr, 1986, 73–77), while the latter occurs in Near Eastern iconography and texts from the fourth to second millennium BC (Anderson *et al.*, 2006). These ancient representations are from elite media in strikingly hierarchical societies and so may represent practices of a minority cultivating on a scale large enough to warrant tillage and threshing with animals. Some Near Eastern sources imply that threshing sledges had symbolic connotations of power (Littauer and Crouwel, 1990; Sherratt, 2006), but contemporary flint inserts with characteristic microwear and impressions of cereal straw apparently chopped with such inserts (Anderson, 2006) support practical rather than solely ceremonial use. Sporadic finds of probable stone inserts and chopped straw, from the eighth millennium BC in the Near East and sixth millennium BC in southeast Europe, likewise suggest threshing with sledges, presumably animal drawn (Anderson, 2003), and so reinforce sparse osteological indications from the same regions for draft cattle from an early stage of the Neolithic.

Draft cattle reduce the risk of sowing too little or too late and increase the potential for overproduction. If not universally accessible, therefore, Neolithic work animals may have exacerbated inequalities of output and over- or underproduction (Sections 2.7 and 3.7) and enabled households with cattle to exchange their services for the manual labor of those without. In the recent past, similar exchanges were common in threshing, but this can be postponed for piecemeal execution by hand, so unequal access to animals for threshing probably played a minor role in *promoting* inequality in the distant past. Nonetheless, evidence for threshing methods may shed indirect light on how widespread was ownership of work animals. Despite indications that straw was threshed for use as fodder, presumably for cattle, from early in the expansion of mixed farming, Neolithic and later archaeobotanical evidence and Roman literary sources both suggest reaping of cereals at variable heights with variable amounts of straw (Section 3.7). While recent farmers also reaped at varying heights, the sparse evidence for antiquity may reflect less use of available straw, implying that, relative to the scale of cereal growing, stall-feeding of large livestock was less common than in the recent past. Patchy ownership of draft animals may thus have been both a source and symptom of economic inequality for much of the history of farming.

In the recent past, even owners of draft animals threshed small batches of crop by hand, partly to avoid damage to grain. Consequently, while farmers frequently grew pulses, easy to thresh but difficult to harvest, on a scale that warranted manual processing, some only sowed cereals – especially wheat, threshed with difficulty – on a scale large enough to fill a threshing floor and thus justify using animals (e.g., 5000 m² in Paliambela). Like tillage, therefore, threshing with animals rather than by hand encourages cropping decisions to be taken for larger land parcels and so may limit crop diversity. The implied choice faced by early farmers, between the time efficiency of using draft animals and the security of growing the full range of available crops, may have reinforced the suggested patchy ownership of work animals.

Secondly, like the cornmill in medieval temperate Europe, the threshing floor was a common point for elite exaction of "surplus" grain from subordinate farmers in the recent Mediterranean and also, arguably, Late Bronze Age southern Greece. While Mycenaean palace scribes mobilized many other resources by setting payment targets and monitoring their fulfillment, this was not the case for the substantial grain harvests recorded in Linear B texts. These grain harvests seem to have been the fruit of a partnership between the palace, which supplied oxen for tillage, and local *damos* communities, which owned the land and probably provided human labor, especially for harvest (Section 3.7). Recent sharecropping, in which two parties divided the processed grain on the threshing floor in agreed proportions, provides a model that accounts parsimoniously for the lack of targets or measures for monitoring production (Halstead, 1999). The so-called Harvesters Vase (e.g., Forsdyke, 1954), apparently illustrating a festive work party for large-scale winnowing, suggests that division of the harvest on the threshing floor was an important ceremonial occasion.

In Late Bronze Age Messenia, various individuals and groups paid flax fiber to the palace of Pylos. These payments, related to landholding, have been interpreted as a levy on fertile plots in well-watered areas particularly suited to growing and retting flax (Foster, 1981, 76). Recent Messenian hill farmers, however, grew flax for fiber on plots of only modest fertility and retted it in small pools, cultivating on a very small scale ("just one corner of a field, about the size of this living room") because harvesting by uprooting (necessary to recover the maximum length of stem) and especially beating out the fibers were so arduous. Circumstantial arguments suggest that individual payments to the palace were not large, the smallest perhaps representing the produce of a plot that could be worked *by hand* in a couple of days. Given the ordeal of processing for fiber, the palace arguably levied flax, not as a tithe or rent on modest allocations of rich land, but as a labor payment for larger allocations of unexceptional land suitable for grain crops (Halstead, 2001, 45–6).

Thirdly, although the contrasting processing requirements of free-threshing cereals and glume wheats notoriously complicate archaeobotanical analysis, they may shed light on changing crop frequencies. In the recent Mediterranean, while free-threshing cereals were usually stored as free grain, glume wheats were sometimes kept as spikelets, between initial threshing to break up the ear and straw and dehusking to free the grain from the glumes. Storage of spikelets spread the labor of dehusking, and spikelets were much less vulnerable than free grain to losses in storage. There is growing archaeobotanical evidence from well-preserved and well-sampled burnt destruction horizons that glume wheats were widely stored as spikelets in prehistory, for example, in southeast Europe from Early Neolithic Slatina in southern Bulgaria (Marinova, 2007), through Final Neolithic and Early Bronze Age Mandalo (Valamoti and Jones, 2003) and Late Bronze Age Assiros Toumba in northern Greece (Jones, 1987b), to Early Iron Age Iolkos in central Greece (Jones, 1982). Glume wheats were gradually displaced by free-threshing wheat across southern Europe, however, during the first millennium BC and early first millennium AD (Section 3.7). This shift doubtless reflects the higher cultural value in the Greco-Roman world of bread, ideally of flour from free-threshing wheat, over flat-breads, groats, and gruels, to which glume wheats were better suited (e.g., Garnsey, 1999, 119–122). It also had practical consequences: free-threshing wheat grain, having a shorter storage life than glume wheat spikelets, was a less dependable staple for self-sufficient farmers but also less heavy and bulky to transport. The emerging importance of free-threshing wheat thus facilitated the movement of grain both in large quantities, which is implied by the growth of towns too large to feed themselves, and over long distances, for which there is sporadic textual (e.g., Garnsey, 1988) and archaeobotanical (e.g., Pals and Hakbijl, 1991) evidence. An expanding grain trade would also have made the reliability of long-term storage less critical, while the high cultural value of bread may partly reflect the practical suitability of free-threshing wheat for feeding *urban* populations.

Fourthly, differences in the degree to which crops were processed before bulk storage have been claimed to account for the contrasting composition of charred plant assemblages (high vs. low ratios of crop grains to weed seeds, of glume wheat grains to glumes, and of large to small weed seeds) from two groups of Iron Age sites in southern England. This model makes the assumption, questioned by van der Veen and Jones (2006), that by-products of routine, poststorage processing for consumption dominate both groups of assemblages. Its attribution of claimed differences in preparation for storage to availability of labor, which in turn reflects organization of processing on a household versus collective level (Stevens, 2003; Fuller and Stevens, 2009), is also questionable. Reciprocal exchanges of labor, for example, in flailing of wheat in Garfagnana or initial threshing of spelt/emmer in Asturias, reduced the tedium of processing and enabled efficiencies of scale, but did not alter the degree of processing before storage. Conversely, additional labor led to more thorough processing, when Asturian households recruited an expert handler of the winnowing sieve, but more careless workmanship, when flailers were hired on a piecework rather than daily basis in Provence.

Nonetheless, processing by-products may shed valuable light on the social scale of agricultural production and consumption among early farmers. Burnt Neolithic "houses" at sites as widely dispersed as Catalhöyük in central Anatolia (Bogaard et al., 2009), Slatina in southern Bulgaria (Marinova, 2007), Lugo di Romagna in northern Italy (Rottoli and Pessina, 2007), and Hornstaad Hörnle 1A in the Alpine Foreland (Maier, 1999) have evidence of intramural grain storage, supporting their identification as "households" (cf. Flannery, 1972). Such well-preserved and well-sampled destruction deposits are rare, and any communal storage facilities located outdoors, suggested on architectural grounds for the earliest Neolithic in the Near East (Bogaard et al., 2009, 650), might be less prone to burning and archaeobotanical recognition. Glume bases discarded after dehusking of glume wheats are found widely on Neolithic sites in Europe, however, in small quantities, suggesting routine (e.g., daily) processing for a small social group (e.g., household) rather than bulk processing for long-term domestic or short-term collective consumption (e.g., Bogaard, 2004, 68). Rare intramural finds of stored grain, commonplace residues from dehusking glume wheats, and changing architecture (e.g., Flannery, 1972; Wright, 2000) thus concur in suggesting that, from an early stage of the Neolithic, stored grain was freed from collective control or obligations to share and that, in much of Neolithic Europe, "houses" may legitimately be regarded as representing some form of "household."

Fifthly, the flexible and opportunistic nature of recent storage practices highlights the danger, without direct evidence, of inferring the contents of containers encountered archaeologically and casts doubt on arguments (e.g., Halstead, 1989; van der Veen and Jones, 2006) that pits, because their effectiveness in controlling pests depends on airtight conditions, served primarily for long-term storage of surplus grain. Moreover, recent farming households often stored staple grain in sacks, wooden chests, baskets, or heaps that are rarely recognized archaeologically, particularly without a conflagration to char their contents. While the *minimum* scale of ancient storage provision may be illuminating (e.g., for Neolithic Catalhöyük – Bogaard *et al.*, 2009), therefore, it is difficult to demonstrate that *actual* storage was *in*sufficient, as in Christakis' (2008) argument – from the capacity of excavated jars – that the palaces of Middle to Late Bronze Age Crete did not redistribute staple grain on a large scale.

Sixthly, as noted earlier, grain for human consumption is generally processed more thoroughly than animal fodder, which is occasionally not threshed and winnowed, often not fine-sieved and especially hand-cleaned, and perhaps normally not dehusked, but the degree of processing is too variable to identify individual archaeobotanical samples safely as fodder or food on this basis (Jones, 1998). Archaeobotanical discrimination between food and fodder grain is rendered more difficult, but ultimately more rewarding, by the recent tendency for poor humans, especially in bad years, to consume incompletely processed grain or grain of a type (e.g., bitter vetch widely, barley in some regions) normally destined for animals, while privileged humans reinforced their status by consuming highly processed grain products (e.g., white flour with a high proportion of bran removed) and grain types (e.g., bread wheat) inaccessible to poorer neighbors. Contextualized archaeobotanical exploration of degrees of processing may thus shed light on the interplay between risk buffering and diacritical strategies, especially once more widespread analysis of charred dung has clarified the range (and degree of processing) of grains fed to livestock. Available data are sparse and of low resolution, but literary sources suggest a hierarchy of grain values (food vs. fodder, rich/urban vs. poor/rustic) for Greco-Roman antiquity (e.g., Garnsey, 1999, 119–122) that broadly matches that of the recent past (e.g., Papa, 1996; Halstead, 2012), while Linear B texts from Late Bronze Age southern Greece indicate differential use (by consumption context, social status, and gender) of two cereals (conventionally identified as "wheat" and "barley") and possibly likewise of flour and groats (Killen, 2004; Isaakidou, 2007). Various forms of preparation of grains for consumption, including coarse and fine cereal groats and split pulses, are known from Late Neolithic or Early Bronze Age contexts in northern Greece (Valamoti *et al.*, 2008; 2011), albeit without contextual hints for or against diacritical use. Bitter vetch, however, was unambiguously a fodder grain – consumed by humans only as a famine food – in the recent past and probably likewise in Greco-Roman antiquity (Hodkinson, 1988; Hillman, 2011), and yet its charred remains have been found in Greece in a fully cleaned state, perhaps intended as food rather than fodder, in contexts ranging chronologically from the Late Neolithic to postpalatial Late Bronze Age (Halstead, 2012). On present evidence, therefore, despite apparent Neolithic use of meat and rare beverages to differentiate commensal occasions (Halstead, 2012; Urem-Kotsou *et al.*, 2002), a clear hierarchy among grain crops developed late in the agricultural history of Greece, perhaps in the later Bronze Age as part of a suite of palatial strategies for mobilizing resources by manipulation of value regimes. More broadly, the reduction of barley grain

181

to low-status rations for livestock and poor humans is perhaps signaled by the sharp decline in the *naked* variety (more easily prepared for human consumption than the *hulled*), which occurs after the Neolithic in the Near East but after the Bronze or even Iron Age in Europe (Lister and Jones, 2013).

Finally, the labor costs of grinding grain by hand deserve comment. On the basis of experiments with a small saddle quern, of the type available before development in the mid-first millennium BC of the rotary quern, Samuel (2010, 464) suggests three hours per day would be needed to grind to flour enough emmer (perhaps 2 kg) for a household. Over a year, this would amount to more than 1000 hours (say 130 man-days) and would match even quite pessimistic estimates of the combined labor requirements for *manual* tilling and sowing, harvesting, and processing for storage of a similar amount of grain (say 800 kg, including seedcorn) (Table 4.1). As Wright (1994) has stressed for the transition from foraging to farming in southwest Asia, therefore, estimation of the labor costs of different subsistence strategies may be misleading if it only considers resource procurement and not processing for

Table 4.1 Estimated annual labor requirement for grinding emmer flour for a household on a saddle quern (after Samuel, 2010) compared with combined labor requirements for *manual* tilling/sowing, reaping, threshing, dehusking, and final cleaning of a similar amount of grain.

Task	Suggested labor productivity	Labor requirement (man-days)
Tillage/sowing of 0.8 ha	0.01–0.03 man-days/ha	27–80
Reaping 0.8 ha	≤0.1 ha/man-day	8–10
Manual threshing of 800 kg	100–300 kg/man-day	3–8
Dehusking of 800 kg	100–300 kg/man-day (??)	3–8
Grain cleaning	Variable	20
Total without grinding to flour		61–126
Grinding to flour	3 hours/day (??2 kg)	130

consumption (cf. White, 1965). Because grinding can be under-taken piecemeal, like dehusking and poststorage grain cleaning (and, less conveniently, initial threshing and winnowing), it is less likely directly to shape decisions on subsistence strategy than tasks such as reaping that take place under time stress during a short seasonal window. On the other hand, three hours per day spent grinding would tie up considerable labor that in the recent past was committed to other tasks (one rationale for the tradition of baking bread at weekly or longer intervals – Dimitriou, 1976–1978, 222). Women normally undertook domestic-scale food preparation in the recent past, and human skeletal evidence from Abu Hureyra in Syria (Molleson, 1989) suggests that grinding was a female task at a very early stage of cereal cultivation. The extent to which women in recent Mediterranean villages engaged in manual agricultural labor was variable, but they widely played a vital role in the key "bottleneck" activity of reaping. More generally, the widespread conviction among work-hardened elderly village women in Greece that their familiar hand-mill could not be used to make flour (and likewise, among glume wheat cultivators across southern Europe, that manual dehusking was not possible) high-lights the extent to which female labor was committed to a range of other domestic and agricultural tasks. If women in early farming communities spent three hours per day making flour on saddle querns, the harvest may have placed even greater restrictions than suggested earlier (Section 3.7) on the scale of cultivation possible with household labor. Alternatively, it is often assumed (because of the late displacement of hard glume wheats by soft bread wheat) that prehistoric farmers largely consumed cereals in the form of groats (e.g., in gruels) rather than flour (for bread). Although groat production is time-consuming on a saddle quern (Wright, 1994, 246, fig. 4), experimental demonstration of the difficulty of pro-ducing uniformly fine flour even on a rotary quern (Samuel, 2010, 462–463) suggests flour-based products may initially have been a relative luxury. Recent advances in archaeobotanical investigation of the final stages of cereal processing for consumption (Valamoti *et al.*, 2008) may thus shed important light on the nature of daily meals, on the rigor of daily "housework" routines, and on the availability of (probably female) labor for agricultural tasks.

References

Amoiralis, G. (1972) Agrotika ethima tis Tinou. *Laografia*, 28, 375–380.

Amouretti, M.-C. (1986) *Le pain et l' huile dans la Grèce antique: de l' araire au moulin*, Les Belles Lettres, Paris.

Anderson, P.C. (2003) Observations on the threshing sledge and its products in ancient and present-day Mesopotamia, in *Le traitement des récoltes: un regard sur la diversité du Néolithique au présent* (eds P.C. Anderson, L.S. Cummings, T.K. Schippers, and B. Simonel), Éditions APDCA, Antibes, pp. 417–438.

Anderson, P.C. (2006) Premiers tribulums, premières tractions animales au Proche-Orient vers 8000–7500 BP? in *Premiers chariots, premiers araires. La diffusion de la traction animale en Europe pendant les IVe et IIIe millénaires avant notre ère* (eds P. Pétrequin, R.-M. Arbogast, A.-M. Pétrequin, *et al.*), Paris, CNRS, pp. 299–316.

Anderson, P.C., Georges, J.-M., Vargiolu, R., and Zahouani, H. (2006) Insights from a tribological analysis of the tribulum. *Journal of Archaeological Science*, 33, 1559–1568.

Bogaard, A. (2004) *Neolithic Farming in Central Europe: An Archaeobotanical Study of Crop Husbandry Practices*, Routledge, London.

Bogaard, A., Charles, M., Twiss, K.C. *et al.* (2009) Private pantries and celebrated surplus: storing and sharing food at Neolithic Çatalhöyük, Central Anatolia. *Antiquity*, 83, 649–668.

Bogaard, A., Jones, G., and Charles, M. (2005) The impact of crop processing on the reconstruction of crop sowing time and cultivation intensity from archaeobotanical weed evidence. *Vegetation History & Archaeobotany*, 14, 505–509.

Camporesi, P. (1980) *Il pane selvaggio*, Il Mulino, Bologna.

Charles, M. (1998) Fodder from dung: the recognition and interpretation of dung-derived plant material from archaeological sites. *Environmental Archaeology*, 1, 111–122.

Christakis, K.S. (1999) Pithoi and food storage in Neopalatial Crete: a domestic perspective. *World Archaeology*, 31, 1–20.

Christakis, K.S. (2008) *The Politics of Storage: Storage and Sociopolitical Complexity in Neopalatial Crete*, INSTAP Academic Press, Philadelphia.

Cimmino, C. (1977) L'agricoltura nel regno di Napoli nell' età del risorgimento: la statistica murattiana del 1811. Le relazioni sulla provincia di Terra di Lavoro. *Rivista Storica di Terra di Lavoro*, 2, 15–143.

D'Andrea, A.C. and Haile, M. (2002) Traditional emmer processing in highland Ethiopia. *Journal of Ethnobiology*, 22, 179–217.

Dantin Cereceda, J. (1941) Distribución geografica de la escanda asturiana. *Estudios Geograficos*, 5, 739–797.

Dennell, R.W. (1976) The economic importance of plant resources represented on archaeological sites. *Journal of Archaeological Science*, 3, 229–247.

Dennell, R.W. (1978) *Early Farming in South Bulgaria from the VI to the III Millennia* BC, British Archaeological Reports, Oxford.

Dimitriou, N. (1976–78) To zumoma kai to fournisma tou psomiou sti Samo. *Laografia*, 31, 219–234.

Duplessy, B., Gabert, A., Valabrégue, J.P. *et al.* (1996) *Le livre de l' épeautre*, Edisud, Aix-en-Provence.

Fernandez Gonzalez, J.R. (1978) *Etnografia del valle de Ancares*, Universidad de Santiago de Compostela, Santiago de Compostela.

Flannery, K.V. (1972) The origins of the village as a settlement type in Mesoamerica and the Near East: a comparative study, in *Man, Settlement and Urbanism* (eds P.J. Ucko, R. Tringham, and G.W. Dimbleby), Duckworth, London, pp. 23–53.

Forbes, H. (1989) Of grandfathers and grand theories: the hierarchised ordering of responses to hazard in a Greek rural community, in *Bad Year Economics* (eds P. Halstead and J. O'Shea), Cambridge University Press, Cambridge, UK, pp. 87–97.

Forsdyke, J. (1954) The 'Harvester' Vase of Agia Triada. *Journal of the Warburg and Courtauld Institutes*, 17, 1–9.

Forte, M.A. (2009) *A Mediterranean Mountain: Landscape and Land Use on the Cairo Massif, Central Italy, 1700–1970* A.D. PhD thesis. University of Sheffield.

Foster, E.D. (1981) The flax impost at Pylos and Mycenaean landholding. *Minos*, 17, 67–121.

Fuller, D.Q. and Stevens, C.J. (2009) Agriculture and the development of complex societies: an archaeobotanical agenda, in *From Foragers to Farmers: Papers in Honour of Gordon C. Hillman* (eds A.S. Fairbairn and E. Weiss), Oxford, Oxbow, pp. 37–57.

185

Gaillard, E.-M. (1997) *Les blés de l' été, 3: au temps des aires*, Les Alpes de Lumière, Salagon.

Garnsey, P. (1988) *Famine and Food Supply in the Graeco-Roman World: Responses to Risk and Crisis*, Cambridge University Press, Cambridge, UK.

Garnsey, P. (1999) *Food and Society in Classical Antiquity*, Cambridge University Press, Cambridge, UK.

Halstead, P. (1989) The economy has a normal surplus: economic stability and social change among early farming communities of Thessaly, Greece, in *Bad Year Economics* (eds P. Halstead and J. O'Shea), Cambridge University Press, Cambridge, UK, pp. 68–80.

Halstead, P. (1990) Waste not, want not: traditional responses to crop failure in Greece. *Rural History*, 1, 147–164.

Halstead, P. (1999) Surplus and share-croppers: the grain production strategies of Mycenaean palaces, in *MELETEMATA. Studies Presented to Malcolm H. Wiener as he Enters his 65th Year* (eds P. Betancourt, V. Karageorghis, R. Laffineur, and W.D. Niemeier), University of Liège, Liège, pp. 319–326.

Halstead, P. (2001) Mycenaean wheat, flax and sheep: palatial intervention in farming and its implications for rural society, in *Economy and Politics in the Mycenaean Palace States* (eds S. Voutsaki and J. Killen), Cambridge Philological Society, Cambridge, UK, pp. 38–50.

Halstead, P. (2012) Feast, food and fodder in Neolithic-Bronze Age Greece: commensality and the construction of value, in Between Feasts and Daily Meals. Towards an Archaeology of Commensal Spaces (ed. S. Pollock). *eTopoi. Journal for Ancient Studies*, special volume 2, pp. 21–51.

Halstead, P. and Jones, G. (1989) Agrarian ecology in the Greek islands: time stress, scale and risk. *Journal of Hellenic Studies*, 109, 41–55.

Hillman, G. (1981) Reconstructing crop husbandry practices from charred remains of crops, in *Farming Practice in British Prehistory* (ed. R. Mercer), Edinburgh University Press, Edinburgh, pp. 123–162.

Hillman, G. (1984) Traditional husbandry and processing of archaic cereals in recent times: part 1, the glume wheats. *Bulletin on Sumerian Agriculture*, 1, 114–152.

Hillman, G. (1985) Traditional husbandry and processing of archaic cereals in recent times: part 2, the free-threshing cereals. *Bulletin on Sumerian Agriculture*, 2, 1–31.

Hillman, G. (2011) The grain from the Granary, in *Well Built Mycenae, 16/17: The Post-Palatial Levels* (ed. E.B. French), Oxbow, Oxford, pp. 748–781.

Hionidou, V. (2011) What do starving people eat? The case of Greece through oral history. *Continuity and Change*, 26, 113–134.

Hodkinson, S. (1988) Animal husbandry in the Greek polis, in *Pastoral Economies in Classical Antiquity* (ed. C.R. Whittaker), Cambridge Philological Society, Cambridge, UK, pp. 35–74.

Isaakidou, V. (2007) Cooking in the labyrinth: exploring 'cuisine' at Bronze Age Knossos, in *Cooking Up the Past: Food and Culinary Practices in the Neolithic and Bronze Age Aegean* (eds C. Mee and J. Renard), Oxbow, Oxford, pp. 5–24.

Jones, G. (1982) Cereal and pulse remains from Protogeometric and Geometric Iolkos, Thessaly. *Anthropologika*, 3, 75–78.

Jones, G. (1987a) A statistical approach to the archaeological identification of crop processing. *Journal of Archaeological Science*, 14, 311–323.

Jones, G. (1987b) Agricultural practice in Greek prehistory. *Annual of the British School at Athens*, 82, 115–123.

Jones, G. (1998) Distinguishing food from fodder in the archaeobotanical record. *Environmental Archaeology*, 1, 95–98.

Jones, G. and Halstead, P. (1995) Maslins, mixtures and monocrops: on the interpretation of archaeobotanical crop samples of heterogeneous composition. *Journal of Archaeological Science*, 22, 103–114.

Jones, M. (1985) Archaeobotany beyond subsistence reconstruction, in *Beyond Domestication in Prehistoric Europe: Investigations in Subsistence Archaeology and Social Complexity* (eds G. Barker and C. Gamble), Academic Press, New York, pp. 107–128.

Karanastasis, A.M. (1952) Oi zevgades tis Ko. I zwi kai oi askholies ton. *Laografia*, 14, 201–303.

Killen, J. (2004) Wheat, barley, flour, olives and figs on Linear B tablets, in *Food, Cuisine and Society in Prehistoric Greece* (eds P. Halstead and J.C. Barrett), Oxbow, Oxford, pp. 155–173.

Kizlaris, T. (1938–1948) Agrotikos vios ton Thrakon. *Laografia*, 12, 386–416.

Lister, D.L. and Jones, M.K. (2013) Is naked barley an eastern or a western crop? The combined evidence of archaeobotany and genetics. *Vegetation History & Archaeobotany*, 22, 439–446.

Littauer, M.A. and Crouwel, J.H. (1990) Ceremonial threshing in the Ancient Near East, I. Archaeological evidence. *Iraq*, 52, 15–19.

Llaty, C. (1997) L' égrenage traditionnel des céréales dans les Alpes du Sud: un 'melting pot' technique, in *Les blés de l' été, 3: au temps des aires* (ed. E.-M. Gaillard), Les Alpes de Lumière, Salagon, pp. 105–114.

Sorting the Wheat from the Chaff

Loukopoulos, D. (1983) *Georgika tis Roumelis*, Dodoni, Athens.

Maier, U. (1999) Agricultural activities and land use in a neolithic village around 3900 BC: Hornstaad Hörnle 1A, Lake Constance, Germany. *Vegetation History & Archaeobotany*, 8, 87–94.

Marinova, E. (2007) Archaeobotanical data from the early Neolithic of Bulgaria, in *The Origins and Spread of Domestic Plants in Southwest Asia and Europe* (eds S. Colledge and J. Conolly), Left Coast Press, Walnut Creek, pp. 93–109.

Megas, G.A. (1946) *Thessalikai oikiseis*, Department of Reconstruction, Athens.

Molleson, T. (1989) Seed preparation in the Mesolithic: the osteological evidence. *Antiquity*, 63, 356–362.

Neira Martinez, J. (1955) *El habla de Lena*, Instituto de Estudios Asturianos, Diputacion de Asturias, Oviedo.

Nesbitt, M. and Samuel, D. (1996) From staple crop to extinction? The archaeology and history of the hulled wheats, in *Hulled Wheats: Promoting the Conservation and Use of Underutilized and Neglected Crops 4* (eds S. Padulosi, K. Hammer, and J. Heller), International Plant Genetic Resources Institute, Rome, pp. 41–100.

Pagkalos, G.E. (1983) *Peri tou glossikou idiomatos tis Kritis, 7: ta laografika*, Kentro Erevnis Ellinikis Laografias, Akadimias Athinon, Athens.

Palanca, F. (1991) Agricultura, in *Temes d' etnografia Valenciana 2: utillatge agrícola i ramaderia* (eds F. Martínez and F. Palanca), Institució Valenciana d' Estudis i Investigació, Valencia, pp. 11–181.

Palmer, C. (1998) 'Following the plough': the agricultural environment of northern Jordan. *Levant*, 30, 129–165.

Pals, J.P. and Hakbijl, T. (1991) Weed and insect infestation of a grain cargo in a ship at the Roman fort of Laurium in Woerden (Province of Zuid-Holland). *Review of Palaeobotany and Palynology*, 73, 287–300.

Papa, C. (1996) The 'farre de Montelione': landrace and representation, in *Hulled Wheats: Promoting the Conservation and Use of Underutilized and Neglected Crops 4* (eds S. Padulosi, K. Hammer, and J. Heller), International Plant Genetic Resources Institute, Rome, pp. 154–171.

Peña-Chocarro, L. (1996) In situ conservation of hulled wheat species: the case of Spain, in *Hulled Wheats: Promoting the Conservation and Use of Underutilized and Neglected Crops 4* (eds S. Padulosi, K. Hammer, and J. Heller), International Plant Genetic Resources Institute, Rome, pp. 129–146.

Peña-Chocarro, L. (1999) *Prehistoric Agriculture in Southern Spain During the Neolithic and the Bronze Age*, Archaeopress, Oxford.

Petropoulos, D.A. (1952) Sumvoli is tin erevnan ton laikon metron kai stathmon. *Epetiris tou Laografikou Arkhiou*, 7, 57–101.

Reynolds, P.J. (1974) Experimental Iron Age storage pits. *Proceedings of the Prehistoric Society*, 40, 118–131.

Rottoli, M. and Pessina, A. (2007) Neolithic agriculture in Italy: an update of archaeobotanical data with particular emphasis on northern settlements, in *The Origins and Spread of Domestic Plants in Southwest Asia and Europe* (eds S. Colledge and J. Conolly), Left Coast Press, Walnut Creek, pp. 141–153.

Russell, K.W. (1988) *After Eden: The Behavioral Ecology of Early Food Production in the Near East and North Africa*, British Archaeological Reports, Oxford.

Samuel, D. (2010) Experimental grinding and ancient Egyptian flour production, in *Beyond the Horizon: Studies in Egyptian Art, Archaeology and History in Honour of Barry J. Kemp* (eds S. Ikram and A. Dodson), American University in Cairo Press, Cairo, pp. 456–477.

Sarpaki, A. (1992) The palaeoethnobotanical approach. The Mediterranean triad or is it a quartet?, in *Agriculture in Ancient Greece* (ed. B. Wells), Swedish Institute at Athens, Stockholm, pp. 61–75.

Sfakianos, N. (1979–81) Paradosiaki tekhniki kai ethima tis kalliergeias kai tis enapothikeusis tou krithariou sti Naxo. *Laografia*, 32, 392–397.

Sherratt, A. (2006) La traction animale et la transformation de l'Europe néolithique, in *Premiers chariots, premiers araires. La diffusion de la traction animale en Europe pendant les IVe et IIIe millénaires avant notre ère* (eds P. Pétrequin, R.-M. Arbogast, A.-M. Pétrequin *et al.*), CNRS, Paris, pp. 329–360.

Shkurti, S. (1979) Le battage des cereales. *Ethnographie Albanaise*, 9, 57–111.

Sigaut, F. (1988) A method for identifying grain storage techniques and its application for European agricultural history. *Tools & Tillage*, 6, 3–32.

Slinis, M.K. (1938–1948) Agrotika ethima Drumou Makedonias. *Laografia*, 12, 92–103.

Spurr, M.S. (1986) *Arable Cultivation in Roman Italy c.200 B.C.–C.A.D. 100*, Society for the Promotion of Roman Studies, London.

Stevens, C.J. (2003) An investigation of agricultural consumption and production models for prehistoric and Roman Britain. *Environmental Archaeology*, 8, 61–76.

Urem-Kotsou, D., Stern, B., Heron, C., and Kotsakis, K. (2002) Birch-bark tar at Neolithic Makriyalos, Greece. *Antiquity*, 76, 962–967.

Valamoti, S.M. and Jones, G. (2003) Plant diversity and storage at Mandalo, Macedonia, Greece: archaeobotanical evidence from the Final Neolithic and Early Bronze Age. *Annual of the British School at Athens*, 98, 1–35.

Valamoti, S.M. and Anastasaki, S. (2007) A daily bread – prepared but once a year. *Petits Propos Culinaires*, 84, 75–101.

Valamoti, S.-M., Samuel, D., Bayram, M., and Marinova, E. (2008) Prehistoric cereal foods from Greece and Bulgaria: investigation of starch micro-structure in experimental and archaeological charred remains. *Vegetation History & Archaeobotany*, 17, 265–276.

Valamoti, S.M., Moniaki, A., and Karathanou, A. (2011) An investigation of processing and consumption of pulses among prehistoric societies: archaeobotanical, experimental and ethnographic evidence from Greece. *Vegetation History & Archaeobotany*, 20, 381–396.

van der Veen, M. and Jones, G. (2006) A re-analysis of agricultural production and consumption: implications for understanding the British Iron Age. *Vegetation History & Archaeobotany*, 15, 217–228.

Vrontis, A.G. (1938–1948) Oi zevgades tis Rodou. *Laografia*, 12, 104–129.

Weinstein, M. (1973) Household structures and activities. *Anatolian Studies*, 23, 271–276.

White, K.D. (1965) The productivity of labour in Roman agriculture. *Antiquity*, 39, 102–107.

Whittaker, J. (1999) Alonia: the ethnoarchaeology of Cypriot threshing floors. *Journal of Mediterranean Archaeology*, 12, 7–25.

Wright, K. (1994) Ground-stone tools and hunter-gatherer subsistence in southwest Asia: implications for the transition to farming. *American Antiquity*, 59, 238–263.

Wright, K. (2000) The social origins of cooking and dining in early villages of western Asia. *Proceedings of the Prehistoric Society*, 66, 89–121.

5

Managing the Land
Coping with Failure and Planning for Success

Despite occasionally claiming that "once sown, wheat doesn't need you until harvest," farmers inspected growing crops en route to other tasks and, if practicable, responded to problems arising from year-to-year variation in weather and pests superimposed upon husbandry practices (e.g., rotation) that varied on a 2–10-year timescale. This chapter explores such reactive measures and also proactive practices on an *interannual* timescale, intermediate between the *annual* round of growing and processing field crops (Chapters 2, 3, and 4), and household strategies on a *generational* timescale (Chapter 6).

5.1 Watching the Corn Grow

The ideal sowing "window," between the first steady autumn rain and the onset of cold weather, was of variable duration, and crops were often sown too early or late, in ground too dry, wet, or frozen

Two Oxen Ahead: Pre-Mechanized Farming in the Mediterranean, First Edition.
Paul Halstead. © 2014 Paul Halstead. Published 2014 by John Wiley & Sons, Ltd.

for thorough tillage and even germination. Konstantinos of Neo Sidirokhori also "left the odd bare patch when sowing early in the morning or late at night." After sowing, therefore, farmers' first concern was the success of germination, and they knew how soon crops should sprout – for example, wheat in lowland northern Greece after 8–10 days in October and 10–12 days in cooler November. Konstantinos had resown bare patches and rarely, like Nikolaos in Kolindros and Nikos in southern Greek Metaxada, whole fields. Early resowing was more likely to succeed (Kostakis, 1976–1978, 89), and Koula in Paliambela recalls her father scratching the surface of recently sown fields to see if germinating seed had survived severe early frosts. Before mechanization, however, many farmers struggled to sow their fields even once, and the window for resowing was especially short to the south, where summer drought curtailed the growing season early.

As the sprouted crop developed through winter, severe frost might cause significant losses, opening gaps in the crop or even destroying whole swathes, as in 1986–1987 in the hills north of Assiros, where wheat sown early recovered thanks to a developed root system, but that sown late was killed on north-facing slopes (where frost was hardest) and hilltops (where wind had blown off protecting snow). Heavy rain caused similar problems. In winter, the streams bordering Paliambela sometimes caused localized damage to crops but downstream below Aiginio flooded fields more frequently and extensively, so that "we sowed wheat in October–November on the off chance and sometimes it did very well, but often we plowed up all or part of the field and in spring sowed it again with maize, beans, or sesame."

In spring, especially where patchy germination or winter losses had left gaps in the crop, warmer weather encouraged growth of weeds that impeded the development, harvesting, processing, and storage of grain crops. Many informants inspected fields, therefore, shortly after sowing and again in March–April. They perhaps weeded moderately infested fields (Section 5.5), but often resowed with summer crops those that were severely affected or used them for fodder. In Aiginio, Dokas recalls, "wheat [in flooded fields] so weed infested that we mowed it [green] for the animals," while Dimos watched a neighbor cut half a dozen sheaves of wheat entangled with wild vetches and tares, before giving up and letting his livestock graze the crop, later burning the stubble to destroy fallen weed seeds. Khristos in nearby Kitros once scythed for his sheep 1.2 ha of weedy lentils on land he had plowed carelessly.

A warm and wet spring might also cause excessive crop growth. In northern Greece, Konstantinos at Neo Sidirokhori reckoned this showed in wheat on particularly fertile land as early as January– February, when sheep grazing lightly could retard growth and reduce the risk of "burning" by late frost. Alexis in Assiros observed that sowing thickly (forcing competition for light) or early favored vigorous growth, as did a mild autumn. He too grazed cereals "to avoid burning by frost," but a commoner rationale was to prevent the crop from becoming so tall in a wet spring that wind or rain beat it down; depending when the crop lodged, its development was impaired and it might fail altogether. Preventive grazing was commonest for free-threshing wheat that usually occupied the most fertile land, but barley, oat, rye, and glume wheats all recovered from early grazing given favorable conditions – unlike pulses (also Gill and Vear, 1966). On heavily manured land at Lazarades in the hills of northern Greece, free-threshing wheat was grazed and rye not, because long rye straw served for roofing sheepfolds.

Cereals only recovered from grazing until "ear emergence" or "stem formation" when they were about shin high (for wheat in lowland Greece usually until March–early April). As ever, Ilias in Metaxada had a mnemonic: "wheat puts on one [straw] node in five months and then five in one month" (so a crop sown in October– November could be grazed until March–April). Even early preventive grazing, however, was a gamble: a crop grazed lightly might lodge if a wet spring followed, but one grazed heavily without subsequent rain might not develop harvestable grain. Farmers considered weather and field quality in judging how hard to graze each crop. In northern Greece, they drove sheep across growing cereals (whole and part fields, ignoring *patches* of excessive growth) for an hour or two to ensure an even, light "trim" ("just a hand"), repeating this if necessary or if the sheep were hungry enough to warrant risking damage. According to the Paliambela *tsípouro* circle, "it was not worth the effort of grazing the one strémma [0.1 ha] you had manured if you only had five sheep; you asked someone with 50 sheep to graze it for a couple of hours for two or three evenings." Herders normally paid a fee, in cash or kind, though some grazed distant plots, unobserved, more heavily than agreed. Goats were less common than sheep on fertile land prone to lodging, but Mitsos considers them a satisfactory substitute: "sheep are better because they graze closely; goats prefer taller plants but were hungry then and did a decent job." Most informants considered cattle unsuitable: being heavier and larger, they trampled the crop. Given reasonable spring rainfall, preventive grazing encouraged tillering, denser and shorter stands, and successful harvests, but Mitsos suffered significant losses after gambling for the sake of his sheep on spring rains that did not arrive.

Excessive early cereal growth was also a concern, as a prelude to lodging rather than frost damage, in the hills of southwest mainland Greece, where mild winters compensated for poor soils. Sheep were banned from land with growing winter crops, making preventive grazing impossible, at Iklaina and Milioti, but flocks were occasionally let into wheat or barley on the best fields at Metaxada and Potamia. With favorable spring rainfall, grazing could again be beneficial, as Panagiotis recalled from a dispute in Potamia after sheep got into a cereal field around Christmas. In these hill villages, however, excessive growth often affected just a single terrace and was grazed by (or trimmed with a sickle to feed) a few house-goats or sheep. Ilias in Metaxada reckoned on cutting a 0.05 ha terrace in half a man-day, though cutting rather than grazing was commoner for *patches* of vigorous growth under trees where sheep slept in summer. Trimming by hand or with a few house-goats, as also at Tharounia in Euboea, reflects both the localized nature of vigorous growth on poor soils and concern to deal with such patches when grain production overall was limited. As in northern Greece, both sheep and goats were considered suitable preventive grazers, but not cattle – for fear of trampling.

194

In central Crete, sprouting cereals were cut to prevent lodging in Epano Simi Viannou in 1932 but perhaps on a new (and hence unusually fertile) field or terrace (Pagkalos, 1983, 7). Lodging was almost unknown in the hill village of Kalo Khorio and uncommon even on the heaviest soils around lowland Knossos. With scarce spring rainfall, cereal stands were unlikely to grow tall, lodge, or recover from grazing. Even informants aware of the practice further north insisted that cereals for grain were not grazed; lodging in a wet spring was far less likely than stunted growth in a drought year. Safer precautions, according to Giorgis in Knossos, were to avoid manuring cereals (Section 5.3.1.4) and delay sowing the heaviest fields. Sparser sowing than in northern Greece also favored tillering over tall growth (Section 2.4). In lowland southeast Italy, excessive cereal growth was variously grazed or trimmed (Spurr, 1986, 64–65). In central Italy, on Monte Cairo, Luigi recalled grazing rye, but not wheat (presumably it did not recover). At Zuheros in the hills of southern Spain, grazing of wheat was again avoided, "because it caused tillering and ears worth nothing." Preventive grazing did not benefit crops struggling with low rainfall or poor soils.

In rainy upland Asturias, spelt/emmer on manured land suffers from lodging rather than drought. A few decades ago, it was grown mainly on poorer outfields where it was less likely to lodge or recover from grazing, but some elderly informants recall preventive grazing, for example, on the rich field of an absentee landowner at Piñera. Nowadays, it is concentrated on heavily manured infield plots with greater risk of lodging, but few villagers have sheep or goats. Leandro in Tiós saw preventive grazing with sheep in his youth and occasionally lets his cows into tall spelt/emmer, keeping them moving to prevent trampling of the crop. Many current plots are also rather small for grazing, and Carmin, after seeing the benefits of an intrusion by her house-goats, now *scythes* spelt/emmer in one tiny garden at Piñera. Most villagers retard spelt/emmer by sowing late or harrowing the emerging crop – measures practicable because of small-scale cultivation – or accept losses from lodging.

Once cereal stems begin to grow upwards, the *maximum* number of plants and grains is set, but not eventual yields. In the

Mediterranean, the greatest concern is usually spring rainfall, especially after insufficient winter precipitation or late sowing and on thin (e.g., Lithourgidis, Damalas, and Gagianas, 2006) or poorly tilled soil. "If it rains in March–April" is a common response in southern Greece to questions about yields. In northern Greece and upland central Crete, where crops ripen later, the refrain is "if it rains in April–May." "The water of May" similarly obsesses farmers around Borja in northern Spain (Carranza Alcalde, 2009, 27–28). Unless spring rainfall makes up any moisture deficit, crops are likely to be stunted and grain yields light, especially if fertile conditions have promoted unsustainable growth. With appropriate infrastructure (mainly in the Iberian Peninsula), scarcity of "God's water" was traditionally compensated by irrigation. Around Borja (Garcia Manrique, 1960, 129; Carranza Alcalde, 2009, 111), as in fourteenth-century AD Valencia (Glick, 1970, 29, 248), staple cereals and vegetables took priority over vines and olives in drought years, when irrigation water too is scarce. Elsewhere in southern Europe, premechanized irrigation was largely restricted to gardens or orchards, and for winter field crops, measures to mitigate late spring or early summer drought were limited to early sowing, weed control, and appeals for rain. In Aragon, northern Spain, icons and relics were paraded and the latter sometimes wetted (Cuadrat Prats, 2008, 43–44; Carranza Alcalde, 2009, 27–29). Prayer was also combined with magic in southeast Europe where a young girl, dressed in leaves, toured the village and was wetted at each house; similar, apparently ancient, ceremonies took place across Turkey and the Near East (Basgöz, 1967; 2007). In Greece, a tortoise was placed upside down under a clod of mud to plead for dissolving rain (Slinis, 1938–1948, 98) or hung in a tree to intercede for its tormentors (Loukopoulos, 1983, 206).

If early sowing, prayer, and magic failed, the harvest might be very thin. On Naxos in summer 1990, barley too stunted to reap was grazed in situ (Figure 5.1). At Kastrisianika on Kithira, Thanasis recalls that "sometimes, on the poorest fields, wheat/barley *smigádi* was too short to harvest and we let the animals graze it, but if tall

Figure 5.1 Cattle grazing drought-stunted barley at Khora, Naxos, Cyclades.

enough to grasp, we reaped it, no matter how poor, because we needed straw for the donkeys over winter." On poor soils in drought years at Vasiliki, east Crete, Peris uprooted cereals, too short to reap with a sickle, as fodder for his work animals. If only one or two plots (perhaps sown late or on soil with poor water retention) were stunted, they might be cut green, a few weeks early, for hay as Mimis described for wheat and barley at Asoutaina in the Messenian hills.

Conversely, if farmers did not retard vigorous early growth and abundant spring rainfall followed, the resulting tall crop was easily flattened by strong wind or rain or, in Asturias, weighed down by the fine June drizzle that collected on spelt/emmer and its scrambling weeds: "el orballo de San Juan estropea el pan" or "spelt spoils if fine spray falls on St John's Day [June 24]." The later in the growing season a crop lodged, the less likely it was to recover, making it difficult to harvest. Anyway, lodged ears often remained undeveloped or spoiled (Percival, 1974, 78) and, at best, were discolored. At Castiglione di Garfagnana, Sergio found dark emmer spikelets looked better after dehusking, but in Asturian Zureda, Severina's lodged spelt/emmer produced black dehusked grain, and in Xomezana, Delfina used her blackest lodged ears as fodder. In southern Spain, Antonio at Zuheros harvested lodged wheat to feed stalled livestock, while the Paliambela *tsípouro* circle left lodged wheat with little or no grain for sheep or pigs to graze in situ. In Cretan Knossos, however, Giorgis had seen livestock reject lodged straw discolored by mold.

Even after good spring and winter growth, desiccating winds might shrivel unripe grain, fungal attack spoil the ear, and hail or locusts or birds decimate a ripe and abundant crop, but heavy losses were sufficiently infrequent that most elderly farmers remember the dates of a handful of severe events. One evening in 1986, the assembled grandfathers outside the cobbler's workshop in Assiros cited 1924 and 1948 as the two worst droughts in their collective memory, spanning seven decades, while a desiccating *lívas* wind around May 20 in 1932 devastatingly caught cereals at the vulnerable milk-ripe stage. In Paliambela, Mitsos remembers a violent April hailstorm in the late 1930s that cut down growing cereals "yis madiám" (like the Biblical laying waste of Midian), while 1936 was particularly bad for rain-induced weed infestation and winter 1989–1990 exceptionally dry. "Hail does favors," striking patchily, as Koula recalls of an April hailstorm around 1955 that leveled crops south and east of Paliambela, but not north and west. Likewise, pests or desiccating winds may only affect some crops, depending on their stage of development. Thus, in early summer of 1991 and 1994, the *lívas* harmed ripe wheat around Assiros less than milk-ripe wheat in the hills to the north, but in 1993, it struck earlier, causing losses around Assiros where the grain was filling, but not to less advanced crops in the hills. In 1988, the *lívas* caught late-sown wheat around Assiros, but not that sown early. Hail, *lívas* winds and locusts thus caused less wholesale losses than severe drought, such that those hardest hit by the 1955 hailstorm in Paliambela worked as harvest laborers, paid in kind, in adjacent villages or for unaffected neighbors. Farmers also salvaged whatever they could with livestock. Crops cut down by the 1930s hailstorm were grazed in situ and, because rain followed in early May, recovered to yield a modest grain harvest for some and a better hay harvest for others. After the 1955 storm, Koula's husband made hay with the destroyed crops, and the following winter, his livestock gave more milk than on their usual diet of straw. The drought of 1989–1990, by contrast, was felt widely in the region and caused almost total failure of winter cereals and severe reductions in pasture across much of southeastern Greece.

As Thanasis noted of 1930s Kithira, "we could not buy bread from the baker and the island did not import grain, so people worked hard to grow their cereals." Farmers monitored growing crops, especially in the first weeks after sowing, in spring when weeds started to flourish, and after extreme weather. There was scope for damage limitation by resowing, preventive grazing, or weeding early in the growing season, while prompt harvesting mitigated hazards near the end (Section 3.2). Rainfall in early summer, too late to save drought-stricken winter crops, might allow sowing of additional maize or sesame – as in Assiros after the 1924 and 1948 droughts. Otherwise, as the growing season advanced, farmers could do little to prevent losses and were often reduced to grazing failed crops or harvesting them for fodder. Crop failure was best averted by thorough seedbed preparation and prompt sowing and by appropriate husbandry over previous years.

5.2 Planning for Success: Fallowing and Rotation

5.2.1 Fallowing

Across the Mediterranean, *cultivated* fallow was until recently common and believed to benefit subsequent crops, as Vangelis in central Cretan Ano Asites explains with a parable:

> An old man went blind. One day, he called his sons and asked them, "have you plowed our fallow field?" When they replied "we have,"

199

he sent them to do it again. Later he asked them the same question, they answered "we have," and he sent them to plow it again. He told them to plow the field five times, and each time, they said, "we have," but they only plowed it four times. At harvest time, the old man told his sons, "take me to the field that we had fallow and put me in the middle." When they did so, he said, "give me a sickle," and reaped what he could from where he sat. Then, he said to his sons, "you lied to me; you did not work the field five times, because I have only cut four, not five, sheaves of barley."

Academics have regarded winter cereals alternating with culti-vated fallow as characteristic of "traditional" Mediterranean agri-culture, reflecting the need to accumulate two years of rainfall for a successful crop (e.g., Semple, 1932; Grigg, 1974, 125). Some elderly farmers had heard this rationale from passing agronomists, but almost all refer to both cultivated and uncultivated fallow as "resting" the land – "do not milk the field every year" (Kostakis, 1976–1978, 83). Pressed to elaborate, some cited improvement of fer-tility: in lowland northern Greece, "before the war [1940s], we left the occasional field fallow because we did not have chemical fertil-izers" (Paliambela) and "cultivated fallow stopped when fertilizers arrived" (Assiros); in the hills of central Greece, "we sowed the good fields every year, but the poorer ones only every second year" (Tharounia); and in lowland central Crete, "just like the crop grows taller where a pile of sticks has been burnt, so the sun burning a plowed field works like fertilizer" (Knossos) and "a dry garden [on cultivated fallow] was like manure" (Aloides).

Some farmers noted that cultivated fallow destroys weeds (e.g., Forbes, 1976a; Halstead and Jones, 1989), while many stressed prac-tical constraints on its application. Those with little land, such as the Paliambela Thracians or poorer Assiros farmers, could not afford regular fallow, though they saw the benefits in larger land-owners' fields. For Nikolaos in Kolindros, fallowing was for those "with lots of land or infertile fields." At Anogia in upland central Crete, Manolis "sowed fields and terraces alike each year; we did not have space for cultivated fallow." His namesake at southeast Cretan Stavrokhori agreed. Conversely, large landowners in early twentieth-century Assiros and Kolindros left fallow both because it boosted yields and because their work animals could not sow all their fields. Some farmers with more modest holdings did likewise, on a small scale, because their small draft *cows* could not plow all their fields at sowing time – although such a pair might also struggle to till fallow in a dry spring and, even more so, to break uncultivated fallow the following autumn (Section 2.6.1). Finally, fields might be left fallow (and perhaps *un*cultivated) because pasture was scarce.

At Mirtos in southeastern Crete, Daskalos observed that, after bare fallow, cereals were higher yielding and withstood drought better: "cereals took a month to become thirsty after cultivated fallow and only 10 days otherwise; well-worked fallow drank whatever rain there was." The destruction of weeds also doubtless improved water retention. Southeast Crete is one of the driest places in Europe, but the common practice among *small*holders here – as elsewhere – of alternating staple cereals with fodder crops rather than fallow argues against accumulated soil moisture as the principal benefit of cultivated fallow. Long-term experiments are, at best, ambivalent on the ability of cultivated fallow to store rainfall for subsequent years (Hudson, 1987, 26; Latta and O'Leary, 2003), and since rainfall is highly variable in dry areas, fields are often fallowed in drought years with minimal water to carry forward. Significantly, adoption of industrial fertilizer, weed killer, and tractors, rather than improved water supply, accompanied the later twentieth-century abandonment of cultivated fallow across the Mediterranean. Elderly farmers with little formal education understood its costs and benefits better than many agricultural scientists.

5.2.2 Crop rotation

Apart from the need to rest or fertilize fields, farmers understood that repeated sowing of the same crop on the same ground favors weeds, pests, and diseases and reduces yields. In addition to alternating winter cereals and cultivated fallow, other two-year and longer rotations were widespread.

Managing the Land

In northern Greece, the classic Mediterranean rotation, described by elderly Assiros residents as the early twentieth-century norm, was best matched by the Ottoman beys' sharecroppers and the largest post-Ottoman landowners (farming 10 ha or more) who alternated winter grain crops with cultivated fallow but planted perhaps half of the latter – subject to manpower and spring rain – with unirrigated summer crops. Surplus-producing farmers with more modest landholdings (5–10 ha) approximated to a three-course rotation of winter wheat, followed by less demanding winter barley or oats for fodder, then cultivated fallow or a summer crop. If it rained in early summer, those with strong work animals might plow up fresh wheat stubble ("while the sheaves were still in the field") before the sun hardened the exposed surface and, after a short summer-long cultivated fallow, sow wheat again, though experienced observers could identify such crops while growing. Those with a smaller holding of 4 ha practiced three-course rotation but normally planted all their "fallow" fields with summer crops. Those with only 2–3 ha had the same aspirations, but some lacked work animals and had to adjust to the availability of hired teams or neighbors willing to engage in sharecropping ("*misiaká*," literally "halves"). The frequency of cultivated fallow and proportion of this unsown thus both declined with decreasing size of landholding.

Of the relatively dependable winter cereals, wheat was in greatest market demand and was sown most extensively at Assiros, especially on larger holdings, while farmers grew various pulses and fodder cereals on a smaller scale, mainly for their own households and livestock. Pulses were sometimes sown in winter with wheat and sometimes later (especially by large landowners – Section 2.3) on cultivated fallow. The less dependable summer crops, for sale and domestic consumption, were at the mercy of spring and early summer rain, although broadcast sesame and planted maize required moisture at slightly different times. "Black Vangelis," in his prime one of the largest local landowners, "sowed a little maize, a little sesame, a little cotton; if one did not grow, the other did." In addition to constraints of landholding, the crops sown by each farmer reflected the needs of work animals (ideally, bitter vetch for cattle, oats for horses) and manpower for labor-intensive summer crops, with further adjustment for interannual variation in weather.

In Paliambela, the Thracian refugees received landholdings at the lower end of the range in Assiros and their children inherited even less, so fallow usually carried summer crops. Mitsos "rarely got much from the maize because it needed summer rain, but it was good for the following wheat." Including rented fields, he devoted perhaps 1.5–2 ha to wheat (for domestic consumption and sale) and slightly more to fodder crops (1 ha to barley, 0.5 ha to oats, 0.5–1 ha to maize) for his working cattle, cash-earning sheep, and fattening pig. Mitsos understood the benefits of rotation ("when I sowed wheat twice, I saw that yields fell") but had little land. Weighing up the strength of each field and when it was last under maize "fallow," he sowed wheat–wheat on his best plots and wheat–barley, wheat–oats, and barley–oats on plots of progressively lower quality. In practice, this rotation "scheme" was even more flexible: most of his fields were roughly 0.5, 1.0, or 1.5 ha in extent and it was not worthwhile sowing winter cereals in units of less than 0.5 ha (Section 4.9); and he did not leave rented fields fallow "since someone else would benefit" (also Palmer, 1998a, 157).

Further afield, the range of crops grown reflected both cultural preferences (e.g., for culinary use of glume wheats) and practical constraints. As dominant winter cereal, free-threshing wheat gave way to barley with increasing aridity (e.g., eastern Crete); to rye with increasing altitude (e.g., the high Pindos of northwest Greece or Monte Cairo in central Italy); and to rye (e.g., the north Greek Kamvounia foothills), barley (e.g., lowland central Crete), or einkorn (e.g., Haute Provence) on poor soils. Preferred summer crops reflected market demand (e.g., Palmer, 1998b, 8), access to land and labor (e.g., cotton vs. tobacco – Section 6.5), soil quality, and, not least, summer rainfall or irrigation potential. For example, maize was mainly rain-fed in lowland northern Greece but largely restricted to irrigated gardens further south, while the distribution of olives and vines is influenced by climate (see Section 5.2.3) and by availability of land and labor, respectively. Given such diversity in crops grown, rotation sequences inevitably vary, but the broad patterns, and parameters that shape them, parallel those outlined for lowland northern Greece.

For example, on steep slopes and infertile soils in the Pindos Mountains in the mid-twentieth century, rain-fed winter cereals widely alternated with uncultivated (grazed) fallow, as at Plikati (1200 m), Agia Paraskevi (1000 m), and Zitsa (700 m), although recently settled Vlach herders in Mavrovouni (800 m) sowed their few fields every year. With rising population in twentieth-century Tsakonia on the southeast Greek mainland, wheat–barley or wheat–pulse rotation displaced alternate fallow (Kostakis, 1976–1978, 84). At Vasiliki in 1930s lowland eastern Crete, when Peris was a teenage helper to his father, wheat or barley alternated with oats (fodder) or pulses (mainly fodder) and only a few fields were fallowed each year, "depending on how many you had and [the strength of] your work animals." At nearby Mirtos, Daskalos' grandfather, a full-time farmer, alternated winter cereals with cultivated fallow, but his father, a part-time farmer with less land, sowed half of his cereals after pulses (e.g., bitter vetch) grown mainly for fodder. Daskalos' contemporaries on Amorgos again rotated cereals with pulses (mainly grass pea and common vetch for fodder), leaving occasional cultivated fallow (or summer gardens) to control weeds. Here, pulses replaced biennial fallow in the 1930s, at the behest of agricultural advisors, to improve livestock production as an alternative "cash crop" to tobacco. Farmers already grew pulses, however, and perhaps expanded cereal–pulse rotation (Halstead and Jones, 1989) because of the prohibition of tobacco growing (on cultivated fallow!) rather than improved agronomic understanding. Giorgos from Methana in southern mainland Greece was one of several informants to insist that "the old ones" had practiced cereal–pulse rotation and understood its benefits long before enlightenment by agronomists.

Elsewhere, longer rotation cycles prevailed. For southern Spain, late nineteenth-century sources report two-year (fallow–winter cereal, pulse–wheat) and three-year (e.g., fallow–pulse–winter cereal) rotations (Peña-Chocarro, 1999, 30–31), while for twentieth-century Zuheros in Andalucia, Antonio described a three-year scheme of cultivated fallow (sometimes with spring-sown chickpea), then wheat or barley, and finally einkorn or lentil. For 1930s central Crete, Giorgis at Knossos and Angeliki at Agia Semni both described a four-year rotation of cultivated fallow–wheat–barley–oat, with bitter or common vetch replacing fallow at Knossos "if a field was exceptionally good." In northern Jordan, with rainfall matching central rather than eastern Crete, the traditional cultivated fallow–winter cereal rotation was intensified through the twentieth century: a summer crop or late winter pulse was substituted for fallow, or a late winter pulse inserted between the winter cereal and fallow made a three-year rotation. Replacement of communal by individual landownership enabled abandonment of fallow, while rising population and smaller landholdings made it advantageous. Farmers with small numbers of livestock mainly sowed the increasingly prominent pulses to compensate for declining fallow pasture and (thanks to employment outside farming) reduced labor for herding (Palmer, 1998b).

The length of rotation cycles thus depended primarily on the abundance and fertility of land and capacity to work it but also on the demands of animal husbandry for fallow grazing or fodder crops and the market for cash crops. While the length of the cycle varied, the most demanding cereal – usually free-threshing wheat – normally followed any fallow period or pulse crop, while the least demanding – such as oats – was sown last. Because difficulty of harvesting restricted their scale (Section 3.3), pulses featured less in rotations in areas of extensive agriculture, such as lowland northern Greece, than of small-scale cultivation, such as the hills of southern Greece (e.g., Forbes, 1976a). Here too, however, the picture is variable, partly because pulses (especially those grown for hay) were often sown under trees such as olives (e.g., on Kithira; at Knossos and Agia Semni in central Crete; at Vasiliki in eastern Crete) for two complementary reasons: first, pulses ripen earlier and have shallower roots than cereals and so are reckoned to compete less with trees for scarce water (for the same reason, barley was preferred to wheat and oats under olives at Skalani, central Crete); secondly, cereals under olives ripen unevenly (those in shade developing later), necessitating piecemeal harvesting, whereas pulses sown for hay were cut and left to dry and those for human consumption perhaps picked fresh, as they ripened.

5.2.3 Fallowing and rotation in space

Crop rotation often exhibits *local* spatial variation. Valley floors often have more fertile and water-retentive soils that are culti- vated more intensively than slopes. Thus, at central Cretan Kalo Khorio, the lower and more level fields were planted with olives, beneath which pulses (which cooked quickly because the olives were manured) alternated with cultivated fallow; on the terraced slopes, winter cereals alternated with fallow, left uncultivated for pasture unless tillage was necessary to control weeds. At Aloides, the lower-lying fields were more or less continuously cultivated, while the higher slopes on the communal "mountain" alternated between pasture and short-term "slash-and-burn" cultivation (Section 6.1.3). Among the lower fields, Sofia's father used two small (each 500 m²), stone-free plots near the village alternately for wheat and a summer garden with watermelons, cucumbers, and the like. His remaining permanent fields on the stony lower slopes, fallowed infrequently "when necessary," he used for other cereals (barley, rye, oats) and pulses (broad beans, lentil, *papoúles* [*Lathyrus ochrus*], *fáva* [probably another *Lathyrus* species], and bitter vetch). He sowed rye and broad beans, considered more demanding than barley or oats, on deeper soils towards the village and, for ease of cooking, grew other food pulses (lentil, *papoúles, fáva*) on a manured plot by a sheepfold and on another with "burnt" soil (probably the site of earlier habitation).

In accidented terrain, rotations might be differentiated by crops' climatic tolerances. For example, on central Italian Monte Cairo, a two-year rotation of winter and summer crops was normal: in winter, free-threshing wheat was sown at lower altitudes, and on sunny slopes, with hardier rye in higher and more shaded loca- tions; in summer, maize and potatoes were commoner in moist conditions at high altitude (Forte, 2009). On the small island of

Kithira, olives near the southeastern shore are sheltered from the north wind that "burns" those on the adjacent central plateau (about 300–400 m OD). Conversely, on Naxos, strong winds stunt or distort tree growth near the coast, largely restricting olives to sheltered valleys inland. Even in gentle terrain, differences in drainage may radically affect land use, as at north Greek Aiginio overlooking the Aliakmon delta. Depending on their fertility, fields in the hills carried various rotations of winter cereals (wheat, barley, oat, rye, einkorn) and pulses (lentil, grass pea, bitter vetch, common vetch), with more or less frequent cultivated fallow or summer crops (chickpea, tobacco, maize). On the plain, prior to drainage, winter cereals (wheat, barley, oat) roughly alternated with spring barley or summer crops (maize, New World beans), although floods often destroyed the former.

Cropping decisions also respected soil type. At Kolofana on Amorgos, red *firóyi* was less drought-prone than grey *psaróyi* and favored for wheat, unless *psaróyi* plots were recently fallowed or manured or *firóyi* plots devoted to pulses. Peas or lentils for food were sown on richer and cleaner fields than common vetch or grass pea for fodder. What was sown where each year thus reflected the quality and cultivation history of individual plots. Some farmers emphasized flexibility rather than a "norm," although data for 71 fields over two harvests included 70% alternation between cereals and pulses, with a fallow year or two consecutive pulses accounting for most aberrations (Halstead and Jones, 1989; Jones and Halstead, 1995).

At north Greek Assiros, the heavy black soils (*kizlátser*) west of the village produced the highest and most reliable wheat yields for those with strong draft animals; lighter soils to east (*kompsáli*) and southwest (*melíki*) were favored for intensively hoed maize and gardens; infertile soils on the plain to the south and hills to the north supported rye; and light *defekiá* patches, where wheat did badly in dry years, produced pulses that cooked easily – as did the *avlés* ["backyards"] that extended perhaps 500 m from the village. The *avlés* had been heavily manured for decades and, thanks to their resulting fertility and tractability and their proximity, were also favored for labor-intensive row crops, such as *okra* (lady's fingers). They encouraged very vigorous growth in cereals, giving rise to their principal use: sown early – as soon as autumn rains permitted – with barley mainly, but also oats and occasionally wheat, to provide "early-bite" grazing (*khasíl*) for sheep. Large landholders owned many *avlés* and most ran big sheep flocks. Some *avlés*, however, belonged to farmers without sheep who sowed wheat for grain, inviting others to graze the crop to avoid lodging; with this precaution, *avlés* sustained two consecutive wheat crops without appreciable reduction in yield.

Distance from the village and the consequently uneven distribution of manure (Section 5.3.1.3) shaped the contrasting cropping regimes on infield *avlés* and arable outfields. The latter gave way in turn, especially on less fertile slopes, to the outermost uncultivated rough grazing. Such zonation was widespread (Chisholm, 1968). At Tharounia on Euboea, small, enclosed plots, valued for their proximity and fertility (from manure of work animals and milked "house-goats" stalled in the village), occupy much of the land "within sight of the village." Some of these plots were vineyards and others (with wells for small-scale irrigation) gardens, but most were *sókhora* (infields) devoted to sown hay crops (barley, oat, bitter vetch, common vetch) for stalled animals, broad beans ("because they cooked better"), and wheat (despite vulnerability to lodging). The much more extensive *exokhórafa* (outfields) were divided, until 1960 when declining population made it unnecessary, into two zones of alternating land use (*zigomeriá*) "above" and "below" the village. Each year, one zone was devoted to winter cereals (barley, oats; wheat on better soils) and pulses (lentils, winged vetchling [*Lathyrus ochrus*], bitter vetch, common vetch) for grain; the other was fallow pasture for *herds* kept outside the village. Human and animal labor permitting, fallow fields were plowed in February–March and some sown with pulses, despite risk of damage by livestock; those left unplowed were harder to cultivate the following autumn. Beyond the *exokhórafa*, the outermost zone of *roumánia* ("forest" outside cultivation) served largely as rough pasture but also for "shifting cultivation" (Section 6.1.3). Over the past half century, with dwindling population, cultivation was abandoned on the *roumánia* and then the *exokhórafa* and is now concentrated on the *sókhora* and gardens (Jones, 2005).

Division of outfields into alternating cultivated and fallow/ pasture zones was widespread in the mountains and hills of Greece, from the high Pindos of northwest Greece (see Section 5.2.2) to upland Arcadia (e.g., Karitaina) and the hills of Messenia (e.g., Asoutaina, Metaxada). At Metaxada, the fallow zone was grazed freely from the end of harvest in June until March, when the best fields were plowed and sown with maize, chickpeas, or New World beans, while poorer land continued to be grazed. Although usually described as time honored ("we found it thus from our forefathers") and consensual, such zones imposed constraints on cropping decisions that must have been especially disadvantageous for those with little land or few livestock. At Tharounia, as cultivation of out-fields declined, collective rotation fell into disuse rather than being formally abandoned. A decade earlier at Asoutaina, however, before emigration relaxed pressure on land, neighbors enforced the agreement by grazing any "illegal" crop.

The distinction between infield and outfield was also widespread, if variable in clarity. Vegetable gardens exploited easily worked *melíki* alluvium 2.5 km south of Assiros and occupied slopes and valleys with spring water for irrigation below hilltop Olimbos on Karpathos, Kalo Khorio on Crete, and Mitata and Viaradika on Kithira. Ideally, however, gardens were concentrated near settlements (e.g., Hillman, 1973a), facilitating intensive husbandry and piecemeal harvesting of fresh produce. Spring-fed, irrigated gardens with vegetables, maize, and New World beans are the norm in and around mixed-farming villages in the Pindos Mountains, but Plikati also had larger infields in the valley below, divided into two zones alternately supporting rain-fed winter wheat and irrigated summer crops. Beyond this infield area, the gentler lower slopes carried the alternating zones of winter crops and fallow grazing mentioned previously, while the steeper slopes bore deciduous oaks managed for leafy hay to feed local sheep and goats over winter (Halstead, 1998). The higher slopes, above an artificially lowered

209

tree line, were grazed in summer mainly by large transhumant flocks. Likewise, in upland Lasithi on Crete, rain-fed winter cereals alternated with irrigated potatoes and New World beans on the basin floor; less demanding winter grain crops (e.g., oat, lentil [which cooked better than when grown on the fields below], common vetch) occupied the terraced lower slopes; and sheep and goats grazed the higher slopes.

Shared irrigation channels and water imposed cultivation zones with sharp limits and common cropping regimes (e.g., Hillman, 1973b, 227, for Aşvan, eastern Turkey). Collective control over cropping is particularly elaborate in some long-standing irrigation systems in lowland Spain, as around medieval Borja in north-central Spain, where water channels roughly parallel to the river Huecha demarcate irrigated *huerta* below from rain-fed *secano* and rough pasture above. While the *secano* is typically under biennial winter cereals and bare fallow, much of the *huerta* comprises paired blocks alternately irrigated in winter and summer. Until demand for local fiber collapsed, the *huerta* typically supported a four-year cycle of hemp–flax–wheat–wheat or hemp–flax–wheat–barley, which latterly gave way to wheat alternating with maize, potatoes, or alfalfa. Planting of olives and vines on the coarser, less water-retentive soils on the margins of the irrigated zone complicated this picture, while viticulture especially expanded and contracted in both *huerta* and *secano* in response to changing demand (Garcia Manrique, 1960). Fluctuating rainfall also caused short-term spatial variability in both irrigation and land use (Section 5.4).

5.2.4   Hedging bets: Mixed cropping

To reduce labor costs and risk of failure, farmers not only planted particular crops in different parts of the landscape but also sowed mixtures of annual crops on the same plot. Mixed wheat/barley or *(s)migádi* was widely sown in southern Greece, because barley better withstood dry years, while a wheat-rich crop in wet years raised the quality of bread or price of surplus grain. For the same reasons, wheat/barley was sown on more varied soils than wheat alone, for which were reserved the heavier, more water-retentive fields at Metaxada in Messenia and recently fallowed, weed-free plots at Kolofana on Amorgos. Kolofana farmers also sowed a mixture of two fodder pulses: grass pea, which livestock preferred, and common vetch, which was higher yielding and less vulnerable to insects (Jones and Halstead, 1995).

At Kastrisianika on Kithira, Yannis' father broadcast a few broad beans in wheat, barley, or common vetch fields to avoid planting a labor-intensive garden crop. In Asturias, some likewise rationalize the sparse scattering of broad beans or peas in glume wheat as enabling small quantities of seed to be *broadcast*; on manured plots, robust broad bean plants also protect host cereals from lodging, but scrambling peas increase this risk. On central Italian Monte Cairo, stiff rye straw protected wheat from lodging in the maslin sometimes sown on high, moist ground (Forte, 2009). Maize and New World beans are widely planted together in the Mediterranean uplands, the former serving as "beanpoles," and in Tharounia, Panagiota plants broad beans with scrambling peas for the same reason. At Kastrisianika, Panagiotitsa sowed shady broad beans with lentils to encourage the latter to grow upwards, making them easier to harvest, and mixed cereal–pulse hay crops (e.g., barley–common vetch at Zoodokhos Pigi, Farsala, in Thessaly) ensure that the pulses grow sufficiently erect to be mown by scythe.

Annual crops were also widely sown under tree crops ("Mediterranean polyculture"), sharing the labor of tillage while exploiting complementary rooting depths and seasonal rhythms (Forbes, 1976b; 1982) and greater market demand for the latter. Over the last century, increasing engagement with a nonlocal market has encouraged denser planting of trees, especially olives, so that annual field crops (except fodder pulses – see the preceding text) are less often sown beneath. The earlier practice of planting trees further apart, often on terrace edges (Figure 5.2) or field boundaries, left more scope for undersowing with winter cereals and thus for hedging bets between yields and prices of grains and fruits or nuts (Section 6.5).

Figure 5.2   Old olive trees on terrace edge at Kavousi, eastern Crete.

5.3   Planning for Success: Manuring

Until the twentieth-century adoption of industrial alternatives, Mediterranean farmers fertilized fields and gardens with silt (Loukopoulos, 1983, 178–179), leaf mold, ash (e.g., Garcia Manrique, 1960, 73), industrial waste, and especially animal dung. Followed by mild winters and abundant spring rainfall, manuring encouraged excessive growth and lodging of cereals; under arid conditions, it "burnt" crops, directly or by encouraging them to outgrow water supply; and it could be rich in weed seeds. Nonetheless, farmers routinely applied manure while attempting to minimize its detrimental effects. Cultivated land was typically manured in three ways: by animals grazing stubble and fallow fields; by animals penned in fields, especially overnight in summer; and by farmers spreading manure from animals stalled overnight or over winter. While the amounts

212

administered varied, informants consistently maintain that grazing had least, penning intermediate, and stall manure most impact, positive and negative. Farmers frequently blame grazing livestock for raiding or trampling adjacent growing crops, but not for causing excessive growth in subsequent crops. They often attribute localized lodging to penning, however, and routinely regulated how much stall manure they spread, and when and where, to avoid damage. Nonetheless, when rationalizing selective distribution of stall manure, most informants cite first limited availability, secondly difficulties of distribution, and only thirdly the fact that some crops benefitted more (or were more highly valued).

5.3.1 Stall manure

Informants across the relatively arid south of Greece consistently described spreading stall manure first on vegetable gardens, secondly on olives and vines, and thirdly, if any remained, on the odd cereal field. On Crete, Giorgis maintained that stall manure should be reserved for olives, vines, and watered gardens, but on the infertile slopes north of Knossos, it also benefitted his cereals, while his insistence that the fertile *leniká* soils overlying Roman Knossos were particularly prone to lodging or "burning" implies that he, or a neighbor, had spread stall manure there too. In Aloides, Sofia's father spread any surplus stall manure on the small plot where he sowed wheat (it also benefitted the following summer garden), but most farmers treated one of their less fertile fields – dung from grazing livestock was not enough. "Burning" was a concern, and in southern Jordan, rain-fed winter cereals benefitted only from grazing animals, but irrigated ones also received stall manure (Charles and Hoppé, 2003, 217). Likewise in southern Greece, watering of vegetable gardens "extinguished the fire" of stall manure, and as Kostis at Kalo Khorio observed, "water and manure make good cabbages for sure" (*koprá kai neró kánei lákhano kaló*). Olives and vines were rain-fed until a few decades ago, however, and both suffered if low rainfall followed manuring. Vegetable gardens were important for household diet, while olive oil and currant grapes were often vital cash crops, but informants almost invariably attributed the low priority of cereal fields to the impossibility of fertilizing large areas with limited manure. Gardens and tree crops were sufficiently small scale for modest amounts of manure to make a significant difference.

In less arid lowland northern Greece, priorities for stall manure were similar: first, vegetable gardens (e.g., Mavrorakhi; Mouries near Kilkis); second, vines (Kolindros) or summer crops (Assiros), especially if grown for market; and, third, if anything remained, cereal fields beginning with the least fertile (Neo Sidirokhori, Assiros, Paliambela). Here, manured cereals risked lodging more than "burning," and the latter from frost more than drought, but again farmers attributed their limited treatment to scarcity of manure and difficulties of transport. In upland Asturias, average annual rainfall is twice that of lowland northern Greece and three times that of eastern Crete and the Cyclades, so manured cereals are at far greater risk of lodging than wilting. Distribution of stall manure prioritized vegetable gardens and staple summer crops (maize and potatoes), with any surplus thrown on hay meadows. Winter-sown spelt/emmer was not manured directly, but rotation with maize or potatoes afforded significant increases in crop height, size of ear, and risk of lodging. Residents accepted this risk, rather than manuring more lightly or adjusting rotation schemes, because maize and potatoes required high fertility and glume wheats otherwise yielded poorly on the upland soils. Ideally, the poorest fields received most manure, although this was variously rationalized as improving yields on poor land or avoiding lodging on rich.

5.3.1.1 Preparation for spreading
Fresh stall manure was usually left to "mature," "ferment," or "digest" before spreading. In rainy Asturias, manure from cattle stalled over winter in the village might be taken piecemeal every few days to nearby fields, or moved in January–February to "cook" in heaps for two to three months until the spring planting of maize and potatoes, or spread in spring straight from a heap in the yard.

In northern Greece, stall manure was collected in the yard or on a nearby field to drain and rot before spreading, usually in the following autumn or winter, although Giorgos in Mavrorakhi let it "boil" for more than a year. In Crete, dung was often rotted – with hearth sweepings and human cess – in a dung pit emptied each year (also central Greece – Loukopoulos, 1983, 177). It was difficult to control the application of dung – particularly if fresh and bound together by straw (litter or bedding) that had not rotted. Dung rotted and drained for several months was lighter and more friable, and so easier to carry and scatter evenly, and lacked the "fire" of fresh, urine-soaked manure that "burnt" crops. The length of time before manure was spread depended on season(s) of stalling, availability of transport, and season of sowing target crops. Nonetheless, maturation was apparently brief in wet Asturias and long in semiarid Crete. As Giorgis in Knossos commented, "it needs a lot of rain to extinguish manure which must be thoroughly digested not to boil the crop. In the old days when we did not water vines or olives, it had to be digested to a fine dust, so we could scatter it thinly – like sowing broadcast; we only spread it more heavily on irrigated gardens, because the water extinguished it and prevented it baking the crops." For the latter reason, Irini's father at Potamos on Kithira watered manure before spreading on his gardens. Worryingly, for archaeologists, some informants avoided mixing in broken crockery because it impeded "broadcasting."

5.3.1.2   Manure of different livestock

For farmers with few livestock, it was often impracticable not to stall different species together and mix their dung, but others with a few working or milking animals at home and a larger single-species herd in a distant fold could use different manures selectively. Valentina in Asturian Zureda considered chicken manure too strong for fields and watered it for application to her garden. Lorenzo at Piazza al Serchio in the Garfagnana hills used sheep manure on his poorest fields "because it was lighter [to carry] and better than cow dung." Candido in Zureda believed that sheep and goat produced better manure than cattle, and cattle much better than pig. Manolis on Naxos also considered pig manure very poor but rated mules and donkeys above sheep, goats, cattle, and poultry. Contradictory evaluations partly reflect whether local rainfall could extinguish the fire of "hot" manure. The quality of manure is also influenced by animals' diet (Ministry of Agriculture and Fisheries (MAF) 1931, 2). For example, Vasilis in southern Greek Arkhaia Nemea preferred dry dung from browsing goats to "muddy" manure from grazing sheep. Stavroula in Messenian Khora drew the same distinction between sheep on dry summer and fresh winter pasture, as did Marí in Asturian Tiós (with seasons reversed) between cattle consuming dry hay in winter and fresh grass in summer. The dung of sheep grazing stubble fields in north Greek Assiros likewise differs dramatically between dry and wet summers. Diet-related differences might influence how manure was used. For example, Nikos in Paliambela spread winter stall manure of cattle on his garden and tobacco fields; the scarcer stall manure from summer, when cattle grazed outdoors by day, was rich in seeds, and this he used for winter cereals that were less vulnerable to competing weeds. Finally, the quality of stall manure, especially of the larger animals, was influenced by the amount of litter – usually cereal straw but also ferns and chestnut leaves in Asturias – added as bedding or to soak up urine and increase bulk.

5.3.1.3 *Transport: Timing, labor, and distance*
Farmers in principle prioritized demanding crops and infertile plots (and, in dry regions, those to be watered) for stall manure, but in practice, its weight and volume imposed constraints. In lowland Greece, manure was usually transported to fields between early summer threshing and autumn sowing, when human (usually male) and pack or draft animal labor was available and stall manure (mainly from winter) was substantially drier and lighter. In winter, muddy tracks were also often impassable for laden carts in the plains. Pack mules and donkeys moved faster and had a wider daily radius than draft cattle pulling carts but carried a smaller load: the

Cypriot folk measures *gomárin* (donkey-load) and *káron* (cartload) represented perhaps 80–100 kg and 300–750 kg, respectively, of manure (Panaretos, 1946, 74).

As a teenage farmhand for a big Assiros landowner, Fotis carried manure by horse-drawn cart to fields up to 2 km away on level ground, but most was dumped within 500 m on the infield *avlés* "because the horses were not strong." Those without a cart moved manure even shorter distances by wheelbarrow. In Aiginio, Dimos and Mavrodis likewise carted manure up to 2–2.5 km, but not uphill. The Paliambela Thracians carried manure to only the gentle slopes within a few hundred meters of the village and rarely more than 500–600 m even on level ground. As Mitsos explained, "I did not have much manure, and in a day, you might manage 5–6 round trips with the cart near the village but only one to a distant field." He also had to cut and transport firewood before autumn plowing and sowing. North Greek farmers with stall manure for winter cereals prioritized the poorest fields *accessible by cart*, usually within a few hundred meters of the village or outlying folds, while more distant fields received dung left by grazing animals. Because transport was difficult, manure from outlying folds was often dumped in adjacent gullies, and in Assiros, occasional flash floods in summer engulfed low-lying houses in a "tsunami" of dung from upstream.

At Tharounia in the hills of Euboea, mules carried manure from work animals stalled in the village, mainly to infield *sókhora* within 500–700 m. Each year, outfields left fallow were fertilized by grazing sheep and goats, while villagers with a flock of sheep, rather than a few house-goats, manured more heavily a few outfields adjacent to their folds (Section 5.3.2). In Asturias, manure was delivered to gardens and fields around or below the village in a small sledge (*carreña*) pulled by two cows or, on narrower paths to distant fields, by a single horse. Uphill, a mule or horse, perhaps borrowed from a neighbor, carried manure in paired esparto baskets. A pack animal carried perhaps a third or half as much as a sledge (and the latter substantially less than a wheeled cart). Most fields were within a few hundred meters of byres in the village, and distant plots were manured where possible from outlying byres. For example, in Tiós, most of Leandro's plots were 10–15 minutes walk from his house and attached byre; a more distant field, 30 minutes away, he manured from a byre in the same area. Outlying byres sheltered cattle that were not working, calving, or being milked and so not needed in the village. This reduced the amount of hay transported down to the village (on sledges drawn by pairs of cows) and made manure more readily available for outlying fields and perhaps hay meadows (Isaakidou, 2011). Conversely, one rationale for dragging hay down from high meadows was to keep more cows in the village and thus increase the availability of stall manure for infields. Someone owning a field but no byre in a distant location sought to exchange manure with a neighbor who owned a nearby byre but no field. Strategic use of outbuildings and cooperation between neighbors significantly reduced transport of manure over difficult terrain, much as elsewhere construction and sharing of outlying threshing floors eased transport of harvested sheaves (Section 3.5). Nonetheless, as Severina in Zureda remarked, "it was easy to spread manure on land near the village, but with more distant fields, you did what you could." Her neighbor, Candido, had spread 14 sledge-loads in one day on land adjacent to the village but considered two round trips realistic for distant fields, implying that manuring of one *dia de bueyes* (800 m^2) with 10–25 sledges (see the following text) needed between one to two days and one to two weeks, depending on distance. As elsewhere, transport constraints sometimes overturned the principle of manuring the poorest soils most heavily.

Stall manure was routinely carried by human hand or back from byre to dung heap and piecemeal from dung heap to garden, but most informants expressed horror at the thought of carrying such weight over longer distances. In the Garfagnana hills, where manure was carried by pack animals and "on the shoulders of Christians," Angelo had done so to fields a kilometer from his byre, but doubtless carried much less than a pack animal, let alone a sledge or cart. From Crete to Asturias, stall manure was difficult to transport and mainly spread near village byres or outlying folds. Industrial alternatives, being dramatically less heavy and bulky, enabled fertilization of distant fields for the first time and contributed to the widespread abandonment of biennial fallow.

5.3.1.4 Stall manure: Rates of application

Whereas industrial fertilizer acts rapidly and briefly, the effect of manure may be greatest in the second year after spreading, obvious for three to five years and perceptible for a decade (also Palmer, 1998a, 149). At Assiros, manure improved yields on the lighter *kompsália* for a few years but was "quickly swallowed up" by the heavier *kizlátser*. The delayed and lasting effect of manure complicated application. In Knossos, where the risk of "burning" was high, Giorgis dispensed manure on vines and olives with an 18-litre can. On fields, manure was first deposited in regularly spaced heaps where, the following spring, patches of luxuriant and perhaps weed-infested crop highlighted its positive and negative effects. In Asturias, each heap represents a sledge-load; in Paliambela, Nikos' father taught him to judge the heaps by eye, forking one off the front and another off the back of the oxcart before moving forward. Farmers adjusted the size and spacing of heaps, taking account of previous results on the same field.

Although manuring rates were adjustable, and volumes partly reflect the amount of added stall litter and duration of storage, order-of-magnitude estimates for different regions are instructive. In rainy upland Asturias, informants in Llanos de Somerón, Tiós, and Zureda cited a norm for maize and potatoes of 25 manure sledges per *dia de bueyes* ($800\,m^2$), although only 10–15 sledges might be available. With a sledge reckoned by two informants to hold 200–300 kg, this amounts to 30–80 tons/ha. Glume wheat rotated biennially with maize or potatoes thus indirectly received 15–40 tons/ha/year – comparable to free-threshing wheat in long-term experiments in Germany (20–30 tons every second year) and England (35 tons annually) (Fraser *et al.*, 2011). Glume wheat was grown on a modest scale, in the mid-twentieth century perhaps 0.2–0.5 ha/household/year, depending on nonagricultural employment. Someone manuring 0.5 ha/year required 60–160 sledge-loads or 15–40 tons, in addition to whatever she/he spread on vegetable gardens, any plots under maize–maize or potato–maize rotation, and perhaps some hay meadow. A stalled cow filled a sledge in eight days (about 30 kg daily, cf. 40 kg for the 1930s United Kingdom – MAF, 1931, 1), on which basis 0.6–1.5 cows stalled for four to five winter months could manure one *dia de bueyes*. Farmers suggested 1–3 stalled cows per *dia de bueyes* allowing for fluctuating numbers kept in the village (cattle not needed were removed to outlying byres) and manuring of gardens. For example, with five to seven cows, a handful of sheep, and one pig overwintered in Xomezana, Inés' husband could not manure four *dias de bueyes* (0.3 ha) per year and used surplus dung from neighbors. Lucino in Llanos needed two to three cows stalled for four to five months for the ideal 25 sledges per *dia de bueyes*; his father kept fewer cows in the village and manured more lightly. A household sowing 0.5 ha of glume wheat biennially thus needed at least 6 and ideally 12–18 winter-stalled cows.

In the equally rainy Garfagnana, before roads and shops relaxed the need for self-sufficiency, Lorenzo worked three hectares as a sharecropping tenant near Piazza al Serchio, growing maize or potatoes followed by two years of bread wheat or emmer and five or six of alfalfa (for hay and pasture). His donkey, 6–7 cows, and 15 sheep (together equivalent to 8–9 Asturian "stalled cows" – Shepherd and Gibbs, 2002) grazed outdoors much of the time and only provided enough stall manure for the 0.3–0.4 ha in maize and potatoes each year. With about 25 "stalled cows" per hectare treated each year, he manured as heavily as his Asturian counterparts, but every eight to nine years rather than biennially, and encountered far fewer problems with lodging of winter cereals.

In lowland northern Greece, 500 m from Paliambela village, Nikos owned two fields together covering 2 ha. Each year, he spread 20–25 cartloads on 0.2 ha (perhaps 40–60 tons/ha), treating each section at roughly 10-year intervals, because lighter manuring was ineffective and heavier treatment was impossible with only five to six cattle stalled for four to five winter months and would risk lodging. Mimis, for the *tsípouro* circle, reckons that two to five cattle manured 0.1–0.3 ha/year at 10-year intervals to avoid lodging. In neighboring

Kolindros, Nikolaos' two oxen and two donkeys (working animals stalled not only in winter) produced enough manure for 0.2–0.3 ha/ year, while Konstantinos' four to five cattle in Neo Sidirokhori fertilized 0.1–0.15 ha of his poorest fields. These north Greek farmers spread the manure of 15–40 "stalled cows"/ha on land sown for *grain*, close to the rate for Asturias (Table 5.1), but again much less frequently. Nikos' manured fields in Paliambela received perhaps 4–6 tons/ha/*year*, compared with 15–40 tons/ha/*year* in Asturias, and his more distant fields, like most arable land in northern Greece, were only fertilized during stubble grazing and perhaps by flocks folded at night in summer. With one head of cattle per hectare of fields (fairly typical for Paliambela), he could only have manured *all* his fields (had they been close enough) at his preferred rate once every 25 years.

Some north Greek fields, however, received much more stall manure. In Paliambela, Mitsos' father concentrated much of the manure from 4–6 cattle and 50–70 sheep (altogether 8 "stalled cows," as the sheep were usually penned only at night) on a nearby field of 0.5 ha, each year spreading perhaps 10 cartloads on 0.1–0.2 ha. He sowed the whole field with barley, grazed by his sheep in March and then left to recover, April–May rainfall permitting, for a reduced but worthwhile grain crop. Koula's husband and brother-in-law used another nearby field of similar size for the same purpose, spreading much of the manure from a byre with up to 11 cattle. In Assiros, a big landowner regularly spread much of the output of 30–40 stalled cows on 0.4 ha within the village, which he sowed with cereals to provide pasture for his lambs and then hay for his work animals. Dimitros, a modest full-time farmer, likewise sowed barley pasture (*khasíl*) for his sheep on 0.3 ha of infield *avlés*, which received the manure from his village byre, housing a horse, four cows, and one or two calves (say, six "stalled cows"). In these cases, farmers spread the manure of at least 10–20 "stalled cows"/ha/*year* and so matched or exceeded the rate on Asturian glume wheat plots (Table 5.1). In Paliambela, just a few of the nearer fields were manured heavily for *khasíl*. At Assiros, stall manure was concentrated on infield *avlés*, over a radius similar to Paliambela, but the

Table 5.1 Estimated application rates of stall manure and dung from folded and grazing livestock.

Location	Crop (rotation)	Manure source/method	Manuring rate Details	Tons/ha/year	"Stalled cows"/ha/year
Stall manure					
Asturias, N Spain	Maize/potato, wheat for grain	Winter-stalled cows	10–25 sledges/0.08 ha/2 years	15–40	6–18
Piazza al Serchio, Garfagnana, N Italy	Maize/potato, two years wheat for grain, five/six years alfalfa for hay	Winter-stalled cows, sheep, and donkey	8–9 "stalled cows"/0.3–0.4 ha/8–9 years		3
Paliambela, N Greece	Sown barley pasture	Winter-stalled cows/sheep	≥10 carts/0.1–0.2 ha/3–5 years	≥10	10–20
	Winter cereals for grain	Winter-stalled cows	10–12 carts/0.1 ha/10 years	4–6	≤1–4
Assiros, N Greece	Sown barley pasture	Winter-stalled horse and cows	6 "stalled cows"/0.3 ha/year		≥20
	Sown barley pasture	All-year sheep fold	150 sheep/0.4–0.5 ha/year		≤40–50 short-term!
Kolindros, N Greece	Sown barley pasture	All-year sheep fold	100 sheep/0.25 ha/2 years		24–30
Tharounia, C Greece	Wheat for grain, fallow pasture	Winter sheep fold	±30 sheep/0.5 ha/2+ years		≤3
Dervenakia, S Greece	Olives and vines	Winter sheep and goat fold	?30 kg/tree	<1.5	

Metaxada, S Greece	Winter cereal, fallow	Winter goat fold	15–20 tons/ha infrequently	? <2
Kastrisianika, S Greece	Olives, some undersown with common vetch	Byre with 2 donkeys and 10 sheep	20 kg/tree/2+ years	<1
Kalo Khorio, Crete	Olives, undersown mainly with pulses	Stall manure	10 tons/ha	<<5
Folded sheep and goats				
Assiros, N Greece	Sown early-bite grazing, several years winter cereals for grain	Summer sheep fold	150–200 sheep/0.7–2ha/several years	11–14 × 1 year
Tharounia, C Greece	Wheat for grain, fallow pasture	Spring pens (one to two weeks)	±30 sheep/0.2–0.3ha/2+ years	≤1
Metaxada, S Greece	Biennial winter cereals for grain	Sheep folded over summer	100 sheep/0.1ha ×4 nights	≤1.5
Tragana, S Greece	Biennial winter cereals for grain	Sheep folded over summer	50 sheep/2ha all summer	≤1
Palaio Loutro, S Greece	Biennial winter cereals for grain	Sheep and goats folded over summer	60–150 sheep and goats/1.5–2ha all summer	≤2–3
Grazing sheep and goats				
Mediterranean	Biennial winter cereal fallow		<0.7	<0.3

number of stalled livestock was an order of magnitude larger and most *avlés* belonged to large landowners with multiple work animals. Cumulative inputs were high, therefore, and these fertile plots were mainly sown with *khasíl* for early-bite pasture/hay, while any wheat for grain was grazed to prevent lodging.

At Assiros "in the old days," herds of 50–500 sheep and goats, too large for housing in the village, spent winter nights in weather- and predator-proof folds (*mantriá*) on the outer edge of the arable zone. From here, some manure was carted away for grain crops, but much was spread heavily by wheelbarrow on neighboring land for *khasíl*. Apostolis' 150 sheep slept year-round on a 0.4–0.5 ha field, sown each autumn for early-bite grazing. He initially spread the manure from his flock (outdoors by day, so equivalent to 20 cows day and night for four to five months or 40–50 "stalled cows"/ha) evenly across the field but after two years feared "burning" the sprouting cereal and restricted treatment to areas of weak growth. A generation previously, Dimitros likewise housed 150 sheep year-round on 0.4 ha sown each year for early-bite grazing but evidently considered their manure excessive for the field, as he threw some into the adjacent ravine until acquisition of a tractor eased transport to more distant plots. Nikos in Kolindros sowed 0.5 ha for early-bite grazing adjacent to his year-round fold, annually spreading the manure of 100 sheep on half of the field, equivalent to 24–30 "stalled cows"/ha/year. In lowland northern Greece, therefore, winter cereals sown for *pasture/hay* (but not *grain*) sometimes received even more stall manure than Asturian glume wheats.

Southern Greek figures for grain crops are elusive, because manure was diverted to tree crops and land was often not measured in areal extent. In Messenian Metaxada, however, 100 mule loads (say, 8–10 tons) from Ilias' winter goat fold (*gréki*) outside the village manured a field of 0.5–0.6 ha. At 15–20 tons/ha, he fertilized more lightly than farmers in Paliambela and also infrequently as he needed manure for his garden, vines, and olives. Tree crops too were manured sparingly. For the pensioners in the Kalo Khorio *kafenío*, "a good mule load of 100 kg would cover 100 m^2" of olives undersown with pulses, amounting to just 10 tons/ha and consistent with Cretan fear of "burning." At Dervenakia in the southeast mainland, Vasilis had a few olives and vines near his permanent winter fold for 100 sheep and goats. The dung he swept up every morning was too little for field crops, but in summer, he spread a basketful (perhaps 30 kg of dried pellets) on one olive or four vine stocks, roughly matching Giorgis' 18-litre can per vine in Knossos. At Kastrisianika on Kithira, the nocturnal output of 2 donkeys and 10 sheep (say, one stalled "cow") gave Thanasis only 10 donkey-loads for 150 olives. Four of his nearer trees shared one load (20 kg/tree) at intervals of more than two years. Olives at Dervenakia, Knossos, and Kastrisianika would have received only 1–2 tons/ha/year even if manured biennially and planted at a dense 100 trees/ha (cf. Foxhall, 2007, 116).

Although comparison with northern Greece is difficult, stall manure was clearly applied more lightly in the south, consistent with greater risk of harmful side effects and also more limited availability. Two informants from central Crete suggested similar outputs of stall manure from working animals: five mule loads (500 kg) per head per year in Kalo Khorio and 15–20 sacks (750–1000 kg) all winter for two oxen *combined* in Knossos. These are strikingly lower than figures from lowland northern Greece and upland Asturias (2–3 tons/stalled "cow") because mild winters and lack of fodder (summer drought made even straw scarce) minimized stall-feeding. Moreover, because drought also restricted pasture for large animals, few farmers kept more than a working pair and many had less: Panagiotitsa and her husband on Kithira had two donkeys, three sheep, and one goat, which manured the garden and some of their olives; and, in Andalucian Zuheros, Antonio's mule, goat, pig, and four to five hens together produced just three 50 kg sacks per year for his garden, olives, and field crops. In not manuring his cereals at Knossos, Giorgis was driven by necessity as well as caution: "with two oxen, how can you manure a 3–4 *strémma* [0.3–0.4 ha] field?" His contemporaries in northern Greece with two oxen expected to do so over three to four years.

In southern Greece, mild winters and scant spring rainfall made sown early-bite pasture less important than further north and less likely to recover for a harvest of ripe grain. On mid-twentieth-century Crete and Kithira, common vetch, cut as hay for stalled livestock, was widely sown under olives, benefitting from manure spread on the latter without competing for space with grain crops. At Mitata on Kithira, however, Fotini's parents also manured 0.1–0.2 ha per year for barley or oats that their livestock grazed briefly, "early, in January–February, so they got enough rain to recover for harvesting [as grain]"; others sacrificed the grain for more extended grazing. Barley and oats are also sown for pasture and fodder at Tharounia on Euboea, on infield *sókhora* manured from village byres. On good plots and with industrial fertilizer, *argasídi* (the local term) can be grazed early and left to recover for hay. A few decades ago, however, the best *sókhora* were devoted to wheat, and with scarce manure on stony ground, *argasídi* could be grazed only fleetingly without jeopardizing the hay crop. That sown pasture was grazed, and probably manured, more lightly in southern than northern Greece may thus be due to constraints of land and manure as much as aridity.

5.3.2   Manuring by folded livestock

At Assiros in early summer, after the cereal harvest, sheep and goats moved from their winter folds onto the stubble fields to graze sprouting weeds and fallen cereal ears. During July and August, sheep often grazed at night and slept through the midday heat in open-sided wood-framed shelters (*tsardákia*), roofed with rye straw. *Tsardákia* were ideally located close to drinking water and fields with rich grazing, but some were near the village so households with scarce labor could complete threshing. Especially through September and October, as the weather cooled, sheep and goats slept at night in flimsier enclosures (*kottária*) of cut thorn bushes that were moved more easily than the winter *mantriá* and early summer *tsardákia*. Once autumn rains started, pasture was more plentiful, so *kottária* were often located to manure a particular field, rather than for access to water and grazing. In Paliambela, the Thracians had modest flocks (mostly 50–100 head), housed within the village over winter, but some used temporary summer folds: for July–August, wood-framed shelters (*tsardákia*) along the stream where the sheep slept by day and, for September–October, moveable thorn bush enclosures (*kórdes*) to manure more distant fields.

Early summer folds in Assiros and Paliambela were swept every morning and the dung was carted or barrowed, ideally to an adjacent field. In September–October, sweeping could be avoided by moving thorn bush enclosures "every 5, 10, 30 days, depending how many sheep you had and how poor the field was," as Apostolis recalled from Assiros. He had been a teenage herder for two farmers who located their early and late summer folds for three months on the same cultivated land. One folded 150 sheep on 0.7 ha, and the other 200 on 1–1.5 ha. If urine voided in these folds compensated for manure lost while grazing outside (more valid for nitrogen and potassium than phosphorus – MAF, 1931), this represented about 11–14 "stalled cows"/ha, albeit for one year only. Such fields were normally sown, as soon as the autumn rains started, with barley or oats for grazing (nutrients are released more rapidly by urine than manure) and in subsequent years with grain crops until they again served as folds. The frequency of folding varied, but those with the biggest flocks and sufficient labor to relocate enclosures also owned extensive arable land and, as Apostolis observed, such fields did not compare with plots close to village byres or winter folds that were manured frequently and used more or less continuously for sown pasture. As the Paliambela *tsípouro* circle commented, a temporary fold "showed in the following cereal crop but only lasted two or three years," whereas stall manure could not be spread again on the same land for 10 years without causing lodging. Here a late summer fold, lasting a few weeks and accommodating up to 150–200 sheep (some Thracians temporarily combined flocks so each owner could work alternate days in the fields), manured just 0.1–0.2 ha, at a similar rate to the summer-long folds at Assiros. The Thracians sowed these manured strips for grain, "whatever you sowed on the rest of the field," rather than pasture, although the crop was often grazed to retard excessive growth or supplement scarce natural pasture, blurring the apparent contrast between Assiros and Paliambela.

Farmers ideally located summer folds on land they owned, or rented for two to three years, to benefit from the dung and urine, but the welfare of their sheep came first. In both Assiros and Paliambela, small-scale farmers often failed to use the manure from their sheep, because they lacked manpower for transport and spreading or because their fields did not provide a well-drained and well-ventilated sleeping area near water and pasture. Farmers without sheep keenly offered alternative locations. Conversely, as a teenager in Kolindros, Iraklis tended 500 sheep for his father who owned enough land (8 ha), mostly in a consolidated block, to leave half fallow each year. Iraklis moved his winter fold every year and summer fold every month, always within the consolidated block, minimizing loss of manure and ensuring relatively even treatment of these fields.

As with spreading of stall manure, there was a strong north–south gradient in intensity of folding. In northern Greece, at lowland Assiros, Kolindros, and Paliambela and in the hills at Lazarades, flocks of up to 200 sheep manured at most 1–1.5 ha over summer, and folds were relocated at weekly to monthly intervals or just from year to year. Further south, smaller flocks manured much larger areas over summer with frequent shifts of fold. At Tharounia in Euboea, where the winter fold for lambing and suckling ewes was located in a large field (say, 0.5 ha) over which accumulated manure was spread with the aid of a pack animal, spring–early summer milking pens were located in smaller fields (say, 0.2–0.3 ha) and moved every week or so to spread manure more widely; over summer, when milking stopped, the sheep slept out wherever they grazed. Frequency of folding depended on the size and distribution of fields and number of sheep (typically two or three dozen) owned by each household, but Konia recalled manuring suitable plots at roughly four-year intervals – enough to cause occasional lodging. In Messenia, Nikos reckoned that 100 sheep manured 0.1 ha in four nights at Metaxada, compatible with Stavroula's estimate that 50 sheep folded on stubble fertilized two hectares over summer at Tragana. In Palaio Loutro, Panagiotis likewise estimated that each summer fold or *tsárko*, housing 60–150 sheep and goats and ideally moved every two days, covered 1.5–2.0 ha over summer, so that much of his father's arable land was fertilized every other year. Although the data are anecdotal and imprecise, farmers clearly folded sheep and goats on grain fields at lower densities and more briefly than in northern Greece.

5.3.3 Manuring by grazing livestock

Manure from grazing and folded sheep was fundamental to arable farming in the Mediterranean (e.g., Marres, 1935, 30; Baticle, 1974, 34) and strengthened the symbiosis between transhumant pastoralists and arable estates in Greece (e.g., Karavidas, 1931). Compared with folding or the spreading of stall manure, grazing livestock distributed dung much more widely and sparsely. The number of animals and duration of grazing on stubble and fallow fields are limited by the quantity and quality of pasture and thus by soil, cropping history, and weather. In the north Mediterranean lowlands, variable summer rainfall makes pasture on new stubble unpredictable, while further south rainfall and pasture are variable in winter and spring and predictably sparse in summer. Moreover, livestock may range widely across stubble and fallow fields (usually a communal resource) and spend part of the year on uncultivated rough grazing or sown pasture. Nonetheless, order-of-magnitude estimates for potential manure inputs are possible.

In Mediterranean regions with an annual rainfall of 400–600 mm (most of those discussed earlier, although upland Asturias and Garfagnana are much wetter, and eastern Crete and southeast Spain drier), the average carrying capacity of *natural* pasture is about 1 adult sheep or goat/ha/year (Le Houerou and Hoste, 1977, 186, fig. 3). Stubble and fallow fields produce younger, more nutritious forage than much uncultivated land, and sheep and goats on new stubble may thrive on fallen ears even in a dry summer with little green pasture. Although arable land can support livestock year-round, numbers depend on the frequency of fallow and whether it is plowed up in the optimal spring grazing season. Even if sheep grazed arable land year-round at 1 sheep/ha and their urine compensated for time spent penned or folded, their manuring capacity while grazing would be 0.3 "stalled cows"/ha/year – an order of magnitude lower than for stall manure and, at least in northern

Greece, folding. Alternatively, if an adult sheep voids 2 kg of dung in 24 hours (Prontzas, 1992, 403, n. 9), flocks grazing year-round on arable land at 1 adult/ha would deposit 0.7 tons/ha/year of fresh dung and urine, again well below the rate at which stall manure was spread on grain fields in Asturias (15–40 tons/ha/year) and northern Greece (4–6 tons/ha/year at Paliambela), although closer to that for olives in southern Greece. In practice, without sown pasture, grazing animals probably manured arable land much more sparsely than estimated here – sparsely enough that farmers across the Mediterranean resorted to folding and spreading of stall manure with attendant risks of lodging, "burning," or weed infestation. While taking mitigating measures (controlled application, delayed sowing, preventive grazing, weeding, watering), farmers accepted these *short-term* risks for *medium-term* gains in fertility and yields.

5.4 Planning for Success, Mitigating Failure: Irrigation

Recent Mediterranean farmers routinely watered small vegetable gardens and orchards in summer from springs, streams, wells, and cisterns but more rarely diverted major watercourses for large-scale irrigation of winter cereals, despite the unreliability of winter–spring rainfall. Capital investment in water capture and distribution is considered in the following text (Section 6.3). Here discussion focuses on how water was allocated between crops, land parcels, and users. Irrigation from shared water sources was governed by rules, customs, or agreements, but water use also reflected interannual variability in availability or need and practical constraints of scale and distance.

Some gardens around Tharounia on Euboea have wells or, latterly, standpipes that primarily water summer vegetables but sometimes also broad beans and peas. These winter pulses largely complete growth before the summer drought, but some villagers water them in March–April if rainfall seems insufficient for flowering or seed development. Voula praises the crops just picked by neighbors who had watered *two rows of broad beans and one of peas*. In 1988, nine watered pulse crops averaged 17 m² and 51 rain-fed over 200 m² (Jones, 2005, 170, table 2). Plots with wells or standpipes are small, but in the dry spring of 2007, eight watered crops averaged 12 m² and three that were rain-fed *despite access to water* averaged 30 m². In circumstances where crop success was not critical, therefore, watering even modest gardens a few minutes walk from home might be prohibitively labor-intensive.

At Vasiliki in eastern Crete, spring-fed channels likewise mainly irrigated vegetable gardens and sometimes broad beans and lentils on the same plots, late in their growth cycle and with clear benefits to yields "if there was enough water; we did not have water to irrigate cereals." Above Khora in Messenia, the Kefalovriso spring normally irrigates summer vegetables and, during a severe drought some decades ago, salvaged rain-fed flax sown in winter in Hariklia's garden, but water was far too scarce for failing winter cereals, even if within reach of irrigation channels. Elsewhere in Greece, premechanized emergency irrigation of winter cereals was attempted only exceptionally on a small scale (Halstead, 1990, 150–151). At Plikati in the Pindos, each year half of the plain below the village was devoted to irrigated summer maize and potatoes and half to rain-fed winter wheat. Wheat, dependent for a good harvest on uncertain May rainfall, would have benefitted from late irrigation using existing channels, but this would have competed for water and labor with higher-yielding summer crops. Likewise, Greek farmers did not normally sow winter cereals on irrigable *gardens*, because (e.g., at Mitata on Kithira) it was not worthwhile on such a small scale: a watered garden of 100 m² in winter cereals might, optimistically, keep a family in bread for two weeks but supply enough accompanying vegetables for a few months. On the substantially drier eastern and southern margins of the Mediterranean, farmers and agronomists agree that supplementary irrigation of rain-fed crops raises and stabilizes yields but delivers poorer returns on water and labor than full irrigation of higher-value crops (Oram and de Haan, 1995, 49–50).

East and central Spain suffers from low and unreliable winter rainfall, but here, the massive medieval expansion of irrigation, associated with introduction of exotic fruit trees and vegetables (Watson, 1983), also raised and stabilized winter cereal yields (Trillo San José, 2004, 54). Around Borja in the Huecha valley of north-central Spain, winter–spring rainfall is modest (*annual* mean 390 mm upstream, less downstream – Martinez Gil and Sanchez Navarro, 1984, 351). Winter cereals grew extensively on the rain-fed slopes, but more dependably in the irrigated *huerta*, where their place was reinforced by tithes and first fruits levied in "prestigious cereals" (Carranza Alcalde, 2009, 33). Higher yields from irrigated winter cereals (e.g., Carranza Alcalde, 2009, 111) presumably spread the considerable costs of running and, after the major floods that were as inevitable as severe droughts, reconstructing the water capture and distribution infrastructure (e.g., Carranza Alcalde, 2009, 23, table 1, 159–164). Rotation with irrigated summer cash crops (e.g., hemp, flax) reduced infestation of winter cereals by wild oats (Garcia Manrique, 1960, 70). Despite detailed regulation, the watering of winter cereals varied significantly from year to year. After snow-free winters on the Moncayo Massif, springs feeding the Huecha and its irrigation channels may dry up, as in 1993–1994 when wheat and barley were not worth harvesting at Borja and severely stunted upstream at Ambel. Conversely, after heavy snowfall, irrigation extends beyond the core *huerta* (watered as of right) to the marginal *orillo* (watered subject to availability), while in a rainy spring, farmers might not water winter crops (e.g., Carranza Alcalde, 2009, 162). Although surplus water in a channel was usually forwarded to its corresponding *orillo*, local regulations or custom stipulated situations in which it could be sold at fixed price or by auction to help fund maintenance (Sindicato de Riegos de Borja, 1927; Carranza Alcalde, 2009, 168). The purchaser gambled, especially with auction, that rain was not imminent and the unpredictable amount of water reaching his land during the block of time bought would benefit his crops. Prohibition on reselling such water or diverting it to another's land prevented profiteering by a wealthy minority, as happened in Alicante (Alberola Romá, 1981, 122).

Other things being equal, irrigated land is close to farming settlements, so intensity of watering, like manuring, declines with distance. Around Borja and neighboring Tarazona, removal of manure from the *huerta* near the town was prohibited (Garcia Manrique, 1960, 73, n. 40). In the mid-nineteenth century, the Borja *huerta* received 280 loads of stall manure per hectare every four years, representing application of perhaps 7 tons/ha/year. This rate, though considered insufficient at the time, is roughly comparable with that for grain production in northern Greece and well in excess of southern Greek levels, perhaps reflecting the capacity of irrigation "to put out the fire" of manure.

5.5 Averting Failure: Weeding

Manure often includes seeds of weeds that compete with crops for light, water, or nutrients; encourage lodging; impede reaping; endanger storage; and perhaps make grain toxic. Before sowing, farmers countered the establishment of weeds by repeated tillage, ideally timed so the final cultivation destroyed emerging seedlings, and by digging untilled patches and breaking clods with mattocks and mallets (Chapter 2). During harvest, some robust weed plants were discarded (Chapter 3), while crop processing removed many weed seeds (Chapter 4). In between, farmers might prematurely cut or graze the weediest growing crops for hay or pasture (see the preceding text) or thin out weed plants.

In Asturias, weeds growing in glume wheat are regularly removed at two stages. In February or March, the ankle-high crop is usually worked with a handheld, two-pronged hoe. Then, in April or May (rarely both), when the crop is taller but normally before the ear emerges, the plot is weeded more selectively by hoe and hand (April) or hand alone (May), focusing on the climbing and clinging bindweeds (*Convolvulus arvensis*, *Bilderdykia convolvulus*), cleavers (*Galium* spp.), tares (*Lathyrus* spp.), and vetches (*Vicia* spp.) that encourage lodging (Figure 5.3). The later weeding is omitted if the crop is very clean, the weather unsuitable (too wet to tread between plants or too dry to uproot them), or labor insufficient, although some households used external labor. For example, Dorin's mother, having only one child, recruited women with insufficient land as

Figure 5.3 Valentina and Antonia uproot bindweeds, cleavers, vetches, and tares by hand in spelt at Zureda, Asturias.

helpers for weeding and harvesting. Alternatively, someone who had borrowed draft cattle might weed in return (without set agreement, "whatever they could manage"). With estimates of 1–8 woman-days per *dia de bueyes* (800 m^2) for February–March hoeing and 0.5–2 woman-days for April–May weeding, depending on whether plots were clean or "full of rubbish," the two operations together were as time-consuming as harvesting (two to seven person-days) and substantially more so than tillage and sowing (one man-day). Whereas the harvest also involved men, weeding was less time-stressed and normally done by women. Nonetheless, Maria's claim that she hoed for a month in Llanos de Somerón is plausible if she spent three to four days on each of six to eight *dias de bueyes*. Hoeing, which could not start until weeds emerged, had to be completed alongside other tasks when the weather was suitable. A few decades ago, when glume wheat was grown on a larger scale (≤0.5 ha/household), an animal-drawn harrow often preceded or, though less effective, replaced the hoe. The later phase of weeding was faster but again time-limited because, once the ear emerged, walking through the crop could do more harm than good; a local saying warns, "go in May with a stick, but in June not even with fist." A debilitating allergic reaction to handling cleavers (*Galium aparine*) forces several women to undertake the later weeding in short spells, making prompt and thorough completion even harder. Both rounds of weeding are slower in heavily infested crops and thus on heavy rather than light soils. By common consent, the effort invested was dictated by weediness rather than distance, although most plots cultivated today are within 30 minutes walk of the village.

Asturian weeding of winter cereals is unusually intensive for southern Europe. In Greece, *hoeing* at ankle or shin height was largely restricted to (and the usual rationale for) row-sown grain crops. This was normal for maize and some other summer crops and not uncommon for the larger-seeded Old World pulses (broad bean, pea, chickpea), especially in gardens, but wheat too was sometimes row-sown (and hoed) rather than broadcast, mainly to secure weed-free seedcorn (Section 2.4). Row sowing and, especially, hoeing were labor-intensive and restricted in scale. Hand weeding, practicable with broadcast as well as row-sown crops, was much commoner. In Greece, this took place between March and May and stopped when the ground became too hard for uprooting or (in cereals) when the ear emerged; in northern Jordan, where ripening is earlier, hand weeding occurred between January and March (Palmer, 1998a, 148). In Greece, at least, weeding usually involved uprooting by bare hand or cutting with a sickle or knife, although more specialized tools were used elsewhere, for example, at Zuheros in Andalucia. Uprooted or cut weeds were consumed by the family (as boiled greens) or its livestock (usually fresh) or left on the edge of the field to wither. As in Asturias, hand weeding was selective in its targets: the bigger and more obvious plants such as red poppies, yellow- or white-flowered relatives of cabbage (*Brassica* spp.) and mustard (*Sinapis* spp.), and tall wild oats; species with noxious seeds, notably corncockle (*Agrostemma githago*); thistles that injured reapers' hands; and vetches (*Vicia* spp.) and tares (*Lathyrus* spp.) that impeded the harvest. Vetches and tares had to be tackled before they entangled the crop and so wheat was weeded before lentil in Assiros, even though the latter was harvested earlier. One of the worst cereal weeds was darnel (*Lolium temulentum*), which was not visually obvious and not easily removed because its slender stems were tough and roots firm.

Some crops were weeded more than others. In southern Spain (Peña-Chocarro, 1996, 133), southern France, and northern Greece, farmers did not weed einkorn because it smothered competitors by tillering strongly (France, Greece) or grew on land too poor for them to flourish (Spain). Emmer and spelt were hand-weeded, however, in Garfagnana and Asturias. Flax, sown densely to develop long stems for fiber, also smothered weeds more successfully than wheat at Korifasio in southern Greek Messenia. Giorgos' oats and rye at north Greek Mavrorakhi were vigorous enough to outcompete weeds, but his wheat did less well on the poor hillslopes and sometimes needed weeding, "provided the [expected] losses to weeds were more than the damage done weeding a broadcast crop." On Kithira, Panagiotitsa weeded wheat, barley, and *smigó* (wheat/barley maslin) for household consumption, but not oats and common vetch for livestock. At Ano Asites in central Crete, Maria likewise weeded wheat and broad beans. Wheat, being less competitive and for human consumption, was thus widely weeded where "lesser" cereals were not, but some farmers weeded the latter if it seemed necessary; Mitsos in Paliambela "started with the wheat, but did the others if they were very bad."

Other important considerations were the scale of the task and availability of labor. In lowland northern Greece, Konstantinos from Neo Sidirokhori hand-weeded his small chickpea crop but for staple wheat relied on thorough cleaning of seedcorn on the threshing floor and harrowing after sowing. In Assiros, Tasoula, whose father – like Konstantinos – farmed enough land to maintain his own draft pair, only recalls pulling other *cereals* from wheat intended for seedcorn. Fotis contrasted smallholders, who were at best self-sufficient in grain and hand-weeded their cereals, with big landowners, who sowed on much too large a scale to contemplate this (and, as they practiced biennial cultivated fallow, had relatively weed-free cereals). Conversely, farmers in the hills of central Greece (Loukopoulos, 1983, 185), at Plikati and Agios Minas in the Pindos Mountains, at Tharounia on Euboea, at Iklaina and Milioti in Messenia, at Aroniadika and Mitata on Kithira, and at Aloides on Crete routinely weeded both cereals and pulses, even if wheat and lentils or peas received more attention than fodder crops (as in northern Jordan – Palmer, 1998a, 148). Weeding was more inclusive than in the northern plains, perhaps partly because smaller-scale cereal growing and sparser crop stands were more manageable with available labor. Under conditions less favorable to cereals, greater concern might also be expected to safeguard vulnerable staple crops, but informants from Crete who did *not* weed cereals offered no such hint: Fountoulonikolis in Kalo Khorio recalled that "the heavy fields produce a lot of weeds, but we didn't weed the cereals [on the lighter slopes] because it was a lot of trouble"; and Nikolis in Skalani asked, "how could you weed ten *strémmata* [1 ha]?" – the area of wheat intensively *hoed* by Nikolaos' father in north Greek Kolindros.

In fact, weeds probably posed fewer problems in southern than northern Greece. Up north, as the Paliambela *tsípouro* circle stressed, weeds flourished in years with abundant spring rainfall, on heavy rather than light soils, and on recently manured land. The same conditions favor a successful harvest, highlighting the importance of weeding. Likewise in southern Greece, Fotini at Kithiran Mitata complained that, without spring rainfall, crops failed and, with it, they were full of weeds that slowed the harvest and work on the threshing floor. Nevertheless, with lower spring rainfall and sparser stall manure, weed growth must have been significantly less vigorous than in northern Greece, as practitioners' accounts of weeding also imply. In northern Greece, weeded plants were often abandoned on the edge of the field to wither, and informants never cited use as fodder or edible greens as a reason for collection. Further south, use of weeded plants was commonplace and "weeding" often rationalized in terms of collecting greens or fodder. In Tharounia, two informants abandoned weeding wheat when they gave up draft cattle (one increased her sowing rate to smother the weeds), while a third decided whether to weed her broad bean garden in light of her goats' fodder requirements.

Weeds were collected for the odd work animal or a few milk sheep or goats and, as in northern Jordan (Palmer, 1998b, 7), were too sparse to feed more than, say, 10 sheep and goats. In most cases, weeds were fed to livestock fresh, although Thanasis at Kithiran Kastrisianika dried batches for stored hay. Greens for human consumption were also an important outcome of southern Greek "weeding," as reflected in Panagiotis' comment that cereals at Potamia in Messenia produced good *lakhaniká* (vegetables), in Panagiotitsa's description of weeding on Kithira as removing "vegetables [eaten] and thistles [discarded]," and in Manolis' statement that crops were *only* weeded at Anogia on Crete to provide greens for human consumption. Indeed, a few southern Greek informants initially denied weeding because my question implied removal of *unwanted* plants. In northern Jordan, some edible weeds are tolerated in crop stands (Palmer, 1998a, 148) and some "wild" edible greens in Greek vegetable gardens are effectively cultivated, although normally self-seeding.

Palmer (1998a, 148) offers figures of 8 and (with difficulty) 1.5 person-days/0.1 ha for hand weeding in northern Jordan, while Maria from Messenian Milioti suggested that one person could comfortably weed more than 0.1 ha per day; the faster figures are compatible with those from Asturias. Most Greek informants were unwilling to offer a figure, however, reflecting great variation in weed infestation, the widespread observation that "we did what we could [with available labor]," and the tendency to weed piecemeal, particularly when foraging for edible greens or fresh fodder (cf. Clark Forbes, 1976). In Greece, women usually undertook both large-scale weeding, by groups of neighbors (for mutual assistance and company) or hired workers, and piecemeal foraging, although married couples also weeded on an intermediate scale.

5.6 Crop Husbandry and Crop Yields

The proactive and reactive husbandry practices described in the preceding text were applied to varying degrees. First, areas with drier summers encouraged more irrigation, lighter manuring, and more

238

cautious preventive grazing. Secondly, labor-intensive application of scarce water and manure declined, and fallowing increased, with distance to fields (Hillman, 1973a, 219–220), while laborious manual weeding, especially of vulnerable summer crops and perhaps winter grains of small-scale farmers, gave way to cultivated fallow on large farms with powerful draft animals. Thirdly, husbandry practices are often interlinked: for example, irrigation enables heavier manuring, which reduces the need for fallowing and increases that for weeding and preventive grazing, while fallowing may increase pasture, livestock numbers, and thus availability of manure. Coupled with constraints of scale and distance, this favors association of intensive methods (rotation, manuring, weeding, watering) with small-scale infields (e.g., broad bean and pea gardens at Tharounia, spelt/emmer plots in Asturias) and of extensive methods (notably cultivated fallow) with large-scale outfields (e.g., winter cereals of large landowners in Assiros). Farmers observed the effects of different husbandry practices on growing and harvested crops. Quantifying their observations is difficult, partly because of how they make and remember them (see the following text) and partly because yields are the outcome of husbandry interacting with environmental conditions that vary locally (e.g., soils, exposure) and interannually (e.g., weather, pests). Nonetheless, focusing on staple winter cereals (without industrial fertilizer, unless stated otherwise), some consistent trends emerge.

In Asturias, informants measured yields of heavily manured and regularly weeded spelt/emmer in *fanegas* (50 kg) of dehusked grain per *dia de bueyes* (0.08 ha). Whether recalling particular harvests from specific fields or generalizing, they consistently regarded two (1250 kg/ha), three (1875 kg/ha), and four (2500 kg/ha) *fanegas/ dia de bueyes* as poor, normal, and good, respectively. At Piazza al Serchio in the gentler Garfagnana hills, much more lightly manured emmer was said to yield 1800–2500 kg/ha of grain *in the glume* or 1100–1500 kg/ha of *dehusked* grain – "poor" in Asturian terms. In Haute Provence, einkorn is rotated with grazed pasture, nitrogen-fixing *sainfoin* (for hay), or multiyear lavender crops but on very marginal land without manure – conditions under which bread wheat fails. Yields of 500–1250 kg/ha of *dehusked* grain thus high-light how undemanding einkorn is; conversely, manure is said to "burn the crop like weed killer" in dry years and cause lodging or shedding of ears in more favorable conditions.

In lowland northern Greece, first harvests of free-threshing wheat on freshly cleared land without manure (Section 6.1.1) were dra-matically ("up to two or three times") better than the long-term average, with yields variously estimated at 800 (Kolindros), 1300–2700 (Paliambela), 2000 (Aiginio), 5000 (Kitros, Kolindros), and 7500 (Aiginio) kg/ha. On established fields at Aiginio, Kolindros, Paliambela, Assiros, and Neo Sidirokhori, estimates for wheat mostly ranged between 400 and 1600 kg/ha, depending on soils, weather, and husbandry. Thus, Mitsos in Paliambela recalls wheat yielding 1000–1300 kg/ha on the best fields (largely without manure) and 650–1000 kg/ha on poorer land in good years ("one year in every three or four when the rains worked out"), but less, especially on poor fields, "in bad years when March–April was dry." In Assiros, Spiros recalled his sharecropper father getting 400–1000 kg/ha after cultivated fallow but 300 kg/ha "on stubble" (directly after a preceding wheat crop), while Black Vangelis claimed yields of 1000–1600 kg/ha on well-plowed fields where he had folded his 300 sheep, as against 600 kg/ha for neighbors with smaller plow animals and no sheep. At Kolindros, Iraklis harvested 650–1300 kg/ha from the block of land fertilized by his winter sheepfold and summer pens but much less on scattered outlying fields manured only by grazing herds; Nikolaos, whose father mainly farmed scat-tered plots distant from his sheepfold, considers 400 kg/ha a plau-sible average. The effects of husbandry could be cumulative, as with the repeatedly manured and very fertile *avlés* at Assiros or *sókhora* at Tharounia. Conversely, yields on the Paliambela Thracians' fields, cleared but rested when they arrived in the 1920s, declined over decades of continuous cultivation with rare fallowing and limited manuring. The less demanding cereals, sown on poorer fields or after nutrient-hungry wheat, coped better with unfavorable conditions: Alexis in Assiros harvested up to 1200 kg/ha of barley and "650 kg, 800 kg at most," of wheat, while Mitsos in Paliambela suggested 1000–1300 kg/ha of barley and 650–1000 kg/ha of wheat on poor land. The field that Mitsos' father manured regularly for early-bite pasture gave as much barley grain in a good year (with March–April rain) as fields that were neither manured nor grazed, but did not recover and yielded poorly in a dry spring.

At Tharounia on Euboea, Konia estimates that she harvested 15–20 sheaves (with six *okádes* of wheat grain each) per 0.1 ha of manured land in the southern zone of alternate-year cultivation and up to 100 sheaves on a 0.4 ha plot in the northern zone. With favorable weather, therefore, yields on manured plots exceeded 1000 kg/ha and perhaps approached 2000 kg/ha. Land manured only by grazing herds, however, bore cereals so short they were harvested by uprooting, and "if you had not plowed the field in winter, while it lay fallow, you were better off not sowing at all." On Kithira, the staple wheat/barley maslin widely alternated with common vetch on marginal land, now mostly under evergreen *maquis* or heather and rock-rose. Per *zevgaréa* (day's plowing) and without stall manure, Thanasis from Kastrisianika reaped from five sheaves in a bad year to 20 in a good year (perhaps 250 and 1000 kg/ha, respectively), while Fotini from Mitata suggests a range of 25–100 *okádes* (say, 200–750 kg/ha). On central Crete, hilly land freshly cleared of shrubs near Ano Asites initially yielded about 1000 kg/ha of wheat (Section 6.1.2). Long-term cultivation yielded well above and below this figure, depending on location and rotation regime. Without stall manure but with cultivated fallow every fourth year, Giorgis harvested 500–600 *okádes* of wheat from 0.4 ha (1600–1900 kg/ha) of his best land in the Knossos valley, which was unusually fertile for central Crete. On the much poorer slopes around Kalo Khorio, where barley alternated with fallow, Kostis reaped four to five (–six) mule loads (each of four sheaves) per day's plowing, matching the upper end of the range for Kithira. At Mirtos in arid southeast Crete, Daskalos' barley *with industrial fertilizer* yielded from 250–300 kg/ha in a bad (rainless) year to 650–700 kg/ha in a good year; in his youth, *without fertilizer*, harvests had been "half or less."

Aşvan in inland eastern Turkey, with an annual rainfall around 430 mm a little wetter than southeast Crete, allows comparison of rain-fed and irrigated yields, both without agrochemicals (Hillman, 1973b, 226–227): 410 kg/ha and 1150 kg/ha, respectively, for two-row spring barley and 630 kg/ha and 1100 kg/ha for winter wheat. The two regimes shared similar rotations, rain-fed cereals typically alternating with fallow or a fodder pulse and irrigated cereals with a summer crop or fodder pulse. Stall manure was concentrated on irrigated land, however, and this, being closer to the settlement, was probably tilled more thoroughly, so differences in yields are not due to irrigation alone. The yield of two-row barley without irrigation highlights the low productivity of spring-sown cereals under scarce rainfall (Section 2.3).

These reported cereal yields from southern Europe and Anatolia consistently highlight the benefits of practices such as manuring, irrigation, or fallowing. Yields as low as 250–500 kg/ha are reported for bad years or areas marginal to cereal growing, but "traditional" husbandry, on land under long-term cultivation without agrochemicals, frequently exceeded one ton and occasionally two tons of grain per hectare. The latter figures are strikingly more optimistic than many early twentieth-century "official" figures for wheat and barley under rain-fed agriculture: around 700 kg/ha (500–1000 kg/ha in different regions) for Greece (Gallant, 1991, 77, table 4.7), 850 kg/ha for Basilicata in southern Italy (Spurr, 1986, 88), and 500–650 kg/ha for Jordan and Palestine (where practitioners' expectations also exceeded official figures – Palmer, 1998a, 155, table 8). In part, this discrepancy is because official figures purport to be *averages* for large regions over several years, whereas "unofficial" figures describe what might be *expected* in good and perhaps poor years, omitting rare bumper and failed harvests. Consideration of how official data were collected, however, casts doubt on their reliability. First, much of the harvest, especially of lesser grains and on small farms, was consumed at source and measured by local officials, at best, during assessment for tithes – normally an approximate process with a bias to *under*estimation. Secondly, in regions of broken relief, where land measurement in areal extent was often impracticable, making area yields unknowable, local officials evidently reported educated guesses or administrative fictions (Forte, 2009).

Conversely, individual farmers routinely measured grain on the threshing floor, even if reluctant to share this information with officialdom, and could provide more contextually nuanced figures, albeit subject to rhetorical manipulation.

Insofar as farmers plan for the expected rather than unexpected, likely yields under more and less favorable conditions are more useful to them (and us) than long-term regional averages – even reliable ones. The kinds of yield data farmers volunteer are instructive. First, while informants may offer improbably high or low figures for rhetorical purposes, serious attempts at generalization tend to start with likely yields under favorable (but imperfect) conditions. Southern Greek olive growers take big trees in good years as their yardstick (Forbes, 1982, 98), presumably because expected yields from small trees or bad years could fall anywhere between this and zero – certainly not from blind optimism as they routinely recite dates of damage by weather or pests. Somewhat similarly, North Greek farmers often report grain yields in terms like "we harvested X tons/ha, but would have got twice that if not for the *lívas*/ hail/locusts in June." In the weeks before harvest, they estimate likely yields from density of crop, size of ear, and fullness of grain (the same methodology underpins some official data!) and, accordingly, usually describe weather and pests as lowering yields in bad years rather than raising them in good while occasionally acknowledging that excellent winter rainfall gifted a bumper harvest or late showers rescued a drought-stricken crop. Secondly, farmers more often volunteer yields for high- (usually free-threshing wheat) than low-status cereals (e.g., oats). It is perhaps easier to predict yields of bread wheat on good land or at the start of a rotation cycle than of oats on poor land or as the last crop before fallow, but farmers often absorb good and bad yields of low-status crops by feeding livestock more or less generously, whereas fluctuations in human dietary staples may result in sale or purchase. The market encourages measurement: on Kithira, says Thanasis, "every house had scales for selling, but at home, you did not weigh – you knew roughly what each chest held," while in Asturian Xomezana, Inés knew how many sacks of glume wheat ears she harvested but "did not measure the [threshed]

243

crop because we did not sell or buy grain." Thirdly, although discussion here has focused on area yields, the ratio of seedcorn to yield was often the traditional currency (Hillman, 1973b, 226; Spurr, 1986, 84–88; Palmer, 1998a, 155). In Greece, my enquiries have been answered in these terms only twice, referring to the early and mid-twentieth century respectively at Agia Paraskevi in the Pindos Mountains and Lazarades further east in the Kamvounia hills, although widespread quantification of land in volume of seedcorn (e.g., the Cretan and Cycladic *mouzoúri* – Petropoulos, 1952) generated yield data of this form. Seed to yield ratios may frustrate the historian, because they reflect sowing rate (often variable and unknown) as well as production per unit area, but make sense to farmers, because they "correct" for variable quality of land (poorer being sown more lightly) and do not presume knowledge of its extent. Area yields are favored where land is sold and rented for cash, generally in terrain where it is also easily measured. Conversely, in early twentieth-century Crete, rent was sometimes pegged to seedcorn (e.g., as *sképas* ["covering"] at Anogia).

5.7 Crop Husbandry and Yields in the Past

Increasingly, isotopic and ecological analysis of on-site crop remains (e.g., Araus *et al.*, 1997; Fraser *et al.*, 2011) and accompanying weed seeds (e.g., Jones *et al.*, 2010), respectively, can discern the husbandry practices discussed earlier. "Every year is not the same," to quote Alexis in Assiros, so practices differ from year to year (and field to field) in timing, intensity, and isotopic or ecological effects. Similar methods may discriminate between good and bad years (cf. Heaton *et al.*, 2009), however, and between social groups with differential access to land (Bogaard, Krause, and Strien, 2011) and may shed light on the distribution and scale of these practices that complements "off-site" mapping of irrigation (Guinot Rodríguez, 2008) and field systems (e.g., Palet and Orengo, 2011), paths radiating from settlements (e.g., Ur, 2003), and surface pottery scatters interpreted as domestic refuse spread with stall manure (e.g., Wilkinson,

1994; Bevan, 2002). Recent practice highlights the difficulty of relating "manuring scatters" to particular forms of land use (Alcock, Cherry, and Davis, 1994): stall manure was variously spread on gardens, orchards, pulses, high-status cereals, poor fields, sown pasture/hay crops, or even unsown meadow; and that spread with little ceramic refuse (e.g., from outlying byres and folds) will not register in surface scatters. Given the difficulty of premechanized transport, however, manuring is a plausible interpretation of the "halos" of surface pottery extending a few hundred meters from ancient rural sites and a little further, declining with distance and slope, from towns such as Boeotian Thespiai (e.g., Bintliff and Snodgrass, 1985; Howard, 2007, 127, fig. 8.28), while crop isotope and weed data may clarify *what* was manured. Hitherto, in the absence of *direct* archaeological evidence for husbandry practices, early farming regimes were often modeled on assumptions about available (usually advancing) technology and know-how, but recent Mediterranean farming highlights how practical constraints (land, labor, climate) may shape husbandry choices and the application of technology and know-how; Williamson (1998) has argued likewise for the early modern agricultural revolution in England. The tension in Mediterranean farming between know-how and practical constraints is briefly explored here for Greco-Roman antiquity and the Neolithic.

In comparing husbandry methods in different regions and interpreting the biological and ecological basis of agricultural observations, the Greco-Roman "agronomist" writers invite analysis in terms of prevailing know-how, leading Isager and Skydsgaard (1992, 199) to label classical Greek agriculture as "rather primitive," whereas White saw Roman "development" in cereal growing (1970a, 289) and "much progress in arboriculture" (1970b, 260). The agronomists describe know-how – primitive or progressive – comparable with that of recent "traditional" farmers (Grigg, 1974, 135), often using similar rationales and imagery. They cover (especially the more extensive Roman sources) almost all the practices discussed in this chapter (Spurr, 1986, esp. 42–43, 56, 64–65, 118–119, 128; White, 1970b, esp. 118–123, 129–131, 153–155): for example, resowing after frost damage to winter cereals (Pliny *Naturalis Historia* 18.183); early preventive grazing, cutting, or harrowing of excessively vigorous cereals (Theophrastus *Historia Plantarum* 8.7.4; Pliny *Naturalis Historia* 18.161, 186); measured spreading of rotted stall manure to avoid lodging, burning, and weed infestation (Columella *de Re Rustica* 2.14.9, 2.15.2); heavier manuring, given sufficient rainfall, of poor land than rich (Theophrastus *Causae Plantarum* 3.9.2, 3.20.2); early and heavy sowing of barley or oats on well-manured land for early-bite grazing or hay (Columella *de Re Rustica* 2.10.31–2.10.32); irrigation of gardens (Cato *de Agri Cultura* 1.7) and orchards (Pliny *Naturalis Historia* 17.249–17.250); weeding of cereals (Xenophon *Oeconomicus* 17.14); and a range of alternative fallowing and rotation regimes (Pliny *Naturalis Historia* 18.187). Some passages report implausible hearsay, whether expressed with caution (e.g., Theophrastus' "they say that in...") or authority (e.g., Columella's high manure output from stalled livestock – Spurr, 1986, 129–130), but the principal question is not whether, but how widely, the methods described were applied. Xenophon (*Oeconomicus* 20.2–5) regarded good farmers as more assiduous, not more knowledgeable, than bad farmers, while Pliny (*Naturalis Historia* 18.38) advised good rather than optimal husbandry unless the latter was possible without external labor. Given how distance and scale of cultivation constrained recent farmers, one might expect – other things being equal – more costly equipment on large classical estates (e.g., Spurr, 1986, 141) and more labor-intensive methods on smaller farms. For Greece, the latter expectation matches the contrast between elite literary emphasis on extensive cereal cultivation with alternate bare fallow and epigraphic evidence of leases documenting cereal–pulse rotation (Jameson, 1977; Amouretti, 1986, 51, 56; Hodkinson, 1988). Roman writers likewise imply a tendency for fallowing on large and more intensive rotations on smaller farms (Spurr 1986, 118), with fallowing requiring more land (Pliny *Naturalis Historia* 18.187) but less labor (Virgil *Georgica* 1.79).

Only archaeological evidence can determine how widely particular practices were applied and by whom (e.g., large- vs. small-scale producers), with implications for both agricultural innovation and how surplus grain was produced to feed cities and finance elite consumption: by intensive husbandry and high area yields (White, 1970a; for the Bronze Age Near East, Wilkinson, 1994) or by extensive, labor-saving methods (Section 2.7; for the Ottoman Cyclades, Davis, 1991). For Greco-Roman antiquity, small rural sites identified by surface survey, whether permanent farmsteads or seasonal shelters (Pettegrew, 2001), would have facilitated intensive cultivation (Alcock, Cherry, and Davis, 1994, 163; Section 5.3.1.3, on outlying barns and byres in Asturias). Temporal and regional variation in their density (e.g., Alcock, 2007; Terrenato, 2007) thus reflects shifting *potential* for intensive farming, while fluctuations in off-site "manuring scatters" are compatible with a trend from intensive Classical–Early Hellenistic farming to extensive agriculture on Late Hellenistic–Roman estates (e.g., Bintliff, Howard, and Snodgrass, 2007, 178–179). More directly, archaeobotanical data from the temperate margins of the Greco-Roman world increasingly demonstrate *extensive* cereal agriculture from the first millennium BC or early first millennium AD (e.g., Jacomet and Brombacher, 2009), contemporary with growing demand for surplus grain (van der Veen and Jones, 2006), although more evidence is needed especially from the Mediterranean.

Farming in Neolithic Europe has particularly attracted models of "primitive" husbandry (Isaakidou, 2011), with slash-and-burn or floodplain cultivation exploiting short-term natural fertility with minimal tillage. Both models are practically (Sections 2.7 and 6.9) and, especially for temperate Europe, empirically implausible (Bogaard, 2004; 2005). Available crop weed evidence suggests long-term cultivation of cleared plots, probably involving intensive tillage and maintenance of soil fertility. In recent Mediterranean farming, intensive husbandry declines with increasing distance to cultivated plots (widely exacerbated by nucleated rural settlement) and scale of cultivation (raised by overproduction for urban markets). Smaller and *relatively* self-sufficient Neolithic settlements faced fewer practical obstacles to intensive husbandry (Bogaard and Isaakidou, 2010).

For example, a household of five, consuming a "generous" 1500 kg of grain and harvesting 1000 kg/ha, would need to sow

1.5 ha annually (Bogaard, 2004, 43, table 2.2) – achievable by sharing draft cows with a neighbor or, at favorable points in the domestic cycle, by hand (Section 2.6.1). A Neolithic "village" of 20–40 households (many were smaller and some probably larger), or 100–200 head, would thus consume the harvest of 30–60 ha each year, implying plots within 300 or 450 m, for a village at the center or edge, respectively, of consolidated cultivated land (cf. Isaakidou, 2008, 102–103, tables 6.1 and 6.2). Over such distances, recent villagers maintained intensive gardens and work animals carried stall manure. On the scale proposed, many plots could have been row-sown, sparing seedcorn and facilitating weeding, and pulses more frequent than today (as Neolithic plant remains from southeast Europe imply), enabling cereal–pulse rotation. Any deficiencies in early tillage equipment (whether digging sticks or cow-drawn ards) would have discouraged regular fallowing. Under such a regime, especially before late Neolithic "marginal colonization" of areas with low rainfall and poor soils, experimental and ethnographic data suggest average yields of 1000 kg/ha were achievable (Bogaard, 2004, 42–43). These calculations make no allowance for seedcorn (modest with row sowing), fallowing (arguably infrequent), or "normal surplus" to buffer bad years (Allan, 1965), but crops could have yielded significantly above 1000 kg/ha if manured.

In *mainland* southern Europe, the enclosures inevitably defending crops from herbivores presumably also, at night, protected from predators any livestock grazing near settlements; folded livestock would have manured arable plots directly, while any dung accumulated in pens could have been spread with sledges (if not carts) drawn by cows (Isaakidou, 2008). Even if diet was mainly grain based, consistent with pathological and stable isotopic evidence from human skeletons, manuring need not have been sparse. First, the highly abrasive diet of Neolithic livestock in southeast Europe (Mainland, 2007; Rivals, Gardeisen, and Cantuel, 2011) suggests a much closer association than today between livestock and disturbed cultivated ground, with more of their dung benefitting crops. Secondly, most Neolithic livestock were reared to a greater age and carcass size than recently (when many infants were culled from dairy herds) and so produced significantly less protein but more manure per head per year. Absolute numbers are unknown, but if each household maintained one adult working/ breeding cow and one younger bovine (a replacement cow or a male for slaughter), it should also have owned several dozen sheep and some pigs and goats to create the sheep-dominated faunal assemblages from southeast European Neolithic villages (Halstead, 1992). With year-round nocturnal folding on arable land, this might make a manuring capacity equivalent to 10–15 winter-stalled cattle per household or 7–10 per hectare sown – within the range for recent intensive spelt/emmer in Asturias. This figure may be excessive, for example, if few households maintained a cow but equally could be an underestimate. Without a grain market, livestock perhaps played a bigger role than recently as a "bank" for surpluses in good years and as emergency food or exchangeable wealth in bad (Section 6.6). Coupled with the prominence of meat in collective commensality (e.g., Halstead and Isaakidou, 2011), this suggests strong practical and ideological incentives for households to expand herds. Either way, with pulses replacing the nutrient-hungry maize and potatoes with which spelt/emmer alternates in Asturias, Neolithic cereal crops may routinely have needed grazing in late winter to avert lodging. These proposed Neolithic husbandry methods might seem more "modern" than "primitive" but presuppose neither complex technology nor obscure know-how. They highlight how radically unfamiliar Neolithic farming may have been in scale and intensity – resembling "gardening" or "horticulture" more than traditional extensive agriculture – and in the close integration of crops and livestock.

An issue not yet considered is changes over time in *potential* crop productivity. The "unofficial" figures cited earlier for free-threshing wheats relate to old long-strawed types, mainly landraces. Until the dramatic improvements of the last decades (e.g., Giunta, Motzo, and Pruneddu, 2007), *maximum* yields may not have changed for centuries (Percival, 1974, 417–418), so the higher reported yields under traditional husbandry were probably matched – under favorable climatic, edaphic, and husbandry conditions – in classical antiquity. Sallares' thesis (1991, 372–389) of significant preclassical improvement in free-threshing wheats, and thus low yield potential in the European Neolithic, lacks empirical support, and early increases in grain size probably reflect husbandry methods rather than yields per se (Fuller, Willcox, and Allaby, 2012, 625); conversely, uncertain Mediterranean rainfall and flexible husbandry probably maintained genetically heterogeneous crops that coped with variable conditions (Calderini and Slafer, 1999; Abbo, Lev-Yadun, and Gopher, 2010). Some consider glume wheats, the dominant preclassical cereals, not to respond to favorable growing conditions, but this impression at least partly reflects their tolerance of, and recent relegation to, marginal climatic and soil conditions (cf. Davies and Hillman, 1988). Percival (1974, 171, 191, 327) cites late nineteenth- or early twentieth-century AD yields for einkorn and spelt on good soils (location unstated) up to 3500 kg/ha of grain in the glume (perhaps ≤2000–2500 kg/ha dehusked grain), while emmer with high nitrogen dressing achieved 4400 kg/ha in the glume (3200 kg/ha dehusked) in modern central Italian experiments (Marino *et al.*, 2009; 2011). Because of their long and (especially einkorn) slender stems, fertilized glume wheats in some experiments suffer from lodging (Troccoli and Codianni, 2005), but preventive grazing might have solved this in the past. Similarly, farmers in Haute Provence report that einkorn lodges on rich or manured ground and burns if low rainfall follows manuring, but in wetter conditions, manured einkorn would have been less prone to burning and could safely have been grazed to avoid lodging. If initial indications of intensive methods in Neolithic southern Europe (Bogaard, 2005) are confirmed, long-term average yields for glume wheats of 1500 kg/ha are not implausible. At any rate, and contrary to what is commonly assumed, average yields are likely to have been significantly higher than in classical antiquity, when extensive agriculture was widespread. Equally, for small-scale Greco-Roman cultivators at least, the assessment (Grigg, 1974, 135; Sallares, 1991, 389) that "yields could have rarely exceeded 650 kg per hectare, except on the better soils" seems pessimistic.

For smallholders reliant on household labor, area yields determined whether or not self-sufficiency was achievable. For the grain supply of urban populations, however, and the contribution of grain sales to elite wealth, the crucial variable was the amount of marketable surplus, and this depended as much on low labor costs as high area yields; modest area yields with modest labor inputs might produce more surplus than high yields with high inputs. This principle will have been exaggerated if, as advocated by Varro (*Res Rusticae* 1.49.1) and implied by earlier Greek inscriptions (Garnsey and Morris, 1989; also Ottoman Crete – Balta, 1992–1994), large landowners profited from grain production primarily by storing surplus from good years with low prices for sale in bad years with high prices. In this context, area yields convey no useful information to the producer, whereas seed to yield ratios arguably provide a more meaningful measure of the extent to which the store of grain is increased or renewed (extending its "shelf life").

References

Abbo, S., Lev-Yadun, S., and Gopher, A. (2010) Yield stability: an agronomic perspective on the origin of Near Eastern agriculture. *Vegetation History & Archaeobotany*, 19, 143–150.

Alberola Romá, A. (1981) Análisis y evolución histórica del sistema de riego en la huerta alicantina. *Anales de la Universidad de Alicante, Revista de Historia Moderna*, 1, 117–140.

Alcock, S.E. (2007) The essential countryside: the Greek world, in *Classical Archaeology* (eds S.E. Alcock and R. Osborne), Blackwell, Oxford, pp. 120–138.

Alcock, S.E., Cherry, J.F., and Davis, J.L. (1994) Intensive survey, agricultural practice and the classical landscape of Greece, in *Classical Greece: Ancient Histories and Modern Archaeologies* (ed. I. Morris), Cambridge University Press, Cambridge, UK, pp. 137–170.

Allan, W. (1965) *The African Husbandman*, Oliver and Boyd, Edinburgh.

Amouretti, M.-C. (1986) *Le pain et l' huile dans la Grèce antique: de l' araire au moulin*, Les Belles Lettres, Paris.

Araus, J.L., Febrero, A., Buxó, R. *et al.* (1997) Identification of ancient irrigation practices based on the carbon isotope discrimination of plant seeds: a case study from the south-east Iberian peninsula. *Journal of Archaeological Science*, 24, 729–740.

Balta, E. (1992–1994) The bread in Greek lands during the Ottoman rule. *Ankara Üniversitesi, Dil ve Tarih-Coğrafya Fakültesi, Tarih Bölümü, Tarih Araştırmaları Dergisi*, 16, 199–224.

Basgöz, I. (1967) Rain-making ceremonies in Turkey and seasonal festivals. *Journal of the American Oriental Society*, 87, 304–306.

Basgöz, I. (2007) Rain-making ceremonies in Iran. *Iranian Studies*, 40, 385–403.

Baticle, Y. (1974) *L'élevage ovin dans les pays européens de la Méditerranée occidentale*, Les Belles Lettres, Paris.

Bevan, A. (2002) The rural landscape of Neopalatial Kythera: a GIS perspective. *Journal of Mediterranean Archaeology*, 15, 217–255.

Bintliff, J.L. and Snodgrass, A.M. (1985) The Cambridge/Bradford Boeotian expedition: the first four years. *Journal of Field Archaeology*, 12, 123–161.

Bintliff, J., Howard, P., and Snodgrass, A. (2007) *Testing the Hinterland: The Work of the Boeotia Survey (1989–1991) in the Southern Approaches to the City of Thespiai*, McDonald Institute for Archaeological Research, Cambridge, UK.

Bogaard, A. (2004) *Neolithic Farming in Central Europe: An Archaeobotanical Study of Crop Husbandry Practices*, Routledge, London.

Bogaard, A. (2005) 'Garden agriculture' and the nature of early farming in Europe and the Near East. *World Archaeology*, 37, 177–196.

Bogaard, A. and Isaakidou, V. (2010) From mega-sites to farmsteads: community size, ideology and the nature of early farming landscapes in western Asia and Europe, in *Landscapes in Transition* (eds B. Finlayson and G. Warren), Oxbow, Oxford, pp. 192–207.

Bogaard, A., Krause, R., and Strien, H.-C. (2011) Towards a social geography of cultivation and plant use in an early farming community: Vaihingen an der Enz, south-west Germany. *Antiquity*, 85, 395–416.

Calderini, D.F. and Slafer, G.A. (1999) Has yield stability changed with genetic improvement of wheat yield? *Euphytica*, 107, 51–59.

Carranza Alcalde, G. (2009) *La Huecha y la Elma. Una historia de riegos y conflictos en el Valle del Río Huecha*, Centro de Estudios Borjanos, Borja.

Charles, M. and Hoppé, C. (2003) The effects of irrigation on the weed floras of winter cereal crops in Wadi Ibn Hamad (southern Jordan). *Levant*, 35, 213–230.

Chisholm, M. (1968) *Rural Settlement and Land Use: An Essay in Location*, 2nd edn, Hutchinson, London.

Clark Forbes, M.H. (1976) Gathering in the Argolid: a subsistence subsystem in a Greek agricultural community. *Annals of the New York Academy of Sciences*, 268, 251–264.

Cuadrat Prats, J.M. (2008) Los condicionantes geográficos en la historia del regadío aragonés, in *¿Agua pasada? Regadíos en el Archivo Histórico Provincial de Zaragoza* (ed. J.M. Ortega Ortega), Gobierno de Aragón, Zaragoza, pp. 37–49.

Davies, M.S. and Hillman, G.C. (1988) Effects of soil flooding on growth and grain yield of populations of tetraploid and hexaploid species of wheat. *Annals of Botany*, 62, 597–604.

Davis, J.L. (1991) Contributions to a Mediterranean rural archaeology: historical case studies from the Ottoman Cyclades. *Journal of Mediterranean Archaeology*, 4, 131–215.

Forbes, H. (1976a) The 'thrice-ploughed field': cultivation techniques in ancient and modern Greece. *Expedition*, 19, 5–11.

Forbes, H. (1976b) 'We have a little of everything': the ecological basis of some agricultural practices in Methana, Trizinia. *Annals of the New York Academy of Sciences*, 268, 236–250.

Forbes, H. (1982) *Strategies and soils: technology, production and environment in the peninsula of Methana*, Greece. PhD thesis. University of Pennsylvania.

Forbes, H. (1992) The ethnoarchaeological approach to ancient Greek agriculture: olive cultivation as a case study, in *Agriculture in Ancient Greece* (ed. B. Wells), Swedish Institute at Athens, Stockholm, pp. 87–101.

Forte, M.A. (2009) *A Mediterranean mountain: landscape and land use on the Cairo Massif, Central Italy, 1700–1970 A.D.* PhD thesis. University of Sheffield.

Foxhall, L. (2007) *Olive Cultivation in Ancient Greece*, Oxford University Press, Oxford.

Fraser, R., Bogaard, A., Heaton, T., and Tsipropoulos, T. (2011) Manuring and stable nitrogen isotope ratios in cereals and pulses: towards a new archaeobotanical approach to the inference of land use and dietary practices. *Journal of Archaeological Science*, 38, 2790–2804.

Fuller, D.Q., Willcox, G., and Allaby, R.G. (2012) Early agricultural pathways: moving outside the 'core area' hypothesis in southwest Asia. *Journal of Experimental Botany*, 63, 617–633.

Gallant, T.W. (1991) *Risk and Survival in Ancient Greece*, Polity Press, Cambridge, UK.

Garcia Manrique, E. (1960) *Las comarcas de Borja y Tarazona y el somontano de Moncayo*, Diputacion Provincial, Zaragoza.

Garnsey, P. and Morris, I. (1989) Risk and the polis: the evolution of institutionalised responses to food supply problems in the ancient Greek state, in *Bad Year Economics* (eds P. Halstead and J. O'Shea), Cambridge University Press, Cambridge, UK, pp. 98–105.

Gill, N.T. and Vear, K.C. (1966) *Agricultural Botany*, 2nd edn, Duckworth, London.

Giunta, F., Motzo, R., and Pruneddu, G. (2007) Trends since 1900 in the yield potential of Italian-bred durum wheat cultivars. *European Journal of Agronomy*, 27, 12–24.

Glick, T.F. (1970) *Irrigation and Society in Medieval Valencia*, Harvard University Press, Cambridge, MA.

Grigg, D.B. (1974) *The Agricultural Systems of the World: An Evolutionary Approach*, Cambridge University Press, Cambridge, UK.

Halstead, P. (1990) Waste not, want not: traditional responses to crop failure in Greece. *Rural History*, 1, 147–164.

Halstead, P. (1992) From reciprocity to redistribution: modelling the exchange of livestock in Neolithic Greece. *Anthropozoologica*, 16, 19–30.

Halstead, P. (1998) Ask the fellows who lop the hay: leaf-fodder in the mountains of northwest Greece. *Rural History*, 9, 211–234.

Halstead, P. and Jones, G. (1989) Agrarian ecology in the Greek islands: time stress, scale and risk. *Journal of Hellenic Studies*, 109, 41–55.

Halstead, P. and Isaakidou, V. (2011) Political cuisine: rituals of commensality in the Neolithic and Bronze Age Aegean, in *Guess Who's Coming to Dinner: Feasting Rituals in the Prehistoric Societies of Europe and the Near East* (eds G.A. Jiménez, S. Montón-Subías, and S. Romero), Oxbow, Oxford, pp. 91–108.

Heaton, T.H.E., Jones, G., Halstead, P. *et al.* (2009) Variations in the $^{13}C/^{12}C$ ratios of modern wheat grain, and implications for interpreting data from Bronze Age Assiros Toumba, Greece. *Journal of Archaeological Science*, 36, 2224–2233.

Hillman, G. (1973a) Agricultural resources and settlement in the Asvan region. *Anatolian Studies*, 23, 217–224.

Hillman, G. (1973b) Agricultural productivity and past population potential at Aşvan: an exercise in the calculation of carrying capacities. *Anatolian Studies*, 23, 225–240.

Hodkinson, S. (1988) Animal husbandry in the Greek polis, in *Pastoral Economies in Classical Antiquity* (ed. C.R. Whittaker), Cambridge Philological Society, Cambridge, UK, pp. 35–74.

Howard, P. (2007) Spatial analysis of Boeotia field-walking survey data, in *Testing the Hinterland: The Work of the Boeotia Survey (1989–1991) in the Southern Approaches to the City of Thespiai* (eds J. Bintliff, P. Howard, and A. Snodgrass), McDonald Institute for Archaeological Research, Cambridge, UK, pp. 111–127.

Hudson, N. (1987) *Soil and Water Conservation in Semi-Arid Areas*, FAO, Rome.

Isaakidou, V. (2008) The fauna and economy of Neolithic Knossos revisited, in *Escaping the Labyrinth* (eds V. Isaakidou and P. Tomkins), Oxbow, Oxford, pp. 90–114.

Isaakidou, V. (2011) Gardening with cows: hoe and plough in prehistoric Europe, in *The Dynamics of Neolithisation in Europe* (eds A. Hadjikoumis, E.N. Robinson, and S. Viner), Oxbow, Oxford, pp. 90–112.

Isager, S. and Skydsgaard, J.E. (1992) *Ancient Greek Agriculture: An Introduction*, Routledge, London.

Jacomet, S. and Brombacher, C. (2009) Geschichte der Flora in der Regio Basiliensis seit 7500 Jahren: Ergebnisse von Untersuchungen pflanzlicher Makroreste aus archäologischen Ausgrabungen. *Mitteilungen der Naturforschenden Gesellschaft beider Basel*, 11, 27–106.

Jameson, M.H. (1977–1978) Agriculture and slavery in classical Athens. *The Classical Journal*, 73, 122–145.

Jones, G. (2005) Garden cultivation of staple crops and its implications for settlement location and continuity. *World Archaeology*, 37, 164–176.

Jones, G. and Halstead, P. (1995) Maslins, mixtures and monocrops: on the interpretation of archaeobotanical crop samples of heterogeneous composition. *Journal of Archaeological Science*, 22, 103–114.

Jones, G., Charles, M., Bogaard, A., and Hodgson, J. (2010) Crops and weeds: the role of weed functional ecology in the identification of crop husbandry methods. *Journal of Archaeological Science*, 37, 70–77.

Karavidas, K.D. (1931) *Agrotika: meleti sigkritiki*, Ministry of Agriculture, Athens.

Kostakis, T.P. (1976–1978) Georgika tis Tsakonias. *Laografia*, 31, 43–150.

Latta, J. and O'Leary, G.J. (2003) Long-term comparison of rotation and fallow tillage systems of wheat in Australia. *Field Crops Research*, 83, 173–190.

Le Houerou, H.N. and Hoste, C.H. (1977) Rangeland production and annual rainfall relations in the Mediterranean basin and in the African Sahelo-Sudanian zone. *Journal of Range Management*, 30, 181–189.

Lithourgidis, A.S., Damalas, C.A., and Gagianas, A.A. (2006) Long-term yield patterns for continuous winter wheat cropping in northern Greece. *European Journal of Agronomy*, 25, 208–214.

Loukopoulos, D. (1983) *Georgika tis Roumelis*, Athens, Dodoni.

Mainland, I. (2007) A microwear analysis of selected sheep and goat mandibles, in *The Early Neolithic on the Great Hungarian Plain: Investigations of the Körös Culture Site of Ecsegfalva 23, Co. Békés* (ed. A. Whittle), Hungarian Academy of Sciences, Budapest, pp. 343–348.

Marino, S., Tognetti, R., and Alvino, A. (2009) Crop yield and grain quality of emmer populations grown in central Italy, as affected by nitrogen fertilization. *European Journal of Agronomy*, 31, 233–240.

Marino, S., Tognetti, R., and Alvino, A. (2011) Effects of varying nitrogen fertilization on crop yield and grain quality of emmer grown in a typical Mediterranean environment in central Italy. *European Journal of Agronomy*, 34, 172–180.

Marres, P. (1935) *Les Grands Causses étude de géographie physique et humaine*, Tours, Arrault.

Martinez Gil, F.J. and Sanchez Navarro, J.A. (1984) Los recursos de agua de la cuenca del río Huecha. Optimización de su uso para el desarrollo del regadío. *Turiaso*, 5, 339–363.

Ministry of Agriculture & Fisheries (MAF) (1931) *Manures and Manuring*, His Majesty's Stationery Office, London.

Oram, P.A. and de Haan, C. (1995) *Technologies for Rainfed Agriculture in Mediterranean Climates: A Review of World Bank Experiences*, World Bank, Washington, DC.

Pagkalos, G.E. (1983) *Peri tou glossikou idiomatos tis Kritis, 7: ta laografika*, Kentro Erevnis Ellinikis Laografias, Akadimias Athinon, Athens.

Palet, J.M. and Orengo, H.A. (2011) The Roman centuriated landscape: conception, genesis and development as inferred from the Ager Tarraconensis case. *American Journal of Archaeology*, 115, 383–402.

Palmer, C. (1998a) 'Following the plough': the agricultural environment of northern Jordan. *Levant*, 30, 129–165.

Palmer, C. (1998b) The role of fodder in the farming system: a case study from northern Jordan. *Environmental Archaeology*, 1, 1–10.

Panaretos, A. (1946) Kupriaka metra, stathma, monades khronou kai skhetikai pros auta lexeis. *Kupriakai Spoudai*, 8, 61–82.

Peña-Chocarro, L. (1996) In situ conservation of hulled wheat species: the case of Spain, in *Hulled Wheats: Promoting the Conservation and Use of Underutilized and Neglected Crops 4* (eds S. Padulosi, K. Hammer, and J. Heller), International Plant Genetic Resources Institute, Rome, pp. 129–146.

Peña-Chocarro, L. (1999) *Prehistoric Agriculture in Southern Spain During the Neolithic and the Bronze Age*, Archaeopress, Oxford.

Percival, J. (1974) *The Wheat Plant*, Duckworth, London.

Petropoulos, D.A. (1952) Sumvoli is tin erevnan ton laikon metron kai stathmon. *Epetiris tou Laografikou Arkhiou*, 7, 57–101.

Pettegrew, D.K. (2001) Chasing the classical farmstead: assessing the formation and signature of rural settlement in Greek landscape archaeology. *Journal of Mediterranean Archaeology*, 14, 189–209.

Prontzas, V. (1992) *Oikonomia kai gaioktisia sti Thessalia (1881–1912)*, Morfotiko Idrima Ethnikis Trapezis, Athens.

Rivals, F., Gardeisen, A., and Cantuel, J. (2011) Domestic and wild ungulate dietary traits at Kouphovouno (Sparta, Greece): implications for livestock management and paleoenvironment in the Neolithic. *Journal of Archaeological Science*, 38, 528–537.

Rodríguez, E.G. (2008) El paisaje de la Huerta de Valencia. Elementos de interpretación de su morfología espacial de origen medieval. *Historia de la ciudad. V. Tradición y progreso*. Valencia, Universidad Politécnica de Valencia, pp. 116–129.

Sallares, R. (1991) *The Ecology of the Ancient Greek World*, Duckworth, London.

Semple, E.C. (1932) *The Geography of the Mediterranean Region: Its Relation to Ancient History*, Constable, London.

Shepherd, M. and Gibbs, P. (2002) *Managing Livestock Manures, Booklet 4: Managing Manure on Organic Farms*, ADAS, Mansfield.

Sindicato de Riegos de Borja (SRB) (1927) *Ordenanzas de riego de la ciudad de Borja y reglamentos del sindicato y jurado*, SRB, Zaragoza.

Slinis, M.K. (1938–1948) Agrotika ethima Drumou Makedonias. *Laografia*, 12, 92–103.

Spurr, M.S. (1986) *Arable Cultivation in Roman Italy c.200 B.C.–C.A.D. 100*, Society for the Promotion of Roman Studies, London.

Terrenato, N. (2007) The essential countryside: the Roman world, in *Classical Archaeology* (eds S.E. Alcock and R. Osborne), Blackwell, Oxford, pp. 139–156.

Trillo San José, C. (2004) *Agua, tierra y hombres en al-Andalus. La dimensión agrícola del mundo Nazarí*, Universidad de Granada, Granada.

Troccoli, A. and Codianni, P. (2005) Appropriate seeding rate for einkorn, emmer, and spelt grown under rainfed condition in southern Italy. *European Journal of Agronomy*, 22, 293–300.

Ur, J. (2003) CORONA satellite photography and ancient road networks: a northern Mesopotamian case study. *Antiquity*, 77, 102–115.

van der Veen, M. and Jones, G. (2006) A re-analysis of agricultural production and consumption: implications for understanding the British Iron Age. *Vegetation History & Archaeobotany*, 15, 217–228.

Watson, A.M. (1983) *Agricultural Innovation in the Early Islamic World: The Diffusion of Crops and Farming Techniques, 700–1100*, Cambridge University Press, Cambridge, UK.

White, K.D. (1970a) Fallowing, crop rotation, and crop yields in Roman times. *Agricultural History*, 44, 281–290.

White, K.D. (1970b) *Roman Farming*, Thames and Hudson, London.

Wilkinson, T.J. (1994) The structure and dynamics of dry-farming states in Upper Mesopotamia. *Current Anthropology*, 35, 483–505.

Williamson, T. (1998) Fodder crops and the 'agricultural revolution' in England, 1700–1850. *Environmental Archaeology*, 1, 11–18.

6

Family Planning
Land, Labor, and Livestock

One morning, Thanasis surprises me by singing "It's a Long Way to Tipperary," heard in 1941 from New Zealand soldiers briefly stationed in Paliambela. The elderly women, waiting for the doctor to measure blood pressure, also remember the soldiers. Two sisters, stern models of propriety, describe making a peephole in the wall of their father's barn to observe the tall, fair-skinned "Englishmen" billeted there. The older sister later married a shepherd and proudly describes exporting cheese (by air!) to Australia, to ex-neighbors driven to emigrate by inadequate landholdings. Other women had grown cash crops to make ends meet. Previous chapters have highlighted how access to land, labor, and livestock (especially work animals) constrained farmers' decision-making. This chapter explores the interplay between capital resources on a generational timescale and the webs of interdependence binding households to each other and to wider communities. First, however, it examines how farming households could extend or effect long-term improvements to

Two Oxen Ahead: Pre-Mechanized Farming in the Mediterranean, First Edition.
Paul Halstead. © 2014 Paul Halstead. Published 2014 by John Wiley & Sons, Ltd.

cultivable land by clearance, deep tillage, terracing, enclosure, drainage, or installing irrigation facilities.

6.1 Clearance

In living memory, scrub and woodland were widely cleared for cultivation in southern Europe. Whether a private or government initiative, individual households usually undertook the task, perhaps helped by kin and neighbors. Political, social, and economic contingencies sometimes triggered clearance, but preexisting vegetation largely determined its difficulty and reflected the ecological variables that shaped potential returns. Accordingly, the following accounts are grouped by type of vegetation cleared.

6.1.1 Uprooting deciduous woodland in lowland northern Greece

In the 1920s and 1930s, livestock grazed the south-facing slope beyond the fields of Paliambela, where deciduous oaks (most of trunk diameter less than 30 cm) and hornbeams (*Carpinus orientalis*) were interspersed with Christ's thorn (*Paliurus spina-christi*), wild pear (*Pyrus amygdaliformis*), Cornelian cherry (*Cornus mas*), and Judas tree (*Cercis siliquastrum*). Vegetation was more open, and grazing richer, than on the shady north-facing slope beyond the watershed. During the 1930s, this common wood pasture was divided into 0.33 ha plots that inhabitants of Paliambela and neighboring Kolindros cleared by hand over a decade.

Aged 14, Manolis lopped branches ahead of his father who dug around trees with a pick and cut the roots so the stumps came free. Grubbing out hornbeams and Cornelian cherry was relatively easy, but oaks and wild pears had bigger roots and the largest stumps were left to rot for a few years before removal. The trunk and thicker branches made valuable firewood, but they burnt light brushwood in situ, sometimes piled over big stumps to kill them and make eventual removal easier. They cleared three plots (1 ha) over winter, working every rain- and snow-free day for six months. Takis and his brother, then young adults, cleared a plot in 20 days, despite a 10 km round trip from Kolindros, but confronted mainly Christ's thorn – deep-rooted oaks would have taken much longer. Two laborers cleared a plot for Antonis' father in 20 days, and decades later, one manually cleared and removed stumps from a wooded 0.08 ha corner of another plot in 10 days. Clearing 0.33 ha of young, light woodland thus needed about 40 man-days. Farmers with grown sons or money to hire laborers cleared plots rapidly, but most had to work around other tasks. Nikolaos' father from Kolindros, despite using paid laborers and his young sons, needed three winters to clear three plots on which the larger trees had been felled, leaving just the stumps. The poorest farmers could only tackle their plot when paid work, including clearance for wealthier neighbors, was unavailable. Vasilis, aged 10, helped his father clear 0.33 ha over two winters, working only when the weather and lack of paid employment permitted.

Growing and processing existing crops occupied the rest of the year, so land was cleared over winter and available for sowing in spring. The first crop was normally sesame or perhaps broomcorn millet that could be sown late and – unlike wheat – grew without a well-worked seedbed ("if the field was a bit wild"). Even with the larger roots removed, newly cleared ground was hard, needing repeated tillage ("at least three times") to break clods, and those with small draft animals often hired a more powerful pair for the first plowing. The first sesame was often sown after one plowing or none – scratching the surface patchily and covering the seed with a mattock. Some farmers worked new clearings entirely by hand: Vasilis' father cleared only 0.05 ha in the first winter and, in late March to early April, dug this, sowed sesame, and harrowed in the seed by dragging wild pear branches; the following spring, he sowed the whole plot with sesame and thereafter with wheat. Sesame "tamed the field," but those without pressing need for a return sometimes left new land bare so the summer sun would help break clods. Tillage mixed in the thick surface layer of fertilizing leaf litter, as well as improving the seedbed.

Stumps left behind did not seriously obstruct tillage, but a pick often preceded the plow for a few years to remove remaining roots and regrowth from stumps. Even after taming with sesame, the first wheat crop was often poor, germinating thinly because of inadequate tillage, but the second usually yielded impressively and was remarkably clean of weeds. To teenage Mitsos, herding sheep nearby, the success of the second and third wheat crops was evident: "they were tall, especially if it rained a lot in April–May, and some grazed them with sheep to avoid lodging"; the stand grew dense, with full ears, and the usual weeds were missing. Thanks to the "manure" from leaf litter, these plots were then sown with wheat without rotation or fertilizer for several years. Yields varied but at least matched the best fields around Paliambela (perhaps 1300 kg/ha in a good year) and were perhaps two or three times higher than for established plots on adjacent slopes (perhaps 900 kg/ha in a good year). High yields lasted for 3–5 or even 10 years without manure, before declining, and weeds increased on a similar timescale.

In nearby communities, Pontic refugees from northern Turkey and Thracians from southern Bulgaria or European Turkey manually cleared much larger areas. In Aiginio, Thracian households each received 4 ha of well-drained slopes and flood-prone plain, comprising a mosaic of clearings, bushes or wet-loving plants, and deciduous trees (oak, Christ's thorn, poplar). The task facing each household varied greatly, as did the workforce: some men worked alone, others with grown sons or brothers, and sometimes groups of neighbors collaborated. Between childhood in Bulgaria and early adulthood as a political prisoner in Greece, Thanasis helped two male relatives fell trees, remove useful wood, burn brushwood, and grub up stumps. Leaving the odd big tree for shade, they cleared one 0.5 ha plot in a month. Mavrodis with three other men cleared 1 ha at 200 m²/day. These estimates of 180–200 man-days/ha exceed those from Paliambela (120/ha) but involved some larger trees. In Kitros, Khristos cleared 3 ha in a few weeks with hired workers, but those dependent on household labor took several years. In Nea Trapezounta, Pontic refugees acquired woodland from an old Turkish estate and grubbed by hand the stumps of trees felled and removed by a merchant. Anestis' father single-handedly brought into cultivation about 0.3 ha per year, taking 11 years to clear 3 ha. Arriving without draft animals, he yoked a cow and donkey to plow "two or three fingers deep" and break up roots before sowing sesame in spring. Khristos in Kitros sowed bitter vetch before his first wheat, while Thanasis in Aiginio first planted maize or cotton on plots available by spring but wheat if he completed clearance later. In Aiginio, Kitros, and Nea Trapezounta, early wheat crops on well-drained fields were again high yielding and weed-free, with yields falling and weeds increasing over the ensuing 5–10 years: for example, on the best fields of one Aiginio Thracian, initial wheat yields of 2000 kg/ha in the early 1930s dropped to 1000–1300 kg/ha in the late 1940s.

North Greek informants burnt brushwood to dispose of material not useful for fuel, incidentally providing warmth on cold days and perhaps preventing regrowth from stumps. They attributed initially high yields to land being "rested" or enriched by decayed leaf litter, and none described wood ash as a useful fertilizer or burning the cleared surface as beneficial. Conversely, citing accounts of clearing deciduous woodland in temperate regions of North America and (mainly on poor soils or steep slopes) Europe, Sigaut (1975) argues that burning sterilized the entire cleared surface to prevent regeneration of woodland plants; with minimal tillage to cover seed sown in the scattered ash (Sigaut, 1975, 213), one or two good clean harvests ensued. In northern Greece, grubbing up roots countered regeneration, and progressive subsurface tillage (creating a good seedbed rather than sterile surface) secured good yields from the second or third year and for several years thereafter.

Some massive returns on seedcorn (e.g., 50–80:1) from shifting slash-and-burn cultivation in Europe may reflect low sowing density rather than high area yields: burnt clearings were sometimes sown by dibbling, which requires less seedcorn than broadcasting (Sigaut, 1975, 141); on clean, fertile new land, heavy sowing to smother weeds was unnecessary and might promote tall crops prone to lodging; and, with unreliable harvests (below), light sowing (compensated by tillering) might be favored to economize on seed-corn (Halstead, 1990a). Reported *area yields* of 1300–1900 kg/ha of wheat *immediately* after burning mature forest in North American New Hampshire and 1350 kg/ha of rye after burning younger woodland in the north French Ardennes (Sigaut, 1975, 19, 152–153) are matched or exceeded by most estimates for *recurring* yields of wheat on tilled clearings in northern Greece (Section 5.6). Moreover, yields in the Ardennes (Cornebois, 1881, 624), as on burnt clearings in northern Europe (Rowley-Conwy, 1981, 88–90), were very unreliable, depending – to eliminate competing forest plants without tillage – on thorough burning which in turn required favorable weather and plentiful fuel (e.g., Cornebois, 1881, 624) and was time-consuming.

6.1.2 Opening up the *maquis* in southern Greece

In terrain less promising than lowland northern Greece, elderly Messenians cleared vegetation ranging from deciduous trees (oaks, hawthorn – *Crataegus* sp.), with most leaf litter and prospect of successful crops, through evergreen trees and shrubs (e.g., holm oak – *Quercus ilex*; prickly oak – *Quercus coccifera*; strawberry tree – *Arbutus unedo*; mastic – *Pistacia lentiscus*) to *phrygana* undershrubs (e.g., rock-rose, heather), with least litter and prospect of success. They felled trees, leaving a few for shade or acorns; dug up stumps; took thicker wood for fuel; and burnt brushwood in situ to kill remaining stumps and provide what they considered (Section 6.1.4) fertilizing ash. Some worked solely by hand, but in Metaxada, Ilias' oxen plowed up shallow-rooted strawberry tree, mastic, and rock-rose before he removed deeper roots with pick and mattock. While some worked single-handed, as when cutting firewood, others joined forces and cleared more land per man-day. At Iklaina, Farmakis alone "with his umbrella" (on rainy days without paid work) cleared 0.5 ha of bushes and trees up to 2 m high over two winters and then, with three or four companions, completed a further 1.2 ha of his *own* land over the following three winters. In Khora, Spanos reclaimed his grandfather's abandoned and overgrown field of 2.5 ha in under three years, working year-round, consistent with Ilias' estimate that he cleared 0.1 ha of bushes with a few large trees in a month. These Messenians encountered fewer and smaller trees but more shrubs and less herbaceous vegetation than their north Greek counterparts. Some of the slow-growing evergreens also have extremely hard wood, and clearance of trees and shrubs apparently needed comparable amounts of labor per unit area in the two regions. Plots with only small undershrubs, such as rock-rose or Jerusalem sage (*Phlomis fruticosa*), were easier: in Kontogoni, Velisaria cleared 0.1 ha of the latter with a mattock in only two days, though she needed two to three days more to remove stones that impeded plowing.

Farmakis first sowed potatoes on one of his new clearings, perhaps to tame the field. Some plots were cleared for cereals and others for olives or vines, but the latter were often sown two or three times with winter cereals or summer row crops until the trees established themselves. Olives grew faster and yielded up to twice as heavily on new clearings as on adjacent old fields. Cereals too grew well and for a few years, especially where leaf mold or ash had been concentrated. Wheat that Nikos sowed on land abandoned for 20 years yielded nearly twice as much as on older fields: "the ears were so heavy that they rubbed against each other in the breeze, shedding grain." Ilias indicated below Metaxada a field his grandfather cleared from woodland. It yielded 60 pack loads of barley sheaves from 0.5 ha in its first year – 6 tons/ha, using Ilias' norms of 6–10 sheaves/load and 5 *okádes* of grain/sheaf. Even if exaggerated, the harvest was impressive because his grandfather had to defend the field at gunpoint from envious neighbors. Informants agreed that without manure but perhaps with alternate fallow, high yields lasted for 3–5 years after scrub and perhaps 10 years where trees had left thick leaf mold, while isolated clearings continued to be fertilized by leaf litter from surrounding trees or bushes and ash from burning of encroaching undershrubs. The first crop was weed-free, and provided manure was not spread, weeds were scarce for three to five years; those that did appear grew vigorously and were enthusiastically gathered as greens for human consumption.

Reclamation of abandoned fields from invading bushes and saplings is also widely recalled in Crete, where the replacement of "Turkish-Cretan" Muslims by Anatolian Christians contributed to the early twentieth-century ebb and flow of cultivation. At Ano Asites, Anastasia and Vangelis recall their father clearing a 4.5 ha field over the winter of 1939–1940, using hired workmen to chop and burn bushes while his oxen pulling an ard (with the "ear" or ridging board removed on one side for maneuverability) broke open ground. He sowed 500 kg of wheat and in May 1941, under Luftwaffe strafing, harvested 5 tons (1 ton/ha). The field yielded four tons the following year and, with wheat giving way to barley, then oats, and finally two fallow years, outperformed established plots until 1949 (when it was planted with olives and vines) and remained weed-free for the first three to four years of continuous cultivation.

At Tharounia on Euboea, Konia likewise harvested weed-free wheat, yielding 1 ton/ha, in the first year after cutting and burning evergreen bushes and aromatic undershrubs on a poor field abandoned 10–15 years previously by her family. Clearance was more widespread in the preceding generation, before urban employment developed, and Kostas' father cut and burnt new plots in both evergreen *maquis* (e.g., strawberry tree bushes) and *phrygana*. Three or four neighbors comfortably cleared more than 0.1 ha of undershrubs per day but were much slower in *maquis* and often removed stumps piecemeal over several years. Some wood was removed for fuel and some burnt in situ as fertilizer: "you cut a good sheaf where you had burnt the brushwood." On Kithira, Fotini's family bought a field, uncultivated for 20–30 years, from a childless man who had neither means nor need to exploit it. After cutting and burning, the first two cereal crops were "a miracle, more than a meter tall," and those in the third and fourth years were above average. As at Tharounia, abandonment and reclamation reflected changes in the labor supply and needs of individual households, rather than a strategy of shifting cultivation.

6.1.3 Shifting cultivation: From Crete to Asturias

At Aloides in lowland central Crete, while privately owned per-manent fields occupied the valley bottom around the village, common land (*aïládes*) on surrounding rocky slopes was alter-nately used for rough grazing and short-term "slash-and-burn" cultivation. In the late 1930s, having too little land to feed his family, Sofia's father reclaimed the overgrown field of an émigré cousin and cleared patches of common land in whichever zone was closed to grazing. On the *aïládes*, the limiting factor was male labor, not land. Over summer, he and his three sons cut and burnt bushes, a meter or more high, and in autumn, aided also by his two daughters, sowed wheat or rye, covering the seed with a mat-tock because there were too many rocks for plowing. "The ash from burning the bushes was like *guano* and the crops grew taller than the rocks." Each plot was sown once or twice and then a new area was cleared. Sowing of the *aïládes* was very different from the discontinuous cultivation of marginal land described for other parts of central and southern Greece. Soil cover was patchy, yields were modest, cultivation was short-lived and so limited to annual field crops, and private ownership was restricted to the crops sown without extending to the plots cleared. Rotating use as common grazing enforced shifting cultivation, but the abundance and poor quality of such land offered little incentive to challenge this regime.

Loukopoulos (1983, 131–132) describes clearance and short-term cultivation of wooded slopes a few decades earlier in the moun-tains of central Greece. While clearing bushes was not difficult, felling mature trees (probably substantially larger than those encountered in northern Greece or Messenia) was very time-consuming, and fires were sometimes started to make the task easier (and justify cultivation in woodland protected by law). The burnt stumps might be left in situ, reducing labor costs and erosion. With steep slopes and heavy rainfall, however, such plots became infertile and were abandoned after a handful of years. Such short-term, shifting cultivation was widespread in the

Mediterranean. In the southern French Alpine foothills, the gentler slopes were sown in alternate years, but the poorest soils were exploited through *essartage* – temporary clearings, fertilized by ash from burnt vegetation and sown for two to four years, usually with undemanding cereals (einkorn, barley, oats, rye – Blanchard, 1945, 321–324). Especially if only partial, such clearings evaded tithe collectors (Duplessy *et al.*, 1996, 56). On the southeast French Maures Massif, nineteenth-century cutting and burning of evergreen trees and bushes, with minimal manual tillage to cover seed, allowed one crop each of wheat then rye, followed by 15–20 years' abandonment for woodland to recover. Where undershrubs prevailed, these were uprooted with an ard, gathered, and burnt, and plots were worked once or twice, sown with wheat followed by rye or oats, and then abandoned for a dozen years. In Corsica, cutting and burning of evergreen bushes was sometimes followed by manual tillage (*maggiere*) and sometimes not (*debbio*), the former giving better yields but requiring more labor (80–140 vs. 60 days/ha). Under both regimes, yields declined steeply over a few years before the land was abandoned to recover (Sigaut, 1975, 26–28). Short-term cultivation is also described in deciduous woodland higher in the Ligurian Apennines of northwest Italy, where felled and burnt grey alder (*Alnus incana*) and beech (*Fagus sylvatica*) provided fertilizing ash for 2–5 years of cereals (protected by fences of thorny undergrowth), followed by 3–12 years of regeneration. Cultivation beyond one year was prohibited, although selective felling apparently spared Turkey oak (*Quercus cerris*, prized for leaf fodder) "standards" and fruit trees (Bertolotto and Cevasco, 2000). Further south on Monte Cairo, a nineteenth-century document describes short-lived cultivation of clearings, abandoned because of soil exhaustion (prohibition of cultivation in public woodland was doubtless also a factor), but eighteenth-century records also cite clearings sufficiently long lasting for planting with olives and vines (Forte, 2009). Elsewhere in Italy, the terminology of clearance suggests that both shifting cultivation with fire (the "red oxen" of the Calabrian mountains) and long-term agricultural colonization, including grubbing as well as cutting and burning, were wide-spread (Sereni, 1981).

In upland Asturias, those in need had the right to clear temporary *boronás* in uncultivated common land beyond the permanent fields. They cut bushes, stripped turf, dug up roots, burnt cleared vegetation, and spread ash as fertilizer (Concepción Suárez, 1992, 313–317). At Zureda, relatively level patches were cleared, fertilized with ash, and planted with glume wheat or potatoes. Scarecrows and fences warded off birds and livestock, respectively, from these vulnerable outlying plots. Candido reckons *boronás* were exhausted after two or three crops, but Severina recalls those with nearby cattle byres extending cultivation with stall manure. For similar eighteenth- and nineteenth-century regimes, the combined labor of paring, burning, and spreading ash amounted to perhaps 35–70 days/ha in Britain, where grassy turf facilitated superficial paring, and 70–140 days/ha in France, where more varied vegetation made the task slower (Sigaut, 1975, 159–161). In France, millet, buckwheat, or root crops might be planted on such plots in summer, with minimal tillage, but autumn-sown cereals again needed more careful preparation. Crops grew particularly well where burning had taken place, despite efforts to spread ash across the whole plot. Of the autumn-sown cereals, some preferred rye because wheat tended to grow too tall and lodge, especially in the first year after burning (Sigaut, 1975, 12–14).

6.1.4 Slashing, burning, and shifting

While clearing new plots in Metaxada, Ilias was one of several informants to find old terrace walls or clearance cairns, indicating prior cultivation. In upland central Greece, Loukopoulos (1983, 127) saw cairns sealed by trees centuries old, but most of the Mediterranean clearance described in Sections 6.1.1–6.1.3 involved young woodland or scrub on land cultivated 10–100 years previously and perhaps, as at Paliambela, used subsequently for pasture and woodcutting. None of this was "pristine" forest, but a lengthy period without cultivation ensured initially abundant and weed-free harvests. Accumulated leaf mold was invariably considered to enhance fertility, and in southern mainland Greece, where farmers spread it on vegetable gardens, some used the same term (*fouskí*) for this and animal manure. Opinions differed, however, on the benefits of ash and burning for subsequent crops. In contrast with descriptions of clearing deciduous woodland in northern Greece, accounts of both medium-term clearance of evergreen woodland and short-term shifting cultivation on the poorest soils repeatedly cite wood ash as a valuable fertilizer, with crops flourishing especially where burning took place. Burning vegetation entails heavy loss of volatile nitrogen, but wood ash is *relatively* enriched in potassium, phosphorus, and other nutrients (e.g., Gillon and Rapp, 1989) and so may beneficially render acid soils more neutral (e.g., Sigaut, 1975, 100; Steensberg, 1979, 38–45). Most of the central and southern Greek clearances described were probably on flysch bedrock (e.g., Zangger *et al.*, 1997, 561), supporting acid soils (Nakos, 1979), whereas the north Greek cases were on younger, alkali bedrock. If *partial* burning also makes nitrogen more available to crops (Sigaut, 1975, 101), it may have been particularly beneficial in clearing broad-leaved evergreen trees and bushes with leaves that decay much more slowly than their deciduous counterparts (cf. van Wesemael, 1993).

The duration of high yields corresponded to the density of cleared vegetation and wealth of accumulated leaf mold, but much of the land cleared within living memory in Greece had fallen out of previous cultivation for reasons other than infertility, including fluctuating household size on Kithira, ethnic conflict in northern Greece and perhaps Messenia, and communal or public ownership. The Cretan *aïlades* would probably not have sustained long-term cultivation, even if privately owned, and clearance of new land allowed Maria's father to abandon some unproductive fields at Milioti in the 1930s, but Ilias in Metaxada insisted that plots were only abandoned if stripped bare by erosion.

6.2 Long-Term Improvement: Deep Tillage, Terracing, and Enclosure

Sofia and her sister in Aloides were hired to prepare vineyards for planting, together digging 2×6 m knee-deep (say 6 m³) per day. Around Knossos, they dug deeper ("up to a meter") and an early twentieth-century estate created extensive vineyards using gangs of cheap workmen. At Ligopsa in the hills of Epirus, the owner of an empty *kafenío* interrupts civil war reminiscences to narrate how, in his youth, "if you wanted to make a vineyard, you invited the whole village and they dug it in two days, after which you laid on a 'table' with meat." Those who could neither hire nor fête their neighbors prepared vineyards slowly. On Kithira, Thanasis inherited his vineyard but watched neighbors make them from scratch, "digging just two, three, four square meters a day with their children." In Paliambela, the Thracian refugees earmarked a south-facing slope for orchards, where each household devoted something like 0.05 ha to vines. Starting in 1937–1938, they dug the whole of each vineyard to 70–80 cm depth, inverting the soil by filling each pit with the spoil from the next one. Working through winter from the end of autumn sowing, groups of two to four men spent a day in turn on the vineyard of each. By autumn 1940, when Mitsos departed for the Albanian front, several vineyards had been planted, but others were not ready. He estimates they dug perhaps 2 m³/man-day. At Gerakies in the Troodos Mountains of 1950s Cyprus, Petros extended and improved a failing vineyard by clearing additional land of bushes and pine trees and then digging the enlarged plot of 0.4 ha down to 80 cm. With 8–10 hired laborers, he took two winters (unencumbered by cereal growing) and hundreds of man-days to complete the task.

On Kithira, the numerous stones turned up by deep tillage were piled on adjacent uncultivated ground. Such piles also result from piecemeal removal over many years during shallow tillage for annual crops, as on Monte Cairo in central Italy where neat retaining walls sometimes prevented collapse on to cultivated ground (Figure 4.6; Forte, 2009). In Roumeli, central Greece, such piles were sometimes moved sideways on to exhausted land, freeing rested land beneath the cairn for cultivation (Loukopoulos, 1983, 126). Deep tillage and unearthing of stones also occurred when slopes were terraced, and similar terms were used for this in Roumeli (*xestremmátisma, kílima* ("turning over," "rolling over") – Loukopoulos, 1983, 122) and Kithira (*xekhónema* ("unearthing")) as for preparing vineyards in Paliambela (*stremmátisma, kílisma*) and on Crete (*kílisma, xekhónema*). Loukopoulos describes how Roumeli farmers built a dry-stone wall with boulders along the lower edge of the field and then deeply turned over the strip of land above, tossing soil downslope against the retaining wall to which they added the exhumed stones. They repeated this process to the top of the field, creating stepped terraces. Terracing improved retention of soil, nutrients, and water and facilitated tillage but impeded access by work animals, unless successive terraces were laid out in zigzag fashion (Loukopoulos, 1983, 124, fig. 24). Landscape archaeologists treat such "braided" abandoned terraces as indicating use for plowed field crops, rather than manually cultivated vines (Rackham and Moody, 1992), although oral testimonies suggest this pragmatic principle was not always obeyed.

On Kithira, Thanasis again acquired ready-made terraces: some his grandfather built in the late nineteenth century and some were older. "Our ancestors built the terraces gradually, to plant olives, before Australia and America opened up [in the twentieth century], when emigration to Smyrna was the only other option." As a teenager, however, he had been employed terracing uncultivated slopes. "We started at the bottom and worked upwards. I dug, throwing the spoil downwards and unearthing stones that they used to build a wall at the bottom, 1 m high on gentle slopes but 1.5–2 m high where it was steeper. Once the wall was finished, we started digging further upslope, unearthing stones for the next one. As soon as a terrace "step" was ready, they planted olives on the outer edge, angled so they shaded the wall, leaving the surface free for sowing wheat or vetch." In addition to such narrow "hillside" terraces on convex slopes, cross-channel terraces subdivide many concave dry valleys

Figure 6.1 Rebuilding a short cross-channel terrace wall at Kastrisianika, Kithira.

on Kithira into broader level fields (Krahtopoulou and Frederick, 2008, 558). Built on gentler slopes, cross-channel terraces created more cultivable land per square meter of retaining wall, and deep digging could be avoided by leaving soil to accumulate gradually behind the terrace wall (Frederick and Krahtopoulou, 2000, 84).

Even without deep tillage and unearthing stones, construction of a durable retaining wall is time-consuming. To rebuild a short wall on a concave slope at Kastrisianika on Kithira (Figure 6.1), Babis placed the largest stones along the bottom, anchoring the all-important corners with small boulders. For successive courses, he then selected stones of a shape that "locked" in place, unable to fall out unless the whole wall collapsed, and carefully maneuvered – if necessary wedged – them so they "slept" immobile on the course below. As he raised the outer face, Babis set large stones at the back of the wall, filled the core with rubble, and poured earth and small stones or potsherds to seal spaces between the stones and help provide a stable foundation for the next layer. Despite having stone to hand from demolishing the wall's sagging predecessor, he needed 10 hours to build a stretch 6 m long of average height 1.25 m. In the Troodos, Petros likewise reckoned on building 7 m² of terrace wall per man-day, with stones available from new vineyards; work proceeded faster with big than small stones. On this basis, it would take five man-days to *re*build a single basal retaining wall for a square 0.1 ha plot but perhaps a month for multiple cross-walls 2 m high on a steeper slope. These figures should be doubled or tripled for new walls, requiring unearthing of stones, and would rise further if blocks of terraces were enclosed by walls or, especially, cut into a hillside.

With cross-channel terraces, retaining walls could be raised piecemeal. On the steep concave slope below his house in Metaxada, septuagenarian Grigoris adds a course every year or two to a retaining wall, as sediment builds up through erosion accelerated by digging. The accumulated sediment will soon make an earlier wall, a few meters upslope, redundant and its stone available for reuse; he has just demolished another redundant wall that shaded his vines. A wall in an adjacent garden, raised piecemeal over 20 years, is now complete, and he has gradually converted several narrow terraces into a few broader, more useful ones. Upslope, a 2 m high retaining wall bulges ominously and cannot be patched but needs demolition and rebuilding. Knowing who built each wall, Grigoris reckons that with annual maintenance, a good wall lasts 80–100 years, although some terraces were rebuilt three times in six decades at Livadi in northern Thessaly (A. Krahtopoulou, personal communication). While less arduous than initial construction, repair and maintenance could thus be time-consuming (*contra* Rackham and Moody, 1992, 130). Ilias argues that cultivation was abandoned sooner on the slope opposite Metaxada than around the village because the former was steeper and its less stable terraces needed more frequent repair. Ease of maintenance, as well as costs and benefits of construction, has surely contributed to the correlation in various parts of the Mediterranean between terracing and gradient or bedrock (Grove and Rackham, 2001, 110;

Figure 6.2   Stone-walled enclosures (*kleistá*), some contiguous, at Diakofti, Kithira.

Krahtopoulou and Frederick, 2008, 559). Grigoris never carried soil uphill to construct or repair terraces. In Asturias, however, nutrient-rich topsoil accumulating at the base of sloping fields was sometimes carried back to the top (Peña-Chocarro, 1999, 39, 61, plate 5.25). On one plot in Zureda, Dorin and Valentina did this every second year, using a pack animal, in advance of the potato crop that alternated with less nutrient-demanding spelt/emmer.

While parts of the southern Aegean are more densely terraced, Kithira is well endowed with dry-stone enclosures (Figure 6.2). These *kleistá*, isolated or contiguous and irregular or rectangular, are scattered across the rocky hills and plateaus above and between the more fertile valleys (Krahtopoulou and Frederick, 2008, 558, fig. 6). In contrast with the Cretan *aïládes* and similar land in many parts of Greece, much agriculturally marginal land on Kithira is divided, perhaps following eighteenth- and nineteenth-century Venetian and British land and fiscal reforms (Leontsinis, 2000, 82–83, 216–218), into privately owned plots marked by small orthostats. Some of these plots were enclosed within and others before living memory. Depending on soil cover, distance from home, and need, some enclosures served just for unsupervised grazing of draft cattle (when not working) or a few sheep and goats, while others were also cultivated. Among the latter, the frequency of sowing and duration of fallow again depended on soil cover and, within living memory, cultivation has denuded some plots. *Kleistá* thus fulfilled three overlapping functions: protecting crops, surrounded by rough pasture, from livestock; enabling livestock to graze unsupervised (perhaps hobbled to prevent them scaling the wall) and so freeing human labor for other tasks; and reserving for the owner's livestock the superior pasture promoted by cultivation. Thanasis and Froso inherited some enclosures and built others, together completing 12–14 m of wall per day. As a teenager, Thanasis helped his father and grandfather build enclosure walls for a neighbor. "My father dug up stones and I carried them five or ten meters to my grandfather. The wall was one meter high and he built 20–22 meters each day." Although enclosure walls needed a face on both sides, they were not subject to lateral pressure like those retaining terraces and so were much quicker to build: 7 m²/man-day *including* acquisition of stones, whereas Babis and Cypriot Petros built 7 m²/man-day of *retaining* wall with stones *already to hand*.

Each of Thanasis' *kleistá* covered 0.1–0.3 ha and so needed at least (if circular) 100–200 m of wall. Others had enclosures of 0.5–1 ha, needing at least 250–350 m of wall. Using Thanasis' labor estimates and his recommended height of 1.20 m (to contain hobbled livestock), building such enclosures needed at least 15–60 man-days, although mutual assistance often lightened the task: "four families got together and 15 or 20 people built 250, 300, 400 meters of wall in a week"; apart from future reciprocation, you could use some of the same wall for a contiguous enclosure. Speed of construction was inversely related to the anticipated use-life, and less durable wooden fences or "dead hedges" of cut branches sometimes replaced dry-stone walls. Prickly oak or Christ's thorn was often cut in northern Greece for temporary sheep or goat pens, lasting a few months (Section 5.3.2), and boundaries of domestic yards, replaced every two years or so. In Paliambela, Mitsos reckons that two people enclosed a 0.1 ha yard or made a temporary fold for 100 sheep in one day. In place of dry-stone walls around permanent enclosures, however, short-lived dead hedges would be a false economy.

6.3 Extending and Improving Cultivable Land: Drainage and Irrigation

Although the Mediterranean is better known for scarcity than surfeit of water, extension or improvement of cultivated land by drainage is widespread. While rich landowners, administrative authorities, and commercial companies have long invested massively in drainage ditches and canalized watercourses (e.g., Braudel, 1975, 66–75), farming households and rural communities have drained land on a smaller scale. In the hills of central Greece, individual farmers improved fields where water collected by manually cutting a network of drains, filled with stones and branches to prevent blockage by soil and leading to a deeper peripheral ditch (Loukopoulos, 1983, 119–120). In the mountains, short drainage channels may divert localized runoff from fields with minimal labor, as around Plikati in the Pindos. In lowland northern Greece, among Thracians allocated land on the floodplain below Aiginio, individual households cut ditches for some plots and groups of households with contiguous land together channeled minor streams. Bigger streams required larger-scale canalization by the local council, however, and flooding by the river Aliakmon needed state intervention.

Low-lying land is also often amenable to irrigation, and again, hydrological and topographic practicalities may demand works transcending a single local community. Such "macroscale" systems, widespread in south and east Spain and involving "several thousand cultivators and a complex canal system, requiring construction of diversion dams . . . and considerable, long-term maintenance . . . typically cover some 50–100 km^2" (Butzer *et al.*, 1985, 485). One example (Section 5.2.3) follows the Huecha for 40 km from springs on the Moncayo Massif to its confluence with the Ebro. As the valley widens, the irrigated area widens from sometimes a single plot in the upper reaches to 2 km above Borja and 5 km below. Water channels hugging the valley side on a gentle gradient run up to 40–70 m above the Huecha at Borja. Each channel shares water between upstream villages and blocks of Borja fields "according to agreements and rights of immemorial origin" (Sindicato de Riegos de Borja, 1927, esp. 4). Construction of this system, partly dating back at least to Moorish rule, required sufficient labor and skill to build water channels on a steady gradient over many kilometers, with occasional tunnels, diversion barriers, and storage tanks. Water is distributed to blocks of land from locked sluice gates, flooding individual fields through temporary breaches in earthen subsidiary channels. If the surface is irregular, shallow furrows created with a hoe may spread water evenly, but this is unnecessary in level fields (Figure 6.3). Sloping surfaces risk water loss, gulleying, and reduced yields due to insufficient or excessive moisture, but most fields receiving higher levels of irrigation have been carefully leveled. As elsewhere in Spain (e.g., Glick, 1970), irrigation at Borja extended to Old World winter cereals as well as summer and tree crops. What individual farmers grew, where, and when was regulated both indirectly, by rights to water, and directly, by restrictions on land use (Sections 5.2.3 and 5.4).

Butzer *et al.* (1985, 485–486) also distinguish "meso-" and "micro-scale" irrigation systems. In the former, exemplified by hill villages above the macroscale system around Valencia, a single community allocates water among up to several hundred cultivators over up to 100 ha. Water from one or more major springs is distributed, mainly in summer, through a network of small channels needing little maintenance. Mesoscale irrigation on Cycladic Naxos distributes spring water to gardens in Kourounokhori, Melanes, and Potamia using short built tunnels, earthen channels, and some modest storage tanks. Until a few decades ago, local Catholic households controlled the system, perhaps constructed by the thirteenth- to sixteenth-century AD Venetian rulers. Within living memory, Old

Figure 6.3   Irrigation at Borja, northern Spain: water spreads (a) evenly and unaided into a level field but (b) unevenly and guided by hoed furrows into a sloping field.

World cereals were not irrigated here, and seventeenth-century documents imply the same (Kasdagli, 1999, 93). Mesoscale systems, usually comprising nothing more elaborate than a branching network of small earthen channels, are widespread in Greece, delivering water to village vegetable gardens (e.g., Grove and

279

Rackham, 2001, 77, fig. 5.5). From a perennial stream skirting Paliambela, the Thracian refugees diverted water along simple earthen channels to summer vegetables in a strip of land set aside for gardens. In mountain villages, springs are commonly tapped to water summer crops, including maize, potatoes, and New World beans, in back gardens and infield plots. In the small plain below Plikati, water was also diverted in summer from the riverbed and distributed to meadows and maize or potato crops by tiny earthen channels that occasionally passed over those diverting winter runoff towards the river.

Finally, in *micro*scale irrigation, one or more cultivators direct water from a spring, well or rain-fed cistern to areas typically smaller than a hectare and sometimes comprising just one garden. This might need minimal capital investment and maintenance – only a short earthen channel, with water easily distributed to each crop row or fruit tree by temporary furrows hoed in the cultivated surface. Digging of wells, however, depending on depth and bedrock, was time-consuming (a few man-weeks) without guarantee of success. Ilias reckoned that most wells dug in Metaxada produced too little water to be worthwhile or too much to be stable; Giono's (1930) tale of well digging in Provence highlights the dangers of the latter. Although non-mechanized micro- and mesoscale irrigation was widespread in Greece, it was normally applied to fruit trees, vegetables, maize, alfalfa, and perhaps Old World pulses grown in gardens, but not staple Old World cereals. The southeast Aegean has rainfall as low and unreliable as southeast Spain, but its short, seasonal streams are less easily controlled than the latter's longer, perennial watercourses.

Microscale systems may need no formal arrangements for sharing water between users. Mesoscale systems too may operate on a first-come, first-served basis, as at Cretan Kalo Khorio where villagers marked their place in the queue with stones, but often the local community allocates turns, especially during summer peak demand. Nocturnal turns may be unavoidable and, during the Axis occupation of Crete, cost the life of a farmer in Ano Asites whose motives for breaking the curfew were misinterpreted. Macroscale systems share water both within and between communities, usually and most simply by allocating blocks of time, as at Borja, although channels may be split to deliver equal or unequal shares of water simultaneously (Glick, 1970, 90, fig. 3). The time allocated to a user is commonly proportional to the area irrigated, effectively linking water rights to land (Glick, 1970, 12, 187), although adjustment is sometimes made for the type of crop or its developmental stage (Loukopoulos, 1983, 215). The communities of users administering such arrangements share both rights to water and obligations to maintain infrastructure (Glick, 1970, 187–188; 1995, 67–75). Such collective control is widely documented among Arab farmers from the Near East to North Africa and Spain but may have indigenous, pre-Roman origins in the west Mediterranean (Richardson, 1983, 38–39), while the diversity of customary and contractual arrangements in highland central Greece indicates local negotiation rather than external imposition (Loukopoulos, 1983, 207–218).

6.4 Counting the Cost of Extension and Improvement

Despite variation in the density of vegetation cleared or steepness of slope terraced and in the composition of a workforce constrained by weather and competing tasks, estimates of the labor needed to extend or improve cultivable land exhibit some consistency. For clearance, Sigaut (1975, 151) estimates 37–38 man-days/ha with steel axes in mature temperate North American woodland, but observation of tall oaks felled with *chainsaws* in the Pindos suggests this is optimistic. Reports from the Ardennes of 63 man-days/ha for gathering and burning brushwood and spreading ash, *without* tree felling or grubbing up stumps (Sigaut, 1975, 152–153), lend credence to north Greek estimates of 120–200 man-days/ha for clearing patchy, young deciduous woodland. Here, big trees were considered more problematic than small, although mature forest would have been easier if large widely spaced trees shaded out undergrowth and especially if their leaf canopy was destroyed by ring barking rather than felling. For clearing evergreens, Messenian figures match those for north Greek deciduous woodland, although

Corsican estimates are lower. Grubbing up stumps was hardest (in Tsakonia, someone looking tired is asked, "have you been removing tree stumps?" – Kostakis, 1976–1978, 53) and leaving these to rot saved considerable time. Following clearance, tillage was minimal in the Ardennes and North America (Section 6.1.1) but thorough in Greece – most time-consuming in the first year and thereafter 6–20 man-days/ha/year, if cross-plowed with a cattle-drawn ard, or 30–100 man-days/ha/year, if dug once by hand (Section 2.6).

For new vineyards, *selective trenching* might match woodland clearance (e.g., Roman figures of 200–240 and 320 man-days/ha to 45–60 and 90 cm – Foxhall, 1990, 448–449). Wholesale deep tillage was much slower: 1500 and 3000 man-days/ha to 45 and 90 cm, using Sofia's estimate of $3 m^3$/day (comparable with recent digging targets of $4 m^3$/man-day in soft rock (McConnell, 1883, 44) and $3–4 m^3$/man-day in rock-free earth (United Nations Food & Agriculture Organisation (FAO) 1986, VI, 6.1.8)); half as long again if farmers with other tasks (not full-time laborers) dug $2 m^3$/man-day, as Mitsos suggested for Paliambela. Having watched vineyard preparation and light woodland clearance, Mitsos was adamant: "digging vineyards so deep was *much* more difficult."

Labor for freestanding dry-stone walls might match manual tillage (60 man-days for a single 1 ha enclosure) or light woodland clearance (190 man-days for ten 0.1 ha enclosures). Constructing a cross-channel terrace wall for a square 1 ha field (100 m long by 1 m high) might require two man-weeks, if stone was to hand, or four otherwise – and could be spread over years. Terracing hillsides, however, required rapid completion of retaining walls combined with deep tillage, and "moving dirt represents the largest portion of labor time" (Kowalewski *et al.*, 2006, 208). Assuming a moderate slope with 1 m high walls and terraces half cut into the slope, excavation to an average depth of 0.5 m would require 1250–1700 man-days/ha, plus perhaps 100–200 man-days to build retaining walls. Seeing abandoned terraces saddens those that built them.

Labor *per hectare drained or irrigated* was particularly variable: if ditches or canals were cut at $3–4 m^3$/man-day, draining a 1 ha plot, with a few shallow brush- or stone-filled field drains (say, 0.5 m wide and deep by 400 m long, needing 17–33 man-days) and deeper ditches round three sides (say, 1 m wide and deep by 300 m long, needing 75–150 man-days), might approximate to light woodland clearance; larger projects, judging by Mussolini's drainage of the Pontine Marshes (330 man-days/ha *plus* heavy machinery – Linoli, 2005), probably matched terracing of hillsides.

Manual extension and improvement of cultivable land are thus labor-intensive to varying degrees: dry-stone enclosures and cross-channel terraces might need inputs similar to manual cultivation, less than woodland clearance or trenching for vines, and dramatically less than wholesale deep tillage or hillside terracing; cutting drains or irrigation channels might match plowing in microscale, but hillside terracing in macroscale systems. Moreover, while cross-channel terraces can be built up gradually and cleared or terraced land planted as work progresses, incomplete macroscale drainage and irrigation projects offer few benefits.

6.5 Subsistence and Cash Crops

Recent smallholders geared to self-sufficiency often exhibited striking crop diversity. In 1930s Aloides, Sofia's father grew 5 cereals and 6 pulses for domestic consumption, while at Olimbos on Karpathos in 1980, a handful of smallholders together grew 10 different Old World pulses (Halstead and Jones, 1989). Practitioners variously rationalize growing "a little of everything" (Forbes, 1976) as meeting a household's diverse needs, maximizing use of its labor, or reducing the risk of overall failure; it did all three. Conversely, farmers growing for market often specialized: smallholders in labor-intensive (below) and big landowners in undemanding crops (e.g., wheat). Another factor was the area of land for which cropping decisions were taken – typically between 300–1000 m^2 (a 10 × 30–100 m sowing strip) and 1000–3000 m^2 (a day's plowing) for farmers with draft cattle, although the desire to thresh most cereals with animals might favor a rather larger area (Section 4.9). Conversely, being slow to harvest but relatively easy to thresh, pulses often occupied a single sowing strip or even one garden furrow and were both cultivated and flailed by hand. Cultivation with draft animals, and especially by hand, thus facilitated small-scale sowing of multiple crops.

Which crops were grown reflected both cultural and practical considerations. For Mediterranean villagers, before agrochemicals and mechanization, cereals (accompanied by dried pulses, vegetables, cheese, and occasionally meat) were the dietary mainstay. The culturally prescribed staple, free-threshing wheat, gave way on high and poorer ground to "lesser" cereals (barley, rye, glume wheats, millets, maize), buckwheat (source of "black bread" in Haute Provence and Piedmont), and potato. Low-status grains have recently recovered ground, thanks to suitability for organic cultivation (e.g., einkorn in Haute Provence) or interest in traditional foods (e.g., emmer or spelt *farro* in Italy, barley rusks in Crete), while continuing cultivation of einkorn and emmer in northern Turkey (Ertug, 2004) and spelt/emmer in Asturias apparently reflects loyalty to tradition, rather than gourmet fashion. Landlords demanding payment in spelt/emmer from maize- and potato-eating tenants and sharecroppers (García Fernández, 1988, 167) probably contributed to the cultural value of Asturian glume wheats. On Crete, spring barley, although lower yielding and less dependable than the staple, autumn variety, was grown on a small scale for its whiter flour. The range of pulses grown exhibited greater regional variability than cereals, partly due to influence of soil quality on cooking times but also perhaps (cause and effect are hard to disentangle) because particular pulse dishes characterized regional cuisine.

Crop choices may change within or between generations as the balance shifts between land, "hands" to work, and mouths to feed. In Paliambela, the first generation of Thracian refugees grew staple wheat, rotated with barley, oats, and maize for fodder. To buy tools, shoes, salt, sugar, and pulses (most of which grew better in neighboring Aiginio), they worked as hired harvesters, herders, and hoers and sold dairy produce, lambs, the occasional calf, and any surplus grain. Tobacco, which a few farmers planted during the 1930s, caught on in the 1950s, when second-generation Thracians inherited landholdings too small to maintain oxen or sustain a family by producing wheat and livestock. "The Australian," then approaching adulthood, thought one morning: "my father has 4 hectares of fields and five children, so I will get next to nothing." He emigrated, to return as a holidaying pensioner. Those who stayed made a living from smaller holdings, plowed by cows rather than oxen, by growing tobacco with high labor inputs and returns *per unit area*. Scheduling clashes led to abandonment of vineyards and fewer livestock (and thus fewer fodder crops), while tobacco sales paid for fertilizer, stronger draft cows, and eventually farm machinery and additional land.

Across the stream marking the boundary with Aiginio, where landholdings were larger, the principal cash crop was cotton, with lower returns and labor inputs per hectare than tobacco. Grapes are also labor-demanding, especially for digging and hoeing and, with currants, for harvesting and drying. Currants were a favored cash crop of smallholders in nineteenth- and early twentieth-century southern Greece and again paid for work animals and improved plows that enhanced cereal cultivation (Psikhogios, 1987, 39). Maize too needs intensive hoeing, before and after planting, and was widely grown – alone or with New World beans and potatoes – as a high-yielding, labor-intensive crop for domestic consumption in mountain villages across the Mediterranean (McNeill, 1992). Requiring labor in spring and late summer, the "dead" periods for winter crops (between sowing and harvesting and between threshing and sowing), tobacco, cotton, grapes, and maize compete with each other, but not with staple winter cereals.

Although tobacco remained the dominant cash crop in Paliambela for 50 years, the amount planted by households varied through the domestic cycle. Chrysoulla grew 2.5 ha of tobacco with the help of three teenage children, to put them through secondary education into jobs off the land. Transplanting tobacco seedlings and "breaking" the leaves left her hobbling on two sticks, but seeing two children in hospital uniform filled her with pride. Conversely, a couple without children planted little tobacco, having neither need nor capacity for more. Although tobacco requires some specialized equipment and knowledge, farmers can expand annual crops in almost immediate response to changing circumstances, whereas perennial tree crops bear fruit after several years. Triantafillos bought a field surrounded by successful cherry orchards, whose owners expressed disbelief when he planted tobacco. "I needed an immediate return to educate my children. After that, I planted cherries." Cherries are *relatively* short-lived and rapidly maturing, as are lavender, grubbed up after 10–15 years in Haute Provence, and vines, that may fruit well from their fifth year (although initial deep tillage strongly discourages short-term planning). Olives, chestnuts, or managed oaks, however, may live for centuries and take decades to achieve mature production levels. In Metaxada, Ilias' grafted wild olives began to fruit after 3–5 years but produced their first useful crop after 10 and "a sack of olives" only after 15. As the saying advises, "plant for your children olive trees, and grapevines that yourself will please" ("vále eliés gia ta paidiá sou, ki ampélia gia tin afendiá sou").

Smallholders heavily dependent on cash crops were vulnerable to fluctuations in both yield and price. In the Pindos, to compensate for scarce cereal-growing land, several elderly informants successfully sold beans, potatoes, walnuts, or wine in local markets for a few years until prices fell. Specialized viticulture for an international market enjoyed a very checkered nineteenth- and early twentieth-century history, as railway construction, growth and contraction of markets and competitors, and spread of the phylloxera pest affected demand or production (Grigg, 1974, 141–144; Morilla Critz, Olmstead, and Rhode, 1999). Ilias' family history illustrates the risks and rewards for a smallholder. In the 1820s, following the Greek War of Independence, his grandfather moved to Metaxada in the Messenian hills. He subsequently acquired a large vineyard in the coastal lowlands, but around 1870, after rain ruined his drying currant crop, he returned to cereals and livestock in Metaxada – "better wheat grain in store than currants on the threshing floor" ("kálio stári sto kasóni pará stafída sto alóni"). By the mid-twentieth century, as some successful currant growers moved to Athens or Patras, hill villagers (including Ilias) again bought land in lowland Messenia but planted olives rather than labor-intensive vines.

Long-lived trees provide a record of changing land use. From above, lowland western Messenia resembles an ocean of olives, with islands of habitation and islets of vineyard. At ground level, most olives are evidently young and closely spaced with a low canopy, having replaced earlier vineyards and cereal fields from the mid-twentieth century onwards, as elderly informants describe. The few old trees, with a high canopy allowing passage beneath by plow animals and grazing sheep or goats, are widely spaced and mostly along field edges, minimizing shading of cereals underneath. The oil from these old trees was valued, because the grandfathers of Ilias and Grigoris *stole* cuttings at night for grafting onto wild root-stock in Metaxada, but their field-edge placement indicates that they supplemented, rather than replaced, staple cereals. As with recent agricultural specialization elsewhere in Europe, the infilling of western Messenia with olives (and earlier reliance on currants) reflects *dependable* and *cheap* bought grain (also Forbes, 1993) but has faced periodic crises of both exchange and production. In early 1940s occupied Greece, the value of olive oil (and other cash "crops," like currants or cheese) relative to grain fell dramatically and farmers cut down olives (e.g., at Stoupa in the rocky Mani peninsula) or grubbed up vines (e.g., at Frilingianika on Kithira) to sow cereals. Nor, despite their longevity, are olives immune to unfavorable weather: hail at flowering time or drought when the fruit fills may reduce yields in an "on" year, which is followed by a low-yielding "off" year; and late frosts, even near the southern Greek coast, or fires in a dry summer may cause damage from which the tree and olive harvest take years to recover. Trunks of old trees bear traces of past amputation after such events. Because the consequences of bad years might last for a decade, and low oil (or high grain) prices even longer, dependence on olives is risky without a very dependable market. Symptomatically, specialized olive growing in the nineteenth-century southern Argolid was an initiative not of small-holders but shipowners, seeking a return cargo on boats carrying grain from the Black Sea (Forbes, 1993).

Nonetheless, perennial cash crops could significantly help small-holders. With his stolen cuttings, Ilias' grandfather initially grafted just two olives to add oil to salads, crushing the fruit with a hand-rolled boulder on a roughly shaped, flat stone still embedded outside his house in Metaxada. As he grafted more trees, much of the oil was sold and pig fat remained the normal cooking medium. Cultivable land was scarce in Metaxada and, in Ilias' lifetime, grain was rarely sold ("there was no surplus"), but tools, a few consumer goods, and, when possible, land were bought by selling oil, wine, cheese, young goats, and the odd calf to consumers in lower-lying villages and towns. Likewise, many elderly smallholders in Crete cooked with pig fat while selling much of their olive crop (Halstead and Isaakidou, 2011a), and limited culinary use of olive oil is reported elsewhere in southern Greece (Forbes, 1993), Italy (Grieco, 1993), and southern France (Comet, 1993). Deep-rooted tree crops have multiple uses for smallholders: they exploit terrain (such as terrace edges) not available for field crops and demand human labor at different times; having a different seasonal rhythm from annual crops, they tend to fail in different years; and the price of their fruits fluctuates on a different cycle from grain. A major problem facing smallholders is their tendency to *sell grain cheap* after bumper harvests and *buy it dear* after poor ones. Cash crop prices are more stable after good harvests, because demand is more elastic than for staples (Jongman and Dekker, 1989, 117), and may rise after good cereal harvests if this raises demand. The distribution of land-holding in Greece indirectly supports the importance of such price buffering. Under Ottoman rule, large estates were heavily concen-trated in the central and northern plains (e.g., McGrew, 1985), partly reflecting their potential for economies of scale in extensive, ox-powered cereal growing on large, contiguous blocks of land. These estates, redistributed among smallholders by the Greek state, rap-idly reformed (McGrew, 1985) – as previously under Ottoman and perhaps Byzantine rule (Vergopoulos, 1975). The cereal-growing plains were not only more attractive to large landowners than dis-sected terrain but apparently more hostile to smallholders. Although probably more susceptible to *total* crop failure than hill farmers (buffered by more diverse terrain, soils, and perhaps crops), farmers in the plains were better placed – other things being equal – for self-sufficiency in staple grains. If specialized in cereal growing, however, they were vulnerable to price fluctuations, especially if they paid rents or taxes in cash and bought grain in bad years. Hill farmers, growing cash crops like olives and vines, were less vulnerable to fluctuating cereal prices and apparently more resilient as independent smallholders.

Because trees mature slowly, they tend to be planted or grafted by farmers with stable rights to land, whether ownership or long-term tenancy. For example, mixed farming combining livestock with polyculture of field and tree crops predominated in early twentieth-century central Italy, where long-term sharecropping tenancies were normal, but cereal monoculture prevailed in the south, where much land was under very short-term (one-year) rental (Silverman, 1968). For the same practical reason, planting trees is not just a response to opportunity, but a statement of intent. Having defeated rival claims to his newly cleared land in Metaxada, Ilias' grandfather planted walnuts, chestnuts, and figs and built cisterns to collect water. These practical and aesthetic improvements are still visible and doubtless signaled a long-term project. He also planted cypresses as future roof beams so that, having raised his children to adulthood, he could establish them in independent households.

6.6   Mixed Farming: Livestock

"We had a donkey, a goat for milk, a few hens for eggs, and every year we fattened a pig." Within living memory, from southern Spain to Cyprus, this was widely considered the minimum for "living like a human." A donkey transported tools and produce between home and distant fields, carried firewood, took cash crops to market, and enabled a wider range of paid jobs. A goat, hen, and pig provided milk, cheese, eggs, fat, and meat that enlivened a tedious diet, enabled acceptable hospitality, and could be bartered: at Nikos' shop-cum-*kafenío* in early twentieth-century Assiros, poor Turkish inhabitants of outlying hamlets exchanged an egg for a box of matches. A few animals also manured the kitchen garden, even if not kept for this purpose.

A few hens foraged around the yard or garden, a child could herd a goat on waste ground, and cereal straw sustained a donkey, but not everyone owned the "minimum" of livestock. Buying a donkey was not cheap: on late 1930s Kithira, 500–1000 drachmas for a good animal, equivalent to two to four months' grain for a couple. Female livestock receiving rich fodder, such as grain, produced more eggs or milk and bigger offspring, while the more grain or acorns a pig ate, the more precious fat it yielded (Halstead and Isaakidou, 2011a). Without access to orchards or woodland, fattening a pig required "as much [grain] as an adult human" and was impossible for the poorest households. In lowland northern Greece, where most farmers ate wheaten bread, household pigs were fattened on maize or barley and routinely slaughtered at twice the weight (say, 80–100 kg) achieved by many on Crete. Here, olive oil could replace lard, but the difference in carcass weight arguably reflected availability of grain, as Kalliopi from east Cretan Stavrokhori indicated: "we fed the pig weeds and carobs, not grain – we didn't have enough grain even for ourselves." North Greek households too could spare grain to varying degrees, so neighbors eyed each other's slaughtered pig competitively. Households with many members or frequent visitors sometimes fattened two or even three pigs. In Paliambela, Tasos' father bought three piglets, expecting to kill one early and lean if grain ran short.

Households owning a donkey and no other draft animals cultivated on a small scale (Section 2.6.1) and, unless specialized in high-value cash crops, could not spare grain for milk or meat production. Households with two draft cattle could cultivate on a larger scale and typically produced a grain surplus – modest with cows and substantial with oxen. Two stalled draft animals produced enough dung for orchards or fields as well as a garden, but purchasing cattle ready for the yoke or rearing calves to a suitable age (ideally three to four years) was expensive. At Paliambela in 1950, a small draft cow cost Mitsos 2000 drachmas, enough for his own annual grain requirement. On Kithira, where some villages had too little pasture for breeding cows, Thanasis recalls a good ox costing 5–6000 drachmas in the 1930s – equivalent to two years' grain supply for a couple. Draft cattle could graze or be stall-fed on straw while idle but needed richer fodder while working, and a pair might consume annually as much grain as one to four adult humans, with bigger rations enabling more work. Many farmers are evasive about how much they fed working animals; in Mitsos' words, "it depended what you had in the barn." Like fattened pigs, well-fed work animals were admired – in Assiros, the miller's exceptionally large and well-fed Serbian carthorse was remembered decades later. Conversely, feeding work animals might be impossible after poor harvests: in nineteenth-century Cyprus, a disastrous drought ended in export of many oxen (Kiriazis, 1931, 92–93). By converting surplus grain into meat, fat, and labor in good years and surviving on short rations or being sold after poor harvests, livestock provided "indirect storage" (Flannery, 1969, 87), even if this was not explicitly recognized (Christakis, 1999, 7).

Such indirect storage was closely related to the hierarchical classification of grains (Section 4.6): free-threshing wheat, pea, lentil, chickpea, black-eyed bean, and New World beans consistently as food; oats, common vetch, and bitter vetch as fodder; and glume wheats (especially einkorn and emmer), barley, rye, millets, maize, broad bean, lupin, and various *Lathyrus* species having intermediate status. Livestock might consume "food" grains on special occasions (e.g., Rhodian oxen received wheat rather than oats or bitter vetch at New Year – Vrontis 1938–1948, 111) but normally only as spoiled (moldy or weevil-infested) stores or crop-processing by-products, while humans ate "fodder" grains only in extreme need. "Intermediate" grains varied in status regionally and temporally: barley was widely food on Crete but almost exclusively fodder in northern Greece; and maize was a common staple of the mid-twentieth-century rural poor in northern Italy and Greece, but Italian *polenta* has since achieved *gourmet* status, while Greek *bobóta* is largely considered inedible. There were food and fodder varieties of some intermediate pulses, the latter having smaller seeds and thicker, darker, more toxic seed coats that discouraged insect pests but reduced palatability to humans. Frequently, however, humans *or* livestock ate intermediate grains, depending on availability. Staple maslins (e.g., wheat, barley) further blurred the distinction between food and fodder, particularly if, as on Amorgos, farmers sieved apart the two components for differential use. The grain hierarchy enhanced livestock productivity after good harvests but protected poorer humans from hunger after bad. First, feeding surplus intermediate grains to livestock avoided "waste," encouraging continued overproduction even after successive good harvests. Secondly, regular reliance on low-status (generally low-risk) staples was discouraged, reserving these as a safety net for bad years. Thirdly, needy farmers exchanged high-status grain on favorable terms, as in 1930s Aloides when Sofia's father disappointed his children by swapping a sack of wheat, bought by a relative in the United States, for two of barley, their normal staple. Fourthly, in severe food scarcity, fodder *crops* provided abundant "famine food" for farmers much as did proscribed *wild foods* for sparse populations of foragers.

A household with, say, 20 female sheep and goats, or 2 breeding cows, or even 1 breeding sow probably sold meat or dairy produce that was surplus to domestic requirements rather than sacrificed to finance essential purchases. Even at this scale, livestock might draw heavily on the "normal surplus" of staple grain resulting from household attempts to achieve self-sufficiency with a margin of safety (Allan, 1965; Forbes, 1982; Halstead, 1990b). In Paliambela, Manolis "had no surplus [grain], because I fed it all to my 4–5 cows." As livestock numbers grew, especially if they were of mixed species with incompatible feeding habits, it was increasingly impracticable for them to accompany a working adult to the fields or be minded by a child or grandparent near home. At least for the summer half year when animals normally grazed outdoors, therefore, those with few livestock often formed combined village herds of sheep and goats, cattle and buffalo, occasionally pigs, and in the uplands horses and mules. Households shared herding (or paying a herder) in proportion to the animals they contributed. Such herds

were widespread from upland Asturias to the Pindos and lowland northern Greece, but unknown in some regions (sometimes
because grazing was sparse or fragmented). Alternatively, animals
might be enclosed. In upland Asturias and Euboea, small infield
plots became enclosed pasture as recent rural depopulation made
labor scarce and land abundant, but on Kithira, such enclosures are
older, partly reflecting the scarcity of pasture around some villages.
For example, in the 1930s, one household at Aroniadika kept its
draft cattle over summer – when not threshing – two hours' walk
away. Animals could be left overnight in such enclosures on Euboea
and Kithira, islands with no large predators, but traditional hedged
or walled enclosures were small and held few animals for short
periods: Thanasis' 0.1 ha enclosures on Kithira each sustained five
sheep for a week, though they recovered for further grazing in
wet years.

Above a variable threshold, a household's livestock warranted
and needed a full-time herder. In Paliambela, Mitsos reckons that
10–20 sheep joined the village herd, 30–40 were minded with a
neighbor of similar means, and 50 were worth herding on their own.
Thresholds were much lower for cattle in northern Greece (say, 1–2
to the village herd, 5–6 in partnership, 10–15 on their own) and
sheep and goats in southern Greece. A man from northerly Assiros
on military service in southerly Messenia met a local man leading
30 sheep and introduced as *kekhagiás* ("livestock owner"), to which
he retorted that back home his father was a *kekhagiás* and had
30 sheep*dogs*. The offspring and/or dairy produce of such herds
was primarily destined for market, to which end their owner
(especially if well endowed with land) probably sowed a significant
area of fodder crops for "early-bite" grazing, hay, or grain, and
straw. Even Mitsos, who started married life with scarce land,
devoted 1 ha to wheat, for domestic consumption, and 1 ha to barley
and oats, to feed his 2 working cows and supplement the diet of his
10–15 sheep.

The largest herds belonged to specialist pastoralists, often seasonally mobile, and some large-scale arable farmers: in early
twentieth-century Assiros, the *tsorbatzídes* who acquired the estates

293

of the beys each had 20–30 cattle and a few hundred sheep or goats. "Middling" households, with enough land to maintain 2 working cattle, used teenage members to accumulate 50–100 sheep – "animal capital" with an annual income that ultimately could finance a dowry, buy land, or pay a doctor (Halstead, 1990b). After two years' schooling, Mitsos started grazing the family's 1 buffalo and 2 oxen, before helping mind the 150 cattle of Paliambela for a summer. His father then bought 20 sheep and for the next six or seven years, Mitsos was a full-time shepherd. The flock grew to 70 by 1939 (when a younger brother took over the sheep and Mitsos started plowing and reaping), reached 80–90 head through the turbulent 1940s, and subsequently helped provide a few fields and animals to Mitsos and his siblings upon marriage. The father was then in his 60s and, needing the remaining unmarried son to help with cultivation, sold the flock.

Livestock were important to arable farmers year-in, year-out: supporting cultivation, as draft and pack animals (Chapter 2, Chapter 3, and Chapter 4), source of manure, and curb on excessive fertility (Chapter 5); supplementing a grain-based diet with dairy produce, eggs, and fat (regularly) and meat (occasionally); and providing produce exchangeable for consumer goods. On an interannual timescale, they converted grain surpluses of modest value and finite life (weevils were an increasing problem in grain over a year old) into more valuable produce or productive assets, thus buffering the effects of variable harvests. On a generational timescale, animal capital accumulated with teenage labor enhanced household reputations: well-fed draft animals or a fat pig indicated a full barn, just as generous hospitality (including cheese and especially meat) implied a well-stocked larder; well-groomed work animals, like children well dressed for church, indicated a "good housekeeper." A farmer known for feeding workers well hired the most reliable plowmen or reapers, while a reputation for industry and full storerooms secured the best marriage partners for one's children. Generous provision of meat and drink to numerous wedding guests particularly enhanced household reputation.

6.7 Labor, Land, and Livestock: The Domestic Cycle

Family households – albeit of variable size, composition, and independence – widely dominated recent farming society in Mediterranean Europe (e.g., Schneider, 1971; Davis, 1977; Pina-Cabral, 1989, 402–403). With individual households vulnerable to death or incapacity of workers, failure of crops, or loss of stores, several informants started work without land or livestock and perhaps responsible for orphaned younger siblings. Households with young children may struggle to feed themselves even in good years, but as older offspring join the workforce, a favorable consumer to worker ratio reduces drudgery and risk. During this phase of the "domestic cycle," many recent Mediterranean households (e.g., Forbes, 1982, 405; see the succeeding text), like Russian peasants (Durrenberger, 1980), increased output. Indeed, the benefits of diversified farming, in spreading demands on household labor (Section 6.5), are usually expressed as avoiding seasonal *under* employment rather than periodic *over*work, as in another Ilias mnemonic: "with some vines and some sheep, ne'er a friend will you keep" ("lígo ambéli, lígi stáni, fílo poté de piánei").

Despite variation in how property was transmitted between generations (e.g., Loizos, 1975; Psikhogios, 1987), recent Mediterranean farmers widely invested teenage and unmarried adult labor in extending or improving arable land, growing labor-intensive cash crops, or accumulating "animal capital" to provide for their children. The contribution of unmarried girls to such tasks varied greatly between regions (Davis, 1977, 43–45; Pina-Cabral, 1989). Men from mixed farming villages in the Pindos worked away for months or years, leaving women responsible for crops and livestock. On Crete, Sofia plowed her father's fields around Aloides and, with other young women, reaped cereals and dug vineyards further away. In lowland northern Greece, while "local" women in Kolindros stayed indoors "like [Moslem] *hanoúmisses*," Thracian wives and daughters in Aiginio and Paliambela helped their husbands and fathers in the fields, but (with rare headstrong exceptions) did not herd livestock.

Asked how a family with only daughters would herd six cows, Mitsos was categorical: "a family without sons would not own six cows. You needed boys to herd cows or sheep. It was a question of honor. The two families here with just daughters had a hard time when I was growing up."

While many rural poor emigrated or eked a living as hired laborers and a few were adopted by childless couples with land, some by hard work and wise or lucky decisions accumulated enough land to raise and marry off a family, as three examples illustrate. Antonio was born in 1903, near Xomezana in upland Asturias, to a newly widowed mother who sold their land to survive. Antonio worked on his godparents' land and, from 14 until his late 20s, as a miner. In the 1930s, he married and moved to Zureda to cultivate his father-in-law's 0.3 ha and other plots that he rented from the absentee landlord and later bought, with the proceeds from rearing and selling calves. He accumulated 1 ha of fields and 3 ha of hay meadow, enough to farm full-time and raise two daughters.

Ilias' grandfather cleared land at Metaxada in the Messenian hills to grow cereals for domestic consumption and planted vines and grafted olives as cash crops (Section 6.5). Over the following century, his descendants planted further olives and vines, periodically removing some because prices fell or the departure of married offspring left too little labor for vines. The grandfather's holding was divided among four children, so Ilias' father, Loukas, received less than 1.5 ha. By sharecropping additional fields and working as a day laborer, he raised a family and accumulated 5 ha that he in turn split between three sons who initially maintained a single household to buy additional land. Once separated, each household had limited labor and land and so downgraded from draft oxen to draft cows and gave up the goats that Ilias had minded through his teens.

Thanasis was born in European Turkey in 1908. Moslem neighbors took him in when his mother died while his father was in an Ottoman forced-labor battalion. He arrived aged 14 in Paliambela. Rejected by his new stepmother, he worked as a full-time farmhand in Kolindros under an agreement giving him four to five female lambs yearly that he herded with his employer's sheep. In 1928, he built a one-roomed, thatched hut and started married life "with borrowed spoons." By 1930, he had enough sheep for an independent flock and in 1934, as a refugee, received 3.6 ha of fields. He bought two oxen with income from his flock, now 70 strong, and hired a teenage shepherd. His fields were poor, however, so he sold the sheep and, with a neighbor, bought a small water-powered cornmill. Although this worked slowly and seasonally, by 1940, the partners had bought an additional hectare, which they farmed with a hired plowman, and Thanasis, a new flock, which he expanded to 150 ewes. Again hiring a young shepherd, he sold cheese and lambs and also butter and calves from a few cows and buffalo. With income from mill, land, and livestock, the partners married off their children, providing each with enough land and livestock to begin another cycle of accumulation.

Antonio, Loukas, and Thanasis each acquired sufficient land and livestock to raise and marry off children. They did so by working for others, especially in early adulthood when they had insufficient land and livestock to occupy or support themselves, and by sale of cash crops or animal produce, especially in midcareer when they had accumulated some capital. Large landowners, such as Antonio's absentee *señores* that "ate and did not work," employed full-time farmhands and, at busy periods, day laborers. More modest farmers provided employment for part of the domestic cycle: Thanasis worked as a farmhand in his teens, hired a shepherd and shared a plowman and a mill-worker in his 20s, and dispensed with the shepherd once his own son was old enough to mind the sheep. Finally, poorer neighbors provided some short-term work: plowing for those with too little land to maintain draft animals or plowing and harvesting for elderly couples with no children or widows with young children. Opportunities to work for others thus arose from both long-term social inequality and shorter-term household dynamics. Likewise, land was available for purchase through both large-scale social changes, such as disinvestment by absentee owners in Asturias, and the vagaries of the domestic cycle, as with the abandoned field on Kithira that Fotini's father bought from a childless farmer (Section 6.1.2).

The basis on which labor was exchanged depended on its duration, the ease of monitoring satisfactory performance, and the circumstances of the parties. Sofia from Cretan Aloides was hired for reaping by the day. At first, as she worked alongside the employer leading the line of reapers, older women warned "don't try to keep up with him or you'll end up dead," but with experience, she cut the expected 20 sheaves per day (Section 3.4). In the more even terrain of lowland northern Greece, the size and yield of fields were easier to estimate and farmers did not normally measure labor in sheaves (or field stooks), although they knew how many they could reap in a day. At Assiros, Fotis and his young wife had no land ("not even a strip to grow our own lentils"), but gained plentiful experience as hired harvest-workers. They reaped fast enough as a pair to harvest the *tsorbatzídes'* large fields on piecework ("by the *strémma*, like gypsy gangs"), rather than working as day laborers alongside middling farmers. At Paliambela, Vangelio reaped on piecework in her early teens, with her parents, and as a young adult, with her husband, but in between, as an unmarried orphan, could not tackle fields single-handed and necessarily worked as a day laborer. Piecework had advantages for those able to reap quickly for many hours but carried risks as with the weedy field that Mitsos and friends unwisely tackled (Section 3.5). Starting married life with very little land, Mitsos took every opportunity for outside work, mainly for elderly neighbors and some larger landowners in Kolindros. Reaping and herding were sometimes paid as piecework but hoeing maize (harder to monitor) by the day. Away from home, workers were paid mainly in cash ("how would you carry grain?") and also fed. Near home, payment was often in kind (e.g., wheat for harvesting, wood for cutting firewood) and daily food negotiable – though feeding well attracted the best workers.

At Assiros, Spiros' father in the 1920s or 1930s paid reapers from a hill village in wheat at the equivalent of 8–12 kg/0.1 ha plus food, while Thanasis around 1950 paid a gypsy team 15 kg/0.1 ha. In the late 1940s, Vasilis earned 13 kg/0.1 ha without food in Kolindros, slightly less (assuming 0.1 ha reaped/man-day – Section 3.5) than the 16 kg of wheat/*day* that Mitsos and Vangelio received in

Paliambela. Koula comments that "[16 kg] of wheat, with the bran removed, would make an oven-load of twelve big loaves, enough to feed a family for a week or Vangelio [known for frugality] for a month." Assuming an annual requirement of 250 kg/adult and remuneration at 15 kg/man-day, a hired reaper should work 17 days to feed himself, 34 days to feed also a wife, and more days than were *locally* available to feed a family. If the daily wage "in the old days" in the southeast mainland was only 4–6 kg (Kostakis 1976–1978, 103, n. 1; cf. 2.5–6 kg/day for flailing in Albania – Shkurti, 1979, 74), 40–60 days of reaping would have been needed to feed just the harvest-worker. Although there were other forms of seasonal employment, life was hard for the landless laborers who waited for work every morning in Kolindros. Antonio recalled that "the day laborers of the *señores* went hungry" in upland Asturias.

A farmer with plow animals tilling for a neighbor without them was often repaid with manual labor: for example, one day's plowing for two to three man-days' harvesting cereals or olives or hoeing maize (Section 2.6.1). Payment in cash, as sometimes on Kithira, might be calculated as the daily manual wage multiplied by the notional equivalence between animal and human labor. The area plowed per day depended on the draft animals, however, and in Kolindros, fewer days of manual labor were exchanged for oxen than for horses and fewer again for cows. A fit plowman with powerful draft animals could, within reason, till a larger area per day by working more hours. Presumably for this reason, such jobs were often "priced" beforehand in days of plowing, especially in irregular terrain where areal measurements were meaningless. Plowing might alternatively be undertaken for some of the harvested grain, the proportion depending on who provided seedcorn and labor for reaping and threshing. Work animals for plowing and, more commonly, threshing were provided even in return for the crop straw (Section 2.6.2).

Longer-term employment took various forms. Fotis lost his mother as a young child and, ejected by his stepmother, became an apprentice farmhand in Assiros to a *tsorbatzís* uncle. Working throughout his teens for board and lodging, he started married life with nothing. The uncle's father, Dimitris, had come in the late nineteenth century to work on a nearby Ottoman estate. The beys employed laborers on six-month contracts but preferred sharecroppers who required little management beyond periodic collection of produce. Dimitris started out in his 20s using the bey's land, oxen, plow, seedcorn, and fodder and borrowing grain for food and so kept only one third of the harvest. Over the next 30 years, he progressively secured his "bread of the year," contributed fodder and seedcorn, acquired his own oxen and plow, and so retained half and then two thirds of the harvest and eventually bought a large block of land. He was one of several sharecroppers who prospered towards the end of Ottoman rule. Others did less well: Eleni's father worked for an Assiros bey before trying sharecropping but hired harvest-workers and so found it uneconomic. According to Spiros, another sharecropper-turned-landowner, the secret of success (apart from avoiding rival Bulgarian and Greek nationalists) was hard work, a large family (free labor), and willingness to gamble. Paid employees were more secure, but sharecroppers had better prospects: "you stole from the bey by threshing at night."

In Greece, annual cultivation agreements usually ran from late October (St Dimitrios' feast), when sowing of winter cereals started, and six-month contracts also from late April (St George's). Herding contracts were frequently for six months, because livestock were stalled over winter or taken to distant pasture in summer. Mitsos minded his own sheep in winter but sometimes hired or shared a shepherd in summer when he could earn more hoeing and reaping – more strenuous tasks that paid better. In the 1950s, the shepherd received for six summer months about 3000 drachmas, enough to buy a ton of wheat flour and thus provide bread for a small family. If he found similar work for the winter and was willing to stay outdoors in all weathers, he might have earned enough also to clothe and house his family. For minding the 150 cows of Paliambela over summer, Giannakos and a neighbor received 5 *okádes* (6.4 kg) of grain *per head*, in total enough for each to feed two adults for a year; similar employment was not available in winter. A hired herder benefitted from the odd twin lamb or kid, born out of sight of the owner, but

300

conversely might be charged for an animal taken by wolves, unless he retrieved the carcass as evidence (e.g., Petsas and Saralis, 1982, 278–279). Until the mid-twentieth century, cows in Greece often just worked and produced calves for market so the village herder at Lazarades in the Kamvounia foothills milked those in his care, making cheese and yoghurt for his family. In lowland northern Greece, however, farmers who ate wheaten bread often paid herders with lesser grains (e.g., maize at Neo Sidirokhori), underlining the latter's unfavorable economic position.

Alternatively, herding labor could be recruited by arrangements resembling sharecropping. In upland Asturias, while some tenant farmers owned cows, others borrowed them from absentee gentry landlords *a medias* ("halves"), feeding and yoking them and sharing with the landlord the proceeds from selling calves. Tio Pipin, a rich villager in Zureda, likewise loaned numerous draft/breeding cows *a medias* to poor households. Inés' husband, a Xomezana farmer of modest means, loaned to poor neighbors the odd cow that they fed, milked, or, if "accustomed," used for draft; he received any calves born and voluntary help in weeding and harvesting (below). Southern Greek arrangements for *misiaká* ("halves," the same term as for 50:50 sharecropping) sheep or goats were more elaborate: one party contributed breeding stock and the other labor; they shared equally the annual yield in cheese, wool/hair, and slaughtered animals (mainly young males and elderly females); and, at the end of the partnership, they split the standing flock. Agreements ran for about five years, so the flock could double in size, and they specified how this would be divided if the partnership was dissolved prematurely (e.g., Messenia (goats at Metaxada, sheep at Potamia and Milioti); central Greece – Loukopoulos, 1930, 162; Sardinia – Mientjes, 2008). Maria started minding *misiaká* sheep in Milioti, aged 10. When the partnership concluded, her father sold his share to rebuild the house. He then took on *afendiká* ("owner's"; in central Greece, *kefaliaká* ("capital") – Loukopoulos, 1930, 159–162) sheep, paying annual interest in money and, at the end of the agreement, returning animals of the same number and age as were originally loaned. Maria noted that her father shared risks and profits equally with *misiaká* sheep but carried all the risk with *afendiká*. He evidently expected more profit with fixed interest and, as five children entered work, was perhaps less risk averse.

Cultivable land could be acquired for short-term use in various ways. The relative benefits of renting and sharecropping depended on the terms offered: Mitsos in Paliambela paid higher rent for a recently fallowed field; and Giorgis in Knossos recalled landowners offering seedcorn or harvest labor to entice sharecroppers onto poor fields. Both concluded, however, that sharecropping was only worthwhile on good land. As farmers accumulated capital – land, labor, livestock, and money – they increasingly benefitted from their efforts, so successful individuals often progressed from paid employment, through sharecropping and then renting, to buying land, perhaps cultivated with hired labor. Thracian refugees arriving in Paliambela with "a cartload of children" drawn by oxen, but without reserves of cash or grain, needed work with immediate returns and so harvested and plowed for others and, in slack seasons, did nonagricultural laboring. Having secured their immediate livelihood, they undertook sharecropping with their oxen, until they had enough cash to rent fields.

Rent was often paid in kind and elderly Assiros informants recalled the early twentieth-century Ottoman beys and Greek *tsorbatzídes* charging 100 kg/ha (one wooden *koútlo* holding 12.5 *okádes* of wheat/"Turkish" *strémma* of 0.16 ha). Although most residents had insufficient land, many lacked draft animals, so demand for rentable land was modest. In 1920s Paliambela, the Thracian refugees initially had draft oxen but no land, so demand was perhaps higher and rents of 100–160 kg/ha are recalled. Lowland north Greek rents in kind are lower than local sowing rates, generally of 150–250 kg (broadly compatible with figures from the Tuscan Garfagnana and around Sault in Haute Provence). Parity between rent and seedcorn on Crete, at Anogia and Ano Asites, probably reflects sparse sowing (e.g., a *mouzoúri* of 17 kg per 0.1 ha in Asites) rather than high rents. With rents not exceeding seedcorn, the cultivator evidently benefitted more from renting than share-cropping except in bad years on poor fields. Sharecropping was sometimes favored because the landowner (e.g., a laborer with too little land for work animals) shared the drudgery of reaping or to help a neighbor in need, but was often enforced by inability to pay rent in advance. Timing of payment varied, but sometimes, Mitsos recalled, "the rent, or at least a downpayment, had to be paid in advance; the owner would not rent [rather than sharecrop] his land if he did not need the money."

Just as those with insufficient land and livestock used their labor to earn their subsistence and, ideally, accumulate capital (land, draft animals, other livestock to generate cash), likewise large-scale owners of land or livestock (both specialized pastoralists (e.g., Nitsiakos, 1997) and mixed farmers) used this capital to extract human labor and money from others. Ownership of work animals also secured access to the land, labor, or produce of those without. Pastoralists with teams of horses toured the lowlands after harvest, threshing in return for a share of the crop (Section 4.2), but mixed farmers normally provided plow animals. At one extreme, the Assiros beys loaned tens of pairs of oxen to sharecroppers. At the other, small landowners with spare capacity plowed for one or two poorer neighbors in return for manual labor or a share of the crop; usually, they accompanied the team, avoiding misuse, and payment was higher with plowman than without (Section 2.6.1). Draft animals were also loaned without owner–plowman: for example, in Metaxada, for the odd day without charge to a neighbor in need or for a year (perhaps 40–50 working days) for a fee (*gómoro*, perhaps 130–150 kg of wheat for two oxen), with the borrower providing fodder and replacing any animal that died or was injured. Although most draft animals belonged to farmers with enough land to occupy and feed them, Vangelis recalls that a few villagers with minimal land ("less than 0.5 ha") at Ano Asites in the mid-twentieth century owned a pair of draft oxen and worked fields rented "with seedcorn" (i.e., for the same amount of grain as was sown). Land, labor, and livestock, therefore, each secured access to other capital resources.

Although the preceding discussion has focused on how farmers accumulated land and livestock, usually this was possible because others *needed* to sell capital resources. For example, in Assiros, Kostas' father sold 10 sheep and the family ate maize after the *lívas* shriveled their wheat in May 1932, while Alexis sold 1 ha of fields to pay debts after the 1963 drought.

6.8 Household and Community

Capital resources of land, labor, and livestock, although substantially controlled by and exchanged between *households*, were also shared and contested more widely, especially within the village communities that dominate Mediterranean rural settlement. Ownership of cultivated land was usually private and of pasture, woodland, and water collective – with important exceptions. Shifting cultivation (legal and illegal) was widespread on common land. On the Cretan *aïládes*, thin soils enforced short-lived cultivation, suppressing conflict between private rights to crops and collective ownership of land, but regional authorities imposed collective organization of shifting cultivation in the Asturian *boronás* (García Fernández, 1988, 130–132) to limit encroachment on communal pasture or woodland. Here, common land set aside for short-term (up to four years) cultivation was often cleared and manured (by grazing livestock) collectively and sometimes the harvest was shared, but usually, individual households tilled and sowed plots allocated by lot and owned the resulting harvest (García Fernández, 1988, 135–136). At Zureda, a communal *permanent* field, donated by an heirless wealthy landowner, is likewise divided among households by lot every four years, and communal fields were also regularly redistributed (*mushá*) in Jordan, perhaps reflecting recent conversion of mobile herders to sedentary mixed farming (Stein, 1984, 14; Palmer, 1999). Conversely, private *unsown* pasture occurs, particularly on previously cultivated land (e.g., infield plots in upland Asturias or at Tharounia) but also rough pasture (e.g., some Kithiran *kleistá*) enclosed to leave livestock unattended. Likewise, although adminis-trators routinely classify trees other than domesticated fruits and nuts as "wild" and thus "public," individual farmers widely planted, protected, trained, and cropped them (e.g., Moreno, 1982) for private use of resin, bark, acorns, and especially leaf fodder.

Given the opposition between cultivated/private and unculti-vated/public, large-scale clearance usually needed official sanction, while small-scale clearances were sometimes short-lived because they lacked authorization. Twentieth-century extension of cultiva-tion in the lowlands was matched by contraction in marginal and upland areas. For example, large parts of the Pindos are now densely forested, with recent mixed farming detectable only in May, when surviving fruit trees blossom, and winter, when leafless old oaks and beeches reveal outlines characteristic of lopping for leafy hay. In some cases, as at Tharounia on Euboea, the oldest inhabi-tants undertook temporary clearance of scrub on distant slopes before watching bushes and trees recolonize first these plots, then permanent fields nearer the village, and finally even infield gar-dens. Abandoned plots reverted – de facto or de jure – to common ownership.

The ebb and flow of cultivation created tensions also between households of conflicting interests. Whether the field, which Ilias' grandfather cleared and defended below Metaxada, threatened his neighbors' interests or was merely envied is unclear. Less ambig-uous was the threat to collective control of pasture at Aetomilitsa in the high Pindos, when two herders with few sheep plowed and sowed flattish ground adjacent to the village. The whole community of transhumant Vlachs grazed here at the beginning and end of summer and responded by grazing flat the growing crops. In low-land Assiros, twentieth-century reforms gave poorer villagers cultivable land, taken initially from the *tsorbatzídes'* extensive fields and later from common rough grazing (Karakasidou, 1997, 167–182). While raising some poorer villagers from insecure laborer to marginally secure independent farmer, this eroded the *tsorbatzídes'* economic dominance not least by limiting – at least in theory – their ability to run large flocks on common pasture.

Some common land was earmarked for specific uses: for example, in Greece, pasture near the village for working cattle or equids that were needed close-by (Section 2.6.2) or coppiced woodland for firewood. These arrangements usually predate collective memory, but an exception illustrates the capacity of local communities to take such initiatives. In the 1920s, Plikati in the Pindos reserved an area near the village for cutting leafy hay (Halstead, 1998) to facilitate overwintering of sheep and goats. The community banned grazing here for a decade, so bushes developed into trees, and prohibited felling of deciduous oaks, the preferred source of leafy hay, such that removal of other species created a pure oakwood. In late summer, from a date declared by the mayor, villagers cut leafy branches at will. Now abandoned and reverting to mixed deciduous woodland, the reserve once needed violent collective defense from the neighboring village.

The most extensive use of common land was as rough pasture, often charged – especially to outsiders – per head of stock and providing significant income for local communities. At Aetomilitsa, an annual assembly assigned grazing areas equitably and sustainably, balancing flock size and pasture quality (Nitsiakos, 1995, 46–50) – much as communities of irrigators shared water in proportion to landholding (Section 6.3). Elsewhere, herders established informal territories that minimized counterproductive competition and conflict (Koster, 1997; Koster and Forbes, 2000). In nineteenth-century Greece, transhumant shepherds renting and manuring over winter the fallow fields of lowland cereal-growing estates prevented poor villagers from grazing livestock and so achieving enough economic independence to reduce the pool of cheap agricultural labor (Karavidas, 1931, 35–37). In early twentieth-century Assiros, *tsorbatzídes* with far more land than they could cultivate used economic dominance, bribery of officials, and violence to discourage poor neighbors from grazing uncultivated fields. Even after land reform, there were combined village herds of cattle, goats, and, briefly, pigs, but not sheep – not because pasture was scarce (Assiros sustained thousands of sheep), but because the *tsorbatzídes* successfully restricted its use (Karakasidou, 1997, 179–181).

Grazing of cultivated land also blurs the distinction between cultivated/private and uncultivated/public. Barley or oats sown as "early-bite" pasture belonged to the cultivator, as did crops grazed because they were at risk of lodging or not worth harvesting for grain (Section 5.1). Farmers in southern Greek Tsakonia sowed field edges to reserve the middle as private pasture (Kostakis, 1976–1978, 47). Even without sowing, tillage may secure private grazing rights, as in the 1980s in parts of eastern Jordan too dry for crops (Andrew Garrard, personal communication). Stubble and fallow fields were also sometimes considered private pasture, as at Kinigou in Messenia, but much more widespread was a collective right, customary or legal, of grazing. Assiros farmers had to remove sheaves to threshing floors by July 20, when winter cereal stubble opened for grazing; from November, winter cereals were again sown and livestock restricted to the village's uncultivated periphery (Karakasidou, 1997, 180), accessing sown pasture and fallow plots only by license or bribery. Here summer crops and fallow plots were scattered among winter cereal fields, but elsewhere, where regular fallowing or rotation of autumn- and spring-sown crops prevailed, communities frequently divided arable land into two or sometimes three blocks (Section 5.2.3), so large areas could be grazed seasonally without damaging field crops.

Perennial tree crops complicated regulation of grazing. Recurrent solutions included pruning trees for a canopy out of reach of livestock (Section 6.5) and banning goats that are agile climbers. Vineyards and orchards were often walled or, as in Assiros, grouped together for protection by a watchtower and warden. Small or young fruit trees among cereal fields depended on the vigilance of herders, although some landowners in the southern Argolid planted olives among cereals to make herders pay a grazing fee rather than face fines for damaging trees (Koster, 1997). Thus, although communal control eased access to pasture, protected crops, and reduced conflict between herders and cultivators, it was open to abuse and perhaps exacerbated economic inequalities. In a community with blocks of land alternately in winter cereals and fallow, a smallholder with limited land could not crop his fields more frequently and, if he lacked teenage children for herding, might not benefit from more accessible pasture.

In addition to collective arrangements and exchanges between households of *one resource for another* (e.g., land for labor), households also pooled resources. Often two farmers, each owning a single cow, made a pair (Section 2.6.1) that they used in turn, either alone or with one partner plowing and the other breaking clods by hand. Such partnerships were for a single season but might continue for years if harmonious – two elderly residents of Anogia in Crete addressed each other as "co-plowman" (*sizeftá*) years after abandoning cultivation. Occasionally, two farmers, each with a draft pair, combined to rent land too extensive for either party alone and collaborated in plowing, sowing, reaping, and threshing. Likewise, two farmers might combine flocks so that one herded and the other attended to crops or one herded lactating females on rich pasture and the other barren animals on poor. Such partnerships too were arranged for a season but might last for years. On a smaller scale, women often pooled milk from a few house-goats and eggs from a few hens so each could in turn prepare the household's supply of cheese or dried cereal products like *trakhanás* (e.g., Koster, 2000, 259). Neighbors or relatives often pooled human labor for tasks like harvesting (Section 3.5) or digging vines, usually in short turns (e.g., "today for me, tomorrow for you" in Spain (Palanca, 1991, 153) and Greece) that minimized risk of nonreciprocation. Collaborative reaping is often rationalized in northern Greece as alleviating tedium, but in the south, where faster ripening places manual harvesting under greater time stress, as enabling timely completion (Section 3.4). Perhaps significantly, reciprocal exchanges of human labor are often described in southerly Crete and Messenia as "loans" (*daneikoús, daneikariés*); to Ilias in Metaxada, these represented a balanced exchange of working days, whereas mutual assistance (*allilovoíthia*) – driven by neighborliness – might not.

Some tedious home-based tasks, such as stripping maize cobs or cleaning wool, were undertaken by lamp-lit nocturnal gatherings of neighbors (Greek *nikhtéria*), drawn by music, drink, snacks, banter, or gossip (Petropoulos, 1943–1944, 70–71; García Fernández,

1988, 165). Food and drink also mobilized labor for heavier tasks, such as digging a new vineyard (Section 6.2; Petropoulos, 1943–1944, 67–68); in Valencia, an elderly farmer who fêted neighbors for digging a garden might say, "the lamb dug it for me" (Palanca, 1991, 38). Reciprocal exchanges of labor could be imbalanced, not least because participants' strength and skill varied, but contributions tended to be measured in man-days rather than work achieved. Reciprocation of labor with food blurred the issue further, because the quality of hospitality expected was frequently calibrated to the host's means (García Fernández, 1988, 171). Ilias described digging wells in Metaxada as "a big job, so everyone would go for a day or two to help and, if he was poor, you also took food [rather than expecting hospitality]." Greek farmers call collaborative work "mutual assistance" (*allilovoíthia*) (Petropoulos, 1943–1944) or "mutual assurance" (*alliloengíisi*), highlighting that balanced reciprocity might become "from each according to his ability, to each according to his need," as in widespread volunteering of human and animal labor on Sundays and feast days to help the elderly, sick, widowed, or poor. On days of rest, when work for oneself drew disapproval, the promise of a party or a reminder in church of moral obligations to the needy could mobilize labor (Petropoulos, 1943–1944, 71; García Fernández, 1988, 169–174). Unilateral assistance also occurred spontaneously on workdays, as Koula in Paliambela recalled: with her husband on military service, during threshing, the owner of an adjacent floor "had several sons and always sent one to help." Stories of cousins or neighbors helping with time-stressed tasks, like harvest or threshing, are widespread.

Elderly informants often describe a past "golden age" of unselfish mutual help, but specific anecdotes document numerous counter-cases arising from political, personal, or economic conflicts. In Greece, mutual assistance was perhaps particularly fragile during the early 1940s famine (cf. Sahlins, 1974, 214): one Assiros resident boasted of exchanging 150 kg of grain for the roof beams and tiles of a neighbor with hungry children; some Paliambela farmers refused to allow gleaning for fear of theft from sheaves; and, more light-heartedly, clucking neighbors for 60 years reminded a Tharounia man of a chicken stolen in his teens. Nonetheless, memories of past solidarity are plausible: prior to mechanization and expanding urban employment, villagers had greater need of, and fewer alternatives to, mutual support; and without television or automobiles, they depended on each other for entertainment, making work parties more attractive and harder to refuse.

Solidarity is implicit even in some interactions involving significant exchanges of resources. The widespread reciprocation of one day's plowing with two or three days' manual labor was far more favorable to the manual worker than a rate based on work achieved (perhaps 1:10 for tillage) or, in many cases, on availability of animal and human labor. Similarly, the 130–150 kg of wheat to rent two oxen for a season in Metaxada was probably recouped in two days' plowing in an average year. At Aroniadika on Kithira in the 1930s, Panagiotitsa's brothers plowed and threshed with their oxen for others, who in turn helped them harvest. "If someone did a day's plowing for you, you paid four days' wages or went to work for them for four days, but between relatives and neighbors, we did not count the days. You went to help someone if you had an obligation or wanted them to be obliged to you." By the late 1940s, Panagiotitsa was married in nearby Kastrisianika. Her husband lacked the pasture to maintain draft cattle and preferred to rent a pair than incur obligations, "but we only kept them for one season and the owners did not want to take anything for them. We went and worked a few days for them and after that they felt obliged to us." Webs of mutual support were thus forged, and not only between close kin and immediate neighbors, by delayed reciprocal assistance (also Galt, 1991, 197). Among herders and between herders and farmers in southern Greece, such delayed reciprocity encompassed diverse goods and services (Koster, 2000). In Asturias, poorer neighbors, who had borrowed cows for milking or draft, weeded or reaped for Inés' husband; the days worked were not agreed beforehand nor apparently counted. Poor neighbors also helped smallholders with weeding in return for just their daily meal. Asturian rural communities (absentee landlords excluded) espoused the principle articulated in the Pindos to explain that neighboring Aristi and Vikos functioned as one community, "you eat so that we eat" (*fáte, na fáme*).

Exchange of food had manifold significance: grain loaned (often interest-free between peers) to the next harvest or labor rewarded with a meal or long-term sustenance averted hunger; "feeding" of workers made employment a social as well as an economic relationship; and commensality reinforced solidarity. Commensality ranged in scale from community-wide celebrations, such as patron saints' *kourbánia* in rural Greece (Georgoudi, 1989) or weddings involving prominent families, to smaller meals accompanying shared labor. In Asturian Zureda, well-fed cats might disappear if opening a new cider barrel triggered a party, but commensality usually involved "farmyard" animals – access to which varied. The weddings of *tsorbatzídes* were keenly anticipated by the poor of Assiros as a rare opportunity to taste meat but also underscored relations of patronage, while provision of livestock for slaughter at the *kourbáni* reflected competition for prestige as much as piety. One local custom, however, symbolized solidarity less ambivalently. Seated cross-legged, Khristos tells how he had barely completed military service, when both parents died, leaving him responsible for three young siblings. His father having just received 5 ha of fields in the 1929 redistribution, Khristos bought a horse and asked neighbors for the can of seedcorn (probably 16 kg) customarily given to new farmers. He sowed 3 ha, so at least 30 neighbors contributed.

6.9   Land, Labor, and Livestock in the Past

Recent farmers' choices of crops, husbandry methods, and processing and consumption practices were strongly shaped by access to labor, land, and livestock. This fluctuated through the domestic cycle and between generations, depending on demographic fortune (health of parents, number and gender of offspring) and household investment of "surplus" teenage-young adult labor in accumulating capital – by extending and improving cultivable land or buying existing plots with income from cash crops or sale of livestock. This concluding section addresses similar issues in the past, considering first the labor costs of agricultural extension and improvement and secondly the possible dynamics of household economies on a generational scale.

Across Europe, the first farmers cleared land for sowing. Ethnographic and experimental observations show that stone axes can fell trees efficiently (Steensberg, 1980; Sigaut, 1975, 217) but offer two contrasting models of forest cultivation: slashing and intensive burning (*temporarily* preventing regrowth of forest plants), followed by sowing with minimal tillage for one or two seasons, or felling with limited burning (to dispose of brushwood and kill stumps), followed by intensive tillage and long-term cultivation (Section 6.1). Despite (questionable – Section 6.1.1) claims that the former model offers higher yields for less labor (e.g., Clark, 1952, 92–97; Sigaut, 1975, 218), charred crop weeds (Bogaard, 2004) and, indirectly, firewood (Kreuz, 1992) unambiguously favor the latter model for Early Neolithic central and probably southeast Europe (Bogaard, 2005). Anyway, recent Mediterranean data identify clearance as more labor-intensive than even manual tillage, and so, unless poor soils or cultural constraints limit cultivation to one or two harvests, the second – archaeobotanically supported – model offers better long-term returns on labor.

Nonetheless, clearance was labor-intensive, with significant implications for agricultural expansion. In recent Greek clearance, households that mobilized several members or additional laborers worked more efficiently and brought new land into cultivation sooner. Similar collaboration presumably facilitated Neolithic clearance, while cattle skulls adorning house facades in southeast Europe (e.g., Koukouli-Chrysanthaki *et al.*, 2005) perhaps reflect large-scale commensal mobilization of labor for house construction. Clearance of new land would have been much easier near home, close to productive fields, stored food, and neighbors, than in establishing a new settlement beyond "commuting" distance from the old, as perhaps occurred when early farming "leapfrogged" between islands or fertile lowland basins. Under these circumstances, the period until the first harvest would have been critical, requiring reliance on foraging (of very variable potential and perhaps demanding mobility incompatible with preparation for cultivation) or transported food – stored grain or lactating domesticates (Rowley-Conwy, 2011). Transport of bulky and heavy grain, beyond seedcorn, would have been impracticable unless putative colonists traveled by sea or river – in which case grain probably competed for cargo space with trussed livestock (Rowley-Conwy, 2011, S436, S439). For crop-based subsistence and seedcorn, colonists comprising only fit adults would have needed to produce at least 250 kg of grain/head/year, initially clearing 0.1–0.3 ha/head (assuming yields of 1–2 tons/ha on fertile land) in perhaps one to three months of hard labor. Whether they felled and burned in summer and tilled in autumn, when the ground was soft, or completed the whole process over winter–spring, recent experience suggests that any crop harvested in the first year will have been sown too late or on inadequately tilled ground to be dependable. The period until the first successful harvest was thus arguably longer and even more problematic than Rowley-Conwy envisages. Whether milking of livestock, transported and hence probably few in number and physiologically stressed, could bridge this gap is questionable. The problem would disappear if colonists received ongoing support from the parent settlement (again much easier by boat) or, conversely, if farming partly spread through adoption by indigenous foragers. Ironically, heavy dependence on reliable harvests strongly favors forest clearance with intensive tillage, whereas a significant role for foragers (or foraging) would lower the premium on harvest success and so make shifting slash-and-burn cultivation, traditionally associated with colonizing farmers, more viable.

Forest clearance apart, the antiquity of agricultural extension and improvement is uncertain (e.g., Foxhall, 2007, 61–72): perhaps later Bronze Age for macroscale drainage in central Greece (e.g., Kienast, 1987) and Greco-Roman antiquity or later for large-scale hillside terracing in southern Greece (Price and Nixon, 2005; Krahtopoulou and Frederick, 2008) and macroscale irrigation in Spain (Butzer *et al.*, 1985). Although know-how is often tacitly considered a limiting factor, Neolithic settlements are often ditched, and early farmers surely practiced small-scale drainage and irrigation at least occasionally. Hillside terracing and *macroscale* drainage or irrigation are an order of magnitude more labor-intensive than clearance, enclosure, or cross-channel terracing, however, and the earliest dated off-site terraces in Greece are, perhaps significantly, of cross-channel type (Krahtopoulou and Frederick, 2008). *Macroscale* drainage and irrigation also need coordination of work at a community or intercommunity level. Even for household initiatives, however, the influence of labor costs depends on the value placed on both labor and returns. Recent household heads commonly regarded unused domestic labor as cost-free and so worth investing in capital projects almost regardless of returns. On Kithira, the concentration of hillside terraces on south-facing slopes (Krahtopoulou and Frederick, 2008, 559) supports Thanasis' claim that land-hungry farmers built them to take a cash crop from frost-sensitive olives planted over the retaining wall while sowing the surface with field crops. Also critical was length of land tenure: in Metaxada, Nikos derided an invitation to terrace a sloping field that he cultivated temporarily as a sharecropper, but Grigoris proudly invested labor in improving the terraced gardens he had inherited and would leave to his children. While contrasting labor requirements are not evidence for dating different forms of agricultural extension and improvement, they do pose fruitful questions of such evidence and may highlight historical contexts in which scarce land, abundant labor, or high cash crop prices encouraged heavy investment (cf. Foxhall, 2007, 72–82).

Farming in Classical (fifth to fourth century BC) Greece, as in the recent past, was organized primarily at a household level and underwent similar cycles of subsistence security and vulnerability over generations as the consumer to worker ratio changed and accumulated property was transmitted to heirs (Gallant, 1991). A clear hierarchy of high- and low-status grains (Garnsey, 1999, 119–122) will have reinforced use of livestock for indirect storage and sometimes replaced starvation with loss of face. Like their recent counterparts, Classical households also sacrificed land, livestock, and labor in bad times (Gallant, 1991) and planted perennial cash crops like olives and vines or built up cash-generating herds in good times. Relevant evidence is largely epigraphic and literary, with an elite bias, but scarcity of specialized olive-processing equipment (Foxhall, 2007, 202) implies that neither elite nor non-elite households produced oil on a scale to match that of some wealthy Roman landowners or even many recent hill farmers. Likewise, elite Classical Greek farmers apparently invested far less labor in preparing vineyards for planting by trenching (Foxhall, 2007, 99) than recent smallholders who practiced wholesale deep tillage, while the herds even of wealthy men in southern Greece (e.g., Athenian Panaitios' 10 adult cattle and 150 adult sheep and goats – Chandezon, 2003) were matched by some recent hill farmers and far exceeded by Assiros *tsorbatzídes*. The apparently modest scale of Classical Greek cash cropping echoes Finley's (1973) insistence on limited market development in antiquity – as do hints that Roman expansion was concentrated on elite estates (e.g., Jongman, 1988; Rodríguez-Ariza and Montes Moya, 2005; Foxhall, 2007).

Through the domestic cycle, Classical Greek farming households thus faced similar stresses to their recent counterparts and, within the constraints of a less developed market economy, exploited similar opportunities to accumulate wealth. To what extent might similar dynamics be relevant to the Neolithic, when markets were lacking, social inequalities less marked, and the boundaries between private and collective ownership perhaps drawn differently? The following paragraphs tentatively explore Neolithic political economy, using southeast Europe to exemplify an argument of wider relevance.

Neolithic settlements in southeast Europe widely took the form of "villages," some forming "tell" mounds through rebuilding in situ of substantial houses and others drifting horizontally through lateral relocation of flimsier dwellings. The former, at least, housed several dozen to a few hundred individuals, enforcing subsistence dominated by staple grains, while archaeobotanical and zooarchaeological evidence from both suggests small-scale intensive crop husbandry, closely integrated with small-scale stock rearing (Section 5.7; Bogaard, 2005). The constituent houses of both types arguably

315

represent *household* units of production, storage, and consumption (Section 4.9), better suited to grain cultivation with heavy labor inputs for delayed returns than are communities with a generalized obligation to share food (Flannery, 1972). *Single* households are viable only in the short term (Sahlins, 1974), however, and the clustering of Neolithic houses in villages, often enclosed within ditches or walls signaling collective solidarity, suggests a dynamic tension between domestic and collective rights and obligations (e.g., Halstead, 2011).

In addition to domestic storage and processing of crops, household ownership of livestock is suggested indirectly by uneven representation of dairy and adipose fat of different domesticates in pots (of a size suitable for family meals) at north Greek Makriyalos and Stavroupoli (Urem-Kotsou, 2006) and by selective consumption of, and working of bone from, large game (subject to sharing among recent foragers) versus small game and domestic animals. Although economies of scale favored *collective* clearance and fencing against wild and domestic animals (Sections 6.1 and 6.2; Fleming, 1985), archaeobotanical hints of long-term, labor-intensive crop husbandry suggest fairly stable use rights to cultivated plots (Bogaard, 2004, 165). Conversely, tells and "flat" enclosures alike created fixed "places" in the cultural landscape (Chapman, 1997), presumably signaling collective defense from neighboring communities, while the longevity at least of tell villages implies, given uneven biological reproduction, collective mechanisms for redistributing ownerless plots among landless households (Isaakidou, 2008, 106). Neolithic land tenure, therefore, probably balanced long-term collective against medium-term domestic control. Tell villages, with houses repeatedly rebuilt in the same "footprint," imply claims to plots over multiple generations, whereas shifting residence on "flat" settlements suggests that rights to land were shorter term (Kotsakis, 1999) or vested in groups of households (cf. Bogaard, Krause, and Strien, 2011).

During labor-stressed phases of the domestic cycle, individual households surely struggled to cope with the incapacity of a working member or a bad harvest, and, again, the longevity of many settlements implies that those in need received help (labor or food as appropriate). This was probably given freely between close kin and for short periods but involved exchange of food for labor over greater social distances and longer periods – if only because consumers were more easily moved to grain than vice versa. Shared regional styles of elaborate ceramic tableware suggest a major role for commensality in cultivating relationships of solidarity, both within and between settlements (e.g., Tomkins, 2007; Urem-Kotsou and Kotsakis, 2007).

While periodic scarcity reinforced mutual dependence, surplus made subsistence support and hospitality possible (Hayden, 2001, 43–44). The highly seasonal Mediterranean climate, leaving limited scope for rain-fed, late sowing to compensate for failed harvests, dictates regular attempts at overproduction (Forbes, 1982). Neolithic households doubtless stored some of the resulting "normal surplus" (Allan, 1965) as insurance for the following year, but the period between low- and high-stress phases of the domestic cycle – and often between good and bad harvests – exceeds the shelf life of grain. Surplus producers thus have powerful incentives to participate in longer-term indirect storage: by supporting needy kin or neighbors in exchange for work or future reciprocation (Allan, 1965); by providing hospitality, to mobilize labor for a task (Dietler and Herbich, 2001) or create symbolic capital with an obligation of reciprocity (Dietler, 2001); or by feeding livestock to enhance their value for work or for consumption in hospitality (Section 6.6). Documenting such practices archaeologically is challenging, but Neolithic burnt dung widely includes grain (e.g., Robinson and Rasmussen, 1989; Charles and Bogaard, 2005; Valamoti, 2007). The age and size of domesticated animal carcasses, and their dispersal apparently before discard, suggest consumption largely in suprahousehold commensality (Halstead and Isaakidou, 2011b), while dental microwear of some animals slaughtered for large-scale commensality at north Greek Makriyalos suggests fattening on a soft diet (Mainland and Halstead, 2005).

The busiest periods for Neolithic grain producers were autumn–early winter sowing or, if draft cattle assisted tillage, early summer harvest. Both became more time-stressed as the severity and duration of summer drought increased from the northern to southern Mediterranean. In the recent past, acutely unequal land ownership ensured a pool of needy laborers for tillage and reaping or, in slack seasons, for forest clearance and house building. Neolithic farmers with surplus probably recruited manual labor with grain after bad harvests but with hospitality involving special beverages (e.g., Urem-Kotsou *et al.*, 2002; Valamoti *et al.*, 2007) or fattened carcasses after good harvests. Feeding surplus grain instead to draft cattle needing training would have represented a longer-term investment, but the narrower the window for sowing and the greater the difficulty of mobilizing labor from neighbors working their own fields, the greater was the advantage of doing so. At Neolithic Knossos, the unusual wealth of evidence for early draft cattle may reflect the narrowness of this window (Isaakidou, 2008), and if only some residents could maintain such animals, the benefits of prompt sowing probably enabled them to exchange tillage for the manual labor (e.g., at harvest) of those less fortunate, as in the recent past, and so perpetuate their greater productivity.

This tentative outline of Neolithic household dynamics has several important implications. First, livestock arguably played a central role not only in crop production (as aid to tillage, source of manure, and defense against lodging) but also in political economy (as means of mobilizing labor, earning prestige, and creating commensal debts) and in linking subsistence and political economy (as vehicles of indirect storage). Inter alia, this accounts plausibly for the integral association of domestic animals with crops in the rapid expansion of mixed farming into Europe from the east Mediterranean (Bogaard and Isaakidou, 2010). Secondly, the imperative to produce fattened livestock and perhaps milk- as well as fruit-based beverages gives "cash crops" a long, premonetary history (Sherratt, 1999), with commensality preceding the market as exchange context. Thirdly, indirect storage, while contributing to short-term subsistence stability, may have promoted longer-term inequality by enabling households that gained prestige through competitive hospitality or achieved overproduction with draft cattle to secure preferential access to others' labor. The durability of such inequality partly depended on the strength of leveling mechanisms. Deliberate burning of houses (Stevanović, 1997) and breaking of grinding stones (Graefe *et al.*, 2009), symbolizing the death of households, perhaps limited (rather than promoted – *pace* Stevanović, 1997) transmission of accumulated wealth and prestige across generations. If "flat" and tell settlements respectively represent collective and domestic control of land between generations, the issue was contested over centuries or millennia in different parts of Neolithic southeast Europe, but the household eventually triumphed, arguably laying the foundations of widening inequality in the Bronze Age.

Whatever the mechanisms by which overtly egalitarian Neolithic societies were transformed into the ostentatiously hierarchical "palatial" polities of later Bronze Age southern Greece, draft cattle (Section 2.7) and diacritical commensality (Section 4.9) played central roles in financing and legitimizing the latter's ruling elites. These elites used preferential access to capital resources of land and livestock to secure human labor, acquiring staple grain and wool under arrangements recalling recent sharecropping (Halstead, 2001). The land on which the palace produced grain apparently belonged to local *damos* communities, however, recalling the success of the wealthy in the recent Mediterranean countryside in gaining preferential access to collective as well as private resources.

References

Allan, W. (1965) *The African Husbandman*, Oliver and Boyd, Edinburgh.

Bertolotto, S. and Cevasco, R. (2000) Fonti osservazionali e fonti testuali. Le 'Consegni dei Boschi' e il sistema dell' 'alnocoltura' nell' Appennino Ligure orientale (1822). *Quaderni Storici*, 103, 87–108.

Blanchard, R. (1945) *Les Alpes occidentales 4: les préalpes françaises du sud*, Arthaud, Grenoble and Paris.

Bogaard, A. (2004) *Neolithic Farming in Central Europe: An Archaeobotanical Study of Crop Husbandry Practices*, Routledge, London.

Bogaard, A. (2005) 'Garden agriculture' and the nature of early farming in Europe and the Near East. *World Archaeology*, 37, 177–196.

Bogaard, A. and Isaakidou, V. (2010) From mega-sites to farmsteads: community size, ideology and the nature of early farming landscapes in western Asia and Europe, in *Landscapes in Transition* (eds B. Finlayson and G. Warren), Oxbow, Oxford, pp. 192–207.

Bogaard, A., Krause, R., and Strien, H.-C. (2011) Towards a social geography of cultivation and plant use in an early farming community: Vaihingen an der Enz, south-west Germany. *Antiquity*, 85, 395–416.

Braudel, F. (1975) *The Mediterranean and the Mediterranean World in the Age of Philip II*, vol. 1, Fontana, London.

Butzer, K.W., Mateu, J.F., Butzer, E.K., and Kraus, P. (1985) Irrigation agrosystems in eastern Spain: Roman or Islamic origins? *Annals of the Association of American Geographers*, 75, 479–509.

Chandezon, C. (2003) *L'élevage en Grèce (fin Ve-fin Ier s. a.C.): l' apport des sources épigraphiques*, Ausonius, Paris.

Chapman, J. (1997) The origin of tells in eastern Hungary, in *Neolithic Landscapes* (ed. P. Topping), Oxbow, Oxford, pp. 139–164.

Charles, M. and Bogaard, A. (2005) Identifying livestock diet from charred plant remains: a Neolithic case study from southern Turkmenistan, in *Diet and Health in Past Animal Populations: Current Research and Future Directions* (eds J. Davies, M. Fabis, I. Mainland *et al.*), Oxbow, Oxford, pp. 93–103.

Christakis, K.S. (1999) Pithoi and food storage in Neopalatial Crete: a domestic perspective. *World Archaeology*, 31, 1–20.

Clark, J.G.D. (1952) *Prehistoric Europe: The Economic Basis*, Methuen, London.

Comet, G. (1993) Le vin et l'huile en Provence medievale, essai de bilan, in *La production du vin et de l'huile en Mediterranee* (eds M.-C. Amouretti and J.-P. Brun), École française d'Athènes, Paris, pp. 343–358.

Cornebois, M. (1881) Notice sur le sartage dans l'arrondissement de Rocroi. *Mémoires de la Société nationale d'agriculture de la France*, 126, 601–642.

Critz, J.M., Olmstead, A.L., and Rhode, P.W. (1999) 'Horn of plenty': the globalization of Mediterranean horticulture and the economic development of southern Europe, 1880–1930. *Journal of Economic History*, 59, 316–352.

Davis, J. (1977) *People of the Mediterranean: An Essay in Comparative Social Anthropology*, Routledge & Kegan Paul, London.

Dietler, M. (2001) Theorizing the feast: rituals of consumption, commensal politics, and power in African contexts, in *Feasts: Archaeological and Ethnographic Perspectives on Food, Politics and Power* (eds M. Dietler and B. Hayden), Smithsonian Institution Press, Washington, DC, pp. 65–114.

Dietler, M. and Herbich, I. (2001) Feasts and labor mobilization, in *Feasts: Archaeological and Ethnographic Perspectives on Food, Politics and Power* (eds M. Dietler and B. Hayden), Smithsonian Institution, Washington, DC, pp. 240–264.

Duplessy, B., Gabert, A., Valabrégue, J.P. *et al.* (1996) *Le livre de l' épeautre*, Edisud, Aix-en-Provence.

Durrenberger, E.P. (1980) Chayanov's economic analysis in anthropology. *Journal of Anthropological Research*, 36, 133–148.

Ertug, F. (2004) Recipies of old tastes with einkorn and emmer wheat. *Tüba-Ar*, 7, 177–188.

Finley, M.I. (1973) *The Ancient Economy*, Chatto & Windus, London.

Flannery, K.V. (1969) Origins and ecological effects of early Near Eastern domestication, in *The Domestication and Exploitation of Plants and Animals* (eds P.J. Ucko and G.W. Dimbleby), Duckworth, London, pp. 73–100.

Flannery, K.V. (1972) The origins of the village as a settlement type in Mesoamerica and the Near East: a comparative study, in *Man, Settlement and Urbanism* (eds P.J. Ucko, R. Tringham, and G.W. Dimbleby), Duckworth, London, pp. 23–53.

Fleming, A. (1985) Land tenure, productivity, and field systems, in *Beyond Domestication in Prehistoric Europe* (eds G. Barker and C. Gamble), Academic Press, London, pp. 129–146.

Forbes, H. (1976) 'We have a little of everything': the ecological basis of some agricultural practices in Methana, Trizinia. *Annals of the New York Academy of Sciences*, 268, 236–250.

Forbes, H. (1982) *Strategies and soils: technology, production and environment in the peninsula of Methana*, Greece. PhD thesis. University of Pennsylvania.

Forbes, H. (1993) Ethnoarchaeology and the place of the olive in the economy of the southern Argolid, Greece, in *La production du vin et de l'huile en Méditerranée* (eds M.-C. Amouretti and J.-P. Brun), École française d'Athènes, Athens, pp. 213–226.

Forte, M.A. (2009) *A Mediterranean mountain: landscape and land use on the Cairo Massif, Central Italy, 1700–1970* A.D. PhD thesis. University of Sheffield.

Foxhall, L. (1990) *Olive cultivation within Greek and Roman agriculture: the ancient economy revisited*. PhD thesis. University of Liverpool.

Foxhall, L. (2007) *Olive Cultivation in Ancient Greece*, Oxford University Press, Oxford.

Frederick, C. and Krahtopoulou, A. (2000) Deconstructing agricultural terraces: examining the influence of construction method on stratigraphy, dating and archaeological visibility, in *Landscape and Land Use in Postglacial Greece* (eds P. Halstead and C. Frederick), Sheffield Academic Press, Sheffield, pp. 79–94.

Gallant, T.W. (1991) *Risk and Survival in Ancient Greece*, Polity Press, Cambridge, UK.

Galt, A.H. (1991) *Far From the Church Bells: Settlement and Society in an Apulian Town*, Cambridge University Press, Cambridge, UK.

García Fernández, J. (1988) *Sociedad y organización tradicional del espacio en Asturias*, Silverio Cañada, Gijón.

Garnsey, P. (1999) *Food and Society in Classical Antiquity*, Cambridge University Press, Cambridge.

Georgoudi, S. (1989) Sanctified slaughter in modern Greece: the 'kourbánia' of the saints, in *The Cuisine of Sacrifice among the Greeks* (eds M. Detienne and J.-P. Vernant), Chicago University Press, Chicago, pp. 183–203.

Gillon, D. and Rapp, M. (1989) Nutrient losses during a winter low-intensity prescribed fire in a Mediterranean forest. *Plant and Soil*, 120, 69–77.

Giono, J. (1930) *Regain*, Bernard Grasset, Paris.

Glick, T.F. (1970) *Irrigation and Society in Medieval Valencia*, Harvard University Press, Cambridge, MA.

Glick, T.F. (1995) *From Muslim Fortress to Christian Castle: Social and Cultural Change in Medieval Spain*, Manchester University Press, Manchester.

Graefe, J., Hamon, C. and Lidström-Holmberg, C. *et al.* (2009) Subsistence, social and ritual practices: quern deposits in the Neolithic societies of Europe, in *Du matériel au spirituel. Réalités archéologiques et historiques des « dépôts » de la préhistoire à nos jours* (eds S. Bonnardin, C. Hamon, M. Lauwers, and B. Quilliec), Éditions APDCA, Antibes, pp. 87–96.

Grieco, A. (1993) Olive tree cultivation and the alimentary use of olive oil in late medieval Italy (ca 1300–1500), in *La production du vin et de l'huile en Méditerranée* (eds M.-C. Amouretti and J.-P. Brun), École française d'Athènes, Athens, pp. 297–306.

Grigg, D.B. (1974) *The Agricultural Systems of the World: An Evolutionary Approach*, Cambridge University Press, Cambridge, UK.

Grove, A.T. and Rackham, O. (2001) *The Nature of Mediterranean Europe: An Ecological History*, Yale University Press, London.

Halstead, P. (1990a) Quantifying Sumerian agriculture – some seeds of doubt and hope. *Bulletin of Sumerian Agriculture*, 5, 187–195.

Halstead, P. (1990b) Waste not, want not: traditional responses to crop failure in Greece. *Rural History*, 1, 147–164.

Halstead, P. (1998) Ask the fellows who lop the hay: leaf-fodder in the mountains of northwest Greece. *Rural History*, 9, 211–234.

Halstead, P. (2001) Mycenaean wheat, flax and sheep: palatial intervention in farming and its implications for rural society, in *Economy and Politics in the Mycenaean Palace States* (eds S. Voutsaki and J. Killen), Cambridge Philological Society, Cambridge, UK, pp. 38–50.

Halstead, P. (2011) Farming, material culture and ideology: repackaging the Neolithic of Greece (and Europe), in *The Dynamics of Neolithisation in Europe: Studies in Honour of Andrew Sherratt* (eds A. Hadjikoumis, E. Robinson, and S. Viner), Oxbow, Oxford, pp. 131–151.

Halstead, P. and Jones, G. (1989) Agrarian ecology in the Greek islands: time stress, scale and risk. *Journal of Hellenic Studies*, 109, 41–55.

Halstead, P. and Isaakidou, V. (2011a) A pig fed by hand is worth two in the bush: ethnoarchaeology of pig husbandry in Greece and its archaeological implications, in *Ethnozooarchaeology: The Present and Past of Human–Animal Relationships* (eds U. Albarella and A. Trentacoste), Oxbow, Oxford, pp. 160–174.

Halstead, P. and Isaakidou, V. (2011b) Political cuisine: rituals of commensality in the Neolithic and Bronze Age Aegean, in *Guess Who's Coming to Dinner: Feasting Rituals in the Prehistoric Societies of Europe and the Near East* (eds G.A. Jiménez, S. Montón-Subías, and S. Romero), Oxbow, Oxford, pp. 91–108.

Hayden, B. (2001) Fabulous feasts: a prolegomenon to the importance of feasting, in *Feasts: Archaeological and Ethnographic Perspectives on Food, Politics and Power* (eds M. Dietler and B. Hayden), Smithsonian Institution Press, Washington, DC, pp. 23–64.

Isaakidou, V. (2008) The fauna and economy of Neolithic Knossos revisited, in *Escaping the Labyrinth* (eds V. Isaakidou and P. Tomkins), Oxbow, Oxford, pp. 90–114.

Jongman, W. (1988) *The Economy and Society of Pompeii*, J.C. Gieben, Amsterdam.

Jongman, W. and Dekker, R. (1989) Public intervention in the food supply in pre-industrial Europe, in *Bad Year Economics* (eds P. Halstead and J. O'Shea), Cambridge University Press, Cambridge, UK, pp. 114–22.

Karakasidou, A.N. (1997) *Fields of Wheat, Hills of Blood*, Chicago University Press, Chicago.

Karavidas, K.D. (1931) *Agrotika: meleti sigkritiki*, Ministry of Agriculture, Athens.

Kasdagli, A.E. (1999) *Land and Marriage Settlements in the Aegean: A Case Study of Seventeenth-Century Naxos*, Hellenic Institute of Byzantine and Post-Byzantine Studies, Venice.

Kienast, H. (1987) Neue Forschungen im Kopais-Becken, in *The Function of the Minoan Palaces* (eds R. Hägg and N. Marinatos), Svenska Institutet i Athen, Stockholm, pp. 121–122.

Kiriazis, N. (1931) Khronografikon simeioma. *Kupriaka Khronika*, 7, 81–91.

Kostakis, T.P. (1976–1978) Georgika tis Tsakonias. *Laografia*, 31, 43–150.

Koster, H.A. (1997) Yours, mine and ours: private and public pasture in Greece, in *Aegean Strategies: Studies of Culture and Environment on the European Fringe* (eds P.N. Kardulias and M.T. Shutes), Rowman and Littlefield, Lanham, pp. 141–186.

Koster, H.A. (2000) Neighbors and pastures: reciprocity and access to pasture, in *Contingent Countryside: Settlement, Economy, and Land Use in the Southern Argolid Since 1700* (ed. S.B. Sutton), Stanford University Press, Stanford, pp. 241–261.

Koster, H.A. and Forbes, H.A. (2000) The 'commons' and the market: ecological effects of communal land tenure and market integration on local resources in the Mediterranean, in *Contingent Countryside: Settlement, Economy, and Land Use in the Southern Argolid Since 1700* (ed. S.B. Sutton), Stanford University Press, Stanford, pp. 262–274.

Kotsakis, K. (1999) What tells can tell: social space and settlement in the Greek Neolithic, in *Neolithic Society in Greece* (ed. P. Halstead), Sheffield Academic Press, Sheffield, pp. 66–76.

Koukouli-Chrysanthaki, H., Aslanis, I., Vaisov, I., and Valla, M. (2005) Promakhonas-Topolniča 2002–2003. *To Arkhaiologiko Ergo sti Makedonia kai Thraki*, 17, 91–110.

Kowalewski, S.A., Feinman, G.A., Nicholas, L.M., and V.Y. Heredia (2006) Hilltowns and valley fields: great transformations, labor, and long-term history in ancient Oaxaca, in *Labor in Cross-Cultural Perspective* (eds E.P. Durrenberger and J. Martí), Altamira Press, Walnut Creek, pp. 197–216.

Krahtopoulou, A. and Frederick, C. (2008) The stratigraphic implications of long-term terrace agriculture in dynamic landscapes: polycyclic terracing from Kythera Island, Greece. *Geoarchaeology*, 23, 550–585.

Kreuz, A. (1992) Charcoal from ten early Neolithic settlements in central Europe and its interpretation in terms of woodland management and wildwood resources. *Bulletin de la Société botanique de France*, 139, 383–394.

Leontsinis, G.N. (2000) *The Island of Kythera: A Social History (1700–1863)*, University of Athens, Athens.

Linoli, A. (2005) Twenty-six centuries of reclamation and agricultural improvement on the Pontine Marshes, in *Integrated Land and Water Resources Management in History* (ed. C. Ohlig), Deutsche Wasserhistorische Gesellschaft, Siegburg, pp. 27–55.

Loizos, P. (1975) Changes in property transfer among Greek Cypriot villagers. *Man*, 10, 503–523.

Loukopoulos, D. (1930) *Poimenika tis Roumelis*, Vivliopoleion I. N. Sideri, Athens.

Loukopoulos, D. (1983) *Georgika tis Roumelis*, Dodoni, Athens.

Mainland, I.L. and Halstead, P. (2005) The diet and management of domestic sheep and goats at Neolithic Makriyalos, in *Diet and Health in Past Animal Populations: Current Research and Future Directions* (eds J. Davies, M. Fabis, I. Mainland *et al.*), Oxbow, Oxford, pp. 104–112.

McConnell, P. (1883) *The Agricultural Notebook*, Crosby Lockwood, London.

McGrew, W.W. (1985) *Land and Revolution in Modern Greece, 1800–1881: The Transition in the Tenure and Exploitation of Land from Ottoman Rule to Independence*, Kent State University Press, Kent.

McNeill, J.R. (1992) *The Mountains of the Mediterranean World*, Cambridge University Press, Cambridge, UK.

Mientjes, A.C. (2008) *Paesaggi pastorali: studio ethnoarcheologico sul pastoralismo in Sardegna*, CUEC Editrice, Cagliari.

Moreno, D. (1982) Querce come olivi: sulla rovericoltura in Liguria tra 18 e 19 secolo, in Boschi: storia e archeologia (eds D. Moreno, P. Piussi, and O. Rackham), *Quaderni Storici*, 49, 108–136.

Nakos, G. (1979) Forest soils of Greece: physical, chemical and biological properties. *Forest Ecology and Management*, 2, 35–51.

Nitsiakos, V. (1995) *Oi orines koinotites tis vorias Pindou*, Plethron, Athens.

Nitsiakos, V.G. (1997) Tsifliki kai tselingato: i sumpliromatikotita duo koinonikooikonomikon skhimatismon, in *Laografika Eteroklita* (ed. V.G. Nitsiakos), Ekdoseis Odysseas, Athens, pp. 88–95.

Palanca, F. (1991) Agricultura, in *Temes d' etnografia Valenciana 2: utillatge agrícola i ramaderia* (eds F. Martínez and F. Palanca), Institució Valenciana d' Estudis i Investigació, Valencia, pp. 11–181.

Palmer, C. (1999) Whose land is it anyway? An historical examination of land tenure and agriculture in northern Jordan, in *The Prehistory of Food: Appetites for Change* (eds C. Gosden and J. Hather), Routledge, London, pp. 288–305.

Peña-Chocarro, L. (1999) *Prehistoric Agriculture in Southern Spain During the Neolithic and the Bronze Age*, Archaeopress, Oxford.

Petropoulos, D.A. (1943–1944) Ethima sinergasias kai allilovoithias tou Ellinikou laou. *Epetiris Laografikou Arkhiou*, 59–85.

Petsas, F.M. and Saralis, G.A. (1982) *Aristi kai ditiko Zagori*, Enosi Aristis-Vikou Zagoriou, Athens.

Pina-Cabral, J. (1989) The Mediterranean as a category of regional comparison: a critical view. *Current Anthropology*, 30, 399–406.

Price, S. and Nixon, L. (2005) Ancient Greek agricultural terraces: evidence from texts and archaeological survey. *American Journal of Archaeology*, 109, 665–694.

Psikhogios, D.K. (1987) *Proikes, foroi, stafida kai psomi: oikonomia kai oikoyenia stin agrotiki Ellada tou 19 aiona*, Ethniko Kentro Koinonikon Erevnon, Athens.

Rackham, O. and Moody, J.A. (1992) Terraces, in *Agriculture in Ancient Greece* (ed. B. Wells), Swedish Institute at Athens, Stockholm, pp. 123–130.

Richardson, J.S. (1983) The Tabula Contrebiensis: Roman law in Spain in the early first century B.C. *Journal of Roman Studies*, 73, 33–41.

Robinson, D. and Rasmussen, P. (1989) Leaf hay and cereals as animal fodder, in *The Beginnings of Agriculture* (eds A. Milles, D. Williams, and N. Gardner), British Archaeological Reports, Oxford, pp. 149–163.

Rodríguez-Ariza, M.O. and Montes Moya, E. (2005) On the origin and domestication of *Olea europaea* L. (olive) in Andalucía, Spain, based on the biogeographical distribution of its finds. *Vegetation History and Archaeobotany*, 14, 551–561.

Rowley-Conwy, P. (1981) Slash and burn in the temperate European Neolithic, in *Farming Practice in British Prehistory* (ed. R.J. Mercer), Edinburgh University Press, Edinburgh, pp. 85–96.

Rowley-Conwy, P. (2011) Westward Ho! The spread of agriculture from central Europe to the Atlantic. *Current Anthropology*, 52, S431–S451.

Sahlins, M. (1974) *Stone Age Economics*, Tavistock Publications, London.

Schneider, J. (1971) Of vigilance and virgins: honor, shame and access to resources in Mediterranean societies. *Ethnology*, 10, 1–24.

Sereni, E. (1981) *Terra nuova e buoi rossi e altri saggi per una storia dell'agricoltura europea*, Einaudi, Torino.

Sherratt, A. (1999) Crops before cash: hunting, farming, manufacture and trade in earlier Eurasia, in *The Prehistory of Food* (eds C. Gosden and J.G. Hather), Routledge, London, pp. 13–34.

Shkurti, S. (1979) Le battage des cereales. *Ethnographie Albanaise*, 9, 57–111.

Sindicato de Riegos de Borja (1927) Sindicato de Riegos de Borja, Ordenanzas de Riego de la Ciudad de Borja y Reglamentos del Sindicato y Jurado. Zaragoza, Sindicato de Riegos de Borja.

Sigaut, F. (1975) *L'agriculture et le feu: rôle et place du feu dans les techniques de préparation du champ de l'ancienne agriculture européenne*, Mouton, Paris.

Silverman, S.F. (1968) Agricultural organization, social structure, and values in Italy: amoral familism reconsidered. *American Anthropologist*, 70, 1–20.

Steensberg, A. (1979) *Draved: An Experiment in Stone Age Agriculture: Burning, Sowing and Harvesting*, National Museum of Denmark, Copenhagen.

Steensberg, A. (1980) *New Guinea Gardens: A Study of Husbandry with Parallels in Prehistoric Europe*, Academic Press, London.

Stein, K.W. (1984) *The Land Question in Palestine, 1917–1939*, University of North Carolina Press, Chapel Hill and London.

Stevanović, M. (1997) The age of clay: the social dynamics of house destruction. *Journal of Anthropological Archaeology*, 16, 334–395.

Suárez, J.C. (1992) *Toponimia Lenense*, Real Instituto de Estudios Asturianos, Oviedo.

Tomkins, P. (2007) Communality and competition. The social life of food and containers at Aceramic and Early Neolithic Knossos, Crete, in *Cooking Up the Past: Food and Culinary Practices in the Neolithic and Bronze Age Aegean* (eds C. Mee and J. Renard), Oxbow, Oxford, pp. 174–199.

United Nations Food & Agriculture Organisation (FAO) (1986) *Watershed Management Field Manual: Slope Treatment Measures and Practices*, Rome, FAO.

Urem-Kotsou, D. (2006) *Neolithiki keramiki tou Makrigialou: diatrofikes sunithies kai oi koinonikes diastasis tis keramikis*. PhD thesis. Aristotle University of Thessaloniki.

Urem-Kotsou, D. and Kotsakis, K. (2007) Pottery, cuisine and community in the Neolithic of north Greece, in *Cooking Up the Past: Food and Culinary Practices in the Neolithic and Bronze Age Aegean* (eds C. Mee and J. Renard), Oxbow Books, Oxford, pp. 225–246.

Urem-Kotsou, D., Stern, B., Heron, C., and Kotsakis, K. (2002) Birch-bark tar at Neolithic Makriyalos, Greece. *Antiquity*, 76, 962–967.

Valamoti, S.M. (2007) Detecting seasonal movement from animal dung: an investigation in Neolithic northern Greece. *Antiquity*, 81, 1053–1064.

Valamoti, S.M., Mangafa, M., Koukouli-Chrysanthaki, H., and Malamidou, D. (2007) Grape-pressings from northern Greece: the earliest wine in the Aegean? *Antiquity*, 81, 54–61.

Vergopoulos, K. (1975) *To agrotiko zitima stin Ellada, i koinoniki ensomatosi tis georgias*, Exandas, Athens.

Vrontis, A.G. (1938–1948) Oi zevgades tis Rodou. *Laografia*, 12, 104–129.

van Wesemael, B. (1993) Litter decomposition and nutrient distribution in humus profiles in some Mediterranean forests in southern Tuscany. *Forest Ecology and Management*, 57, 99–114.

Zangger, E., Timpson, M.E., Yazvenko, S.B. *et al.* (1997) The Pylos Regional Archaeological Project, 2: landscape evolution and site preservation. *Hesperia*, 66, 549–641.

7

Homo agronomicus? Mediterranean Farming, Present and Past

During the fourteenth century BC, as fire overwhelmed mudbrick storerooms at Assiros Toumba in northern Greece, the clay roof collapsed, crushing baskets, bins, and jars but smothering the flames so that charred grain survived until discovery by modern archaeologists. Ilias, raised locally among similar buildings and grain containers, was entrusted with isolating the contents of each container in the biggest storeroom. As a cereal farmer, he recognized barley, became familiar with charred einkorn, and impressively identified the first few grains from one newly exposed jar as "wheat, not what we grow today nor einkorn, two types"; it was a maslin of emmer and spelt, neither of which he had seen before. Present-day analogy was also important after excavation: examination of modern cereal ears enabled identification of a new glume wheat (Jones, Valamoti, and Charles, 2000); isotopic analysis of modern and ancient crops showed that Ilias' emmer and spelt were grown together, rather than mixed in storage (Heaton *et al.*, 2009); and comparison of weeds in nearby fields

Two Oxen Ahead: Pre-Mechanized Farming in the Mediterranean, First Edition.
Paul Halstead. © 2014 Paul Halstead. Published 2014 by John Wiley & Sons, Ltd.

and gardens with those contaminating the Bronze Age crops illumi-
nated how the latter were grown (Jones, 1992).

Explaining to Ilias why Assiros Toumba was important, I summa-
rized Renfrew's "subsistence/redistribution" model (Renfrew, 1972,
480–482) for the Minoan palaces with their monumental storerooms:
elites emerged as managers of redistribution, made necessary by
farmers specializing in crops suited to local conditions. Ilias laughed.
From practical experience, he understood that local environments
and plant ecology *constrain* rather than *determine* what crops grow
where and could not imagine Bronze Age farmers *choosing* to spe-
cialize, given that diversification spreads labor, reduces risk, and
enhances self-sufficiency. Renfrew's contradictory assumptions,
however, were also based on modern observations, so how should
we use analogy?

7.1 Analogies for the Past: "Matters of Fact" and "Matters of Interest"

Prehistorians now widely accept their dependence on present-day
experience, first- or secondhand, to identify and interpret material
remains (e.g., Ascher, 1961; Hodder, 1982). Historians and historical
archaeologists are similarly dependent (e.g., Davis, 1981), despite the
apparent "vocality" of texts (Moreland, 2001, 33–34) and iconography
and the "familiarity" of the recent past (e.g., de Jong, 1996, 335). By
reliance on present analogy, however, we may underestimate or conversely, through the lens of anthropology (e.g., Cohn, 1981; de Jong,
1996), exaggerate the "otherness" of the past (e.g., Hodder, 1982, 39).
In archaeology, two influential solutions have been proposed to this
dilemma.

Binford (1977) distinguished "general theory," which answers "big
questions" (e.g., why did foragers become farmers?), from "middle-
range theory," which infers human behavior (e.g., cultivation) from
material remains (e.g., morphology of cereal ears). Middle-range
theory demands a relationship between material remains and human
behavior that is (i) causal and necessary and thus free of ambiguity or

equifinality; (ii) timeless (the uniformitarian principle), to avoid wrongly reconstructing the past in the image of the present; and (iii) free of assumptions about human behavior (most archaeologists' object of enquiry), to avoid circular argument. For example, attribution of archaeobotanical samples to processing stages, using the size and aerodynamic properties of crop parts and weed seeds (Jones, 1987), meets Binford's exacting standards: the variables analyzed are causally and necessarily related to winnowing, sieving, and sorting; the underpinning laws of physics are unlikely to have changed over the past 10 000 years; and analysis explores the response of plants rather than people to processing. Humans decide where and when processing occurs, however, so the contextual distribution of samples distinguishes producers from consumers (Jones, 1985) or domestic from communal processing (Stevens, 2003) insecurely.

In broad agreement with Binford, Hodder advocates "relational analogy" that specifies a causal link between material remains and inferred behavior (Hodder, 1982, 21) and, echoing historians' concerns (Thomas, 1963, 9), a contextualized argument for relevance. Thus, archaeobotanical methods for identifying crop-processing stages in modern Turkey and Greece are applicable to other times and places, because climate does not determine the size and aerodynamic properties of plant parts (Hodder, 1982, 112). Hodder criticizes Binford's middle-range theory, however, on two counts. First, it addresses only "ecological and functionally adaptive aspects of human behaviour" (Hodder, 1982, 38), leaving much of culture inaccessible. Secondly, Hodder disputes the practicability of isolating the mechanical or biological from the cultural and symbolic: for example, the thoroughness of crop cleaning is partly a cultural choice (Hodder, 1982, 112–113), as with the modern Cretan baker who *adds* chaff to "rustic" barley bread. Nonetheless, although variable thoroughness (for practical and cultural reasons) may obscure the *purpose* of crop cleaning (e.g., for human or animal consumption), it should not prevent archaeobotanists from distinguishing its successive stages (Section 4.9). Hodder's second objection is thus invalid, provided middle-range methods avoid assumptions about human decision-making (Charles and Halstead, 2001, 368–369), but this limits us to recognizing rather than interpreting behavior and so reinforces his first objection. Hodder's own guidelines are less restrictive but thereby risk circular arguments about human behavior.

A productive compromise is to acknowledge both the strength of middle-range theory in generating reliable "matters of fact" about the human past and its limitations in addressing broader "matters of interest" (Wylie, 1989). Recent husbandry involves decision-making, whether discursive or practical (Giddens, 1981), and so offers only heuristic analogies for the distant past, but its heuristic power is greater if it identifies *probable* past practices, or contexts thereof, rather than merely expanding the range of *possibilities*. This is a contentious issue, with anthropologists, historians, and archaeologists variously holding that farmers' decisions are:

- Constrained by identity, status, and values ("cultural reason" (Sahlins, 1976)) and so predictable only with detailed knowledge of a particular culture
- Shaped by "rational" cost–benefit considerations ("practical reason") and so fairly predictable
- Determined by environmental and technological constraints and so highly predictable

These three positions are evaluated here, arguing that *some* husbandry choices of recent premechanized farmers were quite predictable, given knowledge of their practical context. In conclusion, their relevance and heuristic potential, as analogies for the distant past, are discussed.

7.2 Cultural Reason

Premechanized Mediterranean farmers exhibited considerable local and regional variability in tools and practices (e.g., Zojzi, 1976; Shkurti, 1979; Meurers-Balke and Loennecken, 1984; Imellos, 1990–1992; Palanca, 1991). This is particularly clear in northern Greece, where 1920s refugees from Turkey settled among established communities, bringing distinctive toolkits, vocabulary, and ways of performing tasks like sowing and reaping. Refugees and "locals" alike learnt distinctive ways of doing things from an early age. Children helped in the fields, at first minding livestock and younger siblings, gathering ears spilled during harvest, or accompanying pack animals laden with sheaves. By the age of 12, most reaped with a pocketknife or small sickle and some helped with plowing. In Tharounia, Eleni was eight when her father loaded her and a wooden ard on his mule, telling the latter where to go. On arrival, Eleni dismounted, let down and attached the ard, and then "steered" the mule. A passerby, not noticing her, reported the apparent miracle of a mule plowing alone. In Paliambela, Koula received detailed verbal guidelines on reaping (Section 3.4), but most informants learned by example ("do it this way"). Koula's father served a teenage apprenticeship in neighboring Kolindros and so, although a refugee, knew both Thracian and "local" methods, but most farmers acquired skills working with close relatives or neighbors, so communities generally exhibited consistent practices. This shared embodied *habitus* (Bourdieu, 1977) was sometimes reinforced by learning motor habits suited to a particular type of tool or method of working (cf. Gosselain, 1992), as with the "local" sickle and Thracian *leléki* (Section 3.3), and by the exigencies of collaborative work. The sickle and *leléki* were both effective in skilled hands but used side by side could injure workers and produced irregularly sized sheaves that made unstable stooks. Thracian refugees in Paliambela gave their children sickles, to harvest for "local" farmers (Section 3.3). Shared ways of doing were particularly important in collaborative tasks, like reaping (and gathering, stooking, and trans-porting sheaves) or manual flailing.

Thracians and "locals" in northern Greece perceived clear mutual differences, not only in reaping tools and methods but also in pre-ferred work animals, plow types, sheaving practices, and threshing floor equipment. The Thracians regarded draft oxen as the hallmark of a farmer, whereas many "locals" used horses because they farmed land too distant over paths too steep for oxcarts (as in Kolindros) or were smallholders working part-time as carters (as in Assiros).

Preferred work animals in turn accounted for differences in sheaving and stooking (small sheaves for Thracian oxcarts; large for "local" pack animals) and threshing equipment (slow, perhaps unshod Thracian oxen with sledges; faster, shod "local" horses without). Although differences in work animal were influenced by practical considerations (and so less consistent than practitioners' normative accounts implied), this did not diminish their emic importance as identity markers.

When incomers sought locations resembling their original homes, cultural tradition partly dictated practical circumstances. For example, a group from inland northern Turkey, attributing poor health in the refugee camp to lack of the fruit sauces that accompanied staple cereals "back home," chose a small upland basin (Okiouzova, later Skafi) near Kozani, where plums and Cornelian cherries grew wild. The basin supported familiar crops and the departing Muslim inhabitants, reciprocally evicted, advised that maize should be sown when the soil felt warm to bare buttocks! Other refugees from coastal northern Turkey founded Nea Trapezounta near Katerini, clearing fields in a wooded area between sea and mountain – like their homeland. They maintained their culinary tradition, with dairy produce from cows prominent, letting sheep from neighboring villages graze their fields because "we did not speak the language of sheep." Likewise, glume wheats persisted in cultivation for culturally significant foods in Asturias and northern Turkey. Conversely, einkorn, introduced to northern Greece by refugees from Bulgaria and grown on poor land as fodder or hunger food, did not outlast the adoption of industrial fertilizers, and rye, a staple of the Paliambela Thracians in their "homeland" where some fields were infertile, was abandoned for wheat in Greece, perhaps because the new land was richer.

Reasons for local and regional variation in crop and livestock species, tools, and ways of using them thus ranged from unconscious replication of motor habits learnt in childhood, through maintenance of what was familiar and practically viable, to deliberate reinforcement of cultural identity. These differences are of great cultural interest, but need not conflict with practical considerations

(Lemonnier, 1993); on the contrary, consistent learnt procedures may improve efficiency (Arrow, 1962). Cultural traditions described in preceding chapters mostly represent alternatives that, practically, were similarly viable, and it is hard to point to migrant farmers who clung to traditions that were plainly disadvantageous in their new homes. Apart from the 1920s population exchange with Turkey, rural communities in Greece have experienced considerable piecemeal residential mobility over the last two centuries (e.g., Sutton, 1994). The (great-)grandfathers of several informants had migrated between upland and lowland, inland and coast, or north and south Aegean, but their descendants did not farm differently from longer established neighbors. The Vlachs of the Pindos Mountains exemplify the interplay between cultural and practical reason. Some (e.g., at Fourka) had too few livestock for the cultural ideal of specialized pastoralism and supplemented their livelihood by cultivation. At Aetomilitsa, the rest of the community thwarted a similar move, because enclosure threatened collective control of pasture and thus the pastoralist lifestyle (Section 6.8), but the village's location on high, steep slopes is well suited to seasonal herding and poorly to crop husbandry. Conversely, Vlachs nearby in the lower and heavily dissected Eastern Zagori, with limited access to summer pasture, adopted mixed farming and logging and abandoned both pastoralism and Vlach identity.

In addition to normative beliefs about the farming methods of other cultural groups, informants often singled out members of their own community for sloppiness or outstanding workmanship. Quality of workmanship had obvious material consequences. By intensive tillage (plowing, digging up weeds, harrowing), Thodoros at Aroniadika on Kithira compensated with higher area yields for having less land than his father. Careful tillage also yielded cleaner crops, which saved labor in weeding, reaping (particularly critical because time-limited), and processing, and facilitated successful drying and storage. Of the two Paliambela brothers who reaped fast without spilling grain and left stubble that seemed "cut with a spirit-level" (Section 3.4), some neighbors commented that their sheaves of uniform length made stable and weatherproof stooks, but others praised their handiwork simply for looking good. Echoing Malinowski's reaction to the Trobriand ideal of the "good gardener" (Malinowski, 1922), why did many Mediterranean farmers strive for, or admire, unnecessarily neat work? The answer lies partly in superstitious belief that "good" practice, like abstinence or rituals at crucial points in the agricultural calendar, favored positive outcomes and partly in the "cultural capital" earned by evidence of skill or industry (cf. Sutherland and Darnhofer, 2012). As Ilias in Metaxada explained, however, cultural capital also had material consequences. "People went to the mill from all the villages around. The miller saw who brought clean grain in neatly mended sacks and who did not, and people often sought his advice before having dealings with someone they did not know. If the miller had a good opinion of you, you could sell corn at any time of year and could always marry your children to someone suitable." Likewise, someone who plowed or reaped evenly and neatly was evidently skilled and conscientious and easily found employment, just as an employer with a well-stocked larder and reputation for hospitality attracted the best workers (Halstead, 2012). Well-fed and groomed work animals advertised their capacity for work and their owner's full barn, whereas the farmer whose underfed draft animal(s) had to be helped out of the byre in spring was someone to avoid as employer, work partner, or in-law. A shepherd acquaintance with a reputation (probably based on external appearances) for poor dairy hygiene could only sell cheese to strangers.

7.3 Environmental and Technological Constraints

Climate and topography, coupled with "primitive" technology, are sometimes treated as dictating "traditional" Mediterranean land use (Chapter 1). The implied timelessness of alternating cereals and bare fallow, devotion of hill slopes to tree crops, and seasonal transhumance between plains and mountains has encouraged their extrapolation to antiquity (e.g., Isager and Skydsgaard, 1992), but closer examination reveals the influence of historically contingent variables such as scale of land use, form of land tenure, and degree of market integration (Chapters 5 and 6). Nonetheless, variables independent of human decision-making (e.g., climate; soils; hydrology; the physical requirements and tolerances of crops, livestock, and humans) significantly constrain husbandry practices, enhancing their predictability.

For example, thanks to superior strength and stamina, horses or oxen normally outperformed cows, cows outperformed donkeys, and donkeys outperformed humans in tillage. Knowing how much land a premechanized farmer tilled, therefore, enables an educated guess as to the type of labor used. Conversely, knowledge of a farmer's work animals indicates likely scale of cultivation: big animals conferred prestige but needed more fodder and so were usually associated with large-scale cultivation or specialized haulage (Sections 2.1 and 2.3). Similarly, a farmer cultivating on a large scale with work animals probably reaped cereals low, to secure straw for fodder, and threshed with animals, whereas a smallholder tilling manually perhaps reaped high, because straw was not needed, and flailed by hand, because this was unavoidable and, on a small scale, manageable. Such scalar constraints obviously have most predictive value at the extremes: manual flailing might be unattractive for a large household cultivating with two donkeys but prohibitive for one fully exploiting two oxen. The capacity of the labor force was also affected by climatic constraints on the time available for tasks. Thus, the more powerful the animals used for tillage, the more hands were needed for harvest but especially in the south where early summer drought narrowed the window for reaping. Here, drought also delayed autumn sowing and made its early completion doubly important, so that access to draft animals was particularly critical. Further north, because cereals could be cut slightly early and dried in the sheaf, the harvest could be extended and completed by a smaller workforce, although summer rain might make threshing more urgent and, at higher altitudes, necessitate storage of sheaves or ears for piecemeal processing over winter. The more that is known of a farmer's circumstances, the more predictable the husbandry practices: someone cultivating

10 ha with two oxen probably practiced frequent (e.g., biennial) fallow, whereas a neighbor cultivating 2 ha with cows probably rotated crops with infrequent fallow.

Climate, land, and labor thus more or less tightly constrained what was *possible* for recent farmers, not least because many tasks were *necessarily* completed within a seasonal window and because overworking of animals or humans could result in collapse, injury, or death. In addition, some options were feasible to execute but highly risky in outcome. For example, spring sowing of cereals in receding floodwaters provided occasional windfall harvests but often failed or was prevented by the variable extent and timing of flooding and so was not dependable as a regular source of subsistence.

7.4 Practical Reason: Costs, Benefits, and Knowledgeable Farmers

Farmers also faced "real" choices, between alternatives with contrasting, but not determinant, costs and benefits. For example, free-threshing wheat tolerates unfavorable growing conditions less than barley, rye, or oats and so was sown, other things being equal, on better fields. It sometimes occupied worse plots than less demanding cereals but usually for other practical reasons, as when barley was sown on manured land for hay or early-bite grazing. The preceding chapters describe numerous such choices: between leaving a field fallow to control weeds and sowing it to use scarce land fully; between broadcasting to save labor and row sowing to save seedcorn and facilitate weeding; between sowing manured land early and densely, for early-bite grazing, and late and sparsely, to avoid lodging; between uprooting crops, to minimize loss of straw and grain, and cutting them with a sickle, to avoid contaminating grain with stones; between threshing pulses with animals, for speed, and by hand, to minimize damage; and so on. The costs and benefits of such alternatives were routinely understood and frequently acted upon, contrary to widespread dismissal of "traditional" Mediterranean farming as backward (e.g., Grigg, 1974, 125; on Cyprus, Bevan, 1919, 7; on

Greece, Palaiologos, 1833; Strong, 1842, 162), with ignorance, superstition, and conservatism often highlighted as causes. Are my informants, drawn from the last two generations of premechanized farmers, "tarnished" by formal education or advice from agronomists? Or have other commentators overstated their ignorance and conservatism?

Few informants were strictly illiterate, but very few used written guidance on farming. In Assiros, some read occasional letters from relatives in Australia using a pair of cracked reading glasses that sat on a *kafenío* shelf between backgammon boards and playing cards. As young men, they surrendered produce on the threshing floor to pay for purchases on credit, recorded in books only the shopkeepers understood. Before mechanization, agricultural advisors visited rarely, to prohibit tobacco growing or suggest new cash crops, and farmers relied overwhelmingly on what they learned from relatives and neighbors or by personal observation.

Some informants initially struggled with tasks such as plowing in their early teens, when the death of a parent prematurely imposed adult responsibilities, but most learnt the basic skills before they needed to apply them undirected. Skinning and pit roasting a stolen goat while a soldier in the civil war, Ilias told his grateful officer that he had learnt the skills of farmer, herder, and butcher growing up in Metaxada but those of thief in the army. As well as practical skills, childhood equipped him with knowledge of what to plant, where, when, and how: "there was no television and on winter evenings we would gather round the fire and listen to the grown-ups talking and telling stories." Here, he began accumulating his huge repertoire of sayings. Ilias, like Sicilian Padron 'Ntoni in Verga's (1978) *I Malavoglia*, was a particularly enthusiastic exponent of this oral tradition, but farmers of his generation commonly offered sayings, parables, or illustrative stories (e.g., the escaped donkey that "discovered" the benefits of pruning vines) that are more memorable than dry agronomic advice and were clearly considered illuminating. Like their English equivalents (e.g., "red sky at night, shepherd's delight"), rustic sayings are often rendered in verse, with meter and rhyme adding to their mnemonic value.

Answering questions with such aphorisms, or appeals to history ("we have always done it this way"), may create the impression of slaves to tradition, but some informants volunteer the "grandfather response" initially (Alland, 1975, 70) and agronomic cause and effect subsequently. Informants may avoid a cause-and-effect response because it seems too self-evident to be what an educated person is fishing for or, conversely, because it oversimplifies multivariate reality. For example, a farmer might leave a field in cultivated fallow because his work animals could not plow and sow it during autumn, because weeds needed controlling, or to exploit spare household labor by sowing and hoeing a summer cash crop. If all these factors (and others too) are valid, many farmers consider isolating primary causal variables (at my prompting!) pointlessly academic (cf. Mazzocchi, 2006). Likewise, some are reluctant to specify the outcome of a husbandry practice, because "it depends" on unpredictable subsequent weather. Alexis in Assiros was fond of saying "there is no skill in farming," citing years when crops sown too late or on poorly tilled land had yielded better than those sown early or after bare fallow, but he understood that unusual outcomes were no guide to best practice and also maintained that "farming is an entire science."

Some informants were remarkably perceptive observers of plant and animal ecology. A north Greek friend, who started as apprentice shepherd at 11 after a short and undistinguished formal education, now laughs at the ignorance in which, as a teenager, he sold his donkey in a distant village for fear it was pregnant and his role as sire would be obvious. Nonetheless, thanks to a keen eye and quick mind, he knew which weeds improved milk yields and where they grew, entertained his peers with convincing imitations of rutting domesticates, and was always in demand as a hunting companion for his ability to locate scarce game. Dimitrakis on Amorgos was another man of action rather than letters. His analysis of mixed livestock grazing and defecating in a stubble field, however, offered in a rare moment of inactivity, was a close if undertheorized approximation to the Jarman–Bell principle of herbivore feeding ecology (Bell, 1971), with donkeys, cows, and goats replacing the zebra, wildebeest, and gazelle of the Serengeti.

Informants' rationalizations for husbandry practices may be "unscientific" (i.e., incompatible with current scientific thinking), as in some accounts of the benefits of cultivated fallow (Section 5.2.1), but agricultural scientists have also struggled to explain complex processes that cannot be observed (e.g., Morlon and Sigaut, 2008). Anyway, the *effects* of husbandry practices are independent of understanding of the processes involved – one elderly Athenian tavern keeper believed nuclear fission occurred in his barrels but produced outstanding draft wine. Folk agronomy also encompassed a wide range of rituals, including sexual or dietary abstinence before sowing or harvesting, blessing of seedcorn, and arranging tools or sheaves in the shape of a cross. While this might call farmers' rationality into question, they routinely adopted a "belt-and-braces" approach, combining formal religion with sympathetic magic and practical measures (cf. Grøn, Turov, and Klokkernes, 2008, 54), that neither tested the efficacy of appeals to the supernatural nor undermined the application of practical measures.

Ostensibly more problematic is the scheduling of farming and other activities (e.g., felling timber) according to phases of the moon, as a few, mainly elderly, farmers still do and many more recall from childhood. This was not merely groundless superstition: the sap content of wood and hence its suitability for particular uses vary through the lunar cycle (Zürcher, 2001), as do the developmental cycles of many insects (Nowinszky, Petrányi, and Puskás, 2010) and, in some cases, insect damage to young crops (Higuera-Moros, Camacho, and Guerra, 2002). Lunar cycles have complex effects on crop production (Kollerstrom and Staudenmaier, 2001), however, whereas rules of lunar observance are often simple: choose a waning moon for anything intended to last (cutting timber, grafting, storing crops, preserving pig meat) but (less consistently) sow in a waxing moon for rapid growth or beans that cook quickly. Lunar observance may also be impractical for time-stressed tasks. Most Greek informants insisted that grain crops had to be sown when the rains came and harvested when ripe, regardless of the moon, although Cretan Sofia's father advocated a waning moon for the *first* day of sowing. Likewise, at Prasinada in the hills above north

Greek Drama, only the *first* garden produce had to be gathered with the new moon for easy cooking (beans) and freshness (leafy vegetables) or with the old for long storage (garlic, onions, and potatoes). In Asturias, lunar scheduling was advocated quite widely even for sowing (variously waxing or waning) and harvesting (waning moon) of glume wheat, but neither task was time-stressed given small-scale cultivation and slow ripening in damp summers. Nonetheless, most informants considered their modest plots too big for observance to be practicable or, like Leandro, sowed in the approved phase if weather permitted but otherwise exploited the next spell of fine weather rather than delaying until the moon was again favorable. Conveniently, many considered that, as protection against weevils, a waning moon mattered less at harvest than when grain went into store.

While farmers make decisions on the basis of received wisdom, whether local or family tradition or sayings and parables, they also draw on firsthand observation of variations in practice (also Brosius, Lovelace, and Marten, 1986). Many have experimented with alternative crops or methods: some through force of circumstances, as with Asturian Carmin's observation that unintended grazing of young spelt/emmer reduced lodging (Section 5.1), and others because they wished to "try" something novel, as with Asturian Leandro's failed sowing of bread wheat or the theft and successful grafting of olive shoots in Messenian Metaxada. Farmers also accumulated comparative data by observing others. Lowland Greek villagers mobilized to the mountainous Albanian border in 1940 describe unfamiliar practices such as manual threshing of cereals and feeding of livestock with leafy hay, but observations closer to home were more usual. Thanks to fragmented landholding, the frequent combination of arable farming with small-scale stock husbandry, and the importance of communal pasture, many premechanized farmers had ample opportunity during routine movements to observe what their neighbors grew and where, how, and with what success. By the time he graduated from teenage shepherd to adult plowman, Mitsos knew who owned each field around

Paliambela and had watched with interest as men from Kolindros cleared plots in the common wood pasture.

While villagers' formidable intelligence gathering is most obvious in gossip about neighbors' "private" lives (e.g., du Boulay, 1974, 201–229), an impressive volume of information is also accumulated about others' land use. During excavations at Assiros Toumba, Sotiris, a middle-aged villager who spoke only Greek, put down his hand-pick and declared, "I could never speak two languages, I do not have the brain" (plainly unfounded – many of his parents' generation also spoke Bulgarian or Turkish and most of his children's generation English). He had earlier been discussing with another workman, Yannis, something observed in a field some kilometers outside the village. In the gently sloping, cereal-growing landscape around Assiros, field boundaries were often marked by a few stones, while many toponyms referred to features now lost: "the Elms" that succumbed to disease years earlier, "the Tzelepis goat fold" last used two generations ago, and Maro, swept away in her eponymous gulley by a flash flood in time immemorial. Yannis' directions started from the village along the "Turkish gulley," after which I was lost among anonymous dirt tracks. One landmark was a plot where a neighbor's mother-in-law once sowed chickpeas late and yet harvested a good crop. Sotiris remembered the chickpeas and from there was directed to a field included in a neighbor's dowry and thence to a large wild pear tree. They navigated with precision in a relatively homogeneous landscape using a mental cadastral map, on which were superimposed a village genealogy a few generations deep (cf. du Boulay, 1974, 139–140) and a memory of past land use stretching back years and occasionally decades. Such multidimensional mapping, which most academics would find challenging with GIS, was a fairly routine mental exercise for "uneducated" farmers. In a culture where official information is stored and transmitted in writing, however, oral knowledge is undervalued, as much by villagers who rely on it as by educated outsiders who "know many [written] letters."

Even though premechanized farmers gathered and remembered a lot of data on the success or failure of different husbandry practices, it has been argued that quantified analysis of costs and benefits is alien to nonmarket economies (Polanyi, 1957). Informants indeed more readily offer norms of labor productivity for tasks delegated to hired workers (e.g., plowing, reaping) than those undertaken by household members (e.g., weeding, hand-cleaning grain for consumption), albeit partly because piecemeal execution complicates measurement of the latter. Hired labor, especially (but not only) if reciprocated in kind, often involved a morally or socially embedded rate of exchange rather than a disembedded "market rate": for example, one day's work by a plowman and two draft animals (i.e., three workers) for three person-days of manual labor or even, as in Asturias, for unspecified assistance. Likewise, some informants measured produce *for sale* in standard units (kilograms, tons) but that *for household consumption* in approximate units (e.g., sacks). Within the latter category, however, Asturian farmers merely counted sacks of potatoes stored and consumed at home but might measure glume wheat taken to the mill for grinding. Arguably, the crucial issue was whether transactions extended beyond the household rather than whether they involved the market and even the latter often used heaped rather than level measures of volume (Petropoulos, 1952), blurring the distinction between generous reciprocity and calculated market exchange and between folk and standard units.

Moreover, although folk measures like sheaves, baskets, sacks, mule loads, or cartloads were imprecise and their absolute values varied locally, farmers widely and routinely used them in monitoring and planning. For example, Nikos in Kolindros counted sheaves in harvested fields to check whether any were stolen overnight. In Assiros, Fotis counted the stooks (each containing a standard number of sheaves) that he and his wife cut and tied per day as hired reapers to decide whether they would earn more on piecework than by the day. Mikhalis in Paliambela counted stooks to plan how many cart trips he needed from field to threshing floor. His neighbor, Mitsos, is one of many informants who counted sheaves and multiplied by the grain expected per sheaf, to estimate the size of his harvest and thus whether he would buy or sell grain.

In Cretan Aloides, Sofia's father made these calculations in a notebook, but Mitsos was more typical in trusting to memory. Unsurprisingly, farmers varied in their penchant for counting (Mari in Asturian Tiós even knew how many forkfuls of stall manure filled a dung sledge), but some things were also more useful to count than others. For example, farmers were more likely to volunteer a *daily ration* of grain for draft animals during the plowing season than a figure for the amount needed *per year*, in part because the length of the plowing season depended on the weather but also because most farmers fed what they could spare rather than what was ideal. Similarly, sedentary mixed farmers in the Pindos Mountains volunteered the number of leafy hay bundles needed per stall-fed sheep or goat per winter, but not so for grassy hay. Leafy hay was limited by labor for cutting and transport, but grassy hay was much scarcer and the target was to harvest whatever you found (Halstead, 1998).

Despite unstandardized folk metrology, oral information handling, and frequent rationalization of practices in terms of tradition or magic, premechanized farmers *were* rational decision-makers in that they weighed up available alternatives, "the semi-learned grammars of practice" (Bourdieu, 1977, 20), in light of current circumstances and first- and secondhand knowledge of likely costs and benefits. Ilias' extensive repertoire of sayings was not an oral instruction manual, but a reference library of principles to inform decisions. Of course, practitioners varied in knowledge and understanding of these alternatives: Ilias maintained that every village acknowledged one or two senior individuals as sources of wise advice (men advising on different subjects from women). The extent to which farmers applied their knowledge also depended, as with their more literate mechanized counterparts, on variable industry and practical constraints (notably land and labor). Finally, the extent to which "correct" decisions were successful depended on unpredictable variation in weather, pests, the health of household members and livestock, and markets. Nonetheless, practical constraints were sufficiently limiting and decisions sufficiently "rational" that knowledge (the more, the better) of farmers' circumstances enables a plausible guess as to their husbandry practices, and vice versa. The Mediterranean has justly been described as a region of "microecologies" (Horden and Purcell, 2000), while distinctive local traditions add to the resulting diversity of farming practice. Nonetheless, with due allowance for differences between north and south, mountain and plain, coast and inland, and so on, a farmer transplanted from central Greece to southern Italy or from Crete to Provence would largely face familiar challenges and opportunities. On several occasions in Spain and Italy, interviewees have asked me, "how did you know that?" Their accounts sufficiently resembled those previously heard in Greece as to prompt questions from myself that created the illusion of inside knowledge.

7.5 Ancient Farmers: Knowledgeable and Rational?

The level of know-how of recent premechanized farmers differed little from that evident in Greco-Roman literary sources (Section 5.7), which in turn drew on long oral and practical traditions of knowledge (Amouretti, 1986, 225–226). Bronze Age and Neolithic practitioners perhaps had a poorer *scientific* understanding of farming than some Greco-Roman writers, but there is no reason to imagine that they had poorer powers of observation, pattern recognition, or decision-making than their classical and recent counterparts (cf. Mithen, 1990). Moreover, although adapted for elite-sponsored redistribution or exchange, the metrological systems of early literate civilizations include elements suggestive of preliterate popular origins: "practical" units such as load, bowl, and handful (whence the ancient Greek *drachma* coin); the use of finger- or pebble-based counting (Netz, 2002); and multiple systems of numeration and measurement varying both locally and between commodities (Robson, 2000). Even if preliterate farmers lacked the ability to calculate surface area and thus area yields, they doubtless observed differences in height and density of crop stands, in seed to yield ratios, and in numbers of sheaves or volumes of grain yielded per day's plowing or digging. They arguably lacked neither the mental faculties nor the conceptual tools to be as rational decision-makers as their recent counterparts.

7.6 Farming in the Mediterranean: Analogy and Change

Recent premechanized farming in the Mediterranean exhibited considerable diversity, reflecting both regional or local cultural traditions and responses to practical constraints that ranged from regional climatic gradients, shorter-term weather, and local ecological mosaics to variable family size, land tenure, and so on. The opposition between cultural and practical reason should not be overstated, since shared ways of doing things significantly facilitated collaborative work, but local traditions usually represented alternatives of similar viability, making them less "predictable" than responses to known practical constraints. The predictability of such responses depends on the strength of particular constraints and the extent to which farmers made "rational" choices between available alternatives. The rationality of premechanized farmers has often been questioned, partly because educated observers overlook the multiplicity of practical constraints on the former and partly because of incompatibility of expression between traditional and "scientific" knowledge. In routinely drawing on experience and traditional knowledge (e.g., sayings) to choose between alternatives, however, recent farmers were rational decision-makers, and the same may reasonably be assumed for ancient farmers.

To what extent were the *contexts* of recent and ancient decision-making comparable? Since the arrival of farming, the Mediterranean landscape has undergone significant changes in vegetation, soil cover, and so on, but these can be documented and factored into models of past land use. Climate change too is evident, but the inter-annual fluctuations and regional contrasts discussed in Chapter 5 arguably influenced farmers' decisions more. Recent and ancient farmers faced broadly comparable natural constraints.

Available technology has changed. Replacement of stone by bronze and then iron tools perhaps significantly aided reaping by reducing running repairs and extending the reach of sickles, although recent experience warns that skilled hands may use quite different sickles equally effectively. If the earliest farmers lacked wheeled carts (Sherratt, 1981), they probably used sledges, like many recent counterparts. With the striking exception of milling and pressing (Schneider, 2007), however, farmers' equipment changed relatively little during and since Greco-Roman antiquity until the last non-mechanized generation or two widely adopted iron plows. Some iron plows were drawn by a single horse or mule (which could provide both tillage and transport), some *turned* the soil (cultivating more thoroughly than an ard), and all broke less easily on heavy or stony ground. In Assiros, iron plows alone effectively tilled the heaviest and richest soils, but many farmers, here and elsewhere, retained wooden ards for light soils and sowing (Section 2.6.1). Even without subsequent mechanization, wooden ards might well have disappeared as the ideal of modernization left fewer farmers able and *willing* to make and repair them, but the superiority of iron replacements should not be overstated.

Easier to document than technological change is the adoption of new domesticates. The Bronze Age addition of donkey, horse, and mule ultimately transformed rural transport, but how widespread was ownership is unclear. Neolithic grain crops were joined from the Bronze Age onwards by new species (e.g., spelt and common millet, later rice, finally New World maize and beans), but the most radical widespread changes were among the founder species, with the largely Iron Age displacement of glume by free-threshing wheats and of naked by hulled barley, that arguably reflects the emergence of a hierarchy of food and fodder grains (Section 4.9). The progressive enlargement of the crop repertoire with fruits and nuts, vegetables, herbs, and spices underpinned increasing use of diacritical cuisine (e.g., Bakels and Jacomet, 2003; Waines, 2003; Isaakidou, 2007; also ornamental gardens – e.g., Foxhall, 2007) in projecting social and cultural identities. Several of these additions were grown in summer gardens, but they do not indicate Islamic (or even Greco-Roman) "invention" of summer cropping (Watson, 1983) as chickpea occupied this niche from the Early Neolithic (Marinova and Popova, 2008).

Advances in equipment and know-how undoubtedly enriched Mediterranean farming. Insofar as oral history illuminates *long-term* trends, however, it suggests that scholars have overestimated their impact and that the greatest diachronic change in farmers' material conditions were increasingly unequal control of land, labor, and produce (Finley, 1973, 114–115) and perhaps the development of market economies – hotly disputed for Greco-Roman antiquity (Finley, 1973; Morris, Saller, and Scheidel, 2007, 2–6) and widely dismissed for earlier periods (Polanyi, 1957). This underlines both the need to use recent analogy heuristically and its potential to shed light on the broad socioeconomic context of ancient farming. Previous chapters have noted potential insights in various historical contexts, on an annual (Chapters 2, 3, and 4), interannual (Chapter 5), and generational (Chapter 6) timescale. Repetition might imply that analogy can alone reveal how or why people farmed in the distant past, rather than suggesting fruitful questions and likely answers in different practical contexts. Instead, some more general concluding observations are offered on the investigation of ancient farming and its dynamics of long-term change.

First, recent analogy highlights flexibility in farming practice: in an unusually dry or wet autumn, crops might be sown on stubble rather than plowed soil; depending on spring rainfall, a field intended for bare fallow might remain uncultivated or be planted with summer crops; and barley might be given to livestock after a good harvest but kept for humans in a bad year. Accordingly, archaeological (and, where detailed enough, textual) evidence for ancient practices should yield, at best, noisy patterns (e.g., Bogaard, 2004, 124–125; Garnsey, 1992; Kasdagli, 1999, 98).

Secondly (and more conveniently), decisions at any stage of crop production could affect the rest of the cycle: for example, careful cleaning of seedcorn reduced weeds and raised yields, facilitated reaping and processing, and lowered risk of spoilage in store; manuring raised yields for several years. Consequently, practical pressures strongly encouraged thorough workmanship, as did the latter's role as index of dependability in exchanges of personnel or produce. Thanks to their interdependence, practices at one stage (e.g., threshing with animals – Section 4.9) also offer (pre)historians valuable clues to preceding and subsequent stages (Sigaut, 1988).

Thirdly, recent analogy underlines the complexity of predicting past behavior from likely costs and benefits. Recent practitioners were far more sensitive to labor costs of time-limited tasks than those that could be delayed. Thus, although *processing* accounts for much of the labor in exploiting wild cereals (Wright, 1994), efficiency of time-stressed *harvesting* may have been more critical to foragers' decisions. Recent farmers also considered costs and benefits in dealings with outsiders more than within the household. Perhaps partly for this reason, while the extensive surplus-producing estates of the Greco-Roman elite mainly grew cereals, the relatively self-sufficient Neolithic households of southeast Europe also relied heavily on labor-intensive pulses (Section 3.7). Costs and benefits were also judged relative to context-specific expectations. Thus, informants widely claim that manual flailing and especially grinding of household grain supplies are "impossible," but they were unavoidable for some (mainly upland) farmers in the recent past. Finally, recent farmers clearly distinguished between strategies that maximized (e.g., growing currants, renting land) and those that stabilized (e.g., sowing maslins, sharecropping) returns. Some with insufficient land specialized in high-value cash crops (encouraging Renfrew's palatial redistribution model), but most favored diversity and security (consistent with Ilias' skeptical reaction). Whether Greco-Roman *smallholders* specialized in cash crops (available evidence suggests otherwise but is heavily biased towards elite landowners – Section 6.9) would be one measure of the scale and effectiveness of the market in antiquity (cf. Foxhall, 2007; Kehoe, 2007, 553–559).

Fourthly, arguably the greatest factor shaping differences in recent practices was *scale* of husbandry, with large landowners using bigger draft animals, proportionally less manual labor, less intensive rotations, sometimes different reaping and threshing methods, often different crops, and usually more seasonal workers than smallholders. In antiquity too, social hierarchy and unequal access to land and labor enabled and, arguably, were supported by *extensive* agriculture. For example, large- and small-scale husbandry coexisted in later Bronze Age Greece and the Greco-Roman Mediterranean, with extensive husbandry apparently producing much of the surplus that supported "palatial" elites and urban populations. Contrary claims of diachronic *intensification* largely reflect anachronistic expectations of progress in know-how and technology and the didactic tone of some ancient authors that perhaps reflects the difficulty of applying to large estates intensive methods long practiced by small-scale farmers (Section 5.7). The following points also suggest ways in which practicalities of Mediterranean farming perhaps *promoted* increasing inequality.

Fifthly, in recent farming, interannual uncertainties of production threatened the survival of the poor, independence of the better-off, and comfort of the wealthy. In one of Ilias' parables, a rich man asking how much his gold was worth received the answer "one rainfall in May." Common recent buffering strategies included (Forbes, 1989) crop diversification, mixed cropping, and growing low-risk crops, all known from the Early Neolithic (Marinova, 2007); dispersal of land holdings, documented from classical antiquity (Burford Cooper, 1977–1978) and plausible, given nucleated "village" settlement, from the Neolithic; and overproduction of normal surplus, without which early farmers would not have survived inevitable bad years. Grain has a finite storage life, however, and recent producers of normal surplus ideally kept two years' supply but otherwise used it to recruit human labor or as fodder for live-stock (attested from the Neolithic) to improve their carcasses, productivity, and capacity for work (Sections 4.6 and 6.6).

Sixthly, recent analogy highlights how, with generational shifts in the balance between consumers and workers, household economies faced periods of stress but also opportunities, using teenage and young adult labor, to accumulate land and livestock that enabled establishment of new households and also reduced shorter-term risk of hunger. Strategies for buffering bad years were thus entwined with those promoting differential social reproduction between generations, not least through use of livestock to "bank" surplus grain and labor.

Seventhly, livestock were integral to recent arable farming, providing labor and manure and the meat and dairy products that underpinned hospitality and thus social cohesion and competition – again roles plausibly traceable to the Neolithic (Section 6.9). The commensal importance of animal produce, and ability of grain to improve carcass weight and milk yields, helped ensure that normal surplus was not wasted and overproduction not abandoned. Conversely, when other buffering mechanisms were exhausted, the designation of some low-risk grains as fodder helped reserve an emergency grain supply, normally avoided by humans for its negative social connotations. The rapid Early Neolithic spread of *mixed* farming across Europe should thus arguably be understood in terms of the role of livestock in facilitating crop production, buffering crop failure through "indirect storage," and enriching commensality by which households maintained both independence from and solidarity with neighbors. Nonetheless, as a source of agricultural labor, means of converting short-term "normal surplus" into more durable wealth, and key ingredient in competitive and ultimately diacritical commensality, livestock could accentuate inequalities between, as well as stabilize, household economies.

Eighthly, recent farming communities were bound by exchanges of labor, livestock, land, and food on terms ranging from balanced reciprocity between households of similar means to asymmetrical employer–employee or patron–client relationships between unequal parties. In lowland Mediterranean Europe, the seasonal windows for autumn sowing and early summer harvest became significantly narrower from north to south, placing households under increasing time stress and risk of subsistence failure. In the south, coupled with the greater difficulty of rearing and maintaining work animals, this encouraged asymmetrical exchanges of animal for human labor, so that Cretan farmers with modest landholdings employed gangs of reapers matched only by the biggest landowners in northern Greece. Under such severe seasonal labor stress, ownership of work animals by only some households would potentially have promoted acute economic inequality also in the distant past (Section 6.9).

Ninthly, markets, especially those supplying large urban populations, increased farmers' opportunities for specialized surplus production and wealth accumulation but also for economic failure – especially where rents or taxes were monetized and land was alienable. Promotion of economic inequality by variable yields, shifting household composition, seasonal labor stress, "banking" on livestock, and grain hierarchy is accentuated by markets and money, partly because they undermine risk- and benefit-sharing tendencies inherent to other forms of exchange (e.g., in sharecropping) and partly because the wealthy can gain, while the poor lose, from fluctuating prices. Long before markets or money, however, Neolithic farmers produced high-value or value-added "cash crops" (Sherratt, 1999) such as fattened carcasses or special beverages, arguably converting surplus produce or labor into prestige and reciprocal obligations of support. From the Bronze Age onwards, a widening range of nuts, fruits, vegetables, spices, and herbs, together with a hierarchy of staple grains, differentiated special from ordinary meals and high- from low-ranking consumers, reinforcing the linkage between risk avoidance and pursuit of prestige. As this began in a premarket context, the variety of exotic food plants is a questionable index of market development (Kron, 2012), and in terms of widening inequality, Bronze Age elites' strategic manipulation of value regimes (e.g., Halstead, 2012) may have been more fundamental than the growth of a market economy.

Finally, and counter to the practical and antidiffusionist emphasis of the preceding remarks, the hierarchy of grain crops, which latterly reinforced the close linkage between agricultural risk buffering, rearing of livestock, and social inequality and was widespread in hierarchical societies of later Bronze and Iron Age southern Europe, is arguably a better example, than developments in agricultural technology and know-how, for large-scale diffusion of an innovation important to rural economy.

Ancient farmers doubtless varied both in what they knew and, following Xenophon's Isomakhos (*Oeconomicus* 20.2.1–20.2.5), in how assiduously they applied their knowledge. With unpredictable climate and other hazards confounding plans and expectations, they might have subscribed to Alexis' self-deprecating "two oxen ahead and one ox behind," but incomplete knowledge of the future is universal. Ancient farmers, like their modern counterparts, surely responded sufficiently rationally to their circumstances for recent analogy to be an invaluable heuristic tool in investigating their practices. Applications of this principle suggest that ancient farming was in some respects very unfamiliar (e.g., early dominance of small-scale, intensive husbandry) and in others less different (notably less primitive) than scholars have often imagined.

References

Alland, A. (1975) Adaptation. *Annual Review of Anthropology*, 4, 59–73.

Amouretti, M.-C. (1986) *Le pain et l' huile dans la Grèce antique: de l' araire au moulin*, Les Belles Lettres, Paris.

Arrow, K.J. (1962) The economic implications of learning by doing. *Review of Economic Studies*, 29, 155–173.

Ascher, R. (1961) Analogy in archaeological interpretation. *Southwestern Journal of Anthropology*, 17, 317–325.

Bakels, C. and Jacomet, S. (2003) Access to luxury foods in central Europe during the Roman period: the archaeobotanical evidence. *World Archaeology*, 34, 542–557.

Bell, R.H.V. (1971) A grazing ecosystem in the Serengeti. *Scientific American*, 225, 86–93.

Bevan, W. (1919) *Notes on Agriculture in Cyprus and Its Products*, GPO, Nicosia.

Binford, L.R. (1977) General introduction, in *For Theory Building in Archaeology* (ed. L.R. Binford), Academic Press, New York, pp. 1–10.

Bogaard, A. (2004) *Neolithic Farming in Central Europe: An Archaeobotanical Study of Crop Husbandry Practices*, Routledge, London.

du Boulay, J. (1974) *Portrait of a Greek Mountain Village*, Clarendon, Oxford.

Bourdieu, P. (1977) *Outline of a Theory of Practice*, Cambridge University Press, Cambridge, UK.

Brosius, J.P., Lovelace, G.W., and Marten, G.G. (1986) Ethnoecology: an approach to understanding traditional agricultural knowledge, in *Traditional Agriculture in Southeast Asia: A Human Ecology Perspective* (ed. G.G. Marten), Westview, Boulder, pp. 187–198.

Burford Cooper, A. (1977–1978) The family farm in Greece. *Classical Journal*, 73, 162–175.

Charles, M. and Halstead, P. (2001) Biological resource exploitation: problems of theory and method, in *Handbook of Archaeological Sciences* (eds D.R. Brothwell and A.M. Pollard), Wiley, Chichester, pp. 365–378.

Cohn, B.S. (1981) Anthropology and history in the 1980s: toward a rapprochement. *Journal of Interdisciplinary History*, 12, 227–252.

Davis, N.Z. (1981) Anthropology and history in the 1980s: the possibilities of the past. *Journal of Interdisciplinary History*, 12, 267–275.

Finley, M.I. (1973) *The Ancient Economy*, Chatto & Windus, London.

Forbes, H. (1989) Of grandfathers and grand theories: the hierarchised ordering of responses to hazard in a Greek rural community, in *Bad Year Economics* (eds P. Halstead and J. O'Shea), Cambridge University Press, Cambridge, UK, pp. 87–97.

Foxhall, L. (2007) *Olive Cultivation in Ancient Greece*, Oxford University Press, Oxford.

Garnsey, P. (1992) Yield of the land, in *Agriculture in Ancient Greece* (ed. B. Wells), Swedish Institute at Athens, Stockholm, pp. 147–153.

Giddens, A. (1981) *A Contemporary Critique of Historical Materialism, 1: Power, Property and the State*, Macmillan, London.

Gosselain, O.P. (1992) Technology and style: potters and pottery among Bafia of Cameroon. *Man*, 27, 559–586.

Grigg, D.B. (1974) *The Agricultural Systems of the World: An Evolutionary Approach*, Cambridge University Press, Cambridge, UK.

Grøn, O., Turov, M., and Klokkernes, T. (2008) Spiritual and material aspects of everyday ritual negotiation: ethnoarchaeological data from the Evenk, Siberia, in *Six Essays on the Materiality of Society and Culture* (eds H. Glørstad and L. Hedeager), Bricoleur Press, Lindome, pp. 33–57.

Halstead, P. (1998) Ask the fellows who lop the hay: leaf-fodder in the mountains of northwest Greece. *Rural History*, 9, 211–234.

Halstead, P. (2012). Feast, food and fodder in Neolithic-Bronze Age Greece: commensality and the construction of value, in Between Feasts and Daily Meals. Towards an Archaeology of Commensal Spaces (ed. S. Pollock). *eTopoi Journal for Ancient Studies*, special volume 2, pp. 21–51.

Heaton, T.H.E., Jones, G., Halstead, P., and Tsipropoulos, T. (2009) Variations in the $^{13}C/^{12}C$ ratios of modern wheat grain, and implications for interpreting data from Bronze Age Assiros Toumba, Greece. *Journal of Archaeological Science*, 36, 2224–2233.

Higuera-Moros, A., Camacho, M., and Guerra, J. (2002) Efecto de las fases lunares sobre la incidencia de insectos y componentes de rendimiento en el cultivo de frijol (*Vigna unguiculata* (L.) Walp). *Revista Científica UDO Agrícola*, 2, 54–63.

Hodder, I. (1982) *The Present Past*, Batsford, London.

Horden, P. and Purcell, N. (2000) *The Corrupting Sea: A Study of Mediterranean History*, Blackwell, Oxford.

Imellos, S.D. (1990–1992) O N. G. Politis kai ta georgika ergaleia therismou. *Laografia*, 36, 203–206.

Isaakidou, V. (2007) Cooking in the labyrinth: exploring 'cuisine' at Bronze Age Knossos, in *Cooking Up the Past: Food and Culinary Practices in the Neolithic and Bronze Age Aegean* (eds C. Mee and J. Renard), Oxbow, Oxford, pp. 5–24.

Isager, S. and Skydsgaard, J.E. (1992) *Ancient Greek Agriculture: An Introduction*, Routledge, London.

Jones, G. (1987) A statistical approach to the archaeological identification of crop processing. *Journal of Archaeological Science*, 14, 311–323.

Jones, G. (1992) Weed phytosociology and crop husbandry: identifying a contrast between ancient and modern practice. *Review of Palaeobotany and Palynology*, 73, 133–143.

Jones, G., Valamoti, S., and Charles, M. (2000) Early crop diversity: a 'new' glume wheat from northern Greece. *Vegetation History & Archaeobotany*, 9, 133–146.

Jones, M. (1985) Archaeobotany beyond subsistence reconstruction, in *Beyond Domestication in Prehistoric Europe: Investigations in Subsistence Archaeology and Social Complexity* (eds G. Barker and C. Gamble), Academic Press, New York, pp. 107–128.

de Jong, M. (1996) The foreign past. Medieval historians and cultural anthropology. *Tijdschrift voor Geschiedenis*, 109, 326–342.

Kasdagli, A.E. (1999) *Land and Marriage Settlements in the Aegean: A Case Study of Seventeenth-Century Naxos*, Hellenic Institute of Byzantine and Post-Byzantine Studies, Venice.

Kehoe, D.P. (2007) The early Roman empire: production, in *The Cambridge Economic History of the Greco-Roman World* (eds W. Scheidel, I. Morris, and R.P. Saller), Cambridge University Press, Cambridge, UK, pp. 543–569.

Kollerstrom, N. and Staudenmaier, G. (2001) Evidence for lunar-sidereal rhythms in crop yield: a review. *Biological Agriculture and Horticulture*, 19, 247–259.

Kron, G. (2012) Food production, in *The Cambridge Companion to the Roman Economy* (ed. W. Scheidel), Cambridge University Press, Cambridge, UK, pp. 156–174.

Lemonnier, P. (1993) Introduction, in *Technological Choices: Transformation in Material Cultures since the Neolithic* (ed. P. Lemonnier), Routledge, London, pp. 1–35.

Malinowski, B. (1922) *Argonauts of the Western Pacific*, Routledge, London.

Marinova, E. (2007) Archaeobotanical data from the early Neolithic of Bulgaria, in *The Origins and Spread of Domestic Plants in Southwest Asia and Europe* (eds S. Colledge and J. Conolly), Left Coast Press, Walnut Creek, pp. 93–109.

Marinova, E. and Popova, T. (2008) *Cicer arietinum* (chick pea) in the Neolithic and Chalcolithic of Bulgaria: implications for cultural contacts with neighbouring regions? *Vegetation History & Archaeobotany*, 17 (supplement 1), 73–89.

Mazzocchi, F. (2006) Western science and traditional knowledge. *European Molecular Biology Organization Reports*, 7, 463–466.

Meurers-Balke, J. and Loennecken, C. (1984) Zu Schutzgeräten bei der Getreideernte mit der Sichel. *Tools & Tillage*, 5, 27–42.

Mithen, S.J. (1990) *Thoughtful Foragers: A Study of Prehistoric Decision Making*, Cambridge University Press, Cambridge, UK.

Moreland, J. (2001) *Archaeology and Text*, Duckworth, London.

Morlon, P. and Sigaut, F. (2008) *La troublante histoire de la jachère: pratiques des cultivateurs, concepts de lettrés et enjeux sociaux*, Educagri & Quae, Dijon and Versailles.

Morris, I., Saller, R.P., and Scheidel, W. (2007) Introduction, in *The Cambridge Economic History of the Greco-Roman World* (eds W. Scheidel, I. Morris, and R.P. Saller), Cambridge University Press, Cambridge, UK, pp. 1–12.

Netz, R. (2002) Counter culture: towards a history of Greek numeracy. *History of Science*, 40, 321–352.

Nowinszky, L., Petrányi, G., and Puskás, J. (2010) The relationship between lunar phases and the emergence of the adult brood of insects. *Applied Ecology and Environmental Research*, 8, 51–62.

Palaiologos, G. (1833) *Georgiki kai oikiaki oikonomia*, Vasiliki Tipografia, Nafplio.

Palanca, F. (1991) Agricultura, in *Temes d' etnografia Valenciana 2: utillatge agrícola i ramaderia* (eds F. Martínez and F. Palanca), Institució Valenciana d' Estudis i Investigació, Valencia, pp. 11–181.

357

Petropoulos, D.A. (1952) Sumvoli is tin erevnan ton laikon metron kai stathmon. *Epetiris tou Laografikou Arkhiou*, 7, 57–101.

Polanyi, K. (1957) The economy as instituted process, in *Trade and Market in the Early Empires: Economies in History and Theory* (eds K. Polanyi, C.M. Arensberg, and H.W. Pearson), Free Press, New York, pp. 243–270.

Renfrew, C. (1972) *The Emergence of Civilisation: The Cyclades and the Aegean in the Third Millennium BC*, Methuen, London.

Robson, E. (2000) The uses of mathematics in ancient Iraq, 6000–600 BC, in *Mathematics Across Cultures* (ed. H. Selin), Kluwer, Dordrecht, pp. 93–113.

Sahlins, M. (1976) *Culture and Practical Reason*, Chicago University Press, Chicago.

Schneider, H. (2007) Technology, in *The Cambridge Economic History of the Greco-Roman World* (eds W. Scheidel, I. Morris, and R.P. Saller), Cambridge University Press, Cambridge, UK, pp. 144–171.

Sherratt, A. (1981) Plough and pastoralism: aspects of the secondary products revolution, in *Pattern of the Past: Studies in Honour of David Clarke* (eds I. Hodder, G. Isaac, and N. Hammond), Cambridge University Press, Cambridge, UK, pp. 261–305.

Sherratt, A. (1999) Crops before cash: hunting, farming, manufacture and trade in earlier Eurasia, in *The Prehistory of Food* (eds C. Gosden and J.G. Hather), Routledge, London, pp. 13–34.

Shkurti, S. (1979) Le battage des cereales. *Ethnographie Albanaise*, 9, 57–111.

Sigaut, F. (1988) A method for identifying grain storage techniques and its application for European agricultural history. *Tools & Tillage*, 6, 3–32.

Stevens, C.J. (2003) An investigation of agricultural consumption and production models for prehistoric and Roman Britain. *Environmental Archaeology*, 8, 61–76.

Strong, F. (1842) *Greece as a Kingdom; or a Statistical Description of that Country, from the Arrival of King Otho, in 1833, down to the Present Time*, Longman, Brown, Green & Longmans, London.

Sutherland, L.-A. and Darnhofer, I. (2012) Of organic farmers and 'good farmers': changing habitus in rural England. *Journal of Rural Studies*, 28, 232–240.

Sutton, S.B. (1994) Settlement patterns, settlement perceptions: rethinking the Greek village, in *Beyond the Site: Regional Studies in the Aegean Area* (ed. P.N. Kardulias), University Press of America, Lanham, pp. 313–335.

Thomas, K. (1963) History and anthropology. *Past and Present*, 24, 3–24.

Verga, G. (1978) *I Malavoglia*, Biblioteca Universale Rizzoli, Milan.

Waines, D. (2003) 'Luxury foods' in medieval Islamic societies. *World Archaeology*, 34, 571–580.

Watson, A.M. (1983) *Agricultural Innovation in the Early Islamic World: The Diffusion of Crops and Farming Techniques, 700–1100*, Cambridge University Press, Cambridge, UK.

Wright, K.I. (1994) Ground-stone tools and hunter-gatherer subsistence in southwest Asia: implications for the transition to farming. *American Antiquity*, 59, 238–263.

Wylie, A. (1989) Matters of fact and matters of interest, in *Archaeological Approaches to Cultural Identity* (ed. S.J. Shennan), Unwin Hyman, London, pp. 94–109.

Zojzi, R. (1976) Parmenda Shqipëtare dhe proçesi historik i zhvillimit të saj. *Etnografia Shqiptare*, 7, 3–45.

Zürcher, E. (2001) Lunar rhythms in forestry traditions—lunar-correlated phenomena in tree biology and wood properties. *Earth, Moon and Planets*, 85–86, 463–478.

Glossary

ard a simple form of plow that *scratches* a furrow (a true plow turns the soil)

awns bristles on the ears of some cereal varieties

dia de bueyes the *day of oxen* or area that can be plowed by a pair of draft cattle in a day, standardized in the Lena district of Asturias as 800 m² or 0.08 ha

dibbling sowing by dropping seeds into a hole

free-threshing wheats species (e.g., bread and macaroni wheat), threshing of which breaks the ear into free or naked grains and loose *chaff* (including the glumes or husks that enveloped the grains before threshing)

glume wheats species (e.g., einkorn, emmer, and spelt), threshing of which breaks the ear into spikelets with the grain(s) tightly enclosed in husks (glumes), removal of which usually requires further processing

Two Oxen Ahead: Pre-Mechanized Farming in the Mediterranean, First Edition.
Paul Halstead. © 2014 Paul Halstead. Published 2014 by John Wiley & Sons, Ltd.

harrow a toothed tillage implement, dragged across fields usually after sowing to smooth the ploughed surface, break clods, and perhaps cover seedcorn

lodging stem collapse in cereal crops, especially common in tall stands and posing more or less severe problems for the development and harvesting of the grain

maslin a mixed crop, originally wheat/rye, but here referring to various combinations, especially the wheat/barley mixture widely sown in the recent past in southern Greece and variously known as *migádi, smigádi,* or *smigó*

oká(des) an Ottoman unit of mass, latterly standardized as 1.28 kg and now abandoned in Greece, but still the default unit of most elderly Greek farmers' memories

oxen like its equivalents in Greek (*vódhia*), Italian (*buoi*) and Spanish (*bueyes*), strictly refers to castrated adult male cattle, but is often used to describe adult draught cattle, whether male or female

palamariá Greek term for the (usually wooden) *glove* or finger-guard, sometimes worn while reaping with a sickle

row sowing dribbling seeds into a furrow that is then covered over by foot or hoe or plow

strémma(ta) a Greek unit of land area measurement, now standardized as 1000 m² or 0.1 ha, but more variable within the lifetimes of some elderly farmers

summer crops sown in spring(/early summer), growing over summer, and harvested in late summer (NB spring-sown varieties of the winter cereals and pulses are harvested in early summer)

winter crops sown in autumn (/early winter), growing over winter, and harvested in early summer

zevgará or *zevgaréa* a southern Greek term referring to the variable area of land (apparently somewhat larger than the Asturian *dia de bueyes*), that can be plowed by a pair of draft cattle in a day

Index

Two Oxen Ahead: Pre-Mechanized Farming in the Mediterranean, First Edition.
Paul Halstead.© 2014 Paul Halstead. Published 2014 by John Wiley & Sons, Ltd.

Index